P9-CLJ-022

Multinationals, the State, and
Control of the Nigerian Economy

Multinationals, the State, and Control of the Nigerian Economy

Thomas J. Biersteker

PRINCETON UNIVERSITY PRESS

PRINCETON, NEW JERSEY

Copyright © 1987 by Princeton University Press
Published by Princeton University Press,
41 William Street, Princeton, New Jersey 08540
In the United Kingdom:
Princeton University Press, Guildford, Surrey

All Rights Reserved
Library of Congress Cataloging in Publication Data
will be found on the last printed page of this book

ISBN 0-691-07728-2 (cloth) 0-691-02261-5 (pbk.)

Publication of this book has been aided by
a grant from The Andrew W. Mellon Foundation

This book has been composed in Linotron Galliard

Clothbound editions of Princeton University Press
books are printed on acid-free paper, and binding
materials are chosen for strength and durability.
Paperbacks, although satisfactory for personal
collections, are not usually suitable for
library rebinding

Printed in the United States of America by
Princeton University Press, Princeton, New Jersey

For Nancy and Peter

CONTENTS

FIGURES

TABLES

ACKNOWLEDGMENTS

THIS book has been many years in the making, and I owe a debt of gratitude to people on three continents. Most of the research on which it is based was generously supported by a Fulbright senior research award and a grant from the Social Science Research Council. The initial idea for the project, however, grew out of a consulting assignment in Nigeria for the General Electric Company in the summer of 1979. This book goes into considerably greater depth on many fewer issues than were encompassed by that assignment. But that experience was crucial both for my understanding of the inner workings, logic, and concerns of multinational corporations and for access to multinational business managers in Nigeria.

I began with a question drawn from international political economy (that of the balance of bargaining power between host countries and multinationals), but very quickly realized the need to enter the domain of comparative political economy for an analysis of the inner workings and social-class bases of states. Therefore, in return trips to Nigeria I supplemented my interviews with multinationals and held extensive discussions with state officials, representatives of local business and labor associations, and Nigerian managers of indigenized firms.

I have been influenced by (and owe a great intellectual debt to) a number of former students at Yale University. Two former undergraduates, Marc Cohen and Richard Steinberg, were particularly important assistants in and influences on my work. Marc Cohen helped me with the conduct of interviews in Nigeria in 1979 and 1981 and has remained a highly valued reader and critic of my work ever since. Richard Steinberg joined me in Nigeria in 1982 and was critically important for the conduct of remaining interviews and the initial formulation of the structure of the book. Penelope Walker was responsible for arranging the 1979 consulting assignment and has been an important influence on my thinking about the relationship between corporations and states through our many arguments (and agreements).

Ulla Dannebom, visiting Yale for a year from the University of Constanz, undertook the painstaking but vital job of coding the voluminous (and often contradictory) data on incorporated companies in Nigeria, with the assistance and occasional interference of Marc Cohen and myself. Victoria Igel performed valuable bibliographic research on host-country economic nationalism, and Stephen Silvia assisted me with the exploration of the historical sources of contemporary neo-Marxist debates on development. Neil Solomon helped compile the chronology of economic nationalism in Appendix D, and Jean Hoelzel and Pam O'Donnell provided critical clerical and editorial assistance, ranging from the transcription of interviews to the composition of figures and graphs.

Several scholars were also generous in providing me with disaggregated interview data from their research on related topics. I am especially grateful to Ankie Hoogvelt of the Department of Sociology at the University of Sheffield for giving me access to her interviews conducted in Kano during the late 1970s and to Joseph LaPalombara of the Department of Political Science at Yale University for giving me transcripts of interviews from his Conference Board project on elite perceptions of multinationals.

Final preparation of the manuscript would have taken another two years without the assistance of Leigh Payne, who worked her way through the entire manuscript and provided crucial editorial advice; Thomas Hartley, who helped assemble the final manuscript and offered essential advice on the final revisions; and Margaret Santschi, who tracked down all the missing citations. Small but critical amounts of institutional and financial support were provided by Yale's Institution for Social and Policy Studies, its Concilium on International and Area Studies, the University of Sussex Institute of Development Studies, and the University of Southern California's Center for International Studies.

A great many people have read all or part of this book in draft form, and I am indebted to them for their comments. Tom Forrest sent detailed comments that added to, informed, and improved the overall quality of the book. John Harris, Thomas Callaghy, and Pauline Baker also provided extensive comment on the entire manuscript, much of which was incorporated in the final version. Nancy Gilgosch, Susan Woodward, Raphael Kaplinsky, Irving Leonard Markovitz, and Victor Diejemaoh offered thoughtful comments on earlier portions of the work.

In the course of writing this book I have been influenced by discussions in seminars I gave at New York University, Duke University, Harvard University, Columbia University, Cornell University, the Institute of Development Studies at the University of Sussex, and the

University of North Carolina at Chapel Hill. Participation in the Social Science Research Council's conference on the development of capitalism in Kenya, Nigeria, and the Ivory Coast held in Dakar in December of 1980 also influenced the work in subtle but important ways.

Nigeria is a fascinating, complex, and challenging country. The story of its indigenization experience was constructed out of diverse and often contradictory pieces of information. In the course of my research I have worked with, learned from, and spoken to hundreds of people in Nigeria. The individuals cited in the lists of interviews in Appendix A have been generous with their time, their patience, and their insights, and I am grateful to all of them. Some of them provided more assistance and had greater influence on my thinking than others, but to single them out could violate my pledge to maintain the confidentiality of interview information. A number of friends and associates in Nigeria deserve special mention, however. Fred Ekeh, Chairman of the Department of Political Science at the University of Ibadan, provided essential sponsorship for the project, while Adam Sheikh Abdullah of Bayero University, Kano, offered warm hospitality and critical insights during my visit there. Sola Kasim of the Department of Economics at the University of Lagos has kept me supplied with recently published government documents, and Tyler Biggs, Salim Sufi, Kiki Munshi, Richard Ritter, and Lawrence Umeche made my long stays in Lagos more enjoyable.

In one way, this book has been more than a lifetime in the making. I have been taking trips to Nigeria or disappearing into the study to work on it for more years than our three-year-old son has experienced. This book is dedicated to him and to his mother, who has found enough time away from her own busy career for both of us.

ABBREVIATIONS

BNDE	Brazilian National Development Bank
CIC	Capital Issues Commission
CMD	Center for Management Development
ECLA	Economic Commission for Latin America
IFC	International Financial Corporation (of the World Bank)
IMF	International Monetary Fund
ITF	Industrial Training Fund
KSIC	Kano State Investment Corporation
MAN	Manufacturers Association of Nigeria
MNC	Multinational corporation
NACCIMA	Nigerian Association of Chambers of Commerce, Industries, Mines, and Agriculture
NBCI	Nigerian Bank for Commerce and Industry
NEPB	Nigerian Enterprises Promotion Board
NEPD	Nigerian Enterprises Promotion Decree
NIDB	Nigerian Industrial Development Bank
NIEO	New International Economic Order
NIIO	New International Information Order
NIM	Nigerian Institute of Management
NLC	Nigerian Labor Congress
NNDC	New Nigerian Development Corporation
NNIL	Northern Nigerian Investments Ltd.
NNPC	Nigerian National Petroleum Company
NPN	National Party of Nigeria
NPP	Nigerian People's Party
NSE	Nigerian Stock Exchange
NSEC	Nigerian Securities and Exchange Commission
OAU	Organization of African Unity
OPEC	Organization of Petroleum Exporting Countries
PZ	Paterson-Zochinis
SMC	Supreme Military Council
UAC	United Africa Company
UBA	United Bank for Africa
UPN	Unity Party of Nigeria

Multinationals, the State, and Control of the Nigerian Economy

INTRODUCTION

THE issue of control is central to an understanding of the economic and political conflict that separates North from South, rich from poor, the haves from the have-nots in the contemporary world economy. It is related to, but analytically distinct from, the issue of improving the material well-being of the South. For example, nationalization of extractive industries throughout the world took place in part because host states wanted greater control over the natural resources removed from their sovereign territory. OPEC was founded to provide producer states with greater control over the international prices petroleum obtained and over the international markets in which it was traded. Indigenization, divestiture, or mandatory joint-venture programs which swept the globe during the 1970s—from radical developing states to neoprotectionist industrial ones—were also premised on an attempt to obtain greater control over individual enterprises and consequently over the direction of national development.[1] The issue of who should control information (from news to technology) provides the basis of contention between North and South in the interminable, and increasingly inconclusive, United Nations negotiations for a New International Order (whether a New International Information Order or a New International Economic Order). Control over the broad direction of national development is a principal point of contention between debtor states and international financial organizations like the IMF and the World Bank.

In its most general sense, control can be defined as the ability of an actor to determine outcomes in a regularized (but not necessarily institutionalized) manner with a reasonable degree of certainty over matters of importance. Control is rarely absolute and is best described in relative terms. Having relative control of a firm, an economic sector, or a national economy implies having the ability to exert a major or dominant influence on it. It means having the ability to block unwelcome developments or to act unilaterally in important instances.

[1] The Solidarity movement in Poland could also be viewed as an attempt on the part of the working class in that country to obtain control over economic enterprises and consequently (as the ruling oligarchy correctly observes) over the direction of national development.

Thus, having relative control in the national or international political economy means being able to determine outcomes of important matters such as the prices earned by major commodity exports, the predictability of export earnings, the operations of productive enterprises based in one's sovereign territory, or the direction of national development.

Not everyone wants to control the same thing. Significant differences in tastes and cultural preferences exist which prevent conflict over many issues.[2] And there are some things no single actor controls—the open seas, outer space, or the international monetary system. But everyone wants to control at least those things that most directly affect his or her material well-being. The uncertainty that comes from having only limited or tenuous control is disruptive both for the economies of the world and for the political entities that rely on economic performance for survival. This is one of the reasons why international economic issues are often so conflictual in North–South relations. The fact that other sovereign states, international markets, multinational corporations and/or international organizations can all influence the direction of national development, and accordingly disrupt, interfere with, or constrain the exercise of national sovereignty, is a source of constant concern and frustration in the Third World.

Third World governments, business leaders, laborers, and peasants all want greater control over the resources, markets, enterprises, or organizations that affect their economic well-being.[3] However, they would each do very different things if one of them, or if different combinations of them, were to gain control over these entities.[4] They might not manage them any differently from, or necessarily any "better" than, the international corporations and advanced industrial states that currently control some international markets, enterprises, and organizations. At the very least, however, they would like a chance to try. At the same time, multinationals and the states from which they emanate are not taking many chances. They are just as con-

[2] The fact that Saudi Arabia has control over the Kabba in Mecca is of little immediate concern to non-Muslim states and peoples of the world. The fact that it controls nearly a quarter of the world's known oil reserves is a different matter.

[3] In this way they are no different from the neoprotectionist who fears the consequences of growing international interdependence, or the nostalgic American liberal who is not only concerned about the loss of control, but also about who is losing it.

[4] This implies that an understanding of the composition of the coalition that controls the state is essential for an understanding of the consequences of its attempts to obtain control over the resources, markets, enterprises, or organizations that affect it. This will become more apparent in the discussions of Chapters 2 through 6.

cerned with maintaining their control as the have-nots in the current world economy are with obtaining it.

After the Second World War, decolonization was supposed to solve many of these problems for the countries of Africa and Asia by giving them control over their political and economic lives. Since many nationalist leaders held colonialism responsible for the pattern, pace, and direction of development, they expected its termination to end many of the existing barriers to development. At the very least they expected that with independence new groups would assume control of the state and ultimately control the direction of development and national economic policy. However, independence proved a bitter disappointment for many. African and Asian ruling groups and their subject populations soon learned what their counterparts in Latin America already knew too well: Political decolonization was not equal to economic decolonization, and it certainly did not guarantee unfettered economic progress.

Attaining control over the institutions and mechanisms of governance was no small achievement for nationalist leaders, and state control increased over many aspects of the economy as a result of the national planning processes they initiated. However, decolonization alone made little contribution to their control over the pace at which natural resources were extracted from their territory or over the foreign enterprises operating in their countries. State bureaucrats gradually obtained greater control over domestic commodity production and exports, but they had little control over the international markets in which commodities were traded, and no greater access to the technology and information needed for the production, extraction, and marketing of those commodities. At about the same time, multinational corporations began to challenge local business classes with threats of denationalization or stiff competition in limited domestic financial markets. Indigenous businessmen were either losing control of their own enterprises or losing the opportunity to develop them. Finally, despite the fact that decolonization was accomplished in the name of the masses, with very few exceptions laborers and peasants lost some control over the prices their products obtained in the national market and experienced a decline in their general standard of living.

The cumulative impact of these developments led to recurring efforts to attain economic decolonization (i.e. to take national control over natural resources, enterprises, markets, information, and development paths) during the 1960s and 1970s. The Organization of Petroleum Exporting Countries was undoubtedly the most successful of these efforts. The OPEC countries affected prices in the international market, increased their control over the world market in petroleum, renegotiated the terms of their relationship with the multinational oil companies, and became major actors in international financial organizations. However, OPEC has been the exception, not the rule (despite alarmist efforts of a decade ago portraying a growing threat from the Third World). The New International Economic Order negotiations, by contrast, are an unmitigated failure. No one who writes with sympathy for either side in the multilateral negotiations has anything hopeful to say about the process or about the outcomes. The global recession of the early 1980s once again highlighted the vulnerability of most of the world's smaller economies to fluctuations in the economies of the largest countries, and it rejuvenated their desire to control their own economies. Even the newly industrializing countries, whose export-led growth made them the greatest national success stories of the late 1970s, have proven vulnerable to protectionism and the vagaries of the international market in the early 1980s.

Having control, increasing control, or obtaining control is more salient today than it was twenty or even ten years ago. The possibility for change appears to have increased as significant challenges to the legitimacy of the existing system for maintaining control (the liberal regime founded at Bretton Woods) have emerged. The breakdown of the Bretton Woods monetary system, the realization of global resource scarcities, and an enhanced perception of systemic partiality, unfairness, and vulnerability have all contributed to the salience of control as an issue. As interdependence became increasingly apparent—initially as a description of a trend, but subsequently as deliberate policy—it heightened everyone's concern with control. By challenging and eroding national control, interdependence variously provoked neomercantilism, radical self-reliance, and religious anti-Westernism.

In the wake of all this evidence about the centrality of the issue of control, what can we say about the most widespread attempt to obtain control over enterprises and the direction of national development in the last twenty years—the indigenization, divestiture, or mandatory joint-venture programs that nearly every country, irrespective of development path or ideological orientation, has enacted? Do these countries, their indigenous business groups, their working classes, or their peasants have any more control over their economies as a result of these programs?[5]

---

[5] This question should not be confused with the question of whether dependence has

Indigenization programs are measures designed to increase local (state or private) participation in and control of significant economic enterprises or sectors in an economy. They are usually enacted at the national level and are often concentrated in specific sectors of the economy or targeted against specific populations (i.e. either against all foreign companies in general or against a particular nationality of alien entrepreneurs such as the South Asians in East Africa). Nationalization is technically a form of indigenization in which only the state, rather than the state and private individuals in the local business sector, appropriates the shares or assets of the enterprises indigenized.

Indigenization measures are an obvious first step for state or business elites interested in increasing their control over a national economy.[6] From their perspective, the international market may be responsible for many of their development problems, but it is largely unassailable unless they have a successful commodity cartel. Therefore, indigenization allows states or local business classes to do something active, to move against the representatives of foreign capital (the multinational or transnational corporations) captive in their sovereign territory. They usually begin by pursuing personnel indigenization, often by enacting immigration restrictions or stipulating that a certain percentage of senior managers be indigenous. They ordinarily follow this with equity indigenization, requiring that a fixed or gradually increasing percentage of the ownership of enterprises be obtained by the state or local business groups (sometimes in designated sectors such as banking or resource extractive industries and sometimes in the economy as a whole). Eventually, they are likely to complete the package by enacting local-content requirements, stipulating that a certain percentage of the raw materials or inputs used in production by manufacturing enterprises be obtained locally.

Virtually every country in the world, irrespective of its development orientation or level of development, currently has some form of indigenization program. Both socialist Tanzania and capitalist South Korea have mandatory joint-venture programs. Historically, many countries interested in a rapid capitalist development have employed them, Japan and Germany are notable nineteenth century examples. Recently, many advanced industrial countries enacted forms of them

---

been reduced or development has been advanced. The consequences of increased indigenous control of foreign enterprises for dependence and development (as well as the impact of dependence and development on indigenous control) are important, but analytically separable, questions that will be addressed elsewhere in the text.

[6] Labor and the peasantry are often mobilized to support them, but they rarely, if ever, are direct beneficiaries of them.

either as a way of preserving national identity (in the case of Canada) or as a way of supporting declining industries (in the case of recent U.S. labor pressures for local-content requirements in the automobile industry).

My objective in this book is to understand why economic nationalist programs like indigenization have been undertaken, how they have been implemented, and, most important, what has changed as a result. Have states or local capitalists in developing countries obtained or increased their control of significant economic enterprises and consequently of their economic development as a result of indigenization? On which issues (finance, production), at what levels (at the level of the firm, the economic sector, the nation), and for whom (for local business, for state bureaucrats, for the masses) have they done so? Is development enhanced?[7] Is dependence reduced?[8] Although the welfare implications of these programs are important and will be considered in the analysis that follows, my central interest is to determine the direction and magnitude of change (if any) in the control of firms, economic sectors, and the direction of national development. Since indigenization involves an attempt to obtain control over resources, enterprises, and to a lesser degree markets and the means of production, it is important (and appropriate) to examine it in detail.

On the surface, many changes have taken place in the relationship among states, local business, and foreign enterprises in the last decade. The days when multinational corporations indirectly ruled countries are over (e.g. United Fruit in Central America, Firestone in Liberia, Aramco in Saudi Arabia). The creation of wholly owned subsidiaries through direct foreign investment is also a thing of the past. Nearly everywhere they operate, multinational corporations are forced into joint ventures with state or local capital, and increasingly they are being forced to accept minority equity positions. Most multinationals have replaced expatriate managers with local managers in the countries in which they operate. Expatriates are often too expen-

---

[7] Development is defined most broadly here as the process whereby a highly integrated economy and society are created which are capable of substantially providing for the basic needs of the masses of the population. As we shall see in Chapter 1, different theoretical approaches to international political economy have different and mutually exclusive definitions of development.

[8] A country's situation of dependence is defined by the extent to which its significant economic, social, and political developments are (and have historically been) conditioned by, or contingent upon, developments in other countries, usually the advanced industrial ones.

sive to maintain in foreign environments anyway. Local-content requirements are being met in many cases, at least when domestic production is sufficient to meet the annual consumption needs of the
joint-venture producers.[9] Very little new investment is taking place
globally at the present time, and multinational corporations tread
lightly in what many consider a dangerous global climate. From the
perspective of the multinational corporation there is little doubt that
major changes have occurred. Business environments are far more difficult for them today than they were a decade or two ago, regardless
of how well companies are meeting the challenge.

But this is not the impression one gains from speaking with developing-country businessmen, policymakers, or labor representatives.
They are each increasingly frustrated by their inability to determine
outcomes in matters of pressing concern to them. They acknowledge
that changes have taken place in their relationship with multinational
corporations, but many continue to distrust the multinationals and
are not satisfied with the progress they have made in monitoring, participating in, and controlling their operations. Businessmen, policymakers, and laborers are all acutely aware of the extent to which multinational corporations can materially affect their well-being. The
global recession of the 1980s has heightened this perception and the
sense of frustration felt by many of them.

Thus, there is often a direct conflict of interest between the foreign
headquarters of multinational corporations and developing-country
states or local business classes over the issue of control. Company
headquarters want to maintain control over operations in developing
countries, and to keep their subsidiary network intact. By enacting indigenization programs, alliances of state elites and local businessmen
are attempting to obtain greater control over those same operations
to give them a greater ability to determine the direction and pace of
their national development or to receive more of the earnings from
the most profitable enterprises operating in their countries. There are
always some areas of agreement between the multinationals and their
joint-venture partners, but there are also considerable areas of disagreement. This struggle for control is going on wherever international business operates. What is not so clear is who is winning in this
confrontation: the multinationals, the state, local business classes, all
three, or some combination of any two of them. There is little doubt

[9] One of the major constraints on the enforcement of local-content requirements in
many developing countries is the inadequate supply of domestically produced raw materials or other inputs required for production.

that considerable changes are underway in the relationship between these actors, changes that are influenced by, but not entirely dependent upon, global economic trends. Not so clear, however, are the direction and magnitude of these changes. The problems of assessing them are considerable, and will be taken up in the discussion of different contemporary theoretical approaches to international political economy which follows in Chapter 1.

CHAPTER ONE

Assessments of Indigenization: A Critical Review of Six Theoretical Approaches

THERE are as many different perspectives on indigenization and economic nationalism as there are people writing about these topics. However, six distinct theoretical approaches to contemporary international political economy can be identified as important in the discussion of these issues today. Each of these theoretical approaches has different ideas about what development is and what it should be. Each also has a different interpretation of the direction of change in the relationship between rich and poor in the world economy since the mid-1970s. The issue of control is central to many of their concerns, and different perspectives can be defined on the basis of how they deal with it as an issue.

Most North American scholars tend to assess different theoretical perspectives, if they deal with them at all, in isolation, outside of their context, and existing in the objective realm of theoretical social science. At most they see two, and occasionally three, perspectives on any issue, usually a liberal, a conservative, and a radical interpretation. I will attempt to redress this somewhat parochial imbalance by considering a variety of "radical" theories and situating each in its social and political context. There are at least three distinct schools within what is normally regarded as the radical approach that have something important to say about the direction and magnitude of the change between rich and poor in the contemporary world economy. Two of them are from within the dependency tradition and one represents a more classical interpretation of Marxism. And at least three distinct schools currently coexist with roots in the neoclassical economic tradition that also have significant statements to make about the issue. One is the perspective associated with international business and management training in U.S. business schools, the view of what I call "conservative neoclassical realists." Another is a view more commonly associated with the U.S. government, the perspective of liberal internationalists. Structuralist critics occupy a third position, occasionally mediating between radical and neoclassical traditions.

The following review of six theoretical approaches is structured to guide my analysis of the central question posed in the introduction, namely: What are the direction and magnitude of change (if any) in the control of firms or economic sectors, or the pattern of national development since 1970? I am not looking for a "correct" single approach, and do not intend to derive explicit hypotheses from them for a test of each theory. Rather, I am culling the theoretical literature for general guidelines, analytical distinctions, and methodological insights on an important question. In the empirical and theoretical discussions in succeeding chapters, I will construct a synthesis of non-contradictory aspects of these various approaches into an explanation of the sources and consequences of a concrete historical example of the struggle over control: indigenization in Nigeria. In many ways, the construction of this synthesis is the major theoretical and methodological contribution of this work.

CONSERVATIVE NEOCLASSICAL REALISTS

Most American businessmen, and many of their counterparts in Europe and Japan, subscribe to the view that foreign enterprise is essential for the development and economic well-being of the countries in the world and that indigenization programs and other examples of "political interference" are a mistake. They are a mistake, to be sure, for multinational enterprises, but they are also a mistake for countries genuinely interested in development. This is not the view of a disinterested analyst, it is the perspective from which one of the major actors operates.

International-management courses and texts present a more generalized and qualified version of this argument than businessmen operating in a foreign environment on a day-to-day basis. Nonetheless, their basic assumptions, objectives, definitions, and arguments are the same. They are concerned with the problem of maintaining access to Third World markets, or production locations, and throughout the 1970s they were concerned with the growing tendency of governments to impose restrictions on the operations of foreign enterprises in their economies. More recently the attention of both business school analysts and multinational managers has been focussed even more on competition faced by multinationals from other countries and the relationship between business and government in other advanced industrial countries. This has, not surprisingly, been a particularly prominent concern among Americans.

Conservative neoclassical realists contend that the investment and other activities of foreign enterprises are highly beneficial to developing countries. Multinationals not only provide capital, skills, technology, market access, and employment, they also "mobilize local resources that would otherwise not be mobilized—or, at least release foreign exchange available to a country to do the same thing."[1] Some conflict between host-country goals and multinational operations is inevitable, but on balance the trade-off between the costs and benefits to host countries is in favor of the benefits. Multinational executives are more candid and less guarded about their countributions to development. They are convinced that developing countries could not get along without them and that economic development is the creation of private foreign enterprise.

Development is always discussed, but rarely defined, by conservative neoclassical realists. It is an issue that daily confronts the executive of any multinational operation resident in a developing country abroad, whether it comes from the difficulty of getting a ministry to process paperwork or from the experience of getting to work on congested roads. International-management texts discuss development as an objective of host-country governments, but it is not their central concern and is accordingly not discussed explicitly. For the most part, development is equated with industrialization and rapid economic growth. When social development is considered, it is defined as modernization or Westernization. Most managers believe that the development of the local business and government elite can be judged by the extent to which they share the same values and operating procedures as the multinational manager. That is, the more modern they are, the more like us they become.

Conservative neoclassical realists do not think that the degree of change between rich and poor in the world economy has been significant during the last decade. That is one of the reasons they consider themselves realists. While it is certainly true that nearly every economy in the world today has imposed restrictions on the operations of multinational corporations (and the developing countries have usually been at the forefront of this process), the multinational enterprise "is not an unprotected, misused pawn of omnipotent nations; it is a powerful player in the international business game."[2] As far as the multinational managers are concerned, they still control their joint ventures, even in cases where they have lost the majority of the equity involved. In response to the suggestion that they no longer control host-country economies, most neoclassical realists would respond

[1] Robock, Simmonds, and Zwick 1977: 277.
[2] Ibid., p. 245.

that they never did control them. The North–South negotiations for a new international economic order are generally viewed with cynicism and most certainly as a failure, although some writers express concern that they came close, "even without being implemented, to damaging permanently the global economic machine that produced the wealth the Third World so much wants to share."[3] However, by the beginning of the 1980s most individuals associated with this perspective began to think that the realists in the developing countries had prevailed. Economic nationalism, whether expressed through multilateral negotiations or through individual state actions, appeared to be on the decline. It appeared that the pragmatists among the elite in the developing countries had prevailed, and that they had begun to realize that they needed the multinational enterprises more than the multinationals needed them.

Having described the context, general perspective, some of the assumptions, and some of the central definitions of this approach, what can we say about its perspective on indigenization? In general terms indigenization is viewed as an example of host-country political interference, a nationalistic mistake with high costs and low returns to the indigenizing country.[4] These costs are especially high in the case of developing countries, since they have more to gain from the presence of multinational enterprise than their more developed counterparts. Indigenization is an example of national policy enacted as "nations have become increasingly aware of the nature and growing importance of multinational enterprises with global horizons."[5]

No general theory has emerged within this tradition to describe the sources of economic nationalism in developing countries. Most international-management texts are more concerned with elaborating business strategies to respond to economic nationalism than with analyzing its sources. Nevertheless, they do present a general argument about it. Political "interference" such as indigenization is likely "[w]henever foreign-owned firms are perceived, rightly or wrongly, to operate in such a way as to inhibit host-country national economic, political, or social goals."[6] Nationalistic pressures build up to produce

---

[3] Bissell 1978: 240.

[4] The term "political interference" is used to desribe indigenization and other host-country government restrictions on the operations of multinational enterprises in Eiteman and Stonehill 1973: 228–259.

[5] Robock et al. 1977: 221.

[6] Eiteman and Stonehill 1973: 236. Note that it is the perception, rather than the existence, of a conflict between multinational enterprise and host-country goals that is the source of the interference.

controls on foreign ownership, but these pressures do not come from a rationally acting or motivated state:"Few people would attempt to argue that countries act rationally. Pressure groups, coalitions, selective perception, and a range of other behavioral phenomena better explain particular decisions."[7] The major groups or actors to monitor are the parliamentary opposition (if any exists), anarchist or guerrilla groups, students, labor, peasants, ethnic minorities, and occasionally local business groups whose vested interests may be challenged by the presence of multinational enterprise. Often, indigenization programs are enacted by a faltering government in an attempt to rally popular support. Because of their proximity to the issue on a day-to-day basis, most multinational managers are less cautious in their assessment of the sources of economic nationalism. According to a survey conducted of 212 corporate members of the Council of the Americas in 1970:

> The businessmen felt that the major reason for the growing tide of economic nationalism in Latin America stemmed from frustration and dissatisfaction with the slow pace of economic development. These resentments were often encouraged by demagogues and ambitious politicians and then directed against the highly visible U.S. investor, who became the target or whipping boy, rather than at their own leaders who had failed to initiate meaningful reforms.[8]

From the perspective of a conservative neoclassical realist, the objectives of indigenization measures are captured in the preceding quotation. Appeals to nationalism do much to save a faltering regime. They can also launch a self-serving opposition, trying to demonstrate its toughness to the public. Occasionally, indigenization may result from pressures brought by a local business group seeking protection from the competition of multinational enterprise. Although countries may not act rationally, state bureaucrats within them may attempt to promote their own objectives (such as improving foreign exchange position, monetary stability, defense, economic independence, or national prestige) by pursuing indigenization. More cynical observers would add personal aggrandizement to the list of objectives of state officials.

When they assess the outcome of indigenization measures, neoclassical realists see very little to be enthusiastic about. The more successful a country is at altering control of foreign enterprises, the worse off

[7] Robock et al. 1977: 263.
[8] Swansbrough 1973: 69.

it becomes. Fortunately for both the multinationals and for the host countries, most multinationals have been able to retain control of their operations despite their loss of majority equity. And it appears that the pressures for economic nationalism abated somewhat during the global recession of the 1980s.

At the level of the enterprise, therefore, most neoclassical realists do not see significant change. To be sure, some foreign enterprises have been taken over, with dire consequences for the host country (since employment of local nationals as heads of subsidiaries reduces the efficiency of the firm and accordingly its value).[9] However, the countervailing power of the multinational enterprise confronted with host-country nationalism can be considerable. Only the less capable multinational managers are unable to utilize the range of countervailing measures open to them.

Most international-management texts have chapters or sections describing "the means at the command of international firms for adjusting to controls and for exerting countervailing power."[10] Companies can refuse to make new investments, induce home-country support, or deter host-country controls by stimulating local enterprise, developing local allies, sharing ownership through joint ventures, selectively divesting ownership, and acquiring multiple nationality or changing nationality. If a company has not yet established a subsidiary in the indigenizing country, it can choose from a wide variety of defensive entry and operating strategies. And there is always the option of resorting to legal defenses in host-country or international courts.[11] Multinational managers rarely, if ever, admit that they might have lost control over the indigenized enterprises they manage. It would reflect badly on their capabilities if they were to do so. They rather elaborate the complex combinations of strategies they employ to retain control over their operations, strategies tailored to the specific context of their industry, host-country environment, and internal corporate organization.

The consequences of indigenization for particular industries or economic sectors vary according to the degree to which control at the level of individual enterprises has changed hands. There are obvious learning costs associated with indigenization of personnel or equity and these are likely to be reflected in the overall performance of an industry. Unless the technology is widely accessible or easily acquired,

[9] McMillan and Gonzales 1964: 98–106, summarized in Fayerweather 1976: 60.
[10] Robock et al. 1977: 245.
[11] All of these headings correspond to subject headings in ibid., pp. 245–259.

neoclassical realists contend that indigenization will lower productivity in an industry. By reserving certain industries or sectors for indigenous producers with a ban on further foreign investment or a takeover of existing foreign enterprises, indigenization can also begin "dulling the threat of competition" and leave indigenous producers with an unhealthy degree of protection.[12] Although prohibitions on foreign investment may make sense in areas such as national defense, they are simply not justifiable in most industries.

At the national level, neoclassical realists argue that indigenization is likely to discourage foreign investment. Once controls on foreign ownership are instituted, "the inflow of investment will slacken, and if the controls are high enough, or the nationalistic pressures seem likely to produce such controls, the inflow may dry up altogether."[13] This will have obvious adverse effects on development as defined by neoclassical writers, especially since the less developed countries have more to gain from foreign investment in their territory than any other country. Although countries periodically impose restrictions on the operations of multinational corporations in their territories, this trend is not a secular one. An optimal control model can be employed to explain swings in government policy. After controls have been introduced, "Interests from within the country that realize that investment is being forgone are then likely to begin advocating policies that will bring the country back toward its control optima, pointing out the national benefits from doing so."[14] From the vantage point of businessmen operating in the contemporary Third World, the textbook language of optimal control may sound a bit unreal. Nevertheless, their outlook is very much the same. For them, indigenization is a manageable interference in their operations that is not in the best interests of the developing countries. It decreases productivity, retards development, and ultimately impoverishes the bulk of the population. Eventually, more realistic statesmen and policies prevail and more "sensible" programs are enacted.

LIBERAL INTERNATIONALISTS

Liberal internationalists work within the neoclassical tradition and therefore share many of the positions ascribed to the neoclassical realists. They agree that indigenization is a mistake for the developing countries, although they find it more comprehensible. Where they

[12] Schmidt 1978: 281.
[13] Robock et al. 1977: 277.
[14] Ibid.

differ most emphatically with the realists is on the degree of change between rich and poor in the world economy. While the neoclassical realists minimize the significance of indigenization, liberal internationalists point to it as a primary example of the changing power configuration between host countries and multinational enterprises. Host-country governments are increasing their power at the expense of the multinationals and this has significant (and alarming) implications for the growth of protectionism throughout the globe.

Liberal internationalism is most closely associated with the governments of the advanced industrial economies, especially the government of the United States. It is somewhat more academic than the pragmatic, results-oriented view prevalent in business schools or the business world. It reflects the view of academic economists who have spent more time working in the government than working in the private sector. Liberal internationalists are defenders of the post-1945 American-dominated status quo (or regime) against a growing and invidious neomercantilist, protectionist challenge. Like the neoclassical realists, they are concerned with keeping access to Third World markets and production sites. However, rather than concentrate on advice to multinational managers, liberal internationalists concentrate their efforts on governments of both rich and poor countries. Major works within this tradition have emerged in the United States when its commitment to liberal internationalism has been challenged by the American labor movement.[15]

Liberal internationalists agree with neoclassical realists that direct foreign investment is, on balance, good for developing countries. Their analysis is somewhat more guarded, and they do not make inflated claims about the contributions of multinationals to employment or a host country's foreign-exchange position. Instead, they conclude more cautiously:

> The bulk of economic theory and the limited empirical work that has been done suggest that its [foreign direct investment's] aggregate effects are usually positive on national income, jobs, and government revenues in the host countries. However, the contribution of the firms to development, on these criteria, could be improved further. . . . And major doubts remain about the impact of foreign direct investment on both the capital and current accounts of host-country balance-of-payments positions.[16]

[15] Exemplary works in this vein are Vernon 1971 and Bergsten, Horst, and Moran 1978. Both were published in the wake of labor pressures on Congress for restrictive measures on foreign investment and for increased local content.

[16] Bergsten et al. 1978: 368–369.

Because they acknowledge that foreign investment can have some adverse effects on development, liberal internationalists are not surprised by the growth of economic nationalism throughout the world. They are alarmed by this development, however. It makes the task of constructing an international regime in which all can continue to benefit more difficult.

Like the neoclassical realists, liberal internationalists begin their discussion of development in terms of economic growth and performance. The contribution of multinational enterprises to host-country income is the starting point for most discussions of development. But liberal internationalists are likely to go one step further and include consideration of the effects of foreign investment on host-country distribution of income. They are well versed in the common criticism of traditional neoclassical approaches that economic growth does not equal development. "Growth with distribution" better summarizes their conception of what development is.[17]

When they survey the changes that have taken place between rich and poor in the world economy over the last several decades, liberal internationalists are apt to dramatize their significance. Whether they warn about the threat from the Third World or plead for a massive infusion of developmental resources, liberal internationalists contend that the changes are both significant and permanent. Few liberal internationalists argue that the North–South negotiations accomplished anything directly.[18] The more significant trend they see is that developing-country governments are increasing their bargaining power at the expense of that of the multinationals and their home governments. This trend is irreversible, largely because of the increased capability of states to take advantage of significant recent changes in the global economic and political environment.

Because they accept the argument that foreign investment is not an undisguised blessing for developing countries, liberal internationalists see economic nationalism as a rational response for host-country governments. Indigenization programs, in particular, are viewed as a legitimate attempt to promote domestic economic and political objectives. However, they are a mistake, to be sure. They are a mistake because they not only fail to promote these legitimate domestic objectives, but also because they are yet another example of the dangerous

[17] This conception is consonant with the view of development currently predominant within the World Bank, many international aid agencies, and US AID.

[18] They did, of course, provide a forum for discussion, comparison, and suggestion of new host-country policies, a forum that may have significant and far-reaching indirect effects.

barriers to trade that are sweeping the globe. In the long run, even if we are not all dead, we are at least all worse off because of these barriers.

Unlike the neoclassical realists, liberal internationalists do have a general theory to explain the sources of economic nationalism in developing countries. They view the governments in the developing countries as rationally minded nationalists operating in a changing global economic and political environment. The state is the dominant actor and it acts to promote its own interests and its interpretation of the national interest. After inducing foreign investments, the state has proceeded by "then harnessing them to host-country goals."[19] The state is in a better position to do this today because of the increased competition among investors from different countries. As their competition increased,

> the cost of nationalistic demands declined both in absolute terms and in relation to the corresponding rewards in local politics. Sometimes crudely, and sometimes with great sophistication, governments in the developing world began to play foreign companies off against one another, a process that increased when European and Japanese investors began to make offers countering established U.S. companies.[20]

State elites are also more capable of monitoring and regulating multinational enterprises today than they were a decade or two ago. Many have been educated in the same schools in the advanced industrial countries as the multinational managers. They have also learned from the experience of negotiating with multinational enterprises present in their economies over a long period of time. They have learned the important lesson of the obsolescing bargain: "Once foreign investments were sunk, markets explored, and projects producing, local authorities found that they could use the subsidiary as a hostage to levy new requirements on the parent."[21] Finally, there have been significant demonstration effects stemming from the success of economic nationalism in other countries. Indigenization programs in one country have been patterned after similar programs in another, regional integration efforts such as the Andean Common Market have increased the spread of information about particular multinational enterprises, and countries have hired consultants from other countries to develop

[19] Bergsten et al. 1978: 374.
[20] Ibid.
[21] Ibid., p. 373.

their negotiating strategies. Thus, the process has "speeded up over time."[22] This combination of increased competition among investors, the growth of state capabilities, and the expansion of significant demonstration effects has contributed to a situation in which developing-country governments are better able to act as rationally minded nationalists and respond to "the domestic pressure that accompanied social mobilization, urbanization, and industrialization after the Second World War."[23]

Since liberal internationalists view indigenization as an action of rationally motivated states, they are fairly explicit about what they think are the objectives of the exercise. According to Bergsten, Horst, and Moran:

> These goals fall into four categories: (1) domestic economic objectives, such as reducing unemployment or raising tax revenues; (2) external economic objectives, such as improving the balance of payments or breaking into new markets; (3) national ownership of certain economic activities; and (4) indigenous managerial control over certain economic activities.[24]

National ownership of certain activities is especially likely in defense-related activities, utilities, and resource-extractive industries upon which a country depends heavily for its foreign exchange. Indigenous managerial control over certain economic activities is an objective that is closest to our concerns in this study, and it is pursued apparently because the state either assumes that indigenous managerial control is more manipulable or because it is inherently more consonant with government interests.[25]

When they consider the general outcome of host-country policies like indigenization, liberal internationalists emphasize the success of the policies. They admit that "[c]ertainly not all host-country demands have been met, even in part. . . . But even from the failures, host countries learn how best to get foreign investors to serve host-country needs."[26] There has been an important shift in bargaining

[22] Ibid., p. 375.

[23] Ibid., p. 374.

[24] Ibid.

[25] Although their work is not entirely in the liberal-internationalist tradition (it is more a synthesis of liberal internationalism and sophisticated-dependency analysis), Bennett and Sharpe make a useful analytical distinction along these lines in Bennett and Sharpe 1977.

[26] Bergsten et al. 1978: 378–379.

power over time away from the multinational corporation and in favor of host-country governments.

At the level of the firm this transformation is striking. The obsolescing bargain in resource-extractive activities ensures that the multinationals become hostage to host-country governments once their investment is sunk, and they are often forced   to make concessions to those governments. In manufacturing activities, "there is a definite trend toward a sharing of ownership and control."[27] Multinational corporations are being forced into joint ventures, often in a minority position in which they actually lose control. Again, the likelihood that a particular enterprise loses control depends on its position in the product cycle and the sophistication of the technology it employs. However, on balance, the trend toward a loss of control for the multinationals appears inexorable. Even the new investment activities of the multinationals will eventually undergo the same process of loss of control.

The success of indigenization at the level of an industry depends on several factors. For resource-extractive ventures it depends on how far the obsolescing bargain has advanced and on whether an effective cartel has been established to support prices and spread information internationally. For manufacturers it depends on their position in the product cycle and the degree of sophistication of the technology they employ. For both extractive and manufacturing concerns the degree of competition in their industry, whether from indigenous or from other foreign concerns, is also an important factor. That is, the greater the competition in an industry, the greater the erosion of multinational bargaining power in the face of host-country pressure.

The bargaining power of host countries has increased at the expense of the multinational enterprise, since international competition in most industries has increased, cartels are more widespread, information is more readily available, and states are generally more capable. From the perspective of a liberal internationalist, examples of successful nationalistic actions are on the rise. Because their bargaining power is enhanced, host countries are better able to extract concessions from the foreign enterprises, and this provides the host countries with greater control over the direction of their national development. This does not mean that national development will necessarily be enhanced, especially if one includes domestic income distribution in definitions of development, as liberal internationalists do. It only means that developing countries are more responsible for

[27] Ibid., p. 378.

their own development than they were in the past.[28] The host country benefits most when it tries to influence economic performance (through local-content requirements) rather than assume majority ownership of foreign enterprises operating in its territory. In either case, however, the balance of bargaining power has shifted dramatically in favor of the host countries.

STRUCTURALIST PERSPECTIVES

Structuralists occupy a position somewhere between liberal internationalists and more radical views, and they occasionally mediate between the two. Although they are trained and well versed in neoclassical economics, they are far less sanguine about its promises for development. The scholars most identified with this approach are internationalist social democrats,[29] who in many ways have provided the intellectual basis for many established Third World government approaches to development (e.g. national planning, internationally negotiated commodity agreements, etc.). Accordingly, they are generally sympathetic to and supportive of, and have occasionally provided theoretical justifications for, indigenization.

Structuralists are more common in Europe, Canada, and much of the Third World than they are in the United States. Since they are less directly responsible for the creation of the current world economic order, they tend to be more critical of it. They challenge the fairness of the world economy, and in contrast to liberal internationalists, they stress its systemic biases rather than its benefits. Structuralists are probably best known for their critiques of liberal trade theory, as represented by the early works of Hans Singer and Raul Prebisch on the secular decline in the terms of trade for raw-material commodities from developing countries.[30] They tend to be system reformists, and many were associated with the Chenery reforms of World Bank policy and more recently with the Brandt Commission. One contemporary intellectual base of the structuralist view can be found (even with all its diversity) at the Institute of Development Studies at the University of Sussex in England, many of whose fellows have a great deal of di-

[28] Presumably this excuses industrial-country governments and multinational enterprises from any (further?) responsibility for underdevelopment in the Third World. See ibid., p. 381 n. 54.

[29] Gerald Helleiner came very close to stating this explicitly in his introduction to Helleiner (ed.) 1976.

[30] See esp. Singer 1950 and Prebisch 1959. The U.N. Commission on Trade and Development (UNCTAD) has become the institutional manifestation of this view.

rect experience in development as advisors to Third World governments and international organizations.

Although they agree with other neoclassical observers that multinationals have many advantages to offer less developed countries and have been extremely important in their industrialization efforts, structuralists view direct foreign investment as a decidedly mixed blessing which has "considerable potential for both good and evil."[31] But rather than concluding (as liberal internationalists do) that foreign investment is on balance good for developing countries, structuralists emphasize its shortcomings, including its effects on indigenous entrepreneurship, foreign exchange costs, restrictive business practices, training, and consumption and production technologies.[32] They do not reach the conclusion that foreign investment should be terminated in all cases (as most radical analyses contend), but some do go as far as to suggest that "a measure of insulation" from the advanced economies would permit a region like Latin America the opportunity "to deploy the potential for entrepreneurship, skills, and capital formation which it has accumulated over the past 25 years of continuing intimate contact."[33]

For structuralists, the concept of development is inherently normative, and they are centrally concerned with its ends in terms of human living conditions. They go beyond the "growth with distribution" conception of liberal internationalists and stress that development must accomplish the satisfaction of basic needs, incorporating a reduction in absolute levels of poverty, unemployment, and inequality. "If one or two of these central problems have been growing worse, especially if all three have, it would be strange to call the result 'development,' even if per capita income doubled."[34]

Structuralists see the world economy as sharply divided between rich and poor and are sensitive to the "obscene inequalities that disfigure the world."[35] When they consider the degree of change that has taken place between rich and poor in the world economy over the last several decades, they are generally pessimistic. With the possible exception of OPEC (which generated a great deal of interest and enthusiasm from structuralist writers),[36] little of significance has changed in the relationship between rich and poor. Dudley Seers commented,

[31] Hirschman 1971: 226.
[32] Penrose 1976: 147.
[33] Hirschman 1971: 251.
[34] Seers 1972: 123.
[35] Ibid., p. 128.
[36] See esp. the essays by Helleiner, Maizels, Radetzki, Streeten, and Stewart in Helleiner (ed.) 1976.

I am alarmed at the phrase, a "second development decade." Another "development decade" like the 1960's with unemployment rates and inequality rising by further large steps, would be politically and economically disastrous, whatever the pace of economic growth![37]

Many structuralist accounts of the success of the more recent Brandt Commission recommendations are equally pessimistic.[38]

Because they consider nonmarket distortions to be at the source of many of the world economy's structural and systemic biases, structuralists tend to favor intervention in the market—at both the national and the international level—to correct those distortions. Cartels and commodity agreements are the logical prescription of their analysis of trade distortions, while economic nationalism and indigenization follow logically from their analysis of the highly mixed consequences of unregulated foreign investment.[39] Thus, for structuralists, indigenization programs are not only justifiable, they are desirable.

Like the liberal internationalists, most structuralists view rationally motivated governments as the principal source of indigenization. Since there are legitimate conflicts of interest between multinationals and host countries, governments will "want to curb the activities of foreign firms or to reduce the cost of their operations."[40] Since multinationals will act to maximize their own interests in host countries, "It is appropriate, therefore, for the latter to exert their own power in order to obtain a greater gain than they otherwise would get—in other words, to use the power of the state to control the behaviour of multinational corporations."[41] There is, after all, a long history of indigenization efforts. Repurchases of securities by nationals of the borrowing countries in the days of portfolio investment "took place on a large scale in such countries as the United States, Italy, Spain, Sweden, and Japan in the late nineteenth and early twentieth centuries."[42] What has changed today, however, is the fact that with direct foreign investment the transfer of ownership and control requires either the initiative of the parent multinational or concerted action by the state.

[37] Seers 1972: 128.

[38] Seers 1980.

[39] Since both of these interventions ordinarily entail a strengthening of the state, it is obvious why structuralist views resonate so well with Third World technocrats and U.N. system bureaucrats.

[40] Penrose 1976: 149.

[41] Ibid.

[42] Hirschman 1971: 235.

This is what Albert Hirschman meant when he discussed "the 'lost art' of liquidating and nationalizing foreign investments."[43]

Since they assume that some of the benefits of foreign investment will be forthcoming only if governments influence or control multinationals, structuralists are fairly straightforward about the objectives of the exercise. In addition to the political objective of ensuring that key decisions affecting the local economy are not made abroad without consideration of their effects on local development, there are a number of other areas where host countries will want to maximize their own gains. They will particularly want to minimize foreign-exchange costs and ward off monopolistic tendencies (restrictive export, marketing, or sourcing policies) of multinational investors.[44]

Structuralists agree with neoclassical realists that most indigenization programs have not been terribly successful. But unlike other neoclassical writers, structuralists contend that the principal flaws in indigenization stem from the design or implementation of the programs, not from their basic objectives. To ensure that the programs accomplish their objectives, it is necessary that they be coordinated with other policies such as limitations of profit remittances, currency controls, effective training programs, and/or restrictions on tie-in clauses.[45]

At the level of the individual enterprise, most structuralists agree with liberal-internationalists that host countries have improved their bargaining position vis-à-vis foreign corporations in recent years. They caution, however, that "all of this does not mean that governments of the Third World have unlimited bargaining power and can do what they like without a cost to themselves."[46] In the first place, ownership of an enterprise, even 100 percent ownership, is by no means a sufficient condition for control of that enterprise (especially if it remains integrated in a multinational's network). Secondly, the power of the state is severely circumscribed by the bargaining skill of its negotiators. It takes knowledge and skill of a very high order to control an indigenized firm effectively. It also takes a great deal of will on the part of the new joint-venture partners to want to control the operations. It is for this reason structuralists are more optimistic about the effectiveness of indigenization when states, rather than

[43] Ibid., pp. 233–236.

[44] See esp. Penrose 1976: 154–168 for a discussion of these concerns.

[45] See either Hirschman 1971 or Penrose 1976 for a discussion of appropriate ways of combining indigenization with other development objectives.

[46] Penrose 1976: 151.

indigenous businessmen, are the joint-venture partners of the multinationals.[47]

At the sectoral level, structuralists suggest that indigenization is likely to encourage rapid depletion of resources in raw-material-extractive enterprises and discourage the introduction of technological innovation just prior to the transfer of shares.[48] Depletion of resources is less of a problem in manufacturing (where most indigenization is directed). Nevertheless, access to, understanding of, and control over new technology are much greater problems, especially when the government is the recipient of the shares offered. Hirschman suggests that coordination of divestment with other programs (such as a ceiling on profit remittances over the life of the investment, a ceiling acceptable or attractive to the multinational) may be necessary to ensure continued access to new technology in indigenized firms.[49]

At the national level, the consequences of indigenization are likely to be mixed, but beneficial on balance. Inequality is likely to increase, as the shares tend to go to the small group of entrenched capitalists in a position to purchase them. But this tendency can be ameliorated by either state acquisition of shares or deliberate efforts to broaden their distribution. Direct foreign investment in the economy might come to a halt, but this would by no means necessarily be harmful. On the contrary, "it is quite conceivable that a temporary suspension of the flow of private capital toward Latin America would be beneficial rather than calamitous for the area's growth."[50] It would often be even easier to make that claim for the area's development as that concept is defined by structuralist writers. Finally, the amount of experience and training occasioned by participation in joint ventures with foreign enterprises is likely to make a considerable contribution to national development.

"VULGAR" DEPENDENTISTAS

Dependency writers disagree with virtually everything suggested by neoclassical realists, liberal internationalists, and other "bourgeois" social scientists. They come from a completely different epistemological tradition with a very different political agenda. However, they do

[47] Ibid., pp. 148 and 169.
[48] Hirschman 1971: 245.
[49] Ibid., pp. 245–246.
[50] Ibid., p. 251.

agree that indigenization is at best a mistake, at worst another bourgeois mystification for continued imperialistic exploitation.

The dependency tradition is sufficiently broad, differentiated, and influential to warrant a discussion of at least two of its most important variants.[51] Each has its roots in the ECLA critique of Latin American import-substitution industrialization, Marxist analysis, and the direct participation of its theorists in Latin American political and economic controversies. They differ, however in a number of key respects. Let us begin with a discussion of the more strident and probably more influential of the two, the currently out-of-favor, stagnationist view of the so-called vulgar dependentistas.[52] The exemplary writers in this tradition are André Gunder Frank, Theotonio Dos Santos, and to some extent (although in a different geographical context) Samir Amin. Their conception of dependence is most frequently presented as representative of the dependency tradition by its critics from the left[53] or from the right.[54]

There is little doubt that vulgar dependentistas view the activities of multinational enterprises as detrimental to Third World development. Multinationals distort the entire process of development by extracting surplus for export to the metropole, denationalizing domestic industry, utilizing inappropriate capital-intensive technologies, producing largely for the upper classes, enhancing domestic disarticulation, and exacerbating domestic inequality.[55] Multinationals are agents of imperialism and central to neocolonial exploitation in the latest phase of technological industrial dependence.[56]

Their conception of development is quite different from that of the approaches we considered earlier. Development is much more than growth, or growth with distribution. The explanations provided by bourgeois scholars are inadequate because they "very seldom try to grapple with the issue in its totality."[57]

[51] Gabriel Palma suggests a threefold categorization differentiating among Frank and Dos Santos in one school, Sunkel and Furtado in a second, and Cardoso and Faletto in a third in Palma 1978. Although on some issues the differences among these three schools are considerable, for the purposes of this study a distinction between Palma's first school and the others is sufficient.

[52] The term "vulgar dependency" was first used by Fernando H. Cardoso in Cardoso 1977. It was used to differentiate his approach from the less nuanced, more widely read, and more influential dependency work of A. G. Frank (among others).

[53] See esp. the treatment of dependency writings in Brewer 1980 or in Warren 1980.

[54] See esp. Smith 1978.

[55] All of these arguments are made in Frank 1972b: 36–45.

[56] Dos Santos 1970: 232.

[57] Rodney 1974: 13.

Real *development* involves a structural transformation of the economy, society, polity and culture of the satellite that permits the self-generating and self-perpetuating use and development of the people's potential. Development comes about as a consequence of a people's frontal attack on the oppression, exploitation, and poverty that they suffer at the hands of the dominant classes and their system.[58]

Development is more than just economic diversification, industrialization, or political institutionalization. It is the creation of socialism. It is important to note that vulgar dependentistas view the process and pace of capitalist development as fundamentally different in the center and periphery of the world economy. Capitalist development is blocked in the periphery.

When vulgar dependentistas consider the change between rich and poor in the world economy in the last decade, they are likely to belittle its significance. Amin suggests that "the prospects in sight at the present time do not suggest a progressive narrowing of the center-periphery gap, within the context of capitalism."[59] Imperialism is still the dominant feature of the world economy and is responsible for the underdevelopment that continues in its periphery. Formal colonial relations may have disintegrated, but the essential relationship between the rich (exploiters) and poor (exploited) remains essentially unchanged. Old relationships are simply reappearing in new forms: Direct foreign investment has been replaced by licensing arrangements with multinational enterprises and foreign aid has been replaced by commercial bank borrowing. Anyone who fails to see the maintenance of the essential relationship between rich and poor, between metropole and satellite, between center and periphery, is being misled by bourgeois mystification. To quote Frank: "Contemporary underdevelopment is simply a continuation of the same fundamental processes of dependence, transformation of economic and class structure, and lumpenbourgeois policies of underdevelopment which have been in operation throughout our history."[60]

Indigenization is an excellent example of the semblance of change between rich and poor. It consists of the "imposition of certain timid limitations on foreign control"[61] that are largely ineffectual. Multinational enterprises are still able to control all of the significant and

[58] Cockcroft, Frank, and Johnson (eds.) 1972: xvi.
[59] Amin 1976: 38.
[60] Frank 1972a: 92.
[61] Dos Santos 1971: 225.

essential operations of indigenized enterprises through their control of international markets, their technological monopolies, and their deliberate sabotage of the program. Their joint-venture partners from the local bourgeoisie are "merely intermediaries, subordinate allies, in this process of exploitation" who assist them in the subversion of any state-led nationalist objectives that might accompany the program.[62]

The local bourgeoisie is the principal source of indigenization, according to vulgar dependentistas. It uses government cabinets and other instruments of the state to establish "imperialist-nationalist joint ventures."[63] It is during periods of global systemic crisis that the local bourgeoisie attempts to recruit elements of the proletariat and peasantry to support a program of economic nationalism. What the liberal internationalists or structuralists call "increased competition among investors of different nationalities" vulgar dependentistas call "inter-imperialist contradictions during the crisis of capitalism." They are both describing the same phenomenon, and it creates opportunities "for the circumspect and opportunistic policies of decadent classes which rely upon state capitalism and which try to attract the proletariat."[64]

For a vulgar dependentista, the objectives of indigenization programs have nothing to do with development. The bourgeoisie might attempt to generate support for the program in the name of nationalism, progress, or development. Their objectives, however, are far more self-serving. They are the junior partners of imperialism and necessarily favor policies that increase the subjection and dependence of their countries and renew the development of underdevelopment.[65] They will benefit materially from increased participation in joint ventures with multinational corporations, as long as they do not challenge the basic interests of foreign capital operating in their economies. They are the junior partners of imperialism, the basis of a comprador bourgeoisie, not the core of a nationalistic bourgeoisie interested in assuming control of the operations of the multinational enterprises.

Indigenization may be a success for a few well-placed individuals, but it is a failure by any other standard. It certainly does not do a great deal to mitigate the harmful consequences of multinational corporations in underdeveloped countries. Like other intermediate or reformist programs (such as bourgeois nationalism in Latin America

[62] Amin 1980: 21.
[63] Frank 1969: 174.
[64] Dos Santos 1976: 99.
[65] This is paraphrased from Frank 1972a: 16 (his introduction).

during the interwar years), it is utopian—"that is, utopian for the bourgeoisie, but politically suicidal for the people."[66]

At the level of the firm, vulgar dependentistas do not see much change. As already indicated, the joint-venture partners from the local bourgeoisie are not interested in control and play the role of comprador intermediaries by providing access to the local market for the multinationals. André Gunder Frank sarcastically described the emergence of mixed foreign and state capital ventures as follows:

> Who provides the bulk of the capital (the Latin Americans, presumably); who has or achieves effective control of the enterprises, and therefore decides what goods to produce, what industrial equipment and processes to use, when to expand and contract, etc. (the Americans, presumably); and who reaps the bulk of the profits (the Americans, presumably); and who is left with the losses when business is unfavorable (the Latin Americans, presumably)?[67]

The local bourgeoisie is likely to be absorbed in the new joint ventures, and when states try to further the national interest by entering into joint ventures with foreign capital, the only result can be that they "lose even what little political bargaining power they have left in their already all too junior partnership with imperialism."[68] This is a far cry from the argument of the liberal internationalists, with their stress on the significance of enhanced host-country bargaining power.

Although the multinationals might reduce their involvement in some sectors of the economy, those sectors are likely to be less lucrative or less central to their global operations. Low technology assembly for the local market or retail trade might be abandoned for more lucrative or secure activities elsewhere in the economy. When this happens, however, the indigenization of certain sectors is usually "accompanied by a marked lowering in the profitability of these activities, to the advantage of those, whether upstream or downstream, which are controlled by foreign capital."[69] Thus, foreign capital will still retain control over the most dynamic sectors of the economy through its technological advantages, access to finance, and ability to operate on a global scale. As a result of this flexibility, economic nationalism does not pose a serious threat to the multinationals.

At the national level, indigenization is not simply ineffective, it is positively harmful. Majority equity participation may be sought in

[66] Frank 1969: 388.
[67] Ibid., p. 391.
[68] Ibid., pp. 391–392.
[69] Amin 1976: 273.

the name of the national interest, but "[i]t is now clear that these measures only serve to submerge surviving elements of the 'national' bourgeoisie in the imperialist one."[70] That is, those members of the bourgeoisie who have not been denationalized (had their enterprises acquired by multinationals expanding in the local market) have been absorbed into the multinationals' network by entering into joint ventures with them. This eliminates the possibility of national capitalist development, enhances dependence, furthers underdevelopment, and further integrates the country into the world capitalist system:

> neo-imperialism and monopoly capitalist development in Latin America are drawing and driving the entire Latin American bourgeois class—including its comprador, bureaucratic, and national segments—into ever-closer economic and political alliance with and dependence on the imperialist metropolis.[71]

Any remaining elements of the local bourgeoisie are forced to go into nonproductive activities avoided by foreign capital.[72]

As always, workers and peasants suffer the most from these developments. Not only are their countries further absorbed into the capitalist world economy (which necessarily decreases the prospects for genuine development for the masses), but the fraction of the bourgeois class that is not absorbed must resort to superexploitation of the workers and peasants (must "squeeze some additional blood out of that stone")[73] in order to survive.

"Sophisticated" Dependentistas

Sophisticated dependentistas agree with their vulgar counterparts that contemporary development cannot be understood outside the context of the world capitalist system. They also disagree with bourgeois scholarship on most issues, emphasize the unequal and antagonistic social organization of dependent societies, and criticize indigenization programs for their role in maintaining relations of dependence. Where they break most sharply with the vulgar dependentistas is on the issue of the compatibility of dependence and development. As Gabriel Palma has suggested:

[70] Frank 1969: 391.
[71] Ibid., p. 396.
[72] Amin 1976: 245.
[73] Frank 1969: 395.

As foreign capital has increasingly been directed towards manufacturing industry in the periphery, the struggle for industrialization, which was previously seen as an anti-imperialist struggle, has become increasingly the *goal* of foreign capital. Thus dependency and industrialization cease to be contradictory, and a path of 'dependent development' becomes possible.[74]

Thus the sophisticated dependentistas have subsumed what was a paradox or problem for the vulgar dependentistas. This is part of what makes their analysis more sophisticated and more difficult to falsify, and one of the reasons their version of dependency has been less frequently cited as representative of the tradition by its critics.

Sophisticated dependentistas employ a complex dialectical methodology to understand international development that is far less dogmatic than the approach employed by writers like Frank. Their approach, which might also be called the dependent-development approach, is also much in favor among North American social-science consumers of the tradition. Sophisticated dependentistas write within the Marxist tradition, but they are heretical on some crucial points.[75] They acknowledge the possibility (and occasionally stress the importance) of state autonomy and consider Lenin's contributions to a theory of imperialism to be somewhat outdated. (Fernando Cardoso argues that although Lenin made a masterful contribution to theory, international capitalism has undergone significant changes during the twentieth century that need to be taken into consideration.)[76] Like the vulgar dependentistas, sophisticated dependentistas have participated in the debates and controversies surrounding Latin American economic and political development. Some, like Cardoso, have also participated in the political process itself by running for elective office.[77] Finally, sophisticated dependentistas are writing from the periphery of the world economy (unlike many of the classical Marxists we will consider later) and therefore have a direct experience with and stake in the consequences of contemporary dependence.

Although they are less strident than other dependentistas, sophisticated dependentistas are nonetheless highly critical of the developmental contribution of multinational corporations. As the "organi-

[74] Palma 1978: 909.
[75] The nature and magnitude of this heresy will become more apparent in the final section of this chapter, when we consider the classical Marxist approach.
[76] Cardoso 1973: 7–16.
[77] Cardoso ran successfully for the Brazilian Senate in 1982.

zational embodiment of international capital,"[78] the multinationals play a central role in the creation and maintenance of a system of dependent development. Specific situations of dependence vary according to the dialectical relationship between changes in world capitalism and the dynamics of class forces in dependent countries. That is, each country's situation of dependence is historically and contextually specific. Brazil's situation of state-led capitalist dependent development during the 1970s is different from its classic situation of export dependence in the 1930s—and both are different from Peru's situation of dependence in the 1960s. Nevertheless, some generalization about the role of the multinational corporation is possible. Multinationals distort development from what it would be like in their absence by internationalizing the internal market (the internalization of imperialism) and enhancing the disarticulation of dependent societies. Once the veneer is removed, the argument is very much the same as that made by the vulgar dependentistas: Multinationals denationalize dependent economies by displacing local producers, they create few linkages to the rest of the economy, they distort consumption patterns, transfer little technology, and form critical alliances with the state and local bourgeoisie.[79] In the end, the masses suffer from their exclusion from the process of development.[80]

Despite the frequency with which they use the term 'development,' sophisticated dependentistas are surprisingly vague (their critics call them inconsistent) about its definition. In *Dependency and Development in Latin America*, Cardoso and Faletto distinguish development from modernization and define it as entailing "less dependency" as well as "self-sustained growth based on the local capital accumulation and on the dynamism of the industrial sector."[81] In the preface to the English-language edition of the book (written ten years after the original Spanish one), they define "development" more narrowly, as "capitalist development," a form of development that "produces as it evolves, in a cyclical way, wealth and poverty, accumulation and shortage of capital, employment for some and unemployment for others."[82] Development is not merely the achievement of a "more

[78] Evans 1979: 34.

[79] All of these arguments are made by Evans in his case study of Brazil, ibid., esp. chaps. 3 and 4.

[80] Peter Evans writes in ibid., pp. 12–13 (his introduction): "One of the implications of my analysis is that the industrializing elite alliance that currently holds sway in Brazil is inherently incapable of serving the needs of the mass of the population."

[81] Cardoso and Faletto 1978: 10.

[82] Ibid., p. xxiii.

egalitarian or more just society," since these "are not consequences expected from capitalist development, especially in peripheral economies."[83] Although there is an important change in their conception of development (their more recent definition is closer to that of their Marxist critics), in both instances their definitions distinguish development in the center of the world economy from development in its periphery, something also done by the vulgar dependentistas. They also share a commitment to socialism, but their conception of socialism is closer to that of a social democrat than of a Marxist–Leninist revolutionary.

Sophisticated dependentistas want to avoid the pitfalls of stagnation in the arguments of vulgar dependentistas. The "faulty analysis" of vulgar dependentistas has left the impression that "situations of dependency are continuously and necessarily generating more underdevelopment and dependency."[84]

> But to use this approach to point out only the self-perpetuating structural mechanisms implies neglect of the contradictory results of the very process of development as well as the *possibilities* of negation of the existing order also inherent in social processes. It is therefore useful to remember that forms of dependency can change and to identify the structural possibilities for change, pinpointing the alternatives to dependency existing at any given historical moment.[85]

Sophisticated dependentistas thus allow for the possibility of change in the relationship between rich and poor in the contemporary world economy. They also discuss the growth of state power and capabilities, the success of OPEC, the sharpening of intercapitalist contradictions, and the emergence of attempts to eliminate or decrease dependence that can have an effect on this relationship.[86] This means that "[t]here may have been a redefinition of the 'forms of dependency,' in certain Latin American countries there may be 'less dependency,' and the state in these countries may be capable of exercising a greater degree of sovereignty."[87] This is not the central issue, however. The central issue is the nature of class conflicts and alliances, which in turn determines which classes and groups benefit from the change in form of

[83] Ibid.

[84] Ibid., p. x.

[85] Ibid., pp. x–xi.

[86] Cardoso and Faletto discuss these changes in the postscript to the English-language edition of *Dependency and Development*.

[87] Ibid., p. 212.

dependence. Although some change may have taken place in the relationship between rich and poor *countries* in the world economy, that change is not very substantial, and it is by no means very significant for the dominated classes in those countries.

All scholars employing a dependency approach to interpret international political economy are centrally concerned with the issue of control. "Dependency implies vulnerability to the external economy and a significant degree of external control over the local productive apparatus."[88] Indigenization and other programs of economic nationalism are introduced in the name of increasing local control and reducing external vulnerability. However, mandatory joint-venture programs (such as Mexicanization), or their functional equivalent (in the form of the triple alliance in Brazil), have not provided a basis for a less dependent form of development. Rather, they have deepened dependent development in the semiperiphery and have proven to be essential "as a strategy for accumulation in a dependent context."[89] Diversification of the industrial base is one consequence of this strategy of accumulation, but dependent development also has inherent limitations.

Sophisticated dependentistas distinguish themselves from vulgar dependentistas (and from the classical Marxists we will consider later) by allowing for the possibility that states can act relatively independently of dominant social forces. Indigenization programs provide a good illustration of this possibility. State technocrats have expanded their functions to include accumulation and finance (in addition to regulation and planning) "thereby to create a national basis from which to bargain with the multinationals."[90] Occasionally they will be joined by elements of the national bourgeoisie for whom displacement by the multinational enterprises is a major political issue.[91] Whether these programs stem from an alliance of the state and local capital or whether they are principally state-initiated depends on a country's specific situation of dependence. State autonomy is nevertheless a distinct possibility, especially when certain domestic and international conditions prevail.

States are most likely to initiate programs of economic nationalism when they confront:

> The lack of local private investment potential, the political need to prevent multinational corporations from single-handedly appro-

[88] Gereffi and Evans 1981: 58 n. 3.
[89] Evans 1979: 287.
[90] Cardoso and Faletto 1978: 205.
[91] Gereffi and Evans 1981: 49.

priating the most strategic sectors of the economy and their most dynamic branches, and even, at times, the nonexistence of international capital flows to attend to the investment needs of peripheral countries during any given period (since multinationals act on a global scale, aiming at maximizing results and not toward the continuity of local development).[92]

Denationalization, or the fear of displacement by multinationals is most likely to motivate local capital to seek protection in the form of mandatory joint ventures or some other variant of indigenization.

Although they are attempting to incorporate changing relations into their analysis, sophisticated dependentistas do not think that the degree of change from indigenization is significant. At the level of the firm, it is possible that the terms of bargaining have shifted and increased control has been obtained over some issues. This is particularly evident in cases where the state, rather than local entrepreneurs, has entered into participation with the multinationals.[93] As already discussed, states have increased the scope and variety of their activities in recent years. Their technocrats have also improved their capabilities to monitor, regulate, and bargain with the multinationals. Even in cases where local capital has entered into joint ventures with the multinationals, they are no longer simply the junior partners of foreign capital. The multinationals have begun to "share control and returns with a few elite members of the local bourgeoisie."[94]

Despite these developments, however, the emerging triple alliance of foreign capital, local capital, and the state prevents significant change in the functions of the principal actors. The state as entrepreneur or the state in alliance with foreign capital still expresses "a situation of domination, reflects the interests of dominant classes, and expresses their capacity to impose themselves on subordinate classes."[95] Local capital also remains clearly subordinate to both foreign capital and the state. Although foreign capital allows local capital to share some control (over minor issues) in operations, local capital still plays a largely integrative, intermediary role by assisting foreign capital in its attempts to penetrate the domestic market. Local capital is "embedded in local networks in a way that the multinationals cannot be"[96] and it can "provide important informal political resources" that

[92] Cardoso and Faletto 1978: 205.
[93] Evans 1979: 278. On this point, sophisticated dependentistas are very close to the structuralists.
[94] Ibid., p. 304.
[95] Cardoso and Faletto 1978: 209.
[96] Evans 1979: 161.

"can be extremely valuable in dealing with the complexities of the state bureaucracy, ferreting out favorable regulations, or escaping the effects of unfavorable ones."[97] A change in form may well have taken place with the emergence of the triple alliance, but it is not a change of basic functions or relationships. Ultimately, joint ventures between local and foreign capital "do not threaten the multinationals' control over their most important enterprises."[98]

At the sectoral level, the greatest changes have taken place in industries in which state enterprises operate. State technocrats are increasingly capable, and they have increasingly gained confidence in their ability to defend their interests in joint ventures with foreign capital. "The most important resource that local partners may possess is political power, and the local partners with the most direct political leverage are state-owned firms."[99] Industries in which large local businesses operate are also likely to demonstrate more significant changes than industries in which they are absent. Industries in which scale, finance, or advanced technology is essential for successful operation are likely to be affected less by the advent of indigenization.

At the national level, joint ventures have made strategies emphasizing national accumulation more likely. The state has expanded and fortified itself, some of the largest local businesses have been able to build extremely powerful positions, and the multinationals have been forced to modify some of their activities. At the same time, this has meant that dependent development has been enhanced. The triple alliance among multinationals, the state, and a segment of the local bourgeoisie is essential for dependent development. It is a form of development in which the state has become increasingly repressive and introduced policies that exclude the mass of the population from the benefits of economic growth. The process of accumulation under this form of development is still "vulnerable to the effects of disruptions in the international economy, and that vulnerability constitutes the most obvious limitation of the triple alliance."[100]

"CLASSICAL" MARXISTS

Classical Marxists view themselves as the true inheritors (and interpreters) of the Marxist tradition, and they consider dependency writers revisionist and deviationist. For classical Marxists, dependentistas

[97] Ibid., p. 203.
[98] Ibid., p. 209.
[99] Ibid., p. 212.
[100] Ibid., p. 290.

advocate a nationalist mythology that is both misleading and dangerous. In his critical survey of Marxist theories of imperialism, Anthony
Brewer begins his section on modern Marxist theories of development and underdevelopment with a discussion of Paul Baran's work,
which he describes as having "marked an important shift in Marxist
theory, both in its theoretical content and in the problems to which it
was addressed" and which "has become fundamental to subsequent
Marxist thinking about underdevelopment."[101] When he discusses
the work of Frank and the "dependency theorists," he begins by quoting Frank and commenting: "It is essential to realise how drastic a
break with the classical Marxists this is."[102]

Brewer and writers like Bill Warren criticize all dependentistas
(both the vulgar and the sophisticated) for arguing that development
in the center and development on the periphery of the world economy
are fundamentally different. They charge that because dependentistas
assume that peripheral development is distinctive, they miss the principal contradictions in the contemporary world economy (i.e. those
that exist between capital and labor), they idealize the process of development (condemning all capitalist development as distorted or dependent), and they become too nationalistic (and hence too concerned with the loss of *national* control, rather than concerned with
control of the means of production). Classical Marxists contend that
the dependentistas also have great difficulty incorporating major
changes in the relationship between rich and poor countries into their
analysis (such as the new latitude of developing countries in their negotiations with the multinationals, OPEC, the newly industrializing
countries, etc.), and that they attribute to dependence what are the
normal dislocations and distortions of capitalism.

This revived tradition of classical Marxism exists in most parts of
the world today and is exemplified by Laclau's critique in Latin America,[103] the writings of Warren, Brenner, and Foster-Carter in *New Left
Review*,[104] the modes-of-production debate in India during the early
1970s,[105] and recent critiques in the German journal *Peripherie*.[106]
Historically, this split between classical Marxists and dependentistas
can be traced to the Comintern debates on the Eastern question during the 1920s. Otto Kuusinen, a Finnish member of the Executive

[101] Brewer 1980: 132.
[102] Ibid., p. 158.
[103] Laclau 1971.
[104] Warren 1973; Brenner 1977; Foster-Carter 1978.
[105] Alavi 1975; Patnaik 1972; Chattopadhyay 1972.
[106] See, for example, critiques of Dieter Senghaas in *Peripherie* in the early 1980s.

Committee of the Communist International, introduced theses on the Eastern question in the Sixth Congress in 1928 that foreshadow most of the central dependency concepts (unequal exchange, underdevelopment, comprador alliances, and dependent development). Like the debate in the 1920s, the contemporary debate on these issues is concerned with what is to be done. Today's holders of the classical line are concerned that dependency approaches are dangerously misleading:

> We must recognise that opposition to the dominance of the major imperial powers is not necessarily genuine anti-imperialism, and may represent no more than a desire by a newly formed bourgeoisie to establish itself within a world system that it does not wish to change. Socialists have frequently been deceived by anti-imperialist rhetoric into supporting viciously reactionary regimes.[107]

Classical Marxists agree with dependentistas that multinational corporations are exploitative. That is, after all, the nature of capitalism itself. In this way, multinationals are no different from local capitalist firms that are equally exploitative. There is no point in attacking foreign firms "for 'disregarding the needs of the national economy' when there is no reason to suppose that domestic capital would behave any differently."[108] Further, "it is an elementary principle of Marxism that under capitalism exploitation presupposes the advance of the productive forces."[109] Thus, private foreign investment in developing countries is economically beneficial because it advances the productive forces in those countries. It is not a cause of dependence, "but rather a means of fortification and diversification of the economies of the host countries."[110] The denationalization of Latin American economies in the postwar period was only a momentary phase, reflecting the residual effects of U.S. multinational corporate postwar expansion. On balance, foreign private investment since the Second World War has probably created or at least encouraged indigenous capitalism.

When classical Marxists use the term "development," they are referring to capitalist development. Successful capitalist development is development that provides the appropriate economic, social, and political conditions for the continuing reproduction of capital, as a social system representing the highest form of commodity produc-

---

[107] Brewer 1980: 293–294.
[108] Ibid., p. 276.
[109] Warren 1980: 176.
[110] Ibid.

tion.[111] It entails the development of the productive forces, private control of the means of production, the expansion of the exchange of commodities (especially labor), and significant amounts of accumulation. Classical Marxists reject a normative definition of development for a descriptive one:

> If development is defined by reference to the "needs of the masses," then Marxists are unlikely to accept that capitalist development can fit the bill, but this leaves us unable to distinguish between continued stagnation, and development that is successful, in capitalist terms, in that it creates conditions for continued reproduction of capital.[112]

Classical Marxists are concerned about distinguishing between stagnation and successful capitalist development because it has important political implications for them. Whether recent changes between rich and poor in the world economy are examples of stagnation (the dependency view) or of successful capitalist development (the classical Marxist view) suggests who the enemy is, what is to be done, and where one begins to build socialism. Classical Marxists are confident that the change between rich and poor in the world economy in recent decades is significant: "By whatever standard it may be judged, the view that economic relations between rich and poor countries have changed only marginally since independence must be rejected."[113] Capitalism is being expanded into the developing world, as industrialization is shifted from the advanced industrial countries,[114] indigenous accumulation advances,[115] and commodity production is introduced.[116] Exploitation naturally accompanies this expansion, but the ties of dependence are being loosened.

Indigenization and mandatory joint-venture programs are excellent examples of the expansion of capitalism into the developing world. They have provided local capital with a means to accumulate, since they have enabled the ex-colonies to exercise "mounting control over foreign-owned or -controlled economic activity within their borders."[117] The programs have also set in motion a series of forces that will contribute to the formation of a national bourgeoisie.

[111] Warren 1973: 3–35.
[112] Brewer 1980: 291.
[113] Warren 1980: 171.
[114] Warren 1973: 3–41.
[115] Leys 1978.
[116] Williams 1980: esp. chap. 2, pp. 22–67.
[117] Warren 1980: 172.

Classical Marxists are less ambiguous than sophisticated dependentistas about the sources of indigenization. Their argument is closer to that of the vulgar dependentistas, since they suggest that indigenization results from local capital mobilizing state policy to further its own objectives. In the Kenyan case, Leys suggested that the state's initiatives "reflected the existing class power of the indigenous bourgeoisie, based on the accumulation of capital they had already achieved."[118] Warren makes very much the same point, and echoes the argument of liberal internationalists when he argues that local capital is more able to utilize state power when there is substantial competition among manufacturing multinationals in the less developed countries.[119] According to classical Marxists, state autonomy is a myth. The policies of indigenization are enacted at the behest of (or in the interest of) the local capitalist class that controls the state apparatus.

Indigenization may be promulgated in the name of economic nationalism, but when its deeper essences are revealed it is clearly designed to facilitate capital accumulation by the indigenous bourgeoisie. Warren describes it as an attempt to enable new ruling groups to mobilize the state apparatus to suit successful indigenous capitalism.[120] Brewer describes it as an attempt by the state apparatus to promote national capitalist development.[121] Leys concurs when he writes:

> The essential function of the state was to displace monopolies enjoyed by foreign capital and substitute monopolies for African capital, and also to supplement individual African capitals with state-finance capital and state-secured technology, to enable them to occupy the space created for them in the newly-accessible economic sectors.[122]

Not all scholars within the classical Marxist tradition agree entirely with this formulation. Writing about Nigeria, Bjorn Beckman agrees that there is "much evidence to support the proposition that the Nigerian state operates as an organ of the rising domestic bourgeoisie."[123] However, he views the state's role in fostering indigenization as "an attempt to regulate competition between international firms

[118] Leys 1978: 251.
[119] Warren 1980: 175.
[120] Warren 1973.
[121] Brewer 1980: 291.
[122] Leys 1978: 251.
[123] Beckman 1982: 44.

and the rising Nigerian bourgeoisie."[124] The state performs the larger function of serving the needs of capital (maintaining capitalist relations of production) rather than the narrower function of serving the needs of a particular fraction of capital (in this case, that of the national bourgeoisie).

For most classical Marxists, indigenization has enabled the domestic bourgeoisie in less developed countries to extract significant new concessions from multinational enterprises. At the same time, it has contributed to the deepening of capitalist relations of production throughout the Third World. At the level of the firm, "[p]artly owned subsidiaries of multi-national companies tend to come more and more under the control of local shareholders."[125] As control is transferred to indigenous partners or managers, they receive an improved division of the rent (gross profits, interest charges, royalties, and license fees), the already substantial training of indigenous personnel increases, a constant increase in the local content of production takes place, and more modern technology is transferred.[126] Thus, the argument of many classical Marxists about the degree of change at the level of the enterprise is closer to that of liberal internationalists than to that of structuralists and either vulgar or sophisticated dependentistas.

At the sectoral level, classical Marxists contend that indigenization can assist local capital in its efforts to displace foreign capital. Leys describes the process in Kenya where leading African capitalists began their accumulation in one sector (trade or agriculture) and then moved on to another (most recently manufacturing). They were able to initiate a displacement of foreign capital in manufacturing after they accumulated sufficient amounts of capital and after the narrowing scope for further displacement in trade and agriculture became increasingly apparent.[127] This sequence implies that indigenization in the sphere of circulation can evolve into pressure for indigenization in the sphere of production.

At the national level, the most significant and far-reaching consequence of indigenization is that it contributes to the development of capitalism in the developing world. The expansion of import-substitution industrialization and the rapid proletarianization of the peasantry have both contributed significantly to this process. Indigenization aids it further by providing a vehicle through which local capital

[124] Ibid., p. 48.
[125] Brewer 1980: 291.
[126] Warren 1980: 172–174.
[127] Leys 1978: 254.

can accumulate. Even though indigenization involves the acquisition of existing assets, "the significance of these transactions for the long-run potential for further accumulation by indigenous capital remains profound."[128] In addition to providing a base for subsequent accumulation, indigenization has hastened the transfer of modern technology and improved the backward and forward linkages of resource-based enterprises. Indigenization is an example of the important gains obtained whenever "nationalism has forced the pace of economic development."[129] Because it expands capitalism in the developing world, indigenization is historically progressive. At the same time, it is replete with the contradictions that accompany the development of capitalism throughout the world. It may be historically progressive, but it is also (necessarily) highly exploitative.

CONCLUSIONS

There is certainly no unanimity about indigenization or about the direction and magnitude of change that has taken place between rich and poor in the world economy during the last fifteen years. The only thing all six approaches might agree on is that indigenization as pursued by most contemporary developing countries is not a good thing, and that the poorest in the developing world are probably worse off because of it.[130] They disagree about why indigenization is not a good thing, for whom it is not desirable (in addition to "the poor"), and about virtually every other aspect of the program.

The preceding sketches of six alternative theoretical approaches to international political economy introduce a wide variety of positions on indigenization, but they provide only an introduction to the subject. Considerable disagreement also exists within each approach. The differences between Frank and Amin (within the vulgar-dependentista approach) are based on more than differences in geographical context. The same can be said for Leys and Beckman within the classical Marxist approach, or for Bergsten and Vernon within the liberal internationalist one. Table 1.1 summarizes (in an even more abbreviated form) the range of disagreement on these issues among major contemporary approaches to international political economy.

This is the place for an introduction to a critique, not a full critical

---

[128] Ibid., p. 253.

[129] Warren 1980: 185.

[130] This is a minority viewpoint within the classical Marxist tradition exemplified by Beckman in his recent (1982) discussion of Nigeria. Most classical Marxists would contend that indigenization is a good thing, but only because it is historically progressive.

discussion of each of these six approaches. As will become evident in the discussion in the next six chapters, I am not particularly satisfied with any of them, although I find some more satisfactory on certain issues than others. The balance of the text is intended as a critique of, a comment on, and a borrowing from these diverse approaches.[131] Let me begin at this point with a general comment on the utilities of these various approaches for understanding different aspects of indigenization.

Writers in the neoclassical tradition have a more variegated and sophisticated understanding of the motivations and operations of multinational enterprises than most writers within the Marxist tradition. This should come as no great surprise. They are less likely than Marxist writers to make sweeping generalizations about capital and more likely to differentiate among enterprises of different national origin and engaged in different economic activities. They are also more sensitive to the consequences of indigenization at the sectoral level (emphasizing the effects on particular industries or classes of economic activity such as finance, resource extraction, or high-technology manufacturing, for example), rather than dwelling on the effects solely at the enterprise or national level. Liberal internationalists and structuralists tend to differentiate themselves from both the conservative realists and from much of the radical literature by being more sensitive to political changes taking place at the international systemic level.

Where the neoclassical writers are weaker is on the domestic sources of indigenization and on the objectives of the key actors in developing countries. Conservative realists, liberal internationalists and structuralists all have a simplistic, undifferentiated conception of the state and its essential motivations. Despite disclaimers, these approaches conceive of the state as a rational actor operating to maximize its position. Conservative neoclassical realists view the state as attempting to maximize its position with its electorate, while liberal internationalists and structuralists view it as attempting to maximize its position in its bargaining relationship with multinational enterprises. In a view consistent with liberal political thought, each of these schools views the state as an expression of some general will, pursuing a larger national interest distinct from its own. This distinguishes them markedly from those sophisticated-dependency writers who ac-

---

[131] Strictly speaking, this book should not be viewed as a test of these six approaches. I am not trying to determine which approach most closely approximates the "truth." As will become apparent in this conclusion and in the chapters that follow, different theories are useful for understanding different aspects of indigenization.

TABLE 1.1

Alternative Approaches to International Political
Economy on MNCs, Development, North–South
Relations, and Indigenization

	Conservative neoclassical realists	Liberal internationalists	Structuralists
Context	U.S. business Int'l Corporations	U.S. government Academics	U.N. Agencies, European Social Democrats
Attitude on MNCs	Good for LDCs	Good for LDCs	Mixed for LDCs
Definition of development	Modernization	Growth with distribution	Basic needs satisfaction
Degree of North/South Change	Insignificant	Significant	Insignificant
Indigenization			
Sources	Undifferentiated LDCs	Rational governments	Rational governments
Objectives	Nationalism & regime survival	Domestic political & economic objectives of gov'ts	Maximize development objectives
Consequences for firms	No change	MNCs losing control	Little change
Consequences for industries	Production decreases	MNC power least in competitive industries	Loss of access to new technology
Consequences for countries	Worse off	HC bargaining power increased	Marginally favorable
Exemplary statements	Robock, Simmonds, & Zwick	Bergsten, Horst, & Moran	Hirschman Penrose Seers

FC = foreign capital; HC = host country; LC = local capital;
LDC = less developed country; S = state.

"Vulgar" dependentistas	"Sophisticated" dependentistas	Classical Marxists
U.S./European trained academics	Latin American trained academics	European; Marxism
Bad for LDCs	Bad for LDCs	Exploitative, but develop capitalism
Socialism	Autocentric self-reliance	Capitalism
Insignificant	Insignificant	Significant
Local bourgeoisie	State Technocrats & denationalized LC	Local bourgeoisie
Greed	Accumulation & protection from MNC competition	National capitalist development
No change	Insignificant change	MNCs losing some control
MNCs give up weakest activities	Changes in areas between S, LC, & FC	Local accumulation in some areas
Dependence up; development down	Dependent development	Capitalism expanded
Frank Dos Santos Amin	Cardoso Faletto Evans	Warren Brewer Leys

knowledge the possibility (or heresy, according to other Marxists) that the state can act autonomously to further its own objectives.

Liberal internationalists have a more sophisticated understanding (than neoclassical realists) of the significance of global changes on the bargaining capacities of multinationals and host countries. However, they have a more naive, almost myopic, view of the responsive capabilities of multinational enterprises.[132] On this subject the conservative neoclassical realists have a great deal more to say.[133] Structuralists are strongest in their empathetic comprehension of why so many Third World state bureaucracies favor indigenization of some kind.

Writers in the radical, Marxist tradition (the vulgar dependentistas, the sophisticated dependentistas, and the classical Marxists) have a great deal more to say about the sources and objectives of indigenization. One of their central concerns is the role of the state in the process of accumulation in the contemporary developing world, and hence they are sensitive to both how and why economic nationalist programs like indigenization are enacted. Sophisticated dependentistas (and, increasingly, classical Marxists) offer a rich and complex analysis of the interaction of state, local, and foreign capital in the formulation and implementation of indigenization programs. Because of their sensitivity to context, they allow for different coalitions to form and construct policies at different times. They are acutely aware of the ways in which the identity of the formulators of the programs affects the outcome of the indigenization exercise. This gives the radical approaches a greater sophistication not only about who is responsible for indigenization, but also about why the programs are enacted.

Radical approaches are weaker than neoclassical ones when they assess the consequences of indigenization. Many writers associated with these traditions are closed to empirical investigation of the subject. Dependentistas, of the vulgar or sophisticated variety, seem unable to allow for the possibility that indigenization could reduce dependency or promote a form of development that substantially improves upon what currently prevails in much of the developing world (a possibility structuralists readily embrace). Classical Marxists see capitalism being expanded in the developing world, but indigenization is scarcely worth considering beyond its historically progressive role of promoting capitalist relations of production and the exploitation that necessarily accompanies them. For nearly all but a few sophisticated de-

---

[132] See Biersteker 1980: 207–221 for further details of the extent of this tendency.

[133] This is, at least in part, because they teach this in their standard international-management courses.

pendency writers in the Marxist-based radical traditions, the state could never act in a way that would undermine the basis of its existence or that of the ruling classes that control it. Thus, the consequences of indigenization are not particularly interesting. Once you have chosen an approach to understanding the process (whether it is a dependency approach or a classical Marxist one), you have chosen an answer to many of the most interesting questions about indigenization.

Sophisticated dependentistas have the most open (and I would contend, most sophisticated) interpretation of the sources and objectives of indigenization. They at least allow for the possibility of significant state initiative. That is, they entertain the possibility that the state's interests or objectives could go beyond maintaining its own survival and override the objectives of affected interest groups (like capital) in the pursuit of its own conception of development or the national interest. Sophisticated-dependency writers also offer a dialectical method of historical analysis which I will draw on in subsequent chapters. Classical Marxists are more open to the possibility of significant changes taking place as a result of indigenization, at least at the level of the firm and sector of the economy. Like everyone else, I have little positive to say about the vulgar dependentistas, except perhaps that they have provided the most effective polemics on the subject, and that they are centrally concerned with the important issue of control.

In the five empirical and historical chapters that follow, I will examine the sources, the objectives, and the consequences of Nigeria's two-phased indigenization program. With the neoclassical and radical approaches as a guide, I will attempt to provide an answer to the questions posed in the introduction of this book: Why has indigenization occurred? How has it been implemented? and What has changed as a result? Already, it is apparent that it will be necessary to examine the consequences of the program at more than one level of analysis. Thus, the consequences of the Nigerian exercise will be examined at the level of the firm, at the level of the sector of the economy, and at the level of the country as a whole. It is also clear that it will be necessary to differentiate among domestic actors when considering the sources and objectives of the exercise. As a starting point, I will use Evans's distinctions between local capital, foreign capital, and the state. In the course of analysis, however, each of these groups will be further disaggregated for a deeper understanding of the dynamics of the program. Finally, the possibility that the state can act in an autonomous manner, with its own interests and objectives, will be considered explicitly. It is not sufficient to consider the state as an expression of a general will, as a rationally motivated government pursuing an abstraction like the national interest, or as capable of acting only at the behest of some fraction of capital.

In the end, the reasons I have already expressed for my dissatisfaction with each of the six major approaches to contemporary international political economy will become even more apparent. Taken separately, these diverse approaches are inadequate for an understanding of the sources, objectives, and consequences of Nigeria's indigenization program. A broader synthesis of theoretical perspectives is needed to acomplish the central objectives of this book.

Nigeria is an important case to consider because it has a diversified program of indigenization (personnel, equity, and local-content), it modelled its effort after similar programs in other developing countries (notably Brazil and India), it has been a model for other African indigenization programs (Ghana was heavily influenced by Nigeria in its program), and it has gone about as far with indigenization as any other country at a comparable level of development.[134] Since the end of the civil war in 1970, the Nigerian government has placed increasingly stringent requirements on foreign capital operating in the country. Foreign firms have been required to make available shares, part ownership, or managerial positions to Nigerians from the public or the private sector. Beginning with its expatriates-quota system and continuing with the indigenization decrees of 1972 and 1977, Nigeria has embarked on a concerted effort to increase its participation in its own economy. In 1970, nearly 60 percent of the shares in Nigeria's then fledgling industrial sector were in foreign private hands. After only a decade and a half of economic nationalism, only a handful of enterprises engaged in single nonrenewable contracts were exempt from some form of indigenization. Every other foreign concern operating in the country was required to make a minimum of 40 percent of its equity available to Nigerian subscribers, and a majority of the equity of new operations locating in the country was being acquired by the Nigerian state or by indigenous local investors. This transformation is even more remarkable when the phenomenal growth of the

---

[134] Many aspects of the Nigerian case will be better understood if placed in a broader historical context. For the most part, a general familiarity with Nigerian political and economic history is assumed in the discussion in Chapters 2 through 6. For readers lacking that familiarity, a general knowledge of Nigerian history can be obtained from Dudley 1982; Ekundare 1973; and Schatz 1977. For a more extensive review of Nigerian political economy, I recommend Williams (ed.) 1976; Watts 1983; Joseph 1983: 21–38; Lubeck 1977: 5–10; and Forrest 1982.

Nigerian economy during this period is taken into consideration. The process is not yet complete, but it is possible to identify the tendencies, the directions, and the contradictions of the program at the present time.

Each of the six approaches to international political economy discussed in this chapter can be found in Nigeria at the present time. The arguments are made by major actors in the process, by commentators on the exercise, and by academic analysist of the program. The analysis beginning in the next chapter will illustrate some of the deficiencies present in each of them.

CHAPTER TWO

The State as Collaborator:
The First Indigenization Decree

ON 25 February 1972, Nigeria's first Enterprises Promotion Decree was announced by the then head of state, General Yakubu Gowon. It was not the first step, but was a very important one, on a path that would lead throughout the 1970s to one of the most comprehensive mandatory joint-venture programs in Africa, and throughout the Third World. The decree outlined the government's intention to divide the Nigerian economy into three sections, one reserved entirely for Nigerians (Schedule I), one in which Nigerian equity participation must be at least 40 percent (Schedule II), and a third that would be entirely unaffected by the proclamation.

Not long after General Gowon's announcement, Chief Henry Fajemirokun (then president of the influential Lagos Chamber of Commerce) described the 1972 decree as a "simple and unambiguous piece of legislation."[1] On careful examination, however, it was anything but "simple" or "unambiguous." In its final form, the 1972 decree reflected a compromise among certain opposed interests (notably, elements of local capital and elements of foreign capital) and a defeat of others (notably, some elements of the state). The decree does not reveal how local capital captured the state, nor does it demonstrate the unassailable power of foreign capital or the autonomy of state action. Rather, when situated in its appropriate historical context, it becomes clear that the 1972 indigenization decree was a culmination of recurring, and increasing, pressure from local business interests, combined with some strong lobbying from foreign enterprises and some rather independent state initiatives. The state did not initiate the decree, but rather collaborated with local capital in its formulation. The final composition of the decree, as well as its subsequent implementation, reflects this collaboration.

LOCAL CAPITAL

Indigenous business pressure for some form of indigenization (either of personnel, of equity, or of local content) was not a new phenome-

---

[1] Quoted in *Nigerian Business Digest*, November 1973, p. 7.

non in Nigeria. Local businessmen[2] had been writing papers, making representations to government officials, and giving speeches on the subject since before independence in 1960. The earliest proposals called for personnel indigenization, the employment of Nigerians in important positions in economic enterprises operating in the country. The indigenization of the military and the civil service was already well underway by the late 1950s and was taken as a model for the private sector. In particular, the indigenization of the marketing boards (as part of the indigenization of the civil service) was a very important early step for advocates of private-sector personnel indigenization. There was also some early pressure for the provision of government support to local business, initially for financial support (in the form of loans) and later for outright protection against competition from foreign enterprises. Indigenous businessmen wanted to break down the expatriate dominance of certain sectors in the economy, notably produce buying, retail trade, and transportation. Many of these early calls for indigenization (or support to local business) were contained in a continuous barrage of articles published in Nigeria's vibrant local press of the day, especially in the *West African Pilot* and in the *Daily Service*. It is also important to note that most of these pressures came from the South.

The colonial government responded to these pressures with some legislative measures, none of which was very substantial or very far reaching. In 1946, the Nigerian Local Development Boards were established to provide managerial and financial aids to indigenous businessmen. The 1951 Aid to Pioneer Industry Ordinance provided specific incentives for foreign companies employing Nigerians. Statements about immigration policy in 1952 and 1956 included attempts to encourage the employment of indigenous personnel where possible (especially in the distributive trade). As of 1956, only Nigerians could be licensed agents. The 1958 Tax Relief Act, part of the grow-

---

[2] For the purposes of this discussion, local capital will be defined as including all those indigenous businessmen whose logic of accumulation is principally domestic and restricted to Nigeria. This definition applies largely to Nigerian citizens who lack any longstanding commitments or a likelihood to save, invest, and/or accumulate the bulk of their assets outside the country. It includes bankers, lawyers, accountants, manufacturers, consultants, builders, merchants, exporters, and importers. Local capital in Nigeria is divided principally by region (North, West, East), by sector (commerce, production, services), and by scale (those employing more than and fewer than twenty employees). This definition excludes the Levantine community, some of whom became Nigerian citizens after the first indigenization decree and who often behave like members of the Nigerian business community on many issues. They are excluded because their principal base of business operations (including employment, investment, and savings) does not remain in Nigeria.

ing number of legislative incentives to foreign investors passed just prior to independence, required a limited Nigerianization of personnel and even of management of foreign firms interested in obtaining favorable tax treatment from the government.[3] With the exception of the establishment of Local Development Boards in 1946, all of these early government measures addressed only personnel indigenization.

The most significant pre-independence proposals for indigenization were contained in the Report of the Advisory Commission on Aids to African Businessmen submitted to the federal government in 1959. During the 1958 parliamentary debate on the budget, Dr. K. O. Mbadiwe, then Federal Minister of Commerce and Industry, proposed that "Government should step in to set up various agencies to provide Nigerian businessmen with necessary capital, technical knowhow, and management skills for an effective indigenisation programme."[4] As a result, an advisory committee, made up primarily of prominent Nigerians and including a number of the most important indigenous businessmen of the day, was set up to examine ways of assisting indigenous businessmen in Nigeria.

The commission's report is of interest, not because the government acted on its recommendations, but because it expressed concerns of indigenous businessmen which persisted even after independence. It contained a number of far reaching proposals, virtually all of which were eventually enacted in the first indigenization decree in 1972. The commission's report is a clear illustration of the consistency of local businessmen's dissatisfaction with their role in the economy of the country and of their longstanding support for indigenization in Nigeria.

The report specifically attacked the limited contributions of the Syrian and Lebanese entrepreneurs operating in Nigeria, describing them as good in retail trading only. They had "served their usefulness" and "the African must be protected in the field of textile and road transport in which he has acquired efficiency."[5] The case of the European expatriate was different, and "[i]t is really to him that Nigeria must look for partnership which can truly be of mutual bene-

---

[3] Pribor 1979: 4–5. Nigerian commercial entrepreneurs did make some progress in increasing their share of the produce and import trade during the 1950s. The data are scarce and unreliable, and the progress was not substantial. However, the existence of some movement probably spurred demands for more rapid change. See Olakanpo 1963.

[4] Owonuwa 1975: 10.

[5] *Report of the Advisory Committee on Aids to African Businessmen* 1959: 51.

fit."[6] Nevertheless, the commission warned against the creation of "paper" directors who held no shares, attended no meetings, and knew nothing of the company's affairs. Rather, they recommended a more "genuine form of partnership in which the indigenous partner has some of the equity or risk shares and can learn how decisions are made."[7]

There was some suspicion of the number of expatriates employed by foreign enterprises in the country, and the commission recommended the formation of an immigration committee (a precursor of the Expatriate Quota Allocation Board) to screen expatriate applications for admission to the country. The report also proposed that foreign enterprises be moved into areas of economic activity where they could contribute the most to Nigerian development. Thus, in a telling passage that presages the creation of Schedules I and II in the first indigenization decree, the commission commented:

> The only issue outstanding, therefore, is the practical one of continually redrawing the shifting boundary line between the indigenous and the expatriate sectors as the field of indigenous enterprise expands. The two sectors may overlap, depending on the nature of the enterprise and in what part of the country they are located.[8]

Although its recommendations were never acted on or implemented by the government, the commission's report provides a good summary of the concerns and objectives of local capital in Nigeria prior to the first indigenization decree. It was strongly anti-Lebanese, requested state protection in the retail trade in textiles and in road transportation, wanted genuine participation (meaning equity indigenization) with European enterprises, favored an expatriate quota to increase Nigerian employment in upper-level managerial positions, and planned to move foreign enterprises progressively into other sectors of the economy. These are all themes we will return to as we talk about the objectives of local capital in the post-independence period. As we shall see below, they are also all key components of the first indigenization decree.

After independence in 1960, local business proposals for some kind of state assistance increased dramatically. Parliament became an important forum for the presentation of the views of local capital during

[6] Ibid.

[7] Ibid., p. 52.

[8] Ibid., p. 50. The idea of a "shifting boundary" also presages the 1977 indigenization decree, in which the line between foreign capital and local capital was redrawn even further to the advantage of the latter.

the six years of civilian administration between 1960 and 1966. In 1961, the Federal Minister of Economic Development, Alhaji Waziri Ibrahim, presented the first legislative proposals for indigenization. As one of the first indigenous distributors and area managers for the United Africa Company (UAC), Nigeria's largest commercial establishment, Waziri was in a good position to express the interests of an important segment of local capital. Waziri was intensely nationalistic and allegedly thought that UAC should not be engaged in the produce-buying trade, an activity dominated at that time by the large expatriate trading houses like UAC, Paterson-Zochinis (PZ), John Holt Company, and a number of Lebanese merchants.[9] Waziri specifically proposed that expatriate middlemen withdraw from the distributive trade altogether, with the important exception of department-store trading and the sale and servicing of technical goods. The latter two activities were, not coincidentally, the two major areas into which the United Africa Company was diversifying at the time. His recommendations were passed by the parliament and declared the official policy of the government. It is by no means clear that they were implemented, however.

In response to repeated demands for personnel indigenization, demands expressed prominently in the indigenously controlled press of the newly independent country, the 1963 Immigration Act stipulated that no alien could practice a profession without Ministry of Immigration approval. It further established a quota system for employees of newly established multinationals. A government statement on industrial policy issued the following year announced the government's intention to give preference in the awarding of contracts to firms with at least 10 percent indigenous participation and 45 percent local content. Thus, although a comprehensive program of indigenization had yet to be articulated, the post-independence civilian government was responding to local business calls for indigenization with piecemeal legislation to provide incentives for personnel, equity, and even local content indigenization.

In August of 1965, the National Commission on the Nigerianization of Business Enterprises was set up by the federal government to consider a more comprehensive program. The commission's report was never published and never acted upon, as the political crises that culminated in political secession and civil war preoccupied the civil servants and new military leadership of the country. Thus, it was not until near the end of the civil war, during the late 1960s, that con-

[9] Interview with prominent former state official.

certed pressures were again applied by local business groups to reactivate the latent governmental interest in indigenization. These pressures were not prompted by any particular event, but rather had been building for some time (as indicated by their early expression in the 1959 report of the Advisory Commission on Aids to African Businessmen). Proposals for a more comprehensive indigenization program had simply been postponed until after the war.

What were the major reasons for these recurring calls for indigenization from the indigenous private sector? What was the source of their dissatisfaction? At the most general level, local businessmen in Nigeria were simply dissatisfied with foreign control of the economy. They were particularly concerned with foreign domination of the distributive sector, of certain growth areas in industry, and of certain aspects of business operations.

Local capital in Nigeria was (and is) not a monolithic entity, and some important regional and analytical distinctions need to be made. Not only were the concerns of indigenous Kano and Lagos businessmen frequently different, but there were also significant differences between the concerns of independent Nigerian entrepreneurs competing with foreign-owned companies and senior indigenous managers working for multinational corporations. Both are integral parts of local capital and both were dissatisfied with foreign control of the economy. As we shall see, however, the sources of their general dissatisfaction with foreign control (and with what they saw in indigenization) were different. Individual entrepreneurs were primarily concerned with limiting foreign competition or gaining access to profitable ventures, while senior Nigerian managers were more interested in personnel indigenization and effective managerial participation. For the most part, indigenous entrepreneurs took the lead in pushing for indigenization, but they frequently obtained crucial support from local managers as well.

Data on the distribution of shareholding in Nigerian industry in the late 1960s indicate that approximately 60 percent of the shares were held by non-Nigerians.[10] However, even this striking figure underestimates the extent of foreign control of the economy. Nigerian individuals held a majority of the shares in only 2.7 percent of large enterprises, companies whose paid-up capital exceeded 200,000 naira (approximately $280,000).[11] Of the sectors eventually included

[10] Teriba, Edozien, and Kayode 1977: 93–94, citing Registry of Companies data.

[11] Ibid., p. 96. Conversions to U.S. dollars are based on the exchange rate recorded by the International Monetary Fund of $1 = 1.4 naira (two naira equal one of the earlier Nigerian pounds). The naira is divided into 100 kobo.

in Schedule I of the first indigenization decree, approximately 56 percent of their paid-up capital was in Nigerian hands a few years before the decree. In 1967, only 32.4 percent of the paid-up capital in industries eventually listed under Schedule II of the first decree was in Nigerian hands.[12] Table 2.1 illustrates the extent of foreign private ownership of the Nigerian economy between 1963 and 1972, when the first indigenization decree was announced. Although the number had declined somewhat from the levels attained in 1966 and 1968, just under two-thirds of the total capital was still in foreign hands. In addition, it appears that indigenous businessmen also failed to make any appreciable gains during the period considered. Thus, "after a decade of political independence the bulk of the Nigerian modern sector businesses were still owned and directed by foreigners."[13]

The extent of widespread foreign control of the Nigerian economy was not the only source of indigenous businessmen's dissatisfaction. Many were particularly concerned with their inability to purchase shares of the foreign-owned and -managed enterprises, even when they had sufficient capital to buy into them. For example, before indigenization West African Portland Cement gave a portion of its stock to UAC and had it sold to other foreign companies. Indigenous

TABLE 2.1
Source of Paid-up Capital for Nigerian Industries
(in percentages)

	Local capital	Foreign capital	State capital	
			Federal	State
1963	9.8	67.6	3.2	18.7
1964	N.A.	N.A.	N.A.	N.A.
1965	11.1	62.0	4.7	18.5
1966	10.0	70.2	3.7	13.3
1967	12.3	66.1	3.4	14.2
1968	12.7	70.0	4.0	12.6
1969	11.4	64.3	3.9	11.5
1970	9.7	63.0	4.7	10.7
1971	9.3	57.5	4.4	9.9
1972	11.6	58.2	3.5	12.7

SOURCE: *Industrial Survey of Nigeria* (Lagos: Federal Office of Statistics). Published annually; aggregated by the author. As a result of rounding and omission of data categorized as "Other" by the Federal Office of Statistics, rows do not add up to 100%.

[12] Collins 1977: 129.
[13] Ezeife 1981: 164–165.

businessmen resented the fact that they were often barred from actual capital participation,[14] and a number felt at the time that a multinational should make shares available to indigenous people in the host country "as a token of its confidence in the country."[15]

Fear of preemptive displacement by multinational enterprises also proved to be an important source of local-capital dissatisfaction with foreign control of the economy in the 1960s.[16] Akeredolu-Ale presented empirical support for this proposition in his 1971 survey of Lagos State indigenous entrepreneurs, in which he found that most believed that expatriate competition placed important obstacles in the way of their own progress.[17] The preemption of certain spheres of economic activity by foreign enterprises was not the only inhibition to the development of indigenous business in Nigeria, but "[m]any [Nigerian entrepreneurs] may be discouraged from entering and others who do venture have a good chance of ending up frustrated."[18] Some Nigerian entrepreneurs found themselves squeezed by the large trading companies operating in the country (especially the United Africa Company), and therefore resented the predominant position of foreign enterprises because of the restrictions it placed on their own expansion.

> Since the initial advantages enjoyed by foreign business ventures tend to be cumulative, posing with time the problems of unfair competition as far as indigenous business ventures are concerned, the chances of domestic investors emerging as effective imitators of foreign investors are often exaggerated.[19]

Thus, the extent of local capital dissatisfaction with foreign control of the Nigerian economy was widespread, not just because of its magnitude, but, more important, because of its implications for indigenous businessmen, who were prevented from buying shares in profitable companies and preempted from effective competition. Although foreign control of the economy was a central source of local-capital dissatisfaction, the most frequent complaint made by local businessmen during the 1960s was their lack of access to adequate finance and capital for their operations. Many indigenous businessmen

[14] Ogunbanjo 1969: 5.
[15] Interview with former official of an indigenous businessmen's group.
[16] For a definition and discussion of preemptive displacement in Nigeria, see Biersteker 1978: 115–116.
[17] Akeredolu-Ale 1975: 81–83.
[18] Akeredolu-Ale 1972: 256.
[19] Teriba et al. 1977: 111.

have described their lack of access to capital as their greatest single handicap.[20] Akeredolu-Ale reported that 71 percent of his respondents found that access to capital was the most serious difficulty they faced when they commenced operations.[21] This complaint was by no means a new one, since the 1959 Commission on Aids to African Businessmen described at length the lack of access of indigenous businessmen to adequate credit facilities and complained that the banks charged too high a fee for the limited services they provided.[22] In fact, the bulk of the lending to indigenous businessmen in the 1950s came from the European trading companies, not from the banks. The trading firms made loans available to their indigenous suppliers and distributors of course, never to their competitors, yet a further source of local capital dissatisfaction.[23]

Before the first indigenization decree, sixteen commercial banks operated in Nigeria, only three of which were wholly foreign-owned. These three banks, Standard, Barclays, and United Bank for Africa (today known as First Bank, Union Bank, and UBA), accounted for 84 percent of the deposits, 75 percent of the loans, and 85 percent of the international banking transactions at that time.[24] The "big three" foreign-owned and -managed banks were not only the largest commercial banks in the country, but they also operated "practically as if they were e[x]ternal to the Nigerian financial system."[25] Most of their lending went to other expatriate enterprises, rather than to local businessmen. This made good business sense to the bankers, who are by tradition and profession conservative in their lending decisions. Expatriate firms were in general better managed, less of a risk, and therefore more credit worthy. Lending to indigenous businessmen was highly concentrated on a few individuals, those few with "marketable securities such as government bonds, the shares of well-established [foreign-owned] companies, life insurance policies, and documents of title to imported or exported stocks or those awaiting sale."[26] Thus, from the perspective of local capital, the lending policies of the banks

[20] Interview data and Ogunbanjo 1969: 2–3.
[21] Akeredolu-Ale 1975: 76–83. Other factors, notably personnel problems and expatriate competition (discussed above) also proved to be important limitations to local-capital expansion of operations around 1970.
[22] *Report of the Advisory Committee* 1959: 13.
[23] Asabia 1981: 4.
[24] Asabia 1982: 3.
[25] Asabia 1981: 28.
[26] Teriba 1975: 168.

were highly discriminatory in favor of European firms and many of the Lebanese trading companies.

Although precise financial data are difficult to obtain, some writers have estimated that before indigenization, less than 20 percent of the total credit obtained from the expatriate banks was allocated to local capital.[27] Commercial bank loans to indigenous borrowers increased to nearly 50 percent of their total credit by 1970 and increased even further after the introduction of credit guidelines from the Central Bank in 1971.[28] Still, the perception that foreign-owned commercial banks discriminated against local borrowers persisted, and local capital bitterly resented the fact that Nigerian savings held by the "big three" were invested in London and other foreign markets rather than loaned out in Nigeria.[29]

The Nigerian Industrial Development Bank (NIDB) established by the government to promote industrial development in 1964 offered no panacea to indigenous businessmen looking for additional sources of credit. The bank's portfolio was small, especially when compared with that of the big commercial banks. And its lending policy was simply not designed to cater for the small-scale enterprises that predominated among local capital. Most of its lending, like that of the big commercial banks, went to large expatriate-owned and -managed enterprises. Table 2.2 summarizes the number and value of sanctions to foreign, as opposed to indigenous capital between the time of the bank's founding in 1964 to the promulgation of the first decree in 1972.

The reasons for local-capital dissatisfaction with the performance of the NIDB should be clear from Table 2.2. Before 1970, foreign enterprises received the bulk of the funds awarded. In only one year before 1970, in 1966, did local businessmen receive more sanctions than foreign enterprises. However, in that year the value of NIDB sanctions was at its lowest for the decade, at only 727,000 naira (or $1,018,000). Even after 1970, although the number of sanctions received by foreign capital was considerably smaller than the number received by local capital, its percentage of the total value indicates that the change in NIDB lending policy was not as significant in monetary terms as it was nominally.

From the standpoint of indigenous managers, the major source of dissatisfaction with foreign capital stemmed from their limited access

[27] Collins 1977: 130. See also Teriba 1975: 168.

[28] Teriba 1975: 168–169. these guidelines and their implications for indigenization and the control of finance will be discussed more fully below.

[29] Asabia 1981: 4.

TABLE 2.2
Analysis of Sanctions by the NIDB, 1964–72

	No. of sanctions			Value of sanctions		
	Foreign	Indigenous	Total[a]	Foreign	Indigenous	Total[b]
1964	61%	39%	23	61%	39%	3.375
1965	72%	28%	18	77%	23%	2.666
1966	14%	86%	7	1%	99%	.727
1967	67%	33%	9	57%	43%	2.034
1968	75%	25%	8	83%	17%	1.444
1969	70%	30%	20	75%	25%	4.816
1970	18%	82%	28	32%	68%	6.372
1971	10%	90%	40	27%	73%	11.403
1972	7%	93%	14	18%	82%	4.088
Total			167			36.925

SOURCE: "Report of the Industrial Enterprises Panel" (The Adeosun Commission Report), Federal Republic of Nigeria, March 1976 (unpublished), data adapted by the author from Table VII.3.
[a] Total number of sanctions.
[b] Value of the sanctions in thousands of naira.

to senior management positions in the expatriate-dominated modern sector. Throughout the 1960s, personnel indigenization in the private sector had been slow, noticeably slower than the personnel indigenization in the public sector. Most foreign companies were reducing their number of expatriates in senior management positions in the three years prior to the first indigenization decree. In their survey of seventy-five industrial and service firms in 1971, Rimlinger and Stremlau found that between 1968 and 1971 "expatriate staff in the surveyed firms was reduced by 17%."[30] Forty of the companies surveyed reported a decrease in the number of expatriates, fifteen reported an increase, and eight reported no change in the number present.[31] Each of the fifteen firms reporting an increase also expanded its operations during the period. Nevertheless, the total number of expatriates in Nigeria was still very high (some have estimated as high as 20,000 in 1970), and their number had grown since independence.

As a percentage of total private-sector employees, the number of expatriates in Nigeria was small, probably around 3 percent of the total workforce. Their number varied considerably from industry to indus-

[30] Rimlinger and Stremlau 1973: 34. These data refer to sixty-three of the seventy-five firms surveyed. See Rimlinger and Stremlau's note on p. 34 for further details about the sample represented here.
[31] Ibid.

try. In high-technology activities such as petroleum, the number of expatriates to Nigerian employees was predictably high, around 1:6. In low technology areas, such as beer brewing, the number of expatriates was considerably lower, with a ratio of around 1:61.[32] However, the total number of expatriates employed was not at issue for indigenous managers. Their dissatisfaction stemmed from their exclusion from most positions of responsibility within the firms.

Nigerians were largely restricted to middle-level management positions. Only between 15 and 20 percent of the senior managerial positions in the seventy-five firms surveyed by Rimlinger and Stremlau were occupied by Nigerians, and fully one-half of the firms they surveyed had no Nigerian senior managers at all.[33] Those few who advanced to senior management positions found themselves relegated to strategically unimportant positions with little influence and little chance for promotion. The most senior Nigerian managers were stereotypically employed as personnel managers, public relations analysts, legal advisors, and company secretaries.[34] From the perspective of the foreign enterprise, these were the areas in which the Nigerians had a comparative advantage. From the perspective of the indigenous manager, however, this was a source of resentment and dissatisfaction. Nigerian managers felt that foreign firms must take major steps toward Nigerianization on their own, and they were disappointed that the multinationals seemed to respond (and respond grudgingly) only to government regulation.[35]

It is significant to note that the highest ratios of expatriates to Nigerian employees in nontechnical activities appeared in wholesale distribution, an area dominated by Lebanese and Indian businessmen. In many cases, even middle and low-level managerial functions were not indigenized in these firms.[36] When this is added to the fact that Lebanese, Syrian, and Indian businessmen were concentrated in the areas in which indigenous businessmen were most capable of competing successfully, it is not surprising that local businessmen in Nigeria particularly resented "the Levantine community." Wholesale trade, retail trade, road transport, and produce buying all required little technical skill and had a relatively low threshold for entry. They were

---

[32] Rimlinger 1973: 211–212.

[33] Ibid., p. 213. Only one firm had a Nigerian chief executive at the time.

[34] Ibid., pp. 213–214.

[35] Interview with prominent indigenous businessman.

[36] Owonuwa 1975: 49. Owonuwa obtained this information from an analysis of the returns at the Nigerian Enterprises Promotion Board (the NEPB) in April of 1972. Owonuwa was secretary to the NEPB in 1982.

also the traditional areas of Nigerian business activity.[37] Because of their high visibility and because they tended to organize tightly controlled family firms with little or no Nigerian participation and little investment in Nigeria, the Lebanese, Syrian and Indian entrepreneurs were deemed exploiters, and they became a particular target of local capital. It is on this issue that the interests and concerns of both strands of local capital (indigenous entrepreneurs and indigenous managers) most clearly intersected.

The Lebanese had been singled out in the 1959 report of the Commission on Aids to African Businessmen, which criticized their contribution when comparing it with that of the European firms operating in the country. Even ten years after independence, however, indigenous businessmen complained that foreigners were still engaged in small retail-trade activities, and it was widely perceived that the Lebanese owned all the stores.[38] Since they could not invoke the wrath of international organizations like the IMF or the World Bank, and since they had no recourse to a powerful home-country government, the Lebanese, Syrian, and Indian entrepreneurs were far more vulnerable than foreigners based in the multinational corporations from Europe and North America. They were both highly visible and highly vulnerable, and therefore they bore the brunt of the local capital resentment against foreign domination of the Nigerian economy at the time.

Thus, throughout Nigeria's first decade of independence, its local business community was highly dissatisfied with its position in the Nigerian economy. It resented foreign ownership and control of the economy (because of its implications for their access to shares, meaningful employment, and a chance to expand their own operations), and it resented its inability to obtain access to credit, its limited access to senior managerial positions in multinational enterprises, and the entrenchment of Lebanese, Syrian, and Indian merchants in the distributive sector of the economy. As a result of this widespread dissatisfaction, the Nigerian business community made repeated attempts during the late 1960s and early 1970s to direct state policy in its own interests.

In a 1974 speech delivered to the Nigerian Economic Society, P. C. Asiodu, one of Yakubu Gowon's most powerful civilian advisors commented:

[37] Bauer 1954.
[38] Interviews with prominent former state officials.

. . . the current indigenization measures have a long history, and have been adopted in response to well-articulated demands over time by Nigerian businessmen. The agitation was audible even in the colonial era and it became more insistent during the civilian regime. However, it was in the period between 1968 and 1971 that the widest consultations were undertaken leading to the promulgation of the Enterprises Promotion Decree of 1972.[39]

Most of the local-business demands for indigenization during the late 1960s were organized through the Lagos Chamber of Commerce. Although the Lagos Chamber tended to represent the interests of indigenous entrepreneurs, a number of prominent indigenous managers also participated in its deliberations. The Lagos Chamber was the most important single business association in the country because of the economic importance of Lagos and its proximity to the centers of decisionmaking for the federal government of Nigeria. Economic interest groups like the Chamber were especially prominent when the military government was in power, partly because party politics had been banned and partly because other avenues for political involvement at the time were so limited.

The Lagos Chamber of Commerce first admitted African members in 1948 and remained expatriate-dominated throughout the 1960s. More than 75 percent of the members of its governing council were expatriates in 1968. However, in the early 1960s, indigenous businessmen made a calculated decision to form a subgroup within the Chamber to express their interests and initiate proposals for action, rather than create their own business association. They formed Group 15, the Indigenous Businessmen's Group, which became one of the seventeen trade groups whose chairmen make up the bulk of the council of the Lagos Chamber. The membership of this new group was composed primarily of indigenous entrepreneurs engaged in commerce, shipping and clearing of goods, and services. The group did not include many of the indigenous directors of multinational companies, but rather comprised "new capital."[40]

Each separate group of the Chamber holds monthly meetings during which proposals for official Chamber lobbying activities are initiated. Within Group 15, the Indigenous Businessmen's Group, papers advocating indigenization were introduced, and formal proposals for official Chamber action soon followed. Among the most active advocates of indigenization within the group were Chief Henry

[39] Asiodu 1974: 49.
[40] Interview with prominent indigenous businessman.

Fajemirokun, A. S. Guobadia, Chief J. Akin-George, and Chief Ola-dotun Okubanjo. They were individuals who faced their greatest competition from foreign capital, especially small Lebanese enter-prises operating in commerce, shipping, and services. Representatives of the older, wealthier indigenous family enterprises tended to be less enthusiastic about indigenization.

The proposals of the Indigenous Businessmen's Group had to be considered by the council of the Chamber of Commerce before any official Chamber endorsement or action could be taken. The council comprised the officers of the Chamber of Commerce, six members elected at large, and the chairmen of each of the seventeen trade groups, one of which was the Indigenous Businessmen's Group. Since the trade groups were predominantly chaired by expatriate members of the Chamber, the council was controlled by non-Nigeri-ans. It was in the sessions of the council meetings that the indigenous businessmen's proposals for an indigenization program were con-fronted by strong opposition. The relationship between the expa-triate and Nigerian members of the Chamber became antagonistic and several members described the council proceedings during this period as "a three-year battle." The battle began in early 1968 and was not concluded until the end of 1970.

The position of local businessmen during this period was expressed well by C. O. Ogunbanjo, a leading member of the Indigenous Busi-nessmen's Group as well as a director of the British multinational Dunlop. Ogunbanjo was hardly a radical proponent of economic na-tionalism, and his comments probably had greater force with the ex-patriate and governmental communities as a result. In a speech before the Nigerian Institute of Management in 1969, Ogunbanjo encour-aged foreign companies to take the initiative to create more joint ven-tures with local businessmen, urging that "there must be a willingness for Nigerians to participate substantially in the ownership and man-agement of foreign enterprises."[41] He was calling for equity partici-pation and additional employment for Nigerians, and he made a veiled threat that Nigeria might follow the path taken in Nkrumah's Ghana if foreign companies failed to take the lead in the right direc-tion. Ogunbanjo also attempted to influence state officials concerned at the time with the completion of the Second National Development Plan (1970–74), then under preparation.[42] He called for a general policy review which would involve local businessmen and warned

[41] Ogunbanjo 1969: 6.
[42] Ogunbanjo 1982: 10.

against state acquisition of shares of productive enterprises. In a list of specific policy recommendations at the conclusion of his paper, he summarized the dissatisfaction of local capital already discussed in this chapter (access to finance, paper directorships with multinational firms, equity acquisition, etc.) and proposed that retail trading and motor transportation be fully indigenized and that local participation be a condition for investment incentives obtained by multinationals locating in the country.[43]

Ogunbanjo received "100 percent support" from the indigenous business community for his position and was encouraged to circulate his paper to relevent government officials, foreign businessmen, and the press.[44] The proposals were also extremely popular with the public. The foreign business community made no official comment at the time, but continued to oppose the proposals within the Chamber council. An ad hoc committee was formed by the Indigenous Businessmen's Group to develop a more formal proposal for an indigenization program, and the paper was circulated to the especially powerful permanent secretaries (the "super perm secs") within the federal military government.

Ogunbanjo's was one of a number of representations made by the Indigenous Businessmen's Group to government officials. They proceeded to present "a succession of papers" in their lobbying efforts and, from the perspective of at least one leading government official at the time, they were an articulate lobby that applied "steady pressure."[45] None of this was done with the sanction of the council of the Chamber, which remained officially opposed to an indigenization program. This was consistent with the expatriate businessmen's position of a year earlier, when they opposed the inclusion of Part 10 of the 1968 Companies Act (discussed more fully below) which required all foreign enterprises operating in Nigeria to incorporate their subsidiaries in the country as Nigerian companies.

Local businessmen did not rely solely on their formal representations, press releases, and position papers for their lobbying effort. Many had privileged access to top state officials and members of the Supreme Military Council with whom they had special (often commercial) relationships.[46] Senior government officials would often be approached by members of the Indigenous Businessmen's Group "on a personal matter" during which they presented their case for indigen-

[43] Ogunbanjo 1969: 16.
[44] Interview with prominent indigenous businessman.
[45] Interview with prominent former state official.
[46] Interview with prominent indigenous businessman.

ization. These meetings were held secretly and the same indigenous businessmen who during the day joined publicly with their expatriate colleagues or employers in opposition to Part 10 of the Companies Act stated their true convictions and lobbied hard in support of the decree at night.[47] They lobbied first for Part 10 of the Companies Act and subsequently pushed hard for a comprehensive indigenization program.

Eventually, in 1970, the council of the Chamber of Commerce agreed to a resolution supporting indigenization. The resolution called for complete Nigerian ownership of small retail trading activities, certain export/import activities, advertising, and road transport. These were principally areas in which small family-owned Lebanese firms predominated, and hence the large European and North American multinationals, who were well represented in the Chamber, were not affected by the proposal.

The Lagos Chamber of Commerce resolution and the succession of papers from the Indigenous Businessmen's Group did not create the idea of indigenization in Nigeria. As has already been stated, support for an indigenization program had been well established before independence. Rather, the Chamber articulated the argument for a comprehensive program at a particularly critical period. It was joined in this effort by a number of other business associations (including the Nigerian Chamber of Commerce, Mines, and Industry and the Nigerian Chamber of Indigenous Contractors) and by the Nigerian press (especially the *Daily Times*, the *Daily Express*, and the *Morning Post*).

Finally, however, it is important to note that not everyone in the indigenous business community in Nigeria supported indigenization. In addition to some of the directors of multinational enterprises and the older-established trading families already discussed, most of the local businessmen in both the North and the East were not included in the lobbying process. The Indigenous Businessmen's Group of the Lagos Chamber of Commerce was largely a southern, western, and Yoruba-based lobbying group. The distributive trade in the East had long been in indigenous hands; hence it was not especially anxious to reserve a niche for local capital in that area. It is also quite clear that eastern businessmen played no role in the Chamber's deliberations during the Nigerian civil war. Further, there simply was not much interest in indigenization in the North during the late 1960s. Northern businessmen were more concerned with rooting out the southerners (both Ibos and Yorubas) who dominated much of the modern sector

---

[47] Interview with prominent former state official.

of their regional political economy than they were with reducing expatriate involvement in the region. If anything, foreign enterprise was to be preferred to southern enterprise. Northernization was more of a priority than indigenization. The regional basis of support for indigenization becomes significant later, when we talk about the consequences of the first decree and the origins of the second.

In summary, then, what were the principal objectives of the local businessmen who lobbied so hard for an indigenization program? First and foremost, they wanted state support in their bid to take over the distributive trade and the transportation sector in the country. Local capital wanted to reserve a niche free from competition with the Lebanese enterprises that predominated in distribution and transport. They wanted to confine their foreign competition to "areas where we do not operate" in order "to have room to grow."[48]

Second, they wanted to obtain minority participation, not control, of the large and profitable multinational enterprises operating in intermediate industrial activities in Nigeria. Indigenous businessmen wanted to have somewhere between 25 and 40 percent of the equity of these large firms, to have "actual capital participation" and share ownership of them.[49]

Third, indigenous employees of foreign firms wanted more management-level positions and more responsibility associated with those positions. They were tired of paper directorships and joined indigenous entrepreneurs in support of a comprehensive indigenization program. From their standpoint, indigenization would give them an opportunity for both learning and advancement.

Fourth, local capital wanted additional state support for the development of an indigenous private sector. They wanted improved access to finance, training programs, and preferential treatment in the awarding of contracts.

Fifth and finally, they wanted to limit public-sector involvement in the economy (especially in construction, in interstate transport, and in the establishment of new joint ventures with foreign capital).

THE STATE

Although it might appear that the full story of the sources of indigenization has already been told, the state was hardly at the beck and call

[48] Interviews with prominent former state officials.
[49] Ogunbanjo 1969: 5.

of local capital on indigenization.[50] It did not simply carry out the demands of its articulate and impatient indigenous business community. State officials had their own agenda, their own development program, and their own ideas about indigenization. They were aloof from, but not entirely indifferent to, the interests of local capital. As we shall see, they were structurally aware of the presence of local capital, but relatively autonomous in their initiatives and actions.

This relative autonomy stemmed in part from the fact that the military was in power at the time the first indigenization decree was announced. Because the "rivalry and rigidities of party politics" had been eliminated after 1966, it was easier for civil servants and state technocrats to introduce fundamental changes in policy.[51] "The perm secs were the decisionmakers in those days."[52] Most of the new ideas and policy-reform proposals tended to come from the civil service after 1966, a group emboldened by its increased intervention in the economy during the Nigerian civil war. Contact with the indigenous business community existed, but, from the perspective of that community, the contact was "grudging."[53] The top civil servants reacted to the climate of the time, but had the impression they could do anything they wanted: "No military government could run on the pages of the *Daily Times*."[54]

It was widely believed within the civil service that some kind of pressure would be necessary to accomplish indigenization. Political pressure had been necessary for the indigenization of the civil service itself, and therefore it was incumbent upon the political system "to apply to the private sector, strategies and yardsticks similar to

---

[50] For the purposes of this discussion, the state if defined as the institutions of government and its individual representatives which together possess legitimate means of coercion and an ability to tax and plan fiscal policy on a national level. The state provides for the defense, welfare, and security of the entire population and moderates conflicts among fractions of capital. It is also capable of autonomous actions, acting in its own interests, against the prevailing concerns of local capital, foreign capital, labor, or the peasantry. The state in Nigeria is divided principally along the following lines: by function (planning, regulation, production, finance, redistribution, mediation), by ideology (especially with regard to its role in development), by administrative level (SMC, civil commissioners, permanent secretaries), by bureacracy (Finance, Foreign Affairs, Trade), and by generation (senior versus junior-level civil servants).

[51] Ayida 1973: 5. Ayida was permanent secretary in the federal Ministry of Finance at the time. The speech was an important one and has been described by a prominent representative of local capital as "an apologia for the insulation of the top civil servants from popular pressure and influence."

[52] Interview with former advisor to the Gowon government.

[53] Interview with former official of an indigenous businessmen's group.

[54] Interview with prominent former state official.

those which necessitated the Nigerianization of the public sector at Independence."[55]

As we shall see, the civil servants did not operate in a vacuum. They were aware of and responded to explicit interest group pressure, general societal expectations, and their own narrow material and ideological interests.[56] Yet their ideas about Nigerian development were separable from those of the indigenous business community, and they were increasingly able to act on their convictions (largely by decree) after 1966.

Before the military assumed control of Nigeria, state officials initiated elements of a general program of indigenization in the country. The First Development Plan (1962–68) called for economic independence and stated that indigenous businessmen should control an increasing portion of the Nigerian economy. The 1963 Immigration Act and the government's 1964 statement on industrial policy (which when taken together appear designed to encourage personnel, equity, and local-content indigenization) have already been discussed. Around 1964 and 1965 a number of papers were in circulation within the ministries proposing a more comprehensive program of indigenization for the country.[57] However, it is not clear that these proposals (or the declaration in the First Plan, the 1963 act or the 1964 statement, for that matter) were at all separable from the demands emanating from local capital at about the same time.

The same can be said for the creation in 1966 of the Expatriate Quota Allocation Board, since employment was of such concern to local capital. Prior to the establishment of the board, expatriate applications for residence permits in Nigeria were administered by the Ministry of Internal Affairs. In 1966 an interministerial board was established, composed of representatives from eight ministries and the Nigerian Industrial Development Bank. The Expatriate Quota Allocation Board was established at least in part because of local businessmen's complaints about a major influx of Lebanese and Indian merchants engaged in both wholesale and retail sales of textile goods in the Lagos area during 1965 and 1966.[58] However state bureaucrats, especially officials of the Central Bank and in the Ministry of Finance, were worried about the implications of "earnings leakage" for Nigeria's balance-of-payments position. They were concerned that the large

[55] Ayida 1973: 5.

[56] Wilson n.d.: 7.

[57] Interview with former official of an indigenous businessmen's group.

[58] Owonuwa 1975: 29. The same comment was obtained in an interview with a prominent indigenous businessman.

number of expatriates employed in the country sent most of the earnings abroad. Thus, state officials had their own objectives for the creation of the Expatriate Quota Allocation Board, objectives that did not necessarily conflict with (but were different from) those of local capital.

The board assigned terminal dates to specific expatriate positions on a firm-by-firm basis, granting quotas only if no qualified Nigerians were available for the positions. However, it had limited effectiveness, largely because of the small size of its staff and the fact that it had to rely on information supplied by the multinational enterprises, which tended to exaggerate the technical-skill requirements for many of their positions.[59] Still, nearly two-thirds of the firms surveyed by Rimlinger and Stremlau in 1971 reported receiving terminal dates from the board for certain positions.[60]

During the Nigerian civil war, local-business demands for indigenization were not a priority for state officials. Their primary concern was with the war effort. Indigenization was important only to the extent to which it might further the objectives of the federal side in the conflict. The conduct of the war strengthened the powerful federal bureaucrats in Lagos by providing them with experience in centralized decisionmaking and with a nationalistic desire for more control.[61] It also taught them that the multinational oil companies could not be trusted. The oil companies were indecisive at the outset of the war about whether to provide oil revenues to Nigeria or Biafra, and they initially placed their earnings in escrow accounts. That was not the only source of state suspicion of their operations, however. The war also highlighted the fact that the management of these centrally important enterprises was external to Nigeria, since state officials had to guess their contributions to Nigeria's exports and capital flows, and their implications for Nigeria's pricing system.[62] There was high-level resentment of the role of the oil companies at the outset of the conflict, and some officials believed that if they (and the Nigerian public) had had sufficient information about the extent of the oil reserves located offshore in the Bight of Bonny, the Biafran secession might never have taken place.[63]

[59] According to Rimlinger 1973: 210, the multinational enterprises were not necessarily trying to evade the intentions of the government with this practice, but simply attempting to maintain their flexibility.

[60] Ibid., p. 215.

[61] Forrest forthcoming. See also Wilson n.d.: 12.

[62] Interview with prominent former state official.

[63] Ibid.

Part 10 of the 1968 Companies Act was an important precursor of indigenization, and has been variously described as a "prerequisite to indigenization" and "the first aspect of indigenization."[64] The inclusion of Part 10 in what was otherwise largely a copy of the 1948 U.K. Companies Act, "compelled all alien enterprises to register as Nigerian entities."[65] Although this ultimately provided a legal basis for indigenization (i.e. equity could not be acquired if assets were based outside Nigeria), it did not provide a political one. A comprehensive program of indigenization was not the logical next step. In fact, it is not at all clear that state bureaucrats had indigenization in mind when Part 10 was written into the companies legislation.

The civil servants were in the process of updating Nigerian companies legislation in 1967, essentially a routine bureaucratic procedure, when Part 10 was "superimposed" (to use the language of one of the participants). The Minister of Justice at the time, Dr. Elias, and the Economic and Finance Committee of the permanent secretaries in the federal ministries introduced the idea of mandatory incorporation of separate entities of all foreign corporations operating in Nigeria.[66] "We wanted to make it easier to control foreign companies, to get a clear balance sheet from them."[67] They were interested in more than balance sheets, however. They were particularly interested in additional information from the multinational oil companies, the companies that had provoked so much suspicion and resentment at the outset of the civil war. State officials were contemplating nationalization of the petroleum industry at the time, partly because of their dissatisfaction with the recent behavior of the multinational oil companies, partly because of the growing significance of the petroleum sector for government revenues,[68] and partly because of the demonstration effects of petroleum nationalizations in so many of their fellow OPEC members. Therefore, the inspiration for Part 10 of the Companies Act was the avoidance of claims in international courts if and when the Nigerian government decided to nationalize the petroleum companies operating in the country. It was not the first step in a carefully orches-

[64] Interview with former advisor to the Gowon government. A similar sentiment was expressed in Ayida 1973: 5.

[65] Ibid.

[66] It was drafted by lawyers from the Ministry of Commerce.

[67] Interview with prominent former state official.

[68] Petroleum proceeds provided nearly 70 percent of the total federal government revenue in 1970, three full years before the major OPEC-inspired price increases in the wake of the 1973 Mideast war. See Ogbuagu 1981: esp. 90–106 for details.

trated approach to indigenization, and it was not a response to indigenous business pressure.

The first draft of Part 10 was circulated among a few expatriate solicitors who worked with haste over a weekend on revisions to the original language. They clarified some otherwise unanswerable tax problems and circulated the document among leading members of the expatriate business community, especially those associated with the largest British multinationals. Every one of them responded negatively, declaring, "We can't accept that" or "We must reject it outright."[69] The state bureaucrats expected such a reaction, however, and, as one official commented, "We were not deterred. We knew that Nigeria was so important in the region that they would have to stay."[70] They were correct.

Work on the Second National Development Plan (1970–74) was completed during 1968 and 1969. Several new permanent secretaries had been appointed in 1967, and they had indigenization in mind when they wrote the second plan. They consulted with a number of academics and eventually wrote what some observers have described as "a scholarly development plan."[71] When they included indigenization as one of the strategic aims of the second planning period, they were not simply responding to local businessmen's demands. As one senior government official put it, "We were attempting to think in concrete terms regarding the meaning of a mixed economy in Nigeria."[72] State officials were aware of the papers being circulated by the indigenous business community at the time, and even solicited private-sector opinion on certain issues (notably on personnel indigenization). They were also writing their own papers, and as we shall see below, just as in the case of the 1968 Companies Act they also had their own agenda and objectives in mind.

The Second Plan declared that "the interests of foreign private investors in the Nigerian economy cannot be expected to coincide at all times and in every respect with national aspirations. . . . A truly independent nation cannot allow its objectives and priorities to be distorted or frustrated by the manipulations of powerful foreign investors."[73] It was widely believed among senior state officials that left to

---

[69] Interview with former advisor to the Gowon government.

[70] Interview with prominent former state official.

[71] Interview with prominent indigenous businessman.

[72] Interview with prominent former state official.

[73] *Second National Development Plan, 1970–74: Programme of Post-War Reconstruction and Development* 1970: 289. This also sounds like a thinly veiled reference to the multinational oil companies again.

market forces, an unwholesome specialization had emerged, in which foreign capital was concentrated in medium and large-scale enterprises, while local capital was relegated to small-scale activities. Therefore they concluded that only state intervention could alter the situation.

> It is vital, therefore, for Government to acquire and control on behalf of the Nigerian society the greater proportion of the productive assets of the country. To this end, the Government will seek to acquire, by law if necessary, equity participation in a number of strategic industries that will be specified from time to time.[74]

The type of state intervention proposed in this section of the plan did not call for the kind of indigenization envisaged by the local private sector in Nigeria. Rather, it called for the state to "establish the ascendancy of the state sector by widening its areas of influence, operation, and authority."[75]

In particular, the plan called for state acquisition of or dominant participation in the fastest-growing enterprises in the economy, those in industry and mining, possibly in the form of joint ventures with foreign or local capital. It was understood that in these joint ventures "the Government remains the dominant partner."[76] Private investors (either foreign or local) would continue to be welcome in Nigeria, but they would be "partners in progress *led by the public sector*."[77] The plan explicitly rejected local businessmen's call for limited state involvement in the economy, arguing that this view "flows from the narrow conception of the role of Government in national development which is not tenable in Nigerian circumstances."[78] Basically, the state officials did not trust local capital and thought that the type of development the indigenous businessmen would promote would be both inegalitarian and too closely allied with foreign interests.

Several of local capital's proposals for indigenization found their way into the second plan. Personnel indigenization was given top priority, and the plan declared that the government could not "continue to tolerate a situation in which high-level Nigerian personnel educated and trained at great cost to the nation, are denied employment in their own country by foreign business establishments."[79]

---

74 Ibid.
75 Aboyade 1977: 385.
76 *Second Plan* 1970: 289.
77 Ibid. (emphasis added).
78 Ibid.
79 Ibid.

State bureaucrats, of course, had their own reasons for supporting personnel indigenization, concerned as they were with the "earnings leakage" from the large number of expatriates in the country. Similarly, although the plan proposed that foreign capital be restricted to certain sectors of the economy, it is not entirely clear that it did so for the same reasons as the Lagos Chamber of Commerce. Local capital wanted reduced competition and a chance to expand in the distributive sector. The state was more interested in designating areas for its own expansion. As we shall see below, these two objectives are not entirely compatible. Finally, the plan suggested that at least 35 percent of the equity in certain foreign enterprises be held by Nigerians (in food industries, forest products, building materials and construction).[80] However, it made it clear that the participation should be shared by the indigenous public and private sector, not solely reserved for local businessmen.

Thus, although the Second National Development Plan contained significant proposals for indigenization, it is by no means clear that the conception of indigenization considered by state officials bore much resemblance to the conception local capital had in mind. The conceptions were not incompatible, and prospects for collaboration were present. Local businessmen were consulted, and their representations were considered by state officials. They did not control the state, however, and clearly differed on the desirability of state leadership of the direction of national development.

After the work on the Second National Development Plan was completed in 1969, state officials initiated programs and decrees to accomplish their objectives of taking control of the "commanding heights" of the economy and establishing state leadership of the direction of national development. Consistent with these objectives, they began with Nigeria's most important area of economic activity—the petroleum industry. The 1969 Petroleum Decree linked Nigerianization to national control of the industry in line with developments in other OPEC countries.[81] It required new concessions to Nigerianize not fewer than 60 percent of jobs at all levels and not fewer than 75 percent of management positions within ten years of obtaining a lease. This was followed in 1971 by federal government acquisition of minority, and in some cases majority, participation in the petroleum companies operating in Nigeria.

A similar scenario applies to another of Nigeria's crucial economic

[80] Ibid., p. 145.
[81] Forrest forthcoming.

sectors—its commercial banking industry. Banking legislation was introduced in 1969 that required all banks to incorporate in Nigeria and publish audited statements of account in the country. In April of 1970, the Central Bank of Nigeria introduced credit guidelines to commercial and merchant banks operating in the country, stipulating minimum amounts of their total lending which must be committed to particular target sectors of the economy and to particular groups (notably including indigenous private enterprise). By stipulating that 35 percent of commercial lending should be allocated to indigenous firms in 1970, the state simultaneously addressed a central concern of local capital (access to finance) and accomplished an objective of its own (greater control of a strategic economic activity). Early in 1971 Nigeria's three largest expatriate-controlled commercial banks sold token amounts of their equity on the Lagos Stock Exchange. However, this was not enough for state officials, who initiated federal government acquisition of 40 percent of the shares of the big three in April of that year. Although neither General Gowon nor the Civil Commissioner of the Ministry of Finance at the time, Alhaji Shehu Shagari, complained about the policies of these banks when they announced their plans to acquire 40 percent of their share capital, it was widely believed that "the Government may have been influenced by the realisation that although the three banks concerned have all made share issues, only three per cent of their capital is now in local hands."[82] By acquiring a larger share of the equity of these important enterprises, the federal government was able to ensure that its credit guidelines were being followed, improve its monitoring of the banking industry, and assist local capital with improved access to finance. Senior civil servants also suggested that the smaller foreign banks operating in the country follow suit and make a comparable percentage of their equity available for local subscription, but the banks ignored the suggestion.[83] Taken together, the Central Bank's credit guidelines and government acquisition of a major share of the equity of the largest commercial banks ultimately facilitated the indigenization program. However, the measures were not initiated solely for that purpose, since they accommodated the objective of state leadership of the economy as well.

By the middle of 1971 it was clear that the government was preparing a comprehensive indigenization program for the country. The proposals for the program came from the Economic and Finance

[82] *West Africa*, no. 2,862 (21 April 1972), p. 1.
[83] Interview with prominent former state official.

Committee, a group composed of the permanent secretaries of the relevant federal ministries (including Industries, Economic Development, Internal Affairs, and Finance). As has already been discussed,
the permanent secretaries and other top civil servants had between
1968 and 1971 been receiving an increasing number of representations and requests from local capital for some kind of indigenization
program. With the civil war over in 1970, state officials were once
again able to direct their attention to domestic development issues
and began to respond to influential interest groups in the society. The
press had picked up the issue, and a great deal of popular agitation for
some kind of government action against foreign enterprises ensued.[84]
It was politically expedient to act at this point, and state officials were
able to do so without jeopardizing their own agenda for state leadership of national development. In November of 1970 the government
announced its intention to indigenize domestic trading in Nigeria
within four years. This allowed it to make good on a longstanding
commitment to support local capital in this area, and it did not conflict with state plans to expand its role in more strategic areas of the
economy.

The permanent secretaries on the Economic and Finance Committee introduced before the Supreme Military Council their proposals
to create two sectors (or schedules) of economic activities, one reserved entirely for Nigerians and another for 40 percent minority indigenous participation. At the outset, a number of the civilian commissioners on the council opposed the proposals, including Shehu
Shagari, Anthony Enahoro, and J. S. Tarka. They argued that people
in the North and East were not ready for indigenization at this time.
There was no access to capital in the East in the aftermath of the civil
war, and there were not enough people interested in the program in
the North.[85] Sensing that the proposals were about to be defeated,
Abdul Atta, a strong proponent of indigenization and secretary to the
government at the time, passed a handwritten note to General Gowon
advising him to send the proposals back to the Economic and Finance
Committee for further study. Gowon expressed his reservations that
foreign capital might leave Nigeria if the proposals were passed in
their present form, and he wondered whether there would be sufficient capital for indigenous businessmen to buy the shares. Thus, the
proposals were delayed for a time.

Atta had Gowon reschedule a meeting to consider the indigeniza-

[84] Balabkins 1982: 30.
[85] Interview with prominent former state official.

tion proposals at a later time, when he knew that many of the civilian commissioners most strongly opposed to them would be away and unable to attend a meeting. The basic decisions were taken in 1971 (although some aspects of the program had been agreed to earlier in 1970), and in June of 1971 the federal military government enumerated its official objectives and announced its intention to produce an indigenization decree.[86]

There was not unanimity within the state about indigenization. The reservations of some of the civil commissioners have already been discussed. However, even among the permanent secretaries and their top advisors there were important disagreements. Some wanted state participation and leadership throughout the industrial sector, not restricted to the leading, and the largest, high-technology industries such as petroleum, petrochemicals, iron and steel, and fertilizer production (as laid out in the Second Plan). There was also disagreement about whether shares should be held in bulk to ensure that government participation would result in an influence on policy. Some state technocrats favored more control over individual enterprises than others. These differences within the state sector had important implications for the eventual composition and implementation of the program, as we shall see below when we analyze the content of the decree.

There was a long delay between the June 1971 announcement of the Supreme Military Council's agreement to the proposals and the formal promulgation of the decree in February of 1972. This has been attributed to the difficulty of translating the government's objectives into legal language.[87] It is likely, however, that the considerable diversity of opinion, even within the state, created enough infighting to delay the final decree. The proposals were also circulated informally to some members of the Lagos Chamber of Commerce (both indigenous and expatriate members), which also undoubtedly delayed the final announcement.

What, then, were the principal objectives of the state officials who first introduced, then passed, and now had to implement Nigeria's first indigenization decree? First and foremost, they wanted to ensure

[86] "Report of the Industrial Enterprises Panel" 1976: par. 1.1. Five objectives were listed: (1) create opportunities for Nigerian indigenous businessmen; (2) raise the percentage of indigenous ownership of industry; (3) maximize local retention of profits; (4) raise the level of local production of intermediate goods; (5) increase Nigerian participation in decisionmaking in management of the large commercial and industrial establishments. This list includes most (but not all) of my summary of the state's objectives at the end of this section. For more details about the report, see Chapter 3, n. 7.

[87] *West Africa*, no. 2,844 (17 December 1971), p. 1.

that indigenization would be accomplished within the framework of state-led development in Nigeria. They had other measures, such as the banking legislation and the petroleum decrees (and more measures to follow), to accomplish their primary objective of state leadership of the direction of national development.[88] They wanted to be sure, however, that indigenization was consistent with this objective. The benefits to local capital must not be at the expense of the state.[89]

Second, the state wanted to delimit the areas of competition between foreign capital and local capital. The civil servants were dissatisfied with the emerging division of labor between foreign and local capital and wanted to push foreign capital into areas in which it could make its greatest contribution. There was no point in allowing foreign firms to do what Nigerian firms could do, since foreigners were more difficult to control. Thus, foreign companies should be pushed into intermediate and high-technology areas, areas with high management requirements and high risk.[90] This delimiting of areas for foreign capital also served the first objective of state leadership of the economy, since it kept foreign companies out of areas reserved for state corporations.

Third, the state wanted to respond to two important constituencies, local capital and mass public opinion. By creating new opportunites for local capital, the state was able to respond to an influential and growing business class. It was able to do so by squeezing out a vulnerable one, the Lebanese business community.[91] The indigenization decree also served to legitimize the military regime's continued hold on power. After the end of the war effort (for which a military government is well suited and relatively more legitimate) the military leadership needed to demonstrate it could do things that responded to popular demands in other areas as well.[92]

Fourth, state officials, especially those associated with the Ministry of Finance and the Central Bank, had an institutional interest in any

[88] Although they never claimed that indigenization would promote an egalitarian distribution of income in Nigeria (a point of much concern and controversy after the implementation of the decree), the architects of the program justified their intervention in the economy on the basis of their ability to meet the needs and demands of society as a whole. See the discussion of this point, and the implicit critique of local capital, on p. 289 of the *Second Plan*.

[89] There was some dissension on this point among the civil servants, however (interview with prominent former state official).

[90] Collins 1974: 502. See also Hoogvelt 1979: 57 for very much the same point.

[91] State officials also genuinely believed that complaints from the local business community about their inadequate access to finance were legitimate.

[92] Interview with prominent former state official.

measure that would shore up Nigeria's balance-of-payments position. It was widely thought that if personnel indigenization could be advanced, the earnings leakage resulting from having so many expatriates employed in the country could be reduced. Further, if a larger percentage of the shares of enterprises were obtained by indigenous Nigerians, it follows logically that a greater percentage of the profits would be retained locally.[93]

Fifth, at least some state officials wanted to increase local capital's participation in foreign enterprises as a first step toward its eventual assumption of control of them.[94] Indigenization in 1972 was thus seen as a psychological gesture, only a beginning, with participation as the initial stage and effective control as a later one. State officials were afraid that indigenous businessmen would prove unable to manage enterprises adequately, and hence they postponed pushing for managerial control until a later date.

Sixth and finally, the state wanted to prevent a possible flight of foreign capital and reassure the expatriate community that the indigenization program was not the first step on a road of complete nationalization. They promised that no further action would be taken until the end of the Third National Development Plan (in 1980), and General Gowon declared: "We are consolidating our political independence by doing all we can to promote more participation by Nigerians in our economic life while attracting more investment in sectors of the economy where Nigerians are not yet able to rely on themselves."[95] Some of the career civil servants were less concerned than the military leadership about the need to reassure foreign capital. They were convinced that foreign companies would stay and continue to invest in Nigeria once they understood the program.

FOREIGN CAPITAL

Since they were (in theory) the target of indigenization, foreign businessmen were much less involved than either local capital or the state in the formulation of the program.[96] They were by no means quies-

[93] That assumes, of course, that indigenous businessmen are more likely than foreign ones to spend and/or reinvest in Nigeria.

[94] Some state technocrats preferred increasing the state's active participation to increasing local capital's.

[95] General Yakubu Gowon made these comments while speaking at the Royal College of Defense Studies during a state visit to the United Kingdom in June of 1973. They were quoted in Collins 1974: 501.

[96] For the purposes of this discussion, foreign capital will be defined as composed of

cent during the period that led up to the first decree, however, and they did have an influence on its final composition. They began by lobbying against the program, but eventually accepted its inevitability and opted first for appeals for exemptions from aspects of the decree and later for an extension of the deadline for compliance. Large multinational capital should be differentiated from the small-scale operations of the Levantine community in Nigeria. The latter had a much weaker international political base from which to operate and tried to keep a low profile rather than lobby actively against the program.

The opposition of foreign companies to Part 10 of the 1968 Companies Act has already been discussed. The multinational oil companies were particularly opposed to the inclusion of Part 10, perhaps because they realized that it would soon be used against them. However, a more organized and more comprehensive lobbying effort was launched in response to the impending indigenization program. The West Africa Committee, representing the interests of British capital in Nigeria, played an important role in this lobbying effort, as did a few especially prominent and highly visible British firms, notably Nigeria's largest company, the United Africa Company. The West Africa Committee was distrusted by many Nigerians as a colonial remnant,[97] and although it was the largest firm, UAC was only one company. Hence, the bulk of the lobbying effort was undertaken by the Lagos Chamber of Commerce. As long as the Chamber was controlled by expatriates (as it was throughout the 1960s), it was solidly against indigenization. Expatriate members were motivated by the fear that the indigenization of the banking sector in particular might result in the use of finance as a weapon against them. The Chamber regularly sent delegations of expatriates and a few members of the Indigenous Businessmen's Group to convey to top state officials their strong opposition to mandatory joint ventures. The ambivalence of the indigenous businessmen was discussed in the section "Local Capital" above.

In their lobbying against indigenization, the expatriate businessmen argued that Nigerian businessmen were risk-averse and would prefer to invest their money in the more secure real-estate market than in long-term (and riskier) productive investments such as manufac-

---

all those businesses whose logic of accumulation is not restricted to Nigeria. For these enterprises, Nigeria provides either (1) one link in a chain of subsidiaries located throughout the world but based elsewhere (i.e. MNCs), or (2) a temporary base for accumulation, much of which is exported or held abroad (i.e. the Levantine business community). Foreign capital in Nigeria is divided principally by sector, by nation of origin, by scale, and along the lines identified above (i.e. MNCs, Levantine).

[97] Interview with Nigerian journalist.

turing. Accordingly, they predicted that there would be an insufficient number of Nigerians with capital (or an insufficient amount of total local capital) to purchase the number of shares involved.[98] If the government still went ahead with indigenization, the foreign business community argued that productivity and efficiency would certainly fall, because there simply were not enough Nigerians sufficiently qualified to manage the firms.[99] The large trading companies operating in the country at the time (like UAC, John Holt) argued that they should be exempted from the exercise because of the service they provided by ensuring that goods were distributed throughout the nation. They contended that Nigerian distributors would be more parochial than the expatriate trading companies and therefore would be less willing to supply goods outside their own areas (especially if shortages developed).

Although the bulk of their arguments were highly critical of local capital as a credible alternative to foreign capital (e.g. insufficient capital, insufficient interest, insufficient qualifications, or insufficient reliability), the foreign businessmen did join their local counterparts on one issue. They too warned of the dangers of public-sector expansion and encroachment on the areas that they thought should remain under private-sector control. It was on this position (and the fact that the final Chamber resolution on indigenization did not challenge the interests of large foreign capital) that their alliance on indigenization was forged in the Lagos Chamber of Commerce. In an effort to deepen this alliance, expatriates advised Nigerian members of the Chamber that they would be tampering with the good life in Nigeria if they pursued indigenization too vigorously. In the end, if all these arguments should fail, a few foreign businessmen threatened to pull out of Nigeria altogether. They were not very serious, however. When the government finally went through with the first decree and called their bluff, none of the multinational companies left.[100]

After it became obvious that attempts to block indigenization were certain to fail, foreign capital shifted its tack by first agreeing to the Chamber resolution and subsequently proceeding to lobby for specific exemptions from aspects of the program. It was also at this point

[98] They assumed that their own assessment of the fair market valuation of their share capital would be employed if the shares were to be sold.

[99] This is, incidentally, virtually the same argument used by the colonial authorities before independence as to why Nigerians would be unable to govern themselves.

[100] The only foreign enterprises that closed down and left Nigeria after the first indigenization decree were the one-man Lebanese, Syrian, and Greek enterprises in the distributive sector. See Chapter 3 for further details.

that multinational capital began to differentiate itself from the Levantine community. Different industry groupings, including the publishers, insurance companies, advertising agencies, clearing and forwarding agents, and textile manufacturers lobbied for complete exemption or at least exemption from the list of enterprises assigned to Schedule I of the decree, those to become 100 percent Nigerian. The United Africa Company continued to lobby for a special dispensation because of its size and the centrality of its distribution network. However, the most frequent exemption requested was for an extension of the time for compliance with the provisions of the decree. Most foreign companies needed time to diversify their activities, especially those operating principally in areas designated to become fully Nigerian. Some firms required high-level financial restructuring, while others simply needed time to complete long-term diversification plans already underway. This was especially true of the large trading companies, which were increasingly diversifying into joint ventures with MNC manufacturers from Europe and North America, as well as entering into the distribution and servicing of technical equipment.[101] Since many of these diversification programs were already well underway, the foreign companies were less worried about the change brought about by indigenization than they were about the rate at which that change was taking place.

What, then, were the objectives of foreign capital with respect to indigenization? For a time, it wanted to stop the program altogether, since any uncertainty enhances risk, and indigenization presented the specter of both uncertainty and risk. There was no point in encouraging a program that would make its already difficult life in Nigeria any more difficult. This lobbying was going on at a time before joint ventures were as common as they are today.

Second, once indigenization became a near-certainty, they wanted to obtain some specific exemptions from aspects of the program. Some firms wanted their entire sector omitted, some wanted to ensure they avoided Schedule I, some wanted exemptions on the basis of their size, and others chose to lobby for an exemption on the basis of their sectoral contribution.

Third, almost all foreign firms wanted to ensure there would be enough time for their diversification (or expansion) programs, and hence they wanted to delay the implementation of indigenization in

---

[101] Obtaining diversification by progressively moving foreign capital into more advanced production areas was, after all, one of the objectives of the state; hence these requests were not received with much suspicion.

some way. Some favored delaying the initiation of the program for as long as possible, while others favored an extension of their date for compliance with provisions of the decree.

Fourth and finally, foreign capital wanted assurances that it would still be welcome in Nigeria and that no more major changes in its equity position or in its role in the economy would be forthcoming in the immediate future.

THE SCOPE OF THE 1972 DECREE

Some observers have described the 1972 decree as "careless in design" and "sloppy in implementation."[102] We will consider the implementation of the decree in the next chapter, but it would be unfair to describe the first decree as careless in design. In its final textual form it may appear careless, but that is only because it was not dictated by any one of the major actors described up to this point. If local capital had drafted the decree, it would appear more consistent with its objectives. Similarly, if the state officials had not been approached by either local capital or foreign capital, their draft would differ from the final text. The fact is that the objectives of each of the three protagonists are represented in the final decree. Policymaking, in this case the creation of the Nigerian Enterprises Promotion Decree of 1972, was a political process in which the state mediated between the conflicting demands of local and foreign capital, and at the same time attempted to further its own objectives. It is precisely because of this process of policymaking as politics that the decree took the final form that it did. Local capital did not capture the state, the state did not reveal itself to be serving the interests of foreign capital, and the state was not autonomous in its actions.

Earlier in this chapter we considered the variety of ways in which state officials interacted with local and foreign businessmen during the composition of the decree. Their comments and reactions were solicited by state officials at various times, and they were never unwilling to send another delegation or make another representation to the officials responsible for constructing the program. Nigerian labor was virtually excluded from the entire process, but did make some attempts to influence the program after it was first announced in June of 1971. The unions in industries certain to be affected by the decree worried about the prospects of layoffs, should unbought enterprises be closed down. (They seem to have been persuaded by the arguments

[102] Hoogvelt 1979: 57.

of foreign businessmen about the insufficiency of local capital.) Labor was also apprehensive that wages and working conditions would deteriorate once local businessmen assumed control of indigenized enterprises.[103] For the most part, however, the concerns of labor were not very influential, and, as we shall see below, they were not reflected in the final version of the decree that was promulgated in February of 1972.

The 1972 decree essentially divided the Nigerian economy into three parts. One part was reserved entirely for Nigerians, one part was set aside for Nigerian minority equity participation, and one part was not affected at all. All enterprises in businesses assigned to Schedule I of the decree were required to sell 100 percent of their equity to Nigerian subscribers. No new foreign enterpises could be established in those areas after February 1972. Schedule II of the decree listed economic activities in which expatriates would be barred under certain conditions. Small firms, defined as those with equity under 200,000 Nigerian pounds ($608,000) or sales turnover under 500,000 Nigerian pounds ($1,520,000), were required to sell all of their equity to Nigerian subscribers. Large firms, which accounted for nearly all of the enterprises operating in these sectors, were required to make 40 percent of their equity available to Nigerians. The rest of the economy was not affected by the decree at all; as we shall see below, a significant number of economic activities were included.

The classification of economic activities into Schedules I and II was made by the permanent secretaries on the Economic and Finance Committee, in consultation with relevant civil servants in a number of state ministries. Their decision rules combined the scale of the enterprise with the level of technology required for its operation. From this, they constructed a hierarchy of economic activities which assigned activities requiring little capital and little technical expertise to Schedule I, and omitted from either schedule enterprises with large capital needs and requiring a high degree of technical sophistication. There were some notable exceptions, however, as will be indicated in the analysis of the decree which follows.

Schedule I included small-scale, low-technology activities many of which were already nearly 100 percent Nigerian at the time of the announcement of the first decree. Significantly, retail trade throughout the country was reserved for Nigerians (excluding large department stores and supermarkets). The remainder of the list was equally divided between petty manufacturing and service activities. Production

[103] Collins 1974: 505.

of alcoholic drinks, building materials, candles, jewelry, newspapers, garments (not including textile manufacture), and singlets was entirely reserved for Nigerians. Bakeries, electrical assembly, rice milling, and tire retreading were also added to Schedule I. Among the service-sector activities reserved for Nigerians were advertising and public relations; pools, betting, and casinos; cinemas; clearing and forwarding; hairdressing; road transport; laundry; buses and taxis; and radio and television broadcasting.

Schedule II of the decree included largely intermediate-scale and intermediate-technology activities. These were the only areas in which the multinational corporations were affected in any way. Since virtually all MNCs exceeded the size and turnover limits, they were required only to sell 40 percent of their equity to local subscribers.[104] The construction industry was included in Schedule II, as were a few agricultural production and processing activities (including fishing, poultry, meat slaughtering and processing), and the balance of the commercial sector (wholesale distribution, department stores and supermarkets, the distribution of machines and technical equipment, and the distribution of motor vehicles). A number of service activities were also included, namely coastal and inland shipping, real-estate agencies, internal air transportation, interstate bus transportation, shipping, and travel agencies. Most of the activities included in Schedule II were in manufacturing. Beer brewing, boat building, paper conversion, and screen printing on textiles were included, along with the manufacture of tires, soft drinks, cosmetics, furniture, insecticides, bicycles, cement, matches, metal containers, prints, soaps, suitcases, hardware, books, and plywood.

Most of the multinationals in Nigeria at the time were engaged in the high-technology, large-scale operations that were not affected by the first decree. The largest employer in the country, the textile industry, was excluded from either Schedule I or II. Other large industries, such as chemicals, plastics, sugar refining, and telecommunications were similarly excluded. Notably, petroleum, petroleum services, petrochemicals, iron and steel, and fertilizer production (the areas reserved for the state in the Second Plan) were omitted from any mention in the first decree. Banking, insurance, and vehicle assembly, areas of future state investment, were also left out. The mining sector (including tin, coal and columbite) was already mostly state-owned

---

[104] We will discuss in Chapter 3 the controversial determination of these equity and turnover figures, and the reasons why so many multinational corporations wanted time extensions.

and it too was omitted. The decree contained a provision to extend the list of affected enterprises, and at least one prominent state official described it as "a beginning."[105] Whether it was a beginning for the indigenous private sector or for the state was yet to be seen.

The 1972 decree established a board, the Nigerian Enterprises Promotion Board (NEPB), to administer and implement its provisions. It was chaired by the permanent secretary of the Ministry of Industries and contained one representative each from the ministries of Trade, Finance, Economic Development and Reconstruction, and Internal Affairs. Three representatives of development or investment agencies incorporated in Nigeria were also members of the board, and a secretary was appointed from the Ministry of Industries. Administratively, the NEPB had jurisdiction over three divisions: an administrative division, an inspectorate, and a valuation unit. The inspectorate carried out on-site inspections of enterprises, while the administrative unit prepared information for transmission to the board. Since its staff was limited, the NEPB used the Ministry of Industries Inspectorate Division for its controversial valuation of enterprises prior to the establishment of the Capital Issues Commission (CIC) in March of 1973.[106] The CIC and the controversy surrounding its decisions will be discussed further below and in Chapter 3.

The NEPB reported directly to the Federal Commissioner for Industries (a civilian in the military government), who had considerable discretionary power to exempt firms from aspects of the program (especially their classification, their size determination, and their deadline for compliance). He also considered any appeals of NEPB rulings and had the power to overturn them if he and the Federal Executive Council agreed on the matter. Legal appeals were specifically disallowed by the decree, except in cases involving a criminal offense. The NEPB itself also had considerable discretionary power to take over, sell, or dispose of defaulting enterprises without any express provision for compensation.

In anticipation of future implementation problems, the decree specifically prohibited "fronting" (that is, Nigerians operating enterprises on behalf of an expatriate who really manages all essential operations from a back room), and it forbade employment of the previous owner of an indigenized enterprise on a full- or part-time basis. In the spirit of Pan-Africanism, the decree defined all non-Nigerian Africans owning enterprises in the country as "indigenous" as

[105] Interview with prominent former state official.
[106] Ezeife 1981: 173–174.

long as they were from a OAU member state and their home country treated Nigerian businessmen on a basis of reciprocity. A relatively long period, slightly more than two years, was given for firms to comply with the decree, and the appointed day for full implementation was set for 31 March 1974.

The NEPB was not the only organization responsible for the implementation of the 1972 decree. Although they were not mandated by the decree, several other institutions were established or created to facilitate indigenization. Some were created just before the decree (in late 1971) and several were established immediately afterwards, in 1972 and 1973. Since there was widespread concern about the availability of finance and indigenous managerial ability, the federal government of Nigeria moved quickly to create new institutions in each of the problem areas.

In the realm of finance, the government began by providing loans of 54 million naira (or roughly $82.1 million) to indigenous banks to assist them in their expansion and to support the financing of indigenization.[107] The majority of the customers of these banks were petty traders, small businessmen, and other individuals whose financial needs would increase if they participated in the indigenization process.[108] Although the government's acquisition of 40 percent of the equity of the three largest commercial banks in 1971 was not entirely motivated by the indigenization program, it also facilitated the access of indigenous businessmen to capital for the purchase of shares. The government forced the banks to liberalize their credit facilities to local capital by monitoring their adherence to the Central Bank's credit guidelines after 1971. Although the NIDB was primarily concerned with industrialization in Nigeria, it too was instructed to assist in the process by increasing its loans to indigenous businessmen to as much as 80 percent of its portfolio.[109]

Since the NIDB had strong foreign-capital participation (49 percent of its equity was held by the World Bank), an entirely new financial institution, the Nigerian Bank for Commerce and Industry (NBCI), was established to facilitate further the financial implementation of the decree. It was thought that the financing of a new entity

[107] Teriba 1975: 175. The National Bank of Nigeria received 30 million naira (approximately $45.6 million), the Bank of the North 5 million ($7.6 million), the New Nigerian Bank 4 million ($6.1 million), and the African Continental Bank 15 million ($22.8 million).

[108] Ibid.

[109] Ogunsheye 1972: 15.

would be easier than refinancing a "much criticized entity."[110] The NIDB had long been criticized for lending primarily to foreign capital (recall the evidence of this in Table 2.2), and it apparently did not appreciate the creation of a rival government bank. Although plans for the NBCI were first announced in April of 1972, it was not formally established until May of 1973 and only began lending about six months before the March 1974 deadline for compliance. It was established with an authorized share capital of 50 million naira (or roughly $76 million), 60 percent of which was provided by the federal government of Nigeria and 40 percent by the Central Bank.[111] The NBCI was founded principally to assist local capital by identifying viable projects, preparing feasibility studies, offering advice, and lending the necessary funds either for the purchase of indigenized companies (or shares of companies) or for the creation of new enterprises. Because it was exempted from provisions of the banking decree, the NBCI was authorized to offer subsidized interest rates at levels between 6 percent and 8 percent below the rates prevailing at the private commercial banks. It was also empowered to purchase unbought shares of indigenized firms, essentially acting as a buyer of last resort on behalf of the government.[112]

While the NBCI was an important institution from the perspective of local capital, the establishment of the Capital Issues Commission in March of 1973 was of greatest importance to foreign capital. The NEPB relied on the Ministry of Industries Inspectorate Division for its valuation of enterprises to be sold under the decree's provisions throughout 1972, but as its workload began to pick up it became clear that another organization would have to be established. The CIC was empowered to determine the prices at which all foreign enterprises would be sold, as well as the timing of the sale, the price of individual shares, and the terms and conditions of sale (including the manner of selection of buyers and the manner of allotment of shares).[113] The CIC was technically an agency of the Central Bank of Nigeria and was chaired by an official of the bank. It also included representatives from the ministries of Finance, Trade, Industries and Economic Development, from the Lagos Stock Exchange, and from the indigenous busi-

---

[110] Okigbo 1981: 139.

[111] It was intended that 20 percent of the equity would later be transferred to banks, insurance companies, and other private financial companies, but this was never done. See ibid., pp. 139–141, for details.

[112] Ezeife 1981: 174–175. Apparently the fear that there was insufficient local capital available was fairly widespread within the government as well.

[113] Ibid., p. 174.

ness community. Although we will examine its controversial activities in more detail in the next chapter, its interpretation of the provision that the equity and turnover exemptions be based on figures submitted on income-tax returns for the preceding tax years (1968/69, 1969/70, and 1970/71) was a point of major concern to the foreign companies operating in Schedule II.

The government paid less attention to enhancing managerial ability than it did to providing finance, but it established a number of institutions for this purpose. The Industrial Training Fund (ITF), established in 1971, provided a subsidy to employers to support in-house or outside training programs for employees, and it was involved in the training of some lower-level managers. Similarly, the Nigerian Council for Management and Training was "reconstituted and commissioned by the Nigerian Enterprises Promotion Board to formulate policies on management education, training and development and to design suitable training programmes for Nigerian businessmen."[114] Out of its efforts came a number of university short courses and, more important, the Center for Management Development (the CMD). The center held a number of seminars on indigenization and eventually offered a variety of short courses designed to improve the managerial ability of middle-level managers and the new owners of the indigenized firms.

CONCLUSIONS

When the objectives of local capital, the state, and foreign capital are reexamined in light of the scope of the first decree, it becomes clear that the decree itself was the outgrowth of a political process in which the state collaborated with an alliance of elements of local capital against a relatively defenseless fragment of foreign capital, the Lebanese community in Nigeria. There was far more involved than a national government maximizing its position with its electorate or with foreign capital, as most neoclassical writers (conservatives, liberal internationalists, or structuralists) maintain. Every part of the decree, its classification system, its size exemptions, its omitted areas, and its enforcement mechanisms, can be traced to one of the protagonists involved in the process. The 1972 Nigerian Enterprises Promotion Decree fulfilled some of the objectives of each of the major protagonists, but none could be entirely satisfied with the final outcome.

Indigenous entrepreneurs could be pleased that they obtained state

[114] Ibid.

sanction and support in their bid to take over the distributive sector of the economy. There were limits on their participation in this sector, however, since large-scale supermarkets, department stores, whole-sale distribution, and the distribution of machines, technical equipment, and motor vehicles were assigned to Schedule II. Transportation of goods by road was another sector long sought by local capital, but it remained reserved for them only for a limited period. Another of the successes of local capital was to obtain minority participation in the profitable multinational corporations operating in Nigeria. Forty percent of the equity was quite sufficient for an enterpreneur interested in earnings, but not interested in control of the enterprise. However, the range of enterprises included in Schedule II was restricted to the older, more established, and less profitable enterprises, the ones employing a more mature technology. The high-growth, high-technology, high-profit industries were reserved for foreign capital or the state.

Finally, local capital was successful in obtaining a number of state supports, subsidies, and programs designed to facilitate its expansion and development. The Central Bank's credit guidelines, the government's pressure on lending policy after its acquisition of 40 percent of the three largest commercial banks, the grants to indigenous banks, the instructions to the NIDB, and the creation of the NBCI were all designed to facilitate local businessmen's access to finance. The Industrial Training Fund, the Center for Management Development, and the state-funded training programs were all designed to provide similar support in the area of managerial training. However, preferential access to contracts was left out of the indigenization program, and local capital had to find other ways to secure them. Thus, although local capital had some significant success in the composition of the first decree, it was not an unqualified success.

There were also some objectives of one segment of local capital (the indigenous managers) that were denied. Managerial employment in the large modern-sector multinational corporations was not addressed, nor was the issue of meaningful or responsible positions with the firms. The institutional mechanisms for these objectives were already established with the Expatriate Quota Allocation Board, the board was widely criticized for its lenience and frequent exemptions to foreign firms, and it did not coordinate its activities with the NEPB. Local businessmen's attempts to limit public-sector involvement in the economy were even less successful. They did manage to retain for themselves the interstate transport business, but they lost the areas of most rapid growth with the state's expansion into new

TABLE 2.3

A Summary of the Relative Success of Local Capital, Foreign Capital, and the State in the Formulation of the 1972 Nigerian Enterprises Promotion Decree

	Success	Qualified success	Ambiguous	Qualified failure	Failure	Description of outcome
Local capital's objectives						
Take over distributive sector		X				Retail trade assigned to Schedule I, but wholesale trade & dept. stores omitted
Minority participation		X				Many MNCs listed in Schedule II, but most profitable areas of the economy omitted
Managerial employment				X		Omitted from NEPD, but Expatriate Quota Allocation Board already existed
State supports	X					Financial and training supports provided, but not preferential access
Limit public sector				X		Successful only in interstate commerce; many important areas reserved for state
The state's objectives						
State-led development			X			Success or failure depends on perspective within the state (degree of participation necessary)
Delimit areas of FC/LC competition	X					Areas clearly defined by classification of activities in schedules
Respond to constituencies	X					Both local capital and the general public responded to
Improve b.o.p. position					X	Little or no effect
Initiate move to control MNCs				X		A statement is made, but decree contains no enforcement mechanism
Prevent FC flight		X				Accomplished, but largely through outside statements
Foreign capital's objectives						
Stop indigenization					X	Unmitigated failure, more for Lebanese firms than for multinationals
Obtain exemptions		X				Size limitations included; some sectors exempted
Delay compliance	X					Most deadlines extended, giving large MNCs time to diversify
Receive assurances		X				Assurances extended, but they were outside the decree without force of law

B.O.P. = balance of payments; FC = foreign capital; LC = local capital.

joint ventures with foreign capital. Thus, although local capital managed to attain several of its central objectives, it hardly appears that it had captured or controlled the state, as most radical observers maintain, be they dependency writers or classical Marxists.

State officials did not fare appreciably better than local capital with respect to their central objectives. They did manage to delimit the areas of foreign and local capital competition, and they were successful in moving foreign capital into intermediate and high-technology areas. However, it is unlikely that multinational corporations were about to move into the hairdressing or candle-manufacturing business, and many already had diversification programs well underway by the time of the first decree. The state was slightly more successful in its attempt to prevent a flight of foreign capital by giving more than two years for implementation and by providing assurances to foreign capital in a number of speeches and statements. The state was probably most successful in its attempt to respond to its constituencies. By promulgating the indigenization decree, it met the insistent demands of an important constituency, local capital. At the same time the military government gained popular support for its decisive nationalistic contribution to economic decolonization.

Despite these successes, it is less clear that the state accomplished its principal objective: introducing indigenization in the framework of state-led development. A number of well-placed observers who participated in government deliberations at the time have described the 1972 Nigerian Enterprises Promotion Decree as a "radical departure" from the "philosophy of public sector leadership"[115] or "the intentions of the planners"[116] as contained in the Second National Development Plan. From their perspective, the focus on local-capital participation in much of the modern industrial sector (including food, forest products, building materials, and construction) was a departure from the plan's intention to encourage mixed state-local capital ventures in those areas, ventures that would be predominantly directed by the state.[117] This view undoubtedly reflects the perspective of state officials who wanted state participation throughout the manufacturing sector, not restricted to petroleum, petrochemicals, iron and steel, etc. as laid out in the plan. Several senior state officials describe the indigenization decree as generally consistent with the objectives of state-led development. From their perspective, the state accomplished

[115] "Report of the Industrial Enterprises Panel" 1976: par. 1.2. The same point was made by Ezeife 1981: 167.
[116] Aboyade 1977: 379.
[117] Ezeife 1981: 167.

its goal by omitting its participation target industries from either Schedule I or Schedule II.[118] The resolution of this controversy depends on one's perspective on the proper scope of state participation in the economy necessary to maintain its leadership of national development. If state leadership can be obtained with participation in the fastest-growing or largest sectors (in foreign-exchange terms), then the state was successful in achieving its objective with the indigenization program. If state leadership requires broader participation throughout the productive sector of the economy, then it was not. What is clear is that one fragment of the state was defeated during the writing of the first decree, but it returned with a vengeance during the composition of the second decree, as we shall see in Chapter 4.

The state was less successful in improving Nigeria's balance-of-payments position through indigenization. Since personnel indigenization was not addressed in the decree, the earnings leakage lamented in the Second Plan documents was not addressed. Similarly, as we shall see in Chapter 3, there was no guarantee that indigenizing 40 percent of the share capital would result in 40 percent of the profits being retained locally. There were no mechanisms in the decree to ensure that there would be a favorable balance-of-payments contribution from indigenization. Further, since there was no formula for price determination spelled out in the decree, the Ministry of Industries and later the Capital Issues Commission developed their own interpretation of the decree as they implemented its provisions, and there was no guarantee that they considered the balance-of-payments effects of many of their decisions.[119] Finally, it was not clear that the state managed to ensure that the decree was a first step toward eventual Nigerian control of indigenized firms. The authors of the decree did give the NEPB the vague "general power to advance and develop the promotion of enterprises in which citizens of Nigeria shall participate fully and play a dominant role,"[120] but there were no further guidelines to the board on how to ensure full participation or a dominant role. A rhetorical declaration was made, but there is little evidence of any serious implementation of the suggestion. Thus, although several of its objectives were accomplished with the decree, the state may have failed to attain its primary goal, that of leadership of national development. It was hardly oblivious to its principal constituencies (the influence of local capital may have compromised its primary objective), and it cannot be

---

[118] Interviews with prominent former state officials.

[119] See Chapter 3 for details.

[120] Nigerian Enterprises Promotion Decree 1972, Supplement to Official Gazette Extraordinary no. 10, vol. 59, 28 February 1972, Part A, p. A 11.

described therefore as fully autonomous in its actions. The reality of the state's role was somewhat more constrained than liberal-internationalist or structuralist writers would allow and somewhat less constrained than dependency or Marxist writers could imagine.

Foreign capital clearly failed to accomplish its principal objective: stopping the program altogether. The Lebanese traders and petty manufacturers were by far the biggest losers in the exercise. Large multinational capital did, however, manage to accomplish its more modest objectives, and it influenced some important components of the decree. Some industry groupings representing large multinational capital (insurance companies and textile manufacturers) managed to exempt their businesses from the decree, although others (notably advertising agencies, clearing and forwarding agents, and publishers) were less successful. The large European trading firms managed to instill in officials fear about the performance of indigenous distributors, and they obtained size exemptions and classification as Schedule II enterprises. Most foreign firms (both Lebanese and multinational) were also successful in postponing the deadline for compliance with the decree, and they all received assurances about their long-term participation in the economy. Perhaps the most significant accomplishment of foreign capital with respect to the first decree was the apparent persuasiveness of its arguments about the inadequacy of indigenous capital, ability, and reliability. Although it did not dissuade the government from pursuing the program, it did compel it to establish new institutions (NBCI, CMD) and probably reinforced its decision to pursue minority, rather than majority, equity participation. Thus, although foreign companies were unable to stop the program, they were able to influence it in significant ways. The state did not serve the interests of foreign capital by promulgating the decree, even though it treated one fragment (large multinational capital) more leniently than another (the Levantine community). The liberal internationalists' expectations of an inexorable shift in the balance of bargaining power in favor of the state also needs some modification, as we shall see even more clearly in the next chapter.

The state, local capital, and foreign capital each had reasons to be pleased and dissatisfied with the first indigenization decree. The state did not unilaterally initiate the decree, but collaborated with a regional fraction of local capital in its formulation. It was also influenced by large multinational capital on some aspects of the program. The diverse and contradictory sources of the 1972 Nigerian Enterprises Promotion Decree provided the basis both for its implementation and subsequently for its ineffectiveness as a policy.

CHAPTER THREE

Fronting, Commercial Consolidation, and Inequality

THE implementation of the first indigenization decree was even more controversial than its formulation. Nearly everyone in Nigeria, and a great many people outside the country, had a strong reaction to the program. Alison Ayida, the permanent secretary in the federal Ministry of Finance during the formulation of the decree, suggested in 1973 that the program "may yet turn out to be one of the most important landmarks of the military regime."[1] A similar view was expressed by a senior official of the Lagos Stock Exchange in 1982, when he described indigenization as "one of the major developments in the economy during the last decade."[2] Not everyone shared their enthusiasm for the program, or more especially for its implementation. Chief Chris Ogunbanjo, a prominent Lagos-based indigenous businessman, characterized its implementation as something that "took place satisfactorily, but not without criticism from those who claimed to have been deprived of the opportunity of benefitting from the exercise."[3] Some academic observers were more critical, describing indigenization as a program "which had only the concrete, narrow, selfish interests of the petty-bourgeois class at heart."[4] Multinational executives were equally critical of the program, but for very different reasons. One American businessman, long resident in Lagos, described the major beneficiaries of the program as "the people who stole everything from the foreign companies and call it 'indigenization.' "[5]

Despite the lack of consensus among state officials, indigenous businessmen, academic observers, and multinational executives, the initial public response to the first indigenization decree was very favorable.[6] It was not until several years later, after most of the shares had changed hands, that the consequences of the NEPD of 1972 were

[1] Ayida 1973: 5.
[2] Interview with official of the Lagos Stock Exchange.
[3] Ogunbanjo 1982: 10.
[4] Onoge 1974: 59.
[5] Interview with American multinational executive.
[6] Rimlinger 1973: 207.

fully realized. Not only did a very small number of people ultimately benefit from the decree, but the consequences of increased indigenous participation in foreign enterprises also proved disappointing.

At least 952 foreign-owned enterprises were affected by the decree, excluding those exempted for one reason or another by the Nigerian Enterprises Promotion Board.[7] Most of these, 595 of the 952 or about 62 percent, were enterprises operating in Schedule II activities. The remaining 357 firms (or 38 percent of those affected) were located in Schedule I. By the middle of 1975, most of the affected firms had sold their shares to Nigerian subscribers and complied fully with the provisions of the decree, as indicated in Table 3.1. However, Schedule I firms were on average slower to comply than Schedule II firms. The total value of the shares acquired by Nigerians was estimated to be greater than 122 million naira (or approximately $195 million).[8] Most of this was from Schedule II firms, whose shares were valued at 109 million naira, or $174 million. The complying Schedule I enterprises accounted for only 13 million naira, or about $21 million. The total value of the shares acquired was probably even greater than the 122 million naira recorded by the NEPB, since some of the private transfers of shares were never reported to the board. Further, full compliance with the first decree was delayed for so long in some cases that the shares were not transferred until after the promulgation of the second indigenization decree in 1977 and hence are not accounted for in Table 3.1.

By the middle of 1975, 944 of the 952 affected enterprises had been exempted, had fully complied with the decree, or had formally defaulted. Eight cases were still under negotiation and arbitration at that time.[9] Since they were an explicit target of the first decree, it is

---

[7] The source of this information, and of many of the descriptive statistical data on the implementation of the first decree introduced in this chapter, is the unpublished three-volume "Report of the Industrial Enterprises Panel" of 1976. The panel, popularly known as the Adeosun Commission after Chief O. A. Adeosun, its chairman, was appointed by the federal military government in 1975 to investigate the implementation of the first decree. It therefore had access to the complete reports and documentation on hand at the Nigerian Enterprises Promotion Board through the middle of 1975. It is more authoritative and definitive than the secondary literature on this subject and therefore will be relied upon more extensively. To my knowledge, no other scholar writing about indigenization in Nigeria has had full access to this unpublished document.

[8] Conversion is based on the official exchange rate recorded by the International Monetary Fund of 1 naira = $1.5957 at the end of 1975.

[9] The end of June 1975 has been selected as a cutoff point for this discussion, because it coincides with the endpoint used in the Adeosun report and provides a natural break-

TABLE 3.1
The Scope of the First Indigenization Decree

	Schedule I		Schedule II		Total
No. of firms affected	357	(38%)	595	(62%)	952
No. of fully complying firms by mid 1975	209	(28%)	533	(72%)	742
% of firms complying		58%		90%	
Value of shares acquired (in millions of naira)	13	(11%)	109	(89%)	122

SOURCE: Compiled by the author from tables in "Report of the Industrial Enterprises Panel" 1976, from information supplied by the NEPB, and from various secondary sources.

not surprising that Lebanese firms account for 243 (or more than one-fourth) of the total number of affected enterprises. Because of their prominence in the colonial and post-independence economy, British firms accounted for a close second with 228 firms (or approximately 24 percent) of the affected enterprises. When the nationality of affected firms is grouped into meaningful categories based on the analytical distinctions drawn in Chapter 2 (differentiating among multinational capital—predominantly British, European, and North American firms; Levantine capital—predominantly Lebanese, but also including Greek, Syrian, and Jordanian firms; Indian capital; and other capital) some revealing patterns emerge. Nearly half of the firms affected by the first decree were multinational enterprises, 435 or 46 percent of the total affected and whose nationality is clearly identifiable. Nearly 85 percent of these were located in Schedule II activities and required to sell only 40 percent of their equity. The Levantine firms on the other hand were concentrated in Schedule I and hence were required to sell all of their equity to local subscribers. More than half of the enterprises affected in Schedule I activities were originally owned by Levantine capital, as shown in Table 3.2. Indian firms are numerous enough to be separable, but do not tend to be concentrated

---

ing point between the implementation of the first decree and the buildup of pressures for the formulation of the second.

in either Schedule I or Schedule II. They account for 12 percent of the firms affected, 11 percent of those in Schedule I and 13 percent of those in Schedule II.

As indicated in Table 3.2, nearly 79 percent of the firms affected by the decree complied with its terms. Approximately 90 percent of the firms located in Schedule II complied, while only 60 percent of those in Schedule I complied. In both cases, the compliance rate of multinational capital is generally higher (considerably higher in the case of Schedule I firms) than the compliance rate of Levantine and Indian capital. The latter are consistently below the average compliance rate in both schedules for reasons that will become apparent below in the discussion of the strategic responses of foreign capital.

Although a great many industries and enterprises were exempted during the formulation of the first decree, nearly a thousand foreign firms were required to sell a considerable portion of their equity to Nigerian subscribers. Most complied, at least to the satisfaction of the

TABLE 3.2
The Nationality of Affected Enterprises

	Multinational capital	Indian capital	Levantine capital	Other	Total
Schedule I					
Compliances	52	17	98	42	209
Defaults	14	22	77	27	140
Compliance rate	79%	44%	56%	61%	60%
Total affected	66	39	175	69	349[a]
% of total	19%	11%	50%	20%	
Schedule II					
Compliances	342	66	89	36	533
Defaults	27	9	15	11	62
Compliance rate	93%	88%	86%	77%	90%
Total affected	369	75	104	47	595
% of total	62%	13%	17%	8%	
Schedules I and II Combined					
Compliances	394	83	187	78	742
Defaults	41	31	92	38	202
Total affected	435	114	279	116	944[a]
% of total	46%	12%	30%	12%	

SOURCE: Compiled from "Report of the Industrial Enterprises Panel" 1976: vol. II, apps. III–VI.
[a] Does not equal the total number of affected enterprises listed in Table 3.1, since eight cases were still being negotiated or were under arbitration at the end of June 1975, the cutoff point for these data and discussion.

NEPB, and over 122 million naira was provided to the foreign owners for the purchase of part, or all, of their equity. Before we consider the consequences of this transaction at the level of the individual firm, however, let us examine where the money came from, how the NEPB interpreted the decree, and the controversy over how the Capital Issues Commission valued the shares sold publicly.

FINANCING THE DECREE

The value of the shares or part ownership of enterprises acquired by Nigerians reached 122,186,226 naira by the end of 1975.[10] Precisely where the money for this participation came from is less certain, however. There was apparently no lack of money, despite widespread fears that there would not be sufficient local capital to finance the scheme. By the end of 1974 (after the completion of the official implementation period), it was clear that there had been many more local businessmen interested in participating in the program than there were investment opportunities for them. Each of the eighteen foreign enterprises that complied with the decree by making public issues of stock between 1 May 1973 and 31 July 1974 had its offering heavily oversubscribed, ranging from Bata's ratio of 1.08 to Boots's ratio of 11.39.[11] Each share of new stock offered to the Nigerian public received an average of 3.56 applications, with a median number of 2.915 (as summarized in Table 3.3).

Since the Nigerian Bank for Commerce and Industry was created to help finance the indigenization program, it is a logical place to begin a search for the source of funds that fueled it. The bank had been empowered to offer terms to indigenous businessmen that were more generous than those offered by commercial banks, to provide other banking services to clients, and to acquire unbought shares if necessary. By the end of 1975, however, only nine of its sixty projects involved enterprises affected by the indigenization decree. A total of 2,758,000 naira (or approximately $4.4 million) was provided to Nigerian businessmen for the acquisition of foreign enterprises. The bulk of its funds, accounting for 95.1 percent of the bank's approved investment capital, were absorbed by the fifty-one new projects initiated by the NBCI.[12] The NBCI's disbursement of funds to clients was

[10] Compiled from Tables I.1 and I.2 of "Report of the Industrial Enterprises Panel" 1976.
[11] From Table II.4 of ibid.
[12] From Table VI.1 of ibid.

TABLE 3.3
Oversubscription of Public Issues on the Lagos Stock Exchange,
1 May 1973 to 31 July 1974

Firm	No. of applications to No. of shares on offer	Firm	No. of applications to No. of shares on offer
Bata	1.08	John Holt	2.92
CFAO	1.25	UAC	3.10
Blackwood-Hodge	1.57	Guinness	3.26
Metal Box	1.62	Wiggins-Teape	3.50
PZ	1.78	Nigerian Bottling	3.62
Lever Brothers	2.39	Daily Times	4.72
Berger	2.69	Costain	5.98
Nigerian Breweries	2.84	RT Briscoe	7.44
Vono Products	2.91	Boots	11.39

SOURCE: "Report of the Industrial Enterprises Panel" 1976: Table II.4.

also rather slow, but somewhat faster in the case of takeover projects than in the case of new ones.

Given the arguments put forward for its creation, the performance of the NBCI was disappointing. The bank especially created to finance indigenization provided less than 2.3 percent of the capital used to acquire shares or part ownership of affected enterprises. It resembled, and increasingly came to rival, the Nigerian Industrial Development Bank in both its function and its identity.

One of the reasons for its limited role in financing indigenization (and the argument employed in its defense by its personnel) is that the NBCI began operations only six months before the deadline for the implementation of the first decree. However, more than half of the affected enterprises complied with the provisions of the decree during the last six months of the implementation period. Further, many of the companies affected by the first decree were given six-month extensions for compliance, which would have given the NBCI a full year to assist in the financing. More likely, the reason for its limited role stemmed from its intention to create an ongoing role for itself after the completion of the indigenization exercise, an exercise that seemed nearly spent by the time the bank got underway.

Some of its operational policies also inhibited the NBCI from playing a more prominent role in financing the decree. The bank favored productive over service activities in its lending policy,[13] which is fine

[13] Hutchison 1974: 43.

TABLE 3.4

NBCI Takeover Projects versus New Projects, from Inception to
31 December 1975 (in current naira for December 1975)

	No.	Total cost	Approved investment	Disbursement
Takeover projects	9	4,434,500	2,758,000	484,247
New projects	51	293,554,600	56,021,000	5,222,595
Total	60	297,989,100	58,779,000	5,706,842

SOURCE: "Report of the Industrial Enterprises Panel" 1976: vol. I, Table VI.1.

for development purposes but irrelevant to indigenization, since most
of the affected activities were commercial or service ventures. Its preference for limited-liability companies as a form of business organization also prevented it from playing much of a role in Schedule I enterprises, since the limited-liability company was not a popular form of
business organization among Nigerians operating in that schedule.[14]

There was no assurance that Nigeria's commercial banks would assist with the financing of the decree, and they were apparently rather
lukewarm in responding to the needs of Nigerians for funds to purchase wholly or partly foreign-owned enterprises.[15] That was one of
the primary reasons the government created the NBCI. As we saw in
Chapter 2, it also acquired 40 percent of the equity of the big three
commercial banks and drafted the Central Bank's credit guidelines to
ensure that a higher percentage of bank credit would be allocated to
businesses in which Nigerians held a majority of the equity.

The commercial banks proved to be far more important than the
NBCI in the provision of credit to purchase shares. The "Report of
the Industrial Enterprises Panel," hereafter referred to as the Adeosun
Commission report, estimated that "during the period of the indigenization exercise, the Banks supported the purchase of shares to the
tune of 20 million naira (approximately $32 million)."[16] Most of this
money (about 13.8 million naira) was provided for the purchase of
the shares of public companies listed on the Lagos Stock Exchange.
Only 6.2 million naira was loaned for the purchase of privately owned
and traded companies. The Central Bank's credit guidelines undoubtedly played an important role in encouraging this lending, along with

[14] Teriba 1975: 172.
[15] "Report of the Industrial Enterprises Panel" 1976: 1.28.
[16] Ibid.

the NBCI's refusal to loan for the purchase of shares of public companies operating in Schedule II. However, the commercial banks had their own reasons for financing as much as 16.4 percent of the total shares traded. From their discussions with the foreign managers of the indigenized enterprises operating in Schedule II, they knew that many of these firms would soon be increasing their dividends substantially, largely as a hedge against future losses or to get as much capital as possible out of Nigeria while they still controlled the operations. Since the indigenous borrowers would also be beneficiaries of this dividend increase, there was little fear among the commercial bankers about their ability to repay the loans. Hence they were more than willing to extend credit to potential indigenous joint venture partners.[17]

The Nigerian Industrial Development Bank apparently played no role in the financing of the first indigenization decree, except for sponsoring a new issue offered for sale by one of its subsidiaries. It is essentially a development bank, more concerned with new projects than with acquisitions of existing ones. Thus, the Nigerian banking system in its entirety (including government banks like the NBCI and the NIDB and the private commercial banks) accounted for only 18.6 percent of the capital involved in the transfer of shares to indigenous businessmen. The Adeosun Commission estimated that as much as 14 million naira (or about $22.3 million) was provided from private savings and funds from pension and provident funds, bringing the total of funds accounted for to 36.7 million naira (about $58.6 million), or a little over 30 percent of the 122 million naira involved in the transfer. State investment companies like the Kano State Investment Corporation were involved in the acquisition of a few enterprises in the North, but not in a major way. External finance apparently played no major role in the financing of the decree.

This means that as much as two-thirds of the total value of shares or partial ownership that changed hands was transferred on a nominal basis. That is, no money changed hands at all. The foreign partner, forced to sell a portion or all of his business to a Nigerian subscriber, constructed a nominal credit system under which a share of the enterprise would be transferred to his new joint-venture partner to be paid for eventually out of future dividends or profits. As we shall see below, this has important implications for continued foreign managerial control of the enterprise, at least for the immediate future. As shown in

[17] This may be one of the reasons for the widespread oversubscription of public issues.

Table 3.5, probably no more than 30–35 percent of the ownership transferred involved any form of immediate payment.

How the NEPB Interpreted the Decree

The Nigerian Enterprises Promotion Board did not distinguish itself from Nigeria's other regulatory agencies by being particularly efficient. It sent its inspectors out to remind companies of the impending deadlines, arranged meetings between its federal administrators and its state committees, and generated publicity by publishing pamphlets and organizing seminars. However, it lacked the manpower to monitor most of the transfers to ensure that they had actually taken place, that the shares went to bona fide Nigerians, or that the prices paid for the shares were reasonable. Despite these limitations, the board's interpretation of a number of key components of the decree had important implications for its final implementation.

The NEPB had a preference for the formation of public companies, but it left indigenizing companies the option of selling their shares privately. All of the Schedule I firms sold their shares privately, and so did 95 percent of the Schedule II firms. Despite the NEPB's preference and occasional exhortations, the disincentives for going public far outweighed the incentives for listing on the stock exchange. Not only was a public listing more difficult and costly for the indigenizing firms, but it also brought the Capital Issues Commission (discussed below) in on the determination of the value of the acquired assets, the value of individual shares, and their distribution. Private placings were far more difficult to monitor, gave the foreign partner a free hand in the selection of joint-venture partners, and kept the NEPB (or any other government agency) out of the determination of the value of the assets acquired.

TABLE 3.5
Financing Indigenization: Where the Money Came From

	Amount	*% of total*
Banking system	22.7m	18.6
(Government banks)	(2.7m)	(2.2)
(Commercial banks)	(20.0m)	(16.4)
Private savings	14.0m	11.5
Nominal transfers	85.3m	69.9
Total	122.0m	100.0

SOURCE: Assembled by the author.

Although it was eventually criticized widely for failing to ensure a more equitable distribution of shares among the Nigerian public, the NEPB did not concern itself with the distribution of ownership. As V. I. Bello, the former secretary of the NEPB commented:

Although the Board recognizes the existence of this problem, it nevertheless considers that its task, first and foremost, is to ensure the smooth take over of businesses affected by the Decree by Nigerians no matter their states of origin and their numerical strength.[18]

Even if it had wanted to, the NEPB was not empowered to question the basis of allotment of shares in cases where the shares were privately placed. This was true even in cases where there was reasonable doubt about the genuineness of the transaction.[19]

In its operations, the NEPB also failed to coordinate its activities with those of other relevant government agencies in ways that might have furthered the indigenization exercise. For example, quotas for expatriate employment were administered by the Ministry of Internal Affairs and not coordinated with the NEPB. Thus a complying firm might have its expatriate quota increased, reinforcing a tendency to retain effective managerial control in foreign hands. Similarly, restrictive repatriation requirements administered by the Ministry of Finance created incentives for firms to inflate the value of their assets (to ensure that they got at least their "true" value remitted abroad). In many other cases, the limits on repatriation created a significant incentive for firms to delay their compliance with the decree.[20] Finally, the lack of coordination between the NEPB and the Ministry of Internal Affairs on citizenship requirements enabled a number of foreigners to indigenize their enterprises by acquiring Nigerian citizenship. The Federal Commissioner for Industries defended this practice, since the objective of the indigenization exercise was not to drive out foreign businessmen, but rather to get them to reinvest in more sophisticated sectors of the economy.[21] Needless to say, however, by acquiring Nigerian citizenship an affected alien would no longer necessarily have any incentive to diversify into other areas.

[18] Bello 1974: 16.

[19] "Report of the Industrial Enterprises Panel" 1976: par. 1.51(8).

[20] This paid off for a number of firms, when the capital repatriation restrictions were lifted in the 1975/76 budget year in an attempt to encourage noncomplying firms to comply with indigenization. This kind of coordination was long overdue but did not occur until after most firms had already complied.

[21] Owonuwa 1975: 60.

The NEPB tended to be fairly lenient in its granting of time exten-sions to complying firms. The first amendment to the decree an-nounced in June of 1973 allowed firms to apply for exemptions from the decree earlier than four months before the deadline for compli-ance (i.e. four months before 31 March 1974), once it became clear that the board simply could not handle the volume of applications for exemption in time. Subsequently, the deadline for full compliance for all firms was extended another six months, to the end of September 1974. Even after this time, a number of firms were granted extensions for compliance, pending the outcome of the applications of their owners for Nigerian citizenship or, in the case of poorly performing firms that had difficulty finding buyers, pending the discovery of someone interested in purchasing their shares.[22] The frequency of these extensions prompted the Adeosun Commission to conclude that the board's "gentle approach" in implementing the decree (its easy extension of deadlines) allowed clandestine irregularities which defeated the purposes of the decree.[23]

Finally, the NEPB rather liberally granted partial or complete ex-emptions to affected enterprises. At least 68 of the 952 enterprises af-fected by the decree (or slightly more than 7 percent) obtained a par-tial exemption of one kind or another from the NEPB. Thirteen firms were exempted altogether. Table 3.6 summarizes the NEPB's pattern of exemptions and indicates that the largest number were adjustments of capital or turnover estimates of affected Schedule II enterprises. As we shall see in our discussion of the valuation controversy which fol-lows, many Schedule II enterprises had previously minimized their capital or turnover to limit their tax liabilities, and hence fell below the minimum levels established for retaining 60 percent of the shares. Hence they needed to increase capital, turnover, or both to retain par-tial ownership of the indigenized firm, and many applied to the NEPB for an adjustment or exemption of turnover or capital requirements. Accordingly, there was scarcely any Schedule II firm that had to sell more than 40 percent of its equity to local subscribers.[24] Some of the exemptions listed in Table 3.6 involved Nigeria's most prominent firms and had significant long-term implications for Nigerian devel-opment. The largest trading companies like UAC, John Holt, CFAO, and UTC were granted exemptions to continue retailing, and they

[22] Collins 1974: 499.

[23] "Report of the Industrial Enterprises Panel" 1976: par. 1.54(j).

[24] In his early research on indigenization, Collins identified a small number of Sched-ule II firms being closed down but none selling more than 40 percent of their equity (1974: 498–499).

each remain prominent to this day. Decisions on these cases were not delegated solely to the NEPB, but were brought before the Federal Executive Council of the military government for final approval.[25]

THE VALUATION CONTROVERSY

Although the NEPB officially encouraged complying Schedule II companies to go public, only 24 of the 593 complying enterprises (or fewer than 5 percent) ultimately did so. Most of these were already public companies and had no choice but to sell their shares through the Lagos Stock Exchange. Some of the reasons so few complying firms went public were the cost of a public listing, the stringent conditions of entry to the Lagos Stock Exchange, and the unwelcome interference of a government agency in monitoring and regulating the transactions. The main reason so few companies went public, however, was that it cost them so much to lose control over the valuation of their assets.

The Capital Issues Commission had been empowered to determine the price at which the shares offered for sale by a public company would be sold to the Nigerian public, the total value of the shares to be sold, the amount and value of shares sold by public companies already listed on the stock exchange and interested in issuing supplementary offers, and virtually anything else relevant to the sale and dis-

TABLE 3.6
The Pattern of NEPB Exemptions for Affected Enterprises

	No.	%
Granted total exemption	13	16
Granted exemption of capital/turnover requirements	52	64
Allowed to continue retailing	4	5
Exempted if divisions cut back	4	5
Exempted as subsidiary of indigenous firm	2	2.5
Miscellaneous exemptions	6	7.5
Total	81	100

SOURCE: Compiled from "Report of the Industrial Enterprises Panel" 1976: vol. II, app. VII ("List of Enterprises/Individuals Granted Partial or Total Exemption from the Provisions of the NEPD [No. 4] 1972").

[25] Interview with prominent former state official.

tribution of new stock issues. The "valuation controversy" refers to the question of whether the commission was fair in its determination of value of the shares sold by public companies. The CIC claimed it was; the affected companies claimed it was not.

The Capital Issues Commission examined the tax returns of the affected companies and solicited submissions from them before attempting to work out prices it deemed to be fair to both the companies and the general public. It considered a firm's earnings yield (using its average profits over a number of years), its capital gearing and liquidity, its net assets as of its latest balance sheet, its pattern of previous dividend distribution and yield, and its future prospects (based on an evaluation of its management, organization, and operations). It also considered likely developments in the Nigerian economy and the prevailing prices of similar stocks traded on the Lagos Stock Exchange.[26] Formal representations were made by the affected companies, whose representatives were often accompanied by their accountants and merchant bankers.

Most of the affected companies disliked what they viewed as an unwarranted amount of government intervention in the capital market. However, they were even more upset by what they described as the commission's bias against them and charged that the CIC systematically underestimated the value of their shares being issued for sale. They criticized the CIC's evaluation procedures, and argued that its methods of examining balance sheets and tax records in the three-year period before 1972 was flawed because it included two years of the Nigerian civil war, a period when all business activity in the country was severely curtailed.[27] Hence, they argued that the CIC would necessarily underestimate the value of their shares being offered for sale.

Top officials of the Capital Issues Commission agree that they had a few biases, such as a slight preference for companies not planning to transfer the payments for their shares out of the country immediately. They strongly deny the existence of any systematic bias against the foreign companies in the valuation process, however.[28] Members of the commission thought that some of the affected companies were exhausting their accumulated profits in order to increase their short-term dividends immediately before indigenization, and hence their estimates of the value of shares were based on a calculation of the firm's maintainable profit rate.[29] They also took seriously warnings

[26] "Report of the Industrial Enterprises Panel" 1976: par. 2.30.
[27] Owonuwa 1975: 24.
[28] Interview with former state official and member of the CIC.
[29] Rake 1975: 58–59.

that there would be an insufficient amount of capital available for the purchase of shares, and that share offerings would be undersubscribed. There was also a bit of economic nationalism in the thinking of many commission members. Like many other Nigerians, they were of the opinion that foreign companies had made a lot of money from capital raised in Nigeria and had been taking money out of the country for a long time. They felt little or no remorse in rejecting applications from companies asking for a higher valuation.

By the end of 1975 the CIC had valued twenty-four issues and approved supplementary ones for another seven firms. When the prices it approved are compared to the nominal value of the shares being issued, it is difficult to see much sign of systematic bias on the part of the CIC. Table 3.7 shows that of the twenty-four new issues valued by the CIC, in fifteen cases the price approved was greater than the nominal value of the shares. In only five cases was it less than the price approved by the commission. Nevertheless, these valuations were disputed by the affected companies, since even if the approved price is greater than the nominal value, it is not necessarily equal to the market value of the shares, let alone the value accorded to them by the affected firms.

A more convincing case for the systematic undervaluation of shares can be made from an evaluation of the supplementary issues handled by the CIC between 1973 and 1975 (for which there is more information). In all cases, the price approved is less than the price existing on the Lagos Stock Exchange at the date of valuation. It is significantly less, by a factor of almost two in some cases. In all but one case, the price at the end of 1975 was higher (significantly higher in the case of Guinness for example) than the price approved by the CIC. Thus, the Capital Issues Commission valued new stock issues at rates

TABLE 3.7
CIC Applications Determined between 1973 and 1975

Each of 24 companies listed	Nominal value above price approved	Nominal value = price approved	Nominal value below price approved
Offer for sale	1	4	6
Direct sale	4	0	9
Total	5	4	15

SOURCE: Compiled from "Report of the Industrial Enterprises Panel" 1976: Table II.2.

where investors would recover their capital in three or four years.[30] It is no wonder that the commercial banks were so willing to lend capital to Nigerian investors.

Thus, there is something to the contention of foreign companies that their assets were consistently undervalued by the Capital Issues Commission. If the price those shares would earn on an open market had been used for the determination of their value, the affected firms would have received more for their forced sale. The story does not end here, however, with the hapless multinationals being robbed by unreasonable state actions. The valuation process did not take place in a historical vacuum, and there was a considerable degree of justice in the commission's bias.

The main reason so many of the affected Schedule II enterprises were so upset about the valuation was that they were caught in a trap created by their own previous deception. Nigeria's corporate income tax is based on annual turnover. Many of the affected firms had consistently effected a systematic bias of their own—understating their turnover and profitability—to minimize their annual tax liability. When the indigenization decree was announced and the CIC given the role to determine the value of shares sold by public companies, many found themselves in a dilemma. To document the true value of their assets would amount to an admission of their previous illegal undervaluation of turnover and profits for tax avoidance. Most of them would have been able to document their true value, because they kept two sets of books, one for their own accounting purposes and one for

TABLE 3.8
Supplementary Issues Handled by the CIC between 1973 and 1975

Name	Nominal value	Shares issued	Shares previously issued	Price on LSE when valued	Price approved	Price end 1975
Guinness	50 K	2m	1m	1.85	1.00	2.15
Nigerian Bottling Co.	50 K	1.4m	0.37m	1.32	0.90	1.00
CFAO	50 K	1.79m	2.4m	0.80	0.65	0.82
Daily Times	50 K	1.1m	0.23m	1.34	0.85	0.82
Unitex	50 K	0.15m	1.54m	1.07	0.60	0.60
UTC	50 K	0.84m	4.2m	0.55	0.35	0.71
Aluminium Mfg. Co.	50 K	0.03m	0.54m	1.30	0.92	0.99

SOURCE: "Report of the Industrial Enterprises Panel" 1976: Table II.3.

[30] Ibid., p. 58.

the tax authorities. However, none would admit publicly to this practice. The Capital Issues Commission made consistent use of a set of consistently biased documents. The affected companies complained, but had no choice but to "suffer in silence, watching resources being cheaply transferred to lucky new Nigerian shareholders."[31] Thus, although in market terms there is little doubt that the CIC undervalued shares, they were at the same time settling an old score. As we shall see later in the chapter, the net effect was to divert lost tax revenues to local capital.

Having considered where Nigerians obtained the funds for purchasing shares, how the NEPB interpreted the decree, and the role of the CIC in the valuation controversy, we can turn our attention to the consequences of the first indigenization decree. Following the framework developed in Chapter 1, the remainder of this chapter will be devoted to a discussion of the consequences of the decree at the level of the individual firm, at the sectoral level, and at the national level.

CONSEQUENCES FOR THE INDIVIDUAL FIRM

Confronted with indigenization, most foreign companies responded with "countervailing measures" designed to ensure that they retained effective managerial control over the enterprise after compliance with the decree. The acquisition of a majority of the assets of a firm does not automatically translate into the acquisition of effective managerial control of that enterprise, a point emphasized by structuralist writers.[32] There are a great many examples of the divorce between ownership and control in Nigeria. To be sure, maintaining effective managerial control posed a far greater problem for Schedule I firms, required to sell all of their equity to local subscribers, than it did for Schedule II ones, most of which were required to sell only 40 percent of their shares. The modal response of both types of enterprise, as well

[31] O. Aboyade 1977: 382. Both sides in this controversy privately acknowledge the dual accounting practices of the affected firms and suggest they were aware of it when the valuation of assets was being negotiated. Neither the multinational managers nor the members of the Capital Issues Commission admit their knowledge publicly, but rather continue to make eloquent and impassioned arguments on behalf of the legitimacy of their case. They maintain this fiction because the CIC members would not look the ardent nationalists they currently do if it were widely known that they let the multinationals off the hook on tax evasion. Meanwhile, the multinationals like the opportunity to appear the victim and at every available opportunity they remind state officials of how much they suffered at the hands of the CIC. It gives them a little ammunition against other government restrictive policies.

[32] This was an argument most forcefully made by Penrose 1976.

as both types of foreign capital (Levantine and multinational), was to engage in some form of fronting. That is, find a silent partner (or partners), someone who knew and cared little about the business, and create the appearance of a change by having the Nigerian partner visible, taking orders in the front room while the foreign partner (or former owner) manages the firm from the back room. Large multinational capital was not as crude as this, but it acted with the same purpose and effectiveness. Its joint-venture partners were rarely sought for their knowledge and interest in sharing managerial responsibility.

Fronting took many different forms and was just one of the responses of foreign capital to indigenization. To understand the range and complexity of the strategic responses of foreign companies, it is necessary to differentiate both between Schedule I and Schedule II firms and to a lesser extent between Levantine and multinational capital. Schedule I and Schedule II firms were responding to different capital requirements (100 percent and 40 percent, respectively), and, because of their ability to tap the resources of their entire subsidiary network, multinational firms had a broader array of countervailing measures available to them.

Schedule I affected an immense variety of companies, ranging from the sales representatives offices of giant European-based multinationals to one-man Lebanese retailers of textile goods. Most of the 357 affected enterprises were relatively small-scale commercial and transportation firms, and the majority were previously owned by Lebanese and Indian businessmen. Many were family-owned and -managed firms, with relatively little local investment (or reinvestment) in Nigeria.

When confronted with NEPD 1972, one of the first things most Schedule I companies did was to attempt to have their business activities reclassified in some way. Some appealed directly to the NEPB in the hope of having their enterprise reclassified and subsequently either reassigned to Schedule II or exempted from the provisions of the decree altogether. Others tried to rename their existing activities in ways that made them sound as though they were doing something that would lead them to be reclassified. Still others incorporated new companies in Nigeria, with a different name and a different list of activities, just to avoid having to sell all of their equity to local subscribers. If appeals to the NEPB, efforts to rename the activities, or the incorporation of a new company all failed, a well placed bribe might obtain the reclassification sought by the affected firms. The exact number of firms that obtained some kind of reclassification of their activities is not known, but it was probably considerable. The Adeosun report described at least eighty-one exemptions granted by the NEPB, but that number probably underestimates the total number of reclassifications, since the NEPB did not keep records on the matter and would have grouped reclassified firms with other complying enterprises in any event.

Reclassification of activities was the first response of most Schedule I enterprises, but was hardly the only avenue open to them to minimize the effects of the first decree and maintain effective control. Some of the expatriate businessmen responded by applying for Nigerian citizenship. If their applications were granted, they could transfer the ownership to naturalized Nigerians—themselves. If not, they were allowed to continue in operation until their citizenship applications were decided upon, providing them valuable time to develop other strategic responses to indigenization. This was not a response of large corporations, and was principally concentrated among Lebanese family businesses. Typically, only one family member, usually a junior brother, would apply for Nigerian citizenship. If it was granted, he would legally acquire and indigenize the business. His function inside the company did not necessarily change, but the firm would satisfy the requirements of the NEPB. If Nigerian citizenship were unattainable, a few enterprising businessmen found it easier to obtain citizenship in neighboring Niger or Benin. Since they had become citizens of fellow OAU member states that had reciprocal investment agreements with Nigeria, they were treated as indigenous Nigerians by the NEPB.

From her research on indigenization in Kano, Ankie Hoogvelt concluded that fourteen of the forty-nine companies surveyed employed this strategy.[33] When the Lebanese firms are examined separately, it appears that nearly half of them at least tried to obtain Nigerian citizenship.[34] Of the European firms in her sample, only a small Italian construction firm attempted a similar plan, suggesting that both size and nationality had something to do with the use of this strategy.

Although naturalization was a response largely restricted to Lebanese family enterprises, nearly everyone engaged in some form of fronting. Small Levantine capital had everything to lose with a Schedule I classification, and it was most likely to engage in egregious fronting activity. In its most extreme form, the entire transaction might be

[33] Hoogvelt 1979: 61.

[34] Not all were successful, however. Professor Ankie Hoogvelt of the University of Sheffield provided me copies of her disaggregated data on enterprises she interviewed in Kano in 1977 and 1978. It was from these data that I was able to differentiate among Lebanese and multinational responses to indigenization on this issue.

bogus. No shares would be traded, a fictitious Nigerian would be designated recipient, and no share certificates would be issued. In some cases, a salary would be paid to a Nigerian for the use of his (or in at least one case, his wife's) name. The company engaging in this kind of fronting was relying on the inefficiency (or the corruptibility) of the NEPB, and thirty-one examples of this kind of fronting were identified by the Adeosun Commission.[35]

More common were the cases in which a single individual with a questionable involvement in the enterprise was designated the sole purchaser. In one example, 36,750 shares of 2 naira each were allegedly sold to an individual with a vague address in Ajegunle, a notoriously poor Lagos neighborhood. In another case, the wife of a junior police officer was designated the sole purchaser of a huge bloc of shares. Not only are these transactions unlikely, but even if they did occur, it is clear that the recipients would be in no position to participate in the operations in any real way. The Adeosun report listed thirty-four cases of this type of fronting activity.

The classic case of fronting involved the nominal transfer of shares to an individual who performed the actions, but not the functions of genuine ownership. A trusted employee, a former distributor, or someone with a long history of commercial or financial ties would be entrusted to sign the NEPB forms and sit in the front office when necessary. All of the real business would be conducted out of a back office from which the former expatriate owner would continue to operate. Since personnel indigenization was not a part of NEPD 1972 and since there was very little coordination of activities by the NEPB and the Expatriate Quota Allocation Board, it was relatively easy for this type of fronting to take place. It was particularly common among Lebanese firms engaged in the textile trade in Lagos.[36]

If reclassification, naturalization, and/or fronting all failed, the Schedule I company could stall the transfer process by inflating its price to deter buyers for as long as possible.[37] This might give the company enough time to develop an effective front, negotiate for NEPB compliance, or benefit from a hoped-for change in the decree. It also might allow it time to export the bulk of its capital reserves before selling to an indigenous buyer. Because they had few tangible assets to sell, small Lebanese service-sector companies tended to hang on until the bitter end, trying to earn profits for as long as possible.[38]

[35] "Report of the Industrial Enterprises Panel" 1976: Table I.4.
[36] Collins, 1977: 140.
[37] Collins, 1974: 499.
[38] Hutchison 1974: 41.

Once each of these possibilities had been exhausted, Schedule I enterprises could overvalue their assets and sell their inflated businesses privately to willing Nigerians (an option not available to publicly listed Schedule II firms). Since most of the business transfers were private transactions with no valuation by the CIC or the NEPB, it was relatively easy to do this. Some firms (mostly the larger European enterprises) sold only their commercial activities and had themselves declared manufacturers' representatives. For example, G. B. Ollivant, a UAC subsidiary, sold its Nigeradio and Esquire retail shops to Nigerians, but retained an agency to supply goods to them, enabling it to maintain its control over the price, the source, and the quality of the goods sold in the indigenized shops.[39] A variant of this option was to transfer all of the firm's usable assets into a business not affected by the decree and then sell its significantly overvalued shares to local subscribers.

Some entrepreneurs used the capital obtained from the sale of their Schedule I enterprises to finance their move into other areas of the economy. Moving foreign capital into other areas was, after all, one of the explicit objectives of the first decree. However, some of these moves were more apparent than real. They certainly did not necessarily entail a move into more productive activities. The process might simply mean the transfer of foreign capital from the road transportation business to the leasing of motorized vehicles for road transport.[40]

The final option available to an affected firm was to sell its business and leave Nigeria altogether. However, it seems that few, if any, companies actually did this. Nearly a year after the promulgation of the decree, S. K. Okoro, the director of the Investment Center of the Ministry of Industries, was quoted as saying, "To my knowledge, not a single businessman is leaving Nigeria because of the decree."[41] Given the range of potential responses open to Schedule I enterprises alone, his comment is not particularly surprising.

It is impossible to know precisely how common each of the strategic responses summarized in Figure 3.1 actually was. The range and variety of responses for firms required to sell 100 percent of their equity to local subscribers are impressive. It is known that the NEPB granted at least eighty-one exemptions, that at least fourteen firms in Kano alone had employees who received citizenship, that the Adeosun report identified eighty-eight clearcut cases of fronting, and that

[39] "Report of the Industrial Enterprises Panel" 1976: par. 1.55.
[40] "Foreigners Adapt to Nigerian Edict," *New York Times*, 4 February 1973, p. F21.
[41] Ibid.

nearly 70 percent of the transfers of shares were nominal (allowing for easy overvaluation of these nonpublicly listed firms). There is no record of any mass flight of foreign businessmen from the country. What is even more striking about the variety of strategic responses is that they were the countervailing measures of one of the weakest elements of foreign capital in Nigeria—the Levantine community. Contrary to the expectations of liberal internationalists and classical Marxists, foreigners appear to have retained effective control of a surprisingly large number of Schedule I enterprises in the immediate aftermath of the first decree. The range and variety of countervailing measures open to multinational capital concentrated in Schedule II enterprises were even greater.

Nearly 56 percent of the 604 Schedule II enterprises affected by the decree were European-based multinationals, and the majority of those were British. The Lebanese presence in Schedule II was far less prominent than it was in Schedule I, accounting for only 15.6 percent of the total. Seventy-four Indian firms were affected, accounting for 12.3 percent of the total. American and Japanese companies were insignificant by comparison, accounting for only 3.3 percent of the total affected. Table 3.9 summarizes the distribution of affected firms by nationality.

There is a widespread belief in Nigeria that most of the circumvention of the first indigenization decree was accomplished by Lebanese and Indian firms, rather than by the European-based multinational corporations.[42] However, despite some important differences, the European firms were hardly less willing to either circumvent the decree or to consider defensive countervailing measures to minimize its effects on their operations. Much of the following discussion of the countervailing measures of Schedule II enterprises is derived from research interviews conducted in Nigeria with the expatriate managers of fifty-eight of the largest multinationals affected by Nigeria's two indigenization decrees. (For further details on the sampling and research methodology employed in the interviews, see the discussion in Appendix A.) Since many companies were exempted from the first decree (or not fully operational before 1974), the discussion in this section is relevant to only twenty-one.

Like their counterparts in Schedule I, many Schedule II enterprises began by attempting to have their activities reclassified. Even though they had to sell only 40 percent of their shares and therefore had much

[42] Interviews with two prominent indigenous businessmen and an official of an indigenous businessmen's group.

FIGURE 3.1
Strategic Responses of Schedule I Enterprises

Step One   Attempt reclassification
                  Appeal to NEPB
                  Rename existing activities
                  Incorporate new company
                  Bribe

                  If successful, go to Schedule II
                  If not, try Steps Two through Five

Step Two   Take out Nigerian citizenship

                  If successful, sell shares to self
                  If not, try Steps Three through Five

Step Three   Front
                  No purchase; no share certificate; bogus purchase
                  Single purchaser with questionable involvement
                  Sell to reliable employee or distributor

                  If successful, carry on business as usual
                  If not, try Step Four or Five

Step Four   Stall
                  Overvalue assets to deter buyers

                  If successful, try Steps One through Three again, or
                      repatriate capital
                  If not, go to Step Five

Step Five   Overvalue assets and sell privately
                  Sell commercial activities only
                  Sell existing business and diversify
                  Sell enterprise and leave Nigeria

TABLE 3.9
The Nationality of Schedule II Firms

	No. complying	No. defaulting	No. affected	% of total
UK	183	14	197	32.6
EEC	130	11	141	23.3
Lebanese	79	15	94	15.6
Indian	65	9	74	12.3
American	15	2	17	2.8
Japanese	3	0	3	0.5
Other	67	11	78	12.9
Total	542	62	604	100.0

SOURCE: Compiled from "Report of the Industrial Enterprises Panel" 1976: Vol. I, Table I.2; vol. II, app. VI.

less at stake, appeals were made to the NEPB to be classified into one of the many areas of the economy unaffected by the first decree. Because of their links to their European-based parent companies, Schedule II firms were also in a better position to argue that their commercial activities had an important technical component (usually related to servicing).

When reclassification failed, some of the larger firms regrouped and incorporated their Schedule I activities under the umbrella of their Schedule II companies. The United Africa Company, John Holt, and Leventis each received a special dispensation from the NEPB (approved at the level of the Federal Executive Council of the military government).[43] The dispensation enabled them to pull back several of their component companies from Schedule I to Schedule II and retain an important role in commerce in the country. Manufacturers with an established retail network for the distribution and sale of their products manufactured in Nigeria (such as Bata Shoes) were allowed to retain their retail outlets by regrouping them under the umbrella of their Schedule II manufacturing classification.

The largest Schedule II firms were required to sell only 40 percent of their equity to Nigerians, as long as they met certain minimal levels of equity or turnover. Firms with equity or turnover less than the prescribed amounts were required to sell all of their equity to Nigerians. Since so many firms had been undercapitalized for so long (to minimize their tax liability), a number of companies assigned to Schedule

[43] Interview with prominent former state official.

II applied to the NEPB to have their share capital raised above the minimum level of 200,000 Nigerian pounds. By so doing, they would avoid having to sell more than 40 percent of their equity and could thereby retain majority equity. Of the eighty-one exemptions granted by the NEPB, fifty-two (or 64 percent) were exemptions involving either a waiver of the capital requirements or an increase of share capital.[44] European, North American, and Indian capital tended to be large enough to satisfy the minimal capital and turnover requirements before the decree. So the bulk of the applications, nearly all of which were granted, came from Lebanese firms.[45]

Another countervailing measure largely restricted to Lebanese capital was to apply for Nigerian citizenship. It was much less frequent in Schedule II than it was in Schedule I, and was largely restricted to a few family firms. If successful, the application had the same effect. Compliance with the decree could be certified by selling the shares to the single family member who volunteered to take Nigerian citizenship.

Once reclassification or naturalization failed, and once the affected enterprise was able to regroup or increase its share capital to above the minimal requirements, 40 percent of the equity would be sold. Sometimes the assets were overvalued, since they were traded privately, far from the scrutiny of the Capital Issues Commission.[46] This offered promising returns (when real capital actually changed hands); more important, it facilitated the form of fronting widespread among Schedule II firms. The usual pattern was for the shares to be distributed among a small number of joint-venture partners carefully chosen by the expatriate management of the indigenizing firm. Most of the local partners had prior commercial links with the firm, usually as its principal distributors, and were chosen on the basis of their docility rather than their business acumen. Expatriate managers characteristically described their search for "low-profile people," for "a yes-man," or for "very passive people with stature, money, and no interest in significant involvement in the firm."[47]

[44] "Report of the Industrial Enterprises Panel" 1976: vol. II, app. VII.

[45] Owonuwa 1975: 70.

[46] There were exceptions to this pattern, however. One expatriate managing director described his company's practice of keeping its capital exposure and the size of the funds contributed by its indigenous joint-venture partners very low, because "with less capital committed, they are less interested in the business." This multinational's valuation strategy was different, but not its basic objective—to keep indigenous partners uninvolved in the operation.

[47] One American executive said, "We distribute our shares among our friends, people we know well, people with no political drive and no ambition towards management of

There was a great deal of competition among Nigerian entrepreneurs scrambling to be chosen as recipients of the shares of the indigenizing firms. The expatriate management of the firms told them to "just sit and let us make money for you," and the new Nigerian joint-venture partner tended to stay out of day-to-day operations.[48] This is in part due to the fact that the share certificates were viewed by many Nigerians as a symbol of wealth, something to be posted on the office wall of a "big man," rather than as an opportunity to participate in the management of a growing and profitable enterprise.[49] Another reason is that local partners were deliberately chosen by the expatriate management because they were too busy to take an active role, because of their professed indifference to the firm's operations, or because they were in competition with one another and therefore unlikely to cooperate on anything that might challenge the parent company—especially on anything that might jeopardize their access to a constant source of supply of the goods they sold for the bulk of their livelihood.[50]

The European-based multinationals tended to select two or three trusted joint-venture partners, in part to minimize the size of a single individual's shareholding and in part to protect themselves from regional rivalries and an overdependence on a single individual's political and/or economic fortune. In some cases, they distributed their shares even more widely, to as many as twenty-five or thirty-five individuals. Lebanese firms, on the other hand, were more likely to tie themselves to a single individual, often one in a powerful political position in the country. Their objective was the same, however. Joint-venture partners were carefully chosen on the basis of their lack of interest in effective participation in the firm. Although they were more sophisticated than their Schedule I counterparts, Schedule II firms had the same objectives in and net effects from this form of fronting.

For reasons that have already been discussed, very few Schedule II enterprises opted to go public and sell their shares widely to the Nigerian public. The affected firms were required to sell only 40 percent of their equity and therefore retained an uncontested majority equity. Accordingly, they were more concerned with their low valuation.

---

the firm." A few companies paid their directors' fees into accounts located abroad as an incentive to cooperative joint-venture partners.

[48] Banjo 1976: 31. This short article is an excellent summary of the consequences of the first decree from the perspective of an indigenous businessman interested in effective participation in the firm.

[49] Interviews with state official and prominent indigenous businessman.

[50] Hoogvelt 1979: 63.

When they did sell additional shares, however, one expatriate manager suggested that it was "wise to spread the shares as widely as possible."[51] As we shall see in Chapter 5, this became a much more important strategy after the second decree, when firms were required to relinquish a majority of their equity and when so many more were forced into going public.

One countervailing measure that distinguished the responses of multinational capital from Levantine capital was the use of managerial and technical agreements to maintain control over operations. In a few cases, the commercial banks required mangerial contracts with the parent company before they would release funds to local businessmen interested in obtaining finance.[52] The number of technical agreements negotiated between Nigeria and the advanced industrial countries also increased markedly after indigenization, as evidenced by the increase of external payments made for services relative to profits after 1972.[53] As a general rule, the negotiation of managerial and technical agreements between parent and subsidiaries was more common among manufacturing than among commercial multinationals.

As a final resort, a number of firms reorganized their operations in ways that would ensure that indigenization had a minimal effect on their effective control. Some companies decentralized, while others tightened home-office controls. One British firm in the sample interviewed reportedly made its parent company cosignatory on every major capital expenditure after the indigenization of the firm. More expatriates were imported by another company (by legal and illegal means), and many multinationals began to divide their operations into onshore and offshore segments for the first time. Finally, a number of forward-looking manufacturing firms consciously began to train their managers from within the firm, to ensure that the emerging Nigerian executives would eventually be "part of us." One expatriate manager boasted that his company's training programs had "multinationalized" its Nigerian managers.[54]

As summarized in Figure 3.2, there were more countervailing measures open to Schedule II companies than to Schedule I firms. Because so many of them were multinational, they could either invoke the power of the parent company or threaten to invoke the wrath of

[51] Interview with British multinational executive.
[52] Interview with North American embassy official.
[53] Forrest 1982: Table 16.5, p. 327.
[54] Interview with British multinational executive. He actually made a verb out of his company's name to describe the molding of its Nigerian managers through its training programs.

the home-country government. Only the Japanese firms actually used their Lagos embassy on a regular basis to influence the Nigerian government's treatment of them. Every multinational could at least threaten to do this, something that Levantine capital could not credibly attempt. More important, however, multinational enterprises could draw on the resources of their entire subsidiary network to negotiate management and technical agreements, to shift funds and human resources across national boundaries to bolster their positions, to evaluate their responses to other countries' indigenization efforts, to train their indigenous managers to become company people, and to divide their operations readily into onshore and offshore segments.

There were a few important differences among the responses of Schedule II multinationals that corresponded to their sector of operation. As mentioned in the preceding discussion and summarized more concretely in Table 3.10, although nearly all Schedule II firms tried fronting, it was more common among manufacturers. Since so many of the commercial ventures were already public, they spread their shares widely rather than worry about finding the right partners. Manufacturers were also more likely to use management and technical contracts and more likely to adjust their articles of association than were commercial or service-sector companies. They were the only examples in the sample of companies receiving exemptions from the NEPB or deliberately training their managers to identify with the firm and "be one of us." Commercial establishments, on the other hand, were more likely to attempt reclassification, reorganize, regroup, invoke the support of their embassy, or bribe.

What do all of the countervailing measures of Schedule I and Schedule II enterprises mean for effective managerial control of the indigenized firms? Has indigenization had any effect on their operations? To answer these questions, we must again consider the affected enterprises according to the schedule of the decree to which they were assigned. Control is much less of a question when you are only required to sell 40 percent of your equity.

The Nigerian indigenous purchasers of Schedule I enterprises probably acquired effective managerial control over the operations of fewer than half of the 357 firms assigned to the schedule.[55] Exemp-

---

[55] "Effective control requires more than the holding of a simple majority of the equity share capital. It requires the ability to use equity or other means to determine with regularity the outcomes of decisions on the most important questions confronting the management of the firm (i.e. questions concerning production output, technology choice, re-investment, local-content use, export promotion, profits and dividends, local research and development, etc.). Thus, control should be defined in terms of manage-

FIGURE 3.2
Strategic Responses of Schedule II Enterprises

Step One   Attempt reclassification
            Label commercial activities "technical"
            Appeal to NEPB

            If successful, operate as before
            If not, try Steps Two through Eight

Step Two   Regroup
            Incorporate Schedule I activities under Schedule II
                company umbrella

            If successful, sell 40% equity to comply
            If not, see Fig. 3.1

Step Three Increase share capital
            Appeal to NEPB for permission to raise capital or
                turnover figures to avoid selling 100%

            If successful, sell 40% equity to comply
            If not, see Fig. 3.1

Step Four   Apply for Nigerian citizenship

            If successful, sell shares to self
            If not, try Steps Five through Eight

Step Five   Front
            Sell 40% privately to carefully chosen joint-venture
                partners

            If successful, carry on as before indigenization
            If not, try Steps Six through Eight

Step Six   Negotiate management or technical agreement
            Mandate foreign partner's control

            If successful, repatriate capital via fees rather than prof-
            its and carry on as before
            If not, try Steps Seven or Eight

FIGURE 3.2 (*cont.*)

Step Seven   Reorganize the company
  Decentralize, import more expatriates, train local managers to identify with company, or divide into onshore/offshore segments

  If successful, carry on with foreign control
  If not, try Step Eight

Step Eight   Go public and spread shares widely

tions, naturalization, and overt examples of fronting were sufficient for the Adeosun Commission to note that in quite a number of cases, with the approval of the Ministry of Internal Affairs, the original owners and chief executives were allowed to stay on after the end of March 1974.[56] The official explanation for this phenomenon was that to do otherwise would have precipitated the collapse of the indigenized firms, to the detriment to the indigenous buyers of their equity and to the national economy as a whole. The net effect, however, was to ensure that effective managerial control of a majority of the enterprises assigned to Schedule I remained in foreign hands.

There were, however, a number of important cases in which effective managerial control did pass to Nigerians. Nearly 40 percent of the affected enterprises (140 of the 357) defaulted and were therefore subject to closure and/or acquisition by the NEPB or designated indigenous businessmen. Most of these were in commerce (80 percent of the 140), more than two-thirds of which were engaged in the retail and wholesale trade in textiles (75 of the 112 commercial defaulters); most were located in Lagos and Kano (65 percent); and most were previously owned by Lebanese or Indian businessmen (66.4 percent). Control also changed hands when some of the large indigenous holding companies acquired the Schedule I enterprises. Conglomerates like Ibru & Sons preferred to acquire 100 percent of the equity, since they wanted effective control over the firms they planned to incorporate into their subsidiary networks. Classic examples of indigenization, where an indigenous businessman raised his own hard-earned capital to buy out and takeover a small or medium-scale foreign operation, existed, but were extremely rare. Very few indigenous busi-

rial responsibility for financial, technical, and commercial aspects of operations, rather than in terms of responsibility for non-critical functions such as labor relations, product distribution, and advertising" (Biersteker forthcoming).
[56] "Report of the Industrial Enterprises Panel" 1976: par. 5.47.

TABLE 3.10

Responses of Schedule II Multinationals Interviewed

	Commercial	Manufacturing	Service
Fronting	3	7	2
Spread shares	5	6	0
Management contract	1	2	0
Reorganize	2	1	0
Training programs	0	3	0
Bribe	2	1	0
Reclassify	2	0	0
Exemption	0	2	0
Invoke embassy	1	0	0
Total	16	22	2

SOURCE: Interviews conducted by the author. Note that the sample reflects the distribution of foreign business activity in Nigeria in 1972 (i.e. relatively few service-sector activities—only 2 in this sample) and the types of economic activity affected by the first decree (predominantly commerce [9 enterprises] and manufacturing [10]). There are more responses indicated than companies interviewed, since most firms employed more than one strategic response to the first decree.

nessmen raised their own capital (which would at least have given them a greater stake in the control of the venture),[57] and in view of all of the agitation from indigenous businessmen for an indigenization program, a surprisingly small number were interested in assuming all the risks associated with a Schedule I business in Nigeria.

In the majority of cases where effective managerial control of Schedule I enterprises remained unchanged, there is no reason to expect any significant changes in operation. In the smaller number of cases where some significant changes in control did take place (in the case of defaulting firms, acquisitions by indigenous conglomerates, and purchases made from capital raised by indigenous businessmen), a few parallel changes in operations emerged. Many of the Schedule I enterprises acquired were previously controlled by a single individual who had a strong degree of personal control over operations. This made them difficult to takeover, and the new indigenous managers found it nearly impossible to guarantee continuity in management, operations, and performance. As a result, many experienced productivity declines and revenue losses during the first years after indigenization.

Many of the new owners found it difficult to gain access to finance.

[57] Banjo 1976: 32.

The foreign-dominated commercial banks were wary of the adjustment costs and performance possibilities of the newly indigenized firms and tended to switch on their "indigenous service mode" when approached by the new managers.[58] Access to reliable suppliers was an equally important problem for the indigenized commercial enterprises, many of whom found that expatriate suppliers could block their supply and tended to prefer larger (and less risky) accounts with the huge commercial firms that were allowed to regroup after indigenization.

Many of the new indigenous owner-managers inherited companies with no formal organization, no clear delegation of authority, or no clear chain of command. This absorbed much of their energy immediately after they assumed control and also made it difficult for them to establish credibility as effective managers with their inherited employees. Many also found themselves forced to replace supervisors promoted by the previous owner "for their docility and dependence rather than for their initiative and competence."[59] This might enhance their popularity with many of their new employees but it temporarily reduced the productivity of the firm.

Labor was adversely affected by the indigenization of Schedule I enterprises in several different ways. It was not unusual for workers to find their salaries, allowances, and working conditions reduced after indigenous Nigerians assumed control of the firm. More seriously, many even lost their jobs when the new proprietors replaced their existing workforces with relatives[60] or other individuals from their home villages.

Although they affected only a small number of enterprises, there were some important short-term changes in operation after indigenization. The newly indigenized firms tended to have less access to finance, frequent supply interruptions, productivity declines, and reduced labor conditions and renumeration. However, they also presented important opportunities for learning about management, organization, and technology that would otherwise not have existed. It is this counterfactual argument to which we will turn again in subsequent chapters when we assess the long-term significance of indigenization in Nigeria.

Changes in control and operations in Schedule I firms were not as far reaching as might have been expected, and they were even less ap-

[58] Ibid.
[59] Ibid., p. 31.
[60] Sanwo 1975: 36.

parent in Schedule II firms. Expatriates were allowed to retain clear majority control of the ventures with 60 percent of the equity, and hence indigenization had a less immediate effect on control and operations.

There is no example of a change of effective managerial control of any Schedule II enterprise following the first indigenization decree. The Adeosun Commission said that in Schedule II the basic management structure remained the same with only a few additions of Nigerian shareholders on the board of directors. It noted that it was doubtful whether this led to an increase in the number of Nigerians in the highest policy-making bodies of such enterprises.[61] Many companies established two separate boards of directors in the aftermath of indigenization, one a supervisory board and another a management board. The supervisory board contained a few of the firm's executive directors and all of its nonexecutive directors (several of whom were now Nigerian). The management board made virtually all of the decisions that would have any effect on operations and was composed solely of executive directors, nearly all of whom remained expatriate.

All of the twenty-four publicly listed Schedule II enterprises spread their shares widely. Over 300,000 Nigerians applied to the issuing houses for the opportunity to purchase shares, 85,000 of whom were interested in purchasing shares of the United Africa Company. Although the public sale of shares ensured a broader-based Nigerian participation in indigenization than a private sale, it also ensured an atomization of local shareholding. This meant that although a few more Nigerians would be attending shareholder meetings (when they were held),[62] they would be unlikely to exert much influence on the company's management or operations.

As discussed earlier, private placings of shares and part ownership of Schedule II enterprises were far more prevalent than public sales of shares. Over 95 percent of the complying firms engaged in direct negotiations with potential buyers or through established issuing houses to place their shares with a small number of carefully chosen Nigerians. The Adeosun Commission examined the private placement procedures of 384 companies and found an extremely high concentration of share acquisition (discussed in more detail below in the section on the consequences at the national level). In more than 77 percent of the cases examined (296 firms), the 40 percent was distrib-

    [61] "Report of the Industrial Enterprises Panel" 1976: par. 5.46.
    [62] Collins 1977: 139 described Nigerians' complaints about the absence of shareholder meetings and information disclosure by indigenized Schedule II firms in Kano.

uted to not more than five individuals or associations. In nearly 87 percent of the cases (334), fewer than ten individuals acquired all of the shares.[63] Since the Capital Issues Commission was not involved in the transactions, the opportunites for both overvaluation and fronting were considerable.

Most companies chose to expand their capital base rather than divide the existing capital amongst themselves and their new Nigerian partners. Thus, they had an incentive to inflate the value of their assets when they sold to Nigerians, especially when their new joint-venture partners actually contributed some capital to the venture. Fronting was easier with private placings, because the small number of share recipients could be carefully selected to ensure their affinity with their foreign partners. Occasionally, only a single trusted employee would be sold the 40 percent.[64] More commonly, however, the same small number of Nigerian individuals with access to capital would end up purchasing the bulk of the privately placed shares, with the result that they were either too busy or too preoccupied with other (usually commercial) matters to take an active part in management.

In a few cases, the foreign management actually had its control of important matters written into the articles of association of the indigenized company. The expatriates would provide the technology if the Nigerians would take care of all the bureaucratic requirements (necessary contracts, land, legal advice, expatriate permits, foreign-exchange clearance, etc.).[65] Only in the relatively few cases where Nigerians actually put up their own capital for the acquisition of shares did the Nigerian joint-venture partners insist on real participation. They were unable to acquire control, but could make things difficult for the expatriate manager.[66] As we shall see in Chapter 5, this was one of the lessons about indigenization learned (and not forgotten) by expatriate managers after the first indigenization decree.

Since there were no significant changes in control of Schedule II enterprises, it is not surprising that there were few, if any, significant changes in their operations immediately after indigenization. There were, however, a few slight changes that appeared cosmetic at the outset, but grew to have a larger significance over time.

First, although indigenization of personnel was not covered by the first decree, its promulgation convinced a number of expatriate man-

[63] "Report of the Industrial Enterprises Panel" 1976: par. 1.49.
[64] Banjo 1976: 29.
[65] Hoogvelt 1979: 65–66. The same point was made in an interview with a prominent indigenous businessman.
[66] Interviews; three multinational executives reported this experience.

agers that it was time to begin hiring and promoting Nigerians to middle-management (and in a few cases, senior) positions. Expatriates were becoming too expensive to maintain in Nigeria anyway. With a number of Nigerians now positioned on the boards of directors, it was wise to appoint a few more Nigerians to the ranks of management (especially if they were related to the new members of the board). Multinational firms expanded their managerial (and other) training programs after indigenization, although the smaller Lebanese and Indian firms were either less willing or less able to do so.[67] Although these new employees were excluded from critical positions in the firm and largely relegated to personnel, advertising, and marketing positions, they formed an important pressure group within the firm for further personnel indigenization. They were also among the strongest backers of the expansion of the indigenization program brought on by the second decree.

Second, since so many Schedule II enterprises expanded, rather than divided, their equity to comply with the decree, the new capital injection was often used for expansion or improvement of both plant and output. This was usually accomplished by the import of newer, capital-intensive technology which contributed less to unskilled employment than the machinery it replaced or was added to.[68] The reasons for this are many—the newer technology increases productivity, is often readily available from the parent company (especially when the parent has recently upgraded its own facilities with even newer technology), and may be insisted upon by the new Nigerian joint-venture partners (who like the appearance of being associated with a company employing the latest and best technology available).[69] In the long run, however, the introduction of a more capital-intensive technology not only contributed relatively little to Nigerian employment (accepting the counterfactual argument that a more labor-intensive technology is both available and likely to be employed by some enterprises). It also required the introduction of more expatriate technicians and enhanced the parent company's control of the operation through its technological superiority. As we shall see in Chapter 5, this became significant after the second decree, when so many of the multinationals lost majority equity.

Third, galvanized by the prospect of further indigenization, especially in the wake of its spread throughout the developing world in the

[67] Owonuwa 1975: 72–81. See esp. Table 7.

[68] Ezeife 1981: 181. Ezeife suggests that capital was more important than labor for increases in productivity after the decree.

[69] Interviews; four multinational executives reported this experience.

early and mid 1970s, a number of multinationals engaged in commerce diversified into other, more productive activities. In some cases this was a post hoc adjustment on the part of companies interested in legitimizing their false claim to the NEPB that they were already engaged in such activities. In other cases, such as that of Nigeria's largest company, the United Africa Company, diversification first into sales and servicing of technical equipment and later into joint ventures with multinational manufacturing firms was a foresightful corporate strategy that enabled them to stay in the central positions in the Nigerian economy they continue to occupy today.

Most of the other changes in operation induced by the first decree were largely cosmetic. More Nigerians appeared on the boards of directors and began to consume some of the indigenized firms' revenues. The trimmings of their position often included an office and secretary, a car and chauffeur, housing with a night watchman, school fees for their children, and foreign trips—all at company expense.[70] For the most part, however, the Nigerian directors played only a small part in the management of the firm. The only significant exceptions to this were the rare cases where the Nigerian board members were few in number and contributed their own capital and a few cases of joint ventures with elements of the weakest segment of foreign capital (the Lebanese) in Kano.[71]

CONSEQUENCES AT THE SECTORAL LEVEL

Many of the changes at the sectoral level have already been alluded to in earlier parts of this chapter. Since the petroleum industry, banking, insurance, and most of the higher-technology manufacturing activities were excluded from the first decree, the most significant sectoral consequences were to be found in commerce. As many as 54 percent of the Schedule I companies that changed hands during the first de-

[70] Interview with prominent indigenous businessman.

[71] The latter conclusion was obtained from a reanalysis of Ankie Hoogvelt's interview data from Kano, described in her articles on indigenization cited earlier. When the responses to her questions about the degree of activity of Nigerian directors are broken down into Lebanese and multinational capital, some interesting patterns emerge. Nine of the twelve multinationals interviewed (or 75 percent of her sample) reported "no involvement," while only one (or just over 8 percent) reported "regular, active involvement." Among the twenty Lebanese companies for which responses are available, an equal number reported "no involvement" but accounted for only 45 percent of her sample. Three of the Lebanese firms (or 15 percent) reported "regular, active involvement," and eight (or 40 percent) reported that Nigerian directors were active at board meetings.

cree were involved in textile retailing, and it is safe to conclude that although overt fronting was common in this sector, indigenous Nigerian businessmen consolidated their position in textile retailing after the decree. Many of the other real transfers of businesses (whether by sale or by default) similarly involved small-scale commercial enterprises, suggesting that this pattern of commercial consolidation was not restricted to textiles. To evaluate this argument further, however, data on more than just transfers of businesses are needed. Data must also be gathered on the patterns of new incorporations of business enterprises during and immediately after the implementation period to determine whether the opening of certain sectors of the economy to indigenous businessmen encouraged them to venture into new areas. If major shifts in the patterns of new incorporations (or in the total number of enterprises incorporated) can be observed in any sectors after the decree, they would provide a stronger basis for asserting that an effective indigenization of an entire sector had taken place.[72]

Data on almost everything are hard to come by in Nigeria, and even when they are made available they must be scrutinized carefully. Although the Registry of Companies has not been terribly proficient in the maintenance of records on individual enterprises, it has kept up with new incorporations and publishes data on them in its *Directory of Companies in Nigeria*. However, other sources must be culled for information on the ownership and the principal activity of the enterprises incorporated. Appendix B contains a detailed description of data gathered on 2,328 companies operating in Nigeria as of 1980. It was assembled from twelve different business directories, embassy listings, and Nigerian government sources and carefully cross-checked by research interviews where possible.[73] Of the 2,328 companies included in the survey, data on the year of incorporation, principal economic activity, and ownership (whether principally local, foreign, or state) can be obtained for 1,230 of them. It is from this

[72] Effective indigenization of a sector can be said to have taken place when a clear majority of the business activity within a sector has been taken over by indigenous (local and state) enterprises. Ideally, market share should be the critical determinant of the indigenization of a sector, but the paucity of reliable data on market share forces me to look for other indicators of sectoral indigenization.

[73] A complete explanation of the definitions used and the coding rules employed can be found in Appendix B. A word of caution is necessary for the proper interpretation of the data. They account for the incidence of new incorporations only, not their size or, more appropriately, their market share. Hence the patterns described must be interpreted with some caution. Fortunately, the tendencies described are consistent with the assessments of these issues in many of the interviews.

data source, supplemented by research interviews, that the following sectoral analysis of the consequences of the first decree is obtained.

Since the period for the implementation of the first decree coincided with Nigeria's oil boom in the early 1970s, it is not surprising that more new companies were incorporated between 1971 and 1975 than in any other five-year period after 1912 (when the Registry of Companies recorded its first incorporated company in the country). From the sample of 1,230 companies for which complete data on ownership, economic activity, and incorporation date are available, a total of 340 were incorporated during the 1971–75 period.[74] Exactly half of these were indigenous private ventures, while 44 percent were new foreign firms and 6 percent state enterprises. When the new incorporations of local and foreign enterprises are broken down according to sector, some interesting patterns emerge.

A majority of the 170 new indigenous enterprises (53 percent) were engaged in commercial activities; among other sectors the spread was more even. Thirty-five new service-sector firms were incorporated during the period (or 21 percent), twenty-five construction companies (15 percent), and nineteen manufacturing firms (11 percent). Only one new primary-sector company was incorporated.[75] Among the foreign companies incorporated during the period a different pattern emerges. Fifty-two of the 151 new foreign firms (or 34 percent) were in the construction industry, thirty-two (21 percent) were located in service activities, thirty (20 percent) were engaged in some form of commerce, twenty-seven were in manufacturing (18 percent), and ten (7 percent) were established in primary production. The data reinforce the suggestion that the first indigenization decree encouraged the expansion of Nigeria's indigenous private sector into commercial activities. They do not suggest that new foreign enterprises in manufacturing were established (one of the state's principal objectives), but rather reveal the attractiveness of Nigeria's nascent oil-boom economy to foreign service-sector and construction firms. New incorporations are only part of the picture, however, since

[74] The 1970–75 period will be used to evaluated the consequences of the first decree, since, as described in Chapter 2, most members of the indigenous private and state sectors in Nigeria knew of the impending legislation by 1970 and could begin to make their investment plans accordingly. The 1975 cutoff date was chosen because the extensions following the official end of the implementation period at the end of March 1974 expired in that year.

[75] Only large-scale primary enterprises are incorporated and therefore included in the sample of companies. Since most of Nigeria's primary production is still small-scale, the sector as a whole is underrepresented in the sample (in terms of its total contribution to Nigeria's GDP).

TABLE 3.11
Distribution of Newly Incorporated Firms during the
Implementation of the First Indigenization Decree (1971–75)

	Local capital		Foreign capital	
	No.	%	No.	%
Commerce	90	53	30	20
Manufacturing	19	11	27	18
Construction	25	15	52	34
Services	35	21	32	21
Primary	1	0	10	7

SOURCE: Data set described in Appendix B.

they cannot tell us about the cumulative impact of these sectoral shifts, or whether existing foreign enterprises diversified their operations and moved into new sectors. To answer these questions, we have to examine cumulative incorporation data and include information from the research interviews described in Appendix A.

Since the commercial sector was most affected by the first indigenization decree, let us begin our detailed analysis there. At independence in 1960, nearly three-fourths of the incorporated commercial ventures in Nigeria were foreign-owned. Indigenous businessmen expanded their position in the commercial sector in the decade after independence but still accounted for only 45 percent of the companies incorporated in 1970. It was not until after the first indigenization decree that Nigerian businessmen effectively began to dominate the commercial sector of the economy. They collectively accounted for 56 percent of the cumulated commercial ventures in the country in 1975, while foreign enterprises were reduced to 41 percent of the total. (State enterprises made up the balance of commercial firms with 3 percent.) Although the rate of expansion of the indigenous commercial ventures was fairly constant throughout the period, it was after the first decree that they finally surpassed the number of foreign companies engaged in commerce and gained what could be described as a dominant position in the sector.

In 1970, just before indigenization, Nigerian businessmen were most numerous in the retail and wholesale distribution of only nine types of goods (including furniture, glass, paper products, and tobacco). They were about equal with foreign companies in the distribution of building materials and cement, books, timber, metals, and construction materials. The state dominated only in the distribution

TABLE 3.12

Cumulative Incorporation of Commercial Ventures in Nigeria,
1955–75

Year	Local	Foreign	State	Total
1955	7 (23%)	23 (77%)	0 (0%)	30
1960	16 (23%)	51 (74%)	2 (3%)	69
1965	37 (31%)	78 (65%)	5 (4%)	120
1970	89 (45%)	103 (52%)	5 (3%)	197
1975	179 (56%)	133 (41%)	10 (3%)	322

SOURCE: Data described in Appendix B.

of agricultural produce (under its legally mandated monopoly). Foreign companies, from the small Lebanese-owned family enterprise to some of the world's largest multinationals, controlled the distribution of the bulk of the goods in Nigeria. It is not surprising that foreign firms prevailed in the distribution and servicing of technical goods like agricultural equipment, chemicals, machinery, oil equipment, plastics, scientific instruments, computers, and telecommunications. However, they also held a dominant position in the distribution of more mundane goods like textiles, food products, cosmetics, office equipment and shoes.

After indigenization, Nigerian businessmen began to expand their position throughout the commercial sector. There were slight increases in their relative share of the number of incorporated enterprises engaged in the distribution of chemicals, leisure goods, motor vehicles, plastics, scientific instruments, and timber. There were major increases (that is, increases exceeding 20 percent in subsectors with at least ten incorporated firms) in their share of incorporations in building materials and cement, electronic equipment, food products, hardware, textiles, and office equipment. Foreign companies increased their share in only five subsectors in commerce (agricultural equipment, air conditioning, educational equipment, oil equipment, and paper products). In no subsector was there a major increase in foreign-company incorporations after 1970. Figure 3.3 graphically summarizes the shifts and cumulative consequences of new incorporations in Nigeria's commercial sector after the first decree.

It is easy to overemphasize the impact of the first decree using these data. As indicated by Table 3.12, the rate of expansion of indigenous commercial ventures is fairly consistent over time and the decree probably only reinforced (or accelerated slightly) trends already well

FIGURE 3.3
Shifts in the Pattern of New Incorporations in the Commercial Sector after the First Indigenization Decree

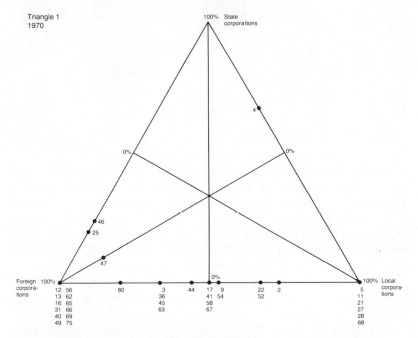

Triangle 1
1970

Key to business activities
2 Agents and general trading companies
3 Agricultural equipment and services
4 Agriculture produce
5 Air conditioning, heating, and refrigeration
9 Building materials and cement (including block molders)
11 Ceramics and sanitary fittings
12 Chain stores
13 Chemicals (batteries, industrial gases, adhesives)
16 Computers
17 Construction plant
21 Educational equipment and training services
22 Electrical and electronic equipment
25 Food and food processing (includes bakeries/

27 Furniture (including interior decorating)
28 Glass
31 Hardware
36 Leather and shoes
37 Leisure goods (includes records, musical instruments)
40 Mechanical engineering plant
41 Metals, metal processing and fabrication
44 Motor vehicles and components
45 Office equipment and supplies
46 Oil and gas exploration and production
47 Oil and gas services and equipment and pipeline contractors (supplying them or distributing their products)

49 Optical and photographic equipment
52 Paper and paper products
54 Pharmaceuticals and medical supplies and services
56 Plastics and plastic products
58 Printing and publishing (books and newspapers)
62 Safety and security equipment
63 Scientific instruments
65 Telecommunications
66 Textiles and clothing and textile equipment
67 Timber industries, sawmills
68 Tobacco
69 Toiletries and cosmetics
75 Technical equipment
80 Diversified

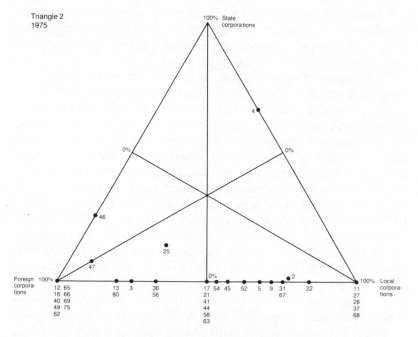

NOTE: Business activities (economic subsectors) are located in the area within the triangles by computing the percentage of incorporated companies in each subsector and plotting them as the intersection of three lines drawn perpendicular to each of the three axes. Thus, if all of the incorporated companies in a particular business activity were predominantly foreign-owned and -controlled, they would appear as a point at the lower left of the triangle. Any change in the percentage of incorporated companies over time is indicated by the movement of the point in the second triangle. The movement (and clustering) of points from Triangle 1 to Triangle 2 illustrates graphically the increased concentration of local capital in business activities in the commercial sector between 1970 and 1975.

In some cases, business activities identified in Triangle 2 are not located in Triangle 1. This is because in the earlier time period there were not sufficient data available to compute the relative share of local, foreign, and state capital. The greater density of Triangle 2 is a graphic representation of the growth of economic activity in Nigeria.

SOURCE: Company data set described in Appendix B.

underway. Other macroeconomic developments such as the expansion of the domestic inflation and the appreciation of the naira during the 1971–75 period served further to expand the role of local capital in commerce. Nevertheless, the general trend suggests that the liberal-internationalist argument about multinational bargaining power being least in highly competitive industries (in this case from local capital) is supported by the Nigerian example.

The manufacturing sector was far less affected by the first indigenization decree. Manufacturing had long been the province of foreign companies, and remained so after the decree. In the sector as a whole, only a slight change in cumulative incorporations was visible. Indigenous businessmen improved their position relative to foreign capital only marginally, with a 2 percent growth in cumulative incorporations. The state sector also increased its share by a comparable amount. Foreign companies, however, still accounted for nearly two-thirds of the total number of incorporated manufacturing firms in 1975. Table 3.13 summarizes these data for the period 1955 to 1975, indicating that the expansion of indigenous business into manufacturing after 1970 was actually slower than its movement between 1965 and 1970. Of course, there was an expansion in the total value of the indigenous ownership of the manufacturing sector in Nigeria after indigenization. Most of that growth was in enterprises fully controlled by foreign companies, however, and thus appropriately coded as "foreign" in the data summarized above. Indigenization can thus be described as having created incentives for indigenous businessmen to invest in foreign-managed manufacturing enterprises and disincentives for them to establish new ventures in that sector in competition with foreign firms. It certainly did not contribute to indigenous control of the sector.

Since changes in the control of the manufacturing sector as a whole are so slight, subsector changes are also rather insignificant. Before indigenization, in 1970, foreign companies dominated in most subsectors in manufacturing. The only areas in which indigenous manufacturers had a firm niche were in the production of carpets, ceramics, and office supplies and in fish processing and sawmills. The state sector had clear dominance in none of the forty-two subsectors reporting incorporated companies in 1970.

By 1975, indigenous businessmen exhibited a major increase (i.e. an increase of 20 percent or more in a subsector with at least ten incorporated companies) in only one area—the production of furniture. In fact, throughout the manufacturing sector as a whole, the number of subsectors in which the share of local capital declined was slightly

TABLE 3.13

Cumulative Incorporation of Manufacturing Ventures in Nigeria, 1955–75

Year	Local	Foreign	State	Total
1955	3 (10%)	23 (79%)	3 (10%)	29
1960	10 (13%)	62 (82%)	4 (5%)	76
1965	36 (20%)	125 (70%)	17 (10%)	178
1970	59 (23%)	181 (70%)	19 (7%)	259
1975	78 (25%)	208 (66%)	27 (9%)	313

SOURCE: Data described in Appendix B.

greater than the number of subsectors in which its share increased.[76] The state sector experienced a similar pattern, except that the number of subsectors in which the state position declined was much greater (declining in six subsectors while increasing in only two).[77]

The indigenization of the commercial (and parts of the service) sector accomplished by the first decree prompted some entrepreneurs to shift into other sectors rather than leave Nigeria altogether. In her study of indigenization and industrialization in Kano, sociologist Ankie Hoogvelt suggested that "foreign capital that was traditionally involved in [these sectors] (especially Lebanese) if it were to stay in Nigeria at all had to concentrate on industry."[78] Her data indicate that, at least for the Kano area, five new manufacturing ventures were formed by Lebanese entrepreneurs with transported capital after 1972.

However, such investment patterns were not limited to the Lebanese. Hoogvelt's disaggregated data suggest that nearly as many new manufacturing concerns were established by multinationals as by Lebanese companies in the Kano area after 1972.[79] From my own data on incorporated companies operating throughout Nigeria (described in Appendix B), there is a visible shift of foreign companies out of

[76] There was a slight decrease in the cumulative incorporations of indigenous firms in nine subsectors (brewing, building materials, ceramics, chemicals, household goods, motor vehicles, office equipment, packaging materials, and rubber goods), while there was a slight increase in eight subsectors (electronic equipment, foods, mechanical engineering plant, metals, paint, plastics, printing, and textiles).

[77] The state sector increased its relative share only slightly in brewing and food processing, while the share declined in building materials, furniture, plastics, printing, rubber goods, and textiles.

[78] Hoogvelt 1979: 66.

[79] See n. 71 for a discussion of Hoogvelt's disaggregated data.

commercial activities and into new areas. However, the multinationals in general were more inclined to move into services and construction than manufacturing, and for the federation as a whole, Lebanese companies did not distinguish themselves by concentrating in manufacturing. They relocated in all sectors of the economy, even in commerce. The patterns Hoogvelt observed in the Kano area may well have been restricted to northern Nigeria.

In the construction and service sectors of the Nigerian economy, indigenous businessmen also expanded their position after indigenization. However, their growth was not as impressive as it was in commerce, and they could not be described as having taken control of either sector. Construction underwent a major boom during the early 1970s, attracting seventy-seven new firms. Local construction firms increased their relative share of the sector by 7 percent, while foreign firms declined by the same amount. The indigenous firms provided no challenge for control of the sector, however, and foreign-owned and -managed construction companies still accounted for 76 percent of the firms after the first decree.

In the service sector as a whole, indigenous companies expanded their relative position by 5 percent, while foreign companies declined slightly, by 2 percent. State involvement was historically greater in services than in any other sector in the Nigerian economy, but its position also declined slightly after 1970, from 16 percent to 13 percent. Private indigenous capital was fairly competitive with state and foreign capital in a number of service-sector areas, and it effectively dominated a number of subsectors in 1970. It was especially prominent in subsectors associated with commerce (such as the operation of commercial institutes, freight forwarding, and customs handling), but also effectively controlled hotels and catering, real estate, transporta-

TABLE 3.14

Cumulative Incorporation of Construction Companies in Nigeria, 1955–75

Year	Local	Foreign	State	Total
1955	0 (0%)	14 (100%)	0 (0%)	14
1960	2 (5%)	36 (95%)	0 (0%)	38
1965	6 (9%)	58 (91%)	0 (0%)	64
1970	16 (16%)	82 (83%)	1 (1%)	99
1975	41 (23%)	134 (76%)	1 (1%)	176

SOURCE: Data described in Appendix B.

tion, travel agencies, and advertising. The state was most important in banking and utilities, while foreign private capital dominated throughout the rest of the service sector.

After indigenization, local capital scored major gains at the expense of foreign capital in the areas of business consulting and publishing. Indigenous businessmen also expanded their position in insurance and shipping, while managing to consolidate their position in freight forwarding. The only service-related area in which foreign capital showed some growth after 1970 was oil and gas services. The state showed slight declines in several of its areas of significant involvement, declines distributed across the service sector as a whole. Since the subsectoral shifts in Nigeria's service sector were fairly extensive, Figure 3.4 summarizes graphically the movement of Nigerian indigenous private capital into the service sector after the first indigenization decree.

Aside from control of certain subsectors, indigenization had some other consequences for Nigeria's service sector. Although banking was specifically excluded from the first decree, the federal government's acquisition of 40 percent of the shares of the largest three foreign commercial banks in 1971 (undertaken in part to facilitate the implementation of the first decree) had an immediate effect on performance within the local private banking community. Since the state sector offered more lucrative salaries, benefits, and prestige, the few banks controlled by local capital lost some of their best personnel to the banks indigenized by the federal government.[80] The banking sector was one of the few subsectors in the Nigerian economy in which the first indigenization decree managed to improve the position of the

TABLE 3.15

Cumulative Incorporation of Service-Sector Ventures in Nigeria, 1955–75

Year	Local	Foreign	State	Total
1955	7 (33%)	7 (33%)	7 (33%)	21
1960	13 (26%)	26 (52%)	11 (22%)	50
1965	32 (34%)	46 (48%)	17 (18%)	95
1970	49 (33%)	77 (51%)	24 (16%)	150
1975	84 (38%)	109 (49%)	29 (13%)	222

SOURCE: Data described in Appendix B.

[80] Okigbo 1981: 116.

FIGURE 3.4
Shifts in the Pattern of New Incorporations in the Service Sector after the First Indigenization Decree

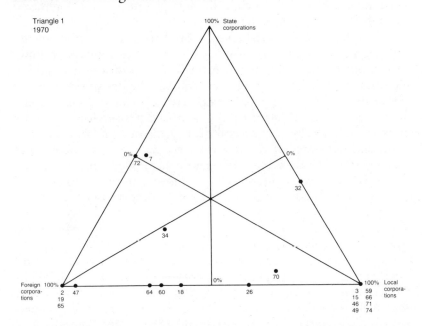

Triangle 1
1970

100% State corporations

0%   0%

0%

Foreign 100%
corpora-
tions   2   47
          19
          65

64 60   18   26

100% Local
corpora-
tions

3   59
15 66
46 71
49 74

Key to business activities
2 Agents and general trading companies
3 Agricultural equipment and services
7 Banks, finance, and investment companies
15 Commercial and industrial institutes and associations
18 Consultants (business) (services include advertising, PR)
19 Consultants (engineering)
26 Freight forwarding and customs agents

32 Hotels and catering
34 Insurance and reinsurance
45 Office equipment and supplies (including cleaning services)
46 Oil and gas exploration and production
47 Oil and gas services and equipment and pipeline contractors (supplying them or distributing their products)
49 Optical and photographic equipment

59 Property or real estate, surveyors
60 Publishing, broadcasting, films, and advertising
64 Shipping, shipbuilding, and shipping services
65 Telecommunications
66 Textiles and clothing and textile equipment
70 Transport
71 Travel and tourism
72 Utilities and public services
74 Advertising

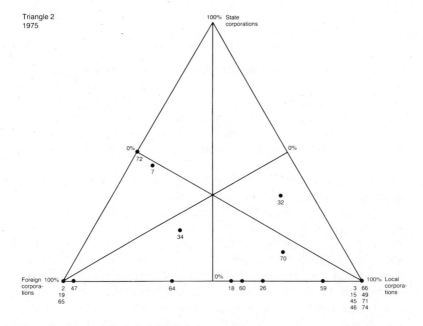

Triangle 2
1975

100% State
corporations

0%

0%

Foreign 100%
corpora-
tions

100% Local
corpora-
tions

0%

72
7
32
34
70

2 47
19
65

64

18 60 26

59

3 66
15 49
45 71
46 74

NOTE: See note to Fig. 3.3, p. 137.
SOURCE: Company data set described in Appendix B.

state sector at the expense of the private sector (both foreign and local).

CONSEQUENCES AT THE NATIONAL LEVEL

Indigenization had a number of rather predictable consequences at the national level (including a temporary decline in new inflows of direct foreign investment and short-term efficiency losses in some industries), but the most striking consequence was its contribution to inequality in Nigeria. A very small number of individuals purchased most of the shares of the 952 enterprises indigenized by the first decree.

By some estimates, less than one-tenth of one percent of the Nigerian public benefited directly from indigenization.[81] In its review of the implementation of the first decree, the Adeosun Commission produced statistics that revealed the extent of the concentration of acquisitions of shares. Only 24 of the 952 indigenized firms were quoted on the Lagos Stock Exchange, and they registered over 300,000 applications for subscription. But 928 of the enterprises (over 97 percent) placed their shares privately, either through direct negotiations with prospective buyers or through professional advisors (such as issuing houses, commercial banks, stockbrokers, solicitors, and accountants). From a sample of 384 of these private placings involving Schedule II enterprises, the Adeosun Commission found that in nearly 30 percent of the cases (for 115 firms) all of the shares were acquired by a single individual. Only two individuals received all of the shares in 75 other enterprises, for a cumulative total of nearly 50 percent of the firms in the sample. If their sample is representative (and it does account for 41 percent of the total private placings from the first decree), it would imply that, at most, 932 individuals acquired the shares offered by almost half of the enterprises indigenized. Even the estimate of 932 is probably inflated, because it assumes that different individuals were involved in the acquisition of the shares of each company. In fact, there was considerable overlap in the accumulation of shares.

By the estimate of one of the members of the Adeosun Commission, as few as twelve individuals or families acquired the bulk of the enterprises affected by the first decree.[82] From my own perusal of the list of names contained in Volume III of the commission's report

[81] Sanwo 1975: 36.
[82] Interview with prominent former state official.

TABLE 3.16
Concentration of Share Acquisition
from Private Placings

No. of shareholders	No. of companies	Cumulative total
1	115	115 (30%)
2	75	190 (49%)
3–5	106	296 (77%)
6–10	38	334 (87%)
11–20	20	354 (92%)
21–30	14	368 (96%)
31–40	12	380 (99%)
41–50	2	382 (99%)
51–100	2	384 (100%)

SOURCE: "Report of the Industrial Enterprises Panel"
1976: par. 1.49.

(where each Schedule II firm is listed, along with the names of individuals receiving the shares and the amounts they paid for those
shares), the concentration is quite striking. I would expand the list of
names from twelve to about twenty individuals or family groups, but
not much further. In one case, at least seventeen companies were acquired by a single individual.[83] Others acquired as many as fourteen,
thirteen, or nine enterprises. Although thousands of names appeared
in Volume III, very few recurred with this frequency. The identity of
the individuals, families, and groups of companies is irrelevant for our
purposes, but it is fair to say that they are among the most prominent,
highly visible, and occasionally outspoken members of Nigeria's contemporary economic elite. Many are officials in indigenous business
associations, industrial leaders, or self-appointed spokesmen for the
private sector. Of the top thirty, only two were military officials, while
well over half (56 percent) were Yoruba entrepreneurs from the Lagos
area.

This last point implies that the inequality engendered by the first
indigenization decree existed not only at the national level (between
rich and poor), but also emerged at the regional level. Of the most
prominent thirty individuals (or family groups) acquiring shares, seventeen (or 56 percent) were Lagos-based westerners. Eight (or about
27 percent) were northerners, while three (10 percent) were eastern-

[83] The total is probably more, since his group of companies acquired enterprises under other names.

ers, and 2 (for about 7 percent) were midwesterners. Similar results (especially the predominence of the West) have been reported by Aboyade,[84] Collins,[85] and Hoogvelt[86] in their analyses of the first decree. In general, data from Volume III of the Adeosun Commission report suggest that the shares were more widely dispersed in the East than in either the West or North. (Traditional rulers in the North appear far more active in the acquisition of shares than their counterparts in the South, and in the Kano area in particular Hoogvelt notes that only six persons acquired 50 percent of the shares of firms she studied.)[87] All of the empirical evidence available supports the contention that the first indigenization decree enhanced inequality and worsened the distribution of income at both the national and regional levels in Nigeria.

The reasons for this inequality at both the national and regional levels are not very hard to come by. The creation of the group of entrepreneurs who subsequently became known as "the Mr. 40 percenters" was encouraged by the fact that nearly all of the indigenized enterprises sold their shares privately. Thus, there was no way to either monitor or affect the distribution of shares. The NEPB was not empowered to question the basis of the allotment of share capital to indigenous subscribers.

The fact that many foreign companies had a strong incentive to sell their shares to a small number of well-known, trusted, or manipulable individuals (discussed previously as "fronting") also contributed to the high concentration of share acquisition. Even those companies not looking for fronts—but wanting the security of selecting individuals with important political positions (or connections)—found only a small number of well-placed candidates to whom they could sell their shares.[88]

Finally, very few indigenous entrepreneurs had access to finance to enable them to purchase shares. Even fewer had proven credit records that would enable them to borrow from the major banks. The NBCI made no loans of less than 30,000 naira (or almost $48,000), effectively eliminating all but a tiny fraction of the Nigerian private sector. Only those individuals and institutions with substantial investments

[84] Aboyade 1977: 381.

[85] Collins 1974: 500 and 1977: 129, 138.

[86] Interview with Hoogvelt. She described the anxiety among northerners that Lagos would become a base for multinationals, Kano being relegated to a location for their subsidiaries.

[87] Hoogvelt 1980: 259–260.

[88] Hoogvelt 1979: 62.

were in any position to participate actively in the first indigenization exercise.

Many of the same factors explain the regional inequalities exacerbated by the first decree. The number of private placings meant that the NEPB could not impose a federal character on the distribution of most of the shares. Individuals in Lagos had better access both to sources of finance and to the major enterprises being indigenized. Most of the Schedule II companies were based in Lagos, as were many of the smaller Schedule I firms. Investment expertise and experience were also concentrated in Lagos. People in the North were generally less experienced with (and less interested in) large-scale Schedule II ventures, especially in the larger multinationals engaged in manufacturing. In the East, as Paul Collins has described it, "foreign enterprise (in the trading and service sector) never got a foothold as elsewhere while in other fields all enterprise remains hampered by the infrastructure damaged in the civil war."[89]

It is fairly easy to document the extent of inequality occasioned by the first indigenization decree, as well as offer reasons for it. However, it is not so easy to assess its desirability. On the surface, anything that exacerbates inequality or the maldistribution of income can be (and usually is) readily condemned. However, what if it serves an important ancillary function such as contributing to the creation of a national bourgeoisie or, as classical Marxists suggest, providing a basis for national accumulation? The members of the Adeosun Commission recognized this as a possibility when they commented that the participation of only a small number of individuals (those with substantial investments) was neither unexpected nor necessarily undesirable.[90]

To assess whether the decree "marked a significant step in the accumulation and concentration of wealth" in Nigeria,[91] we must return to the interview data described in Appendix A and the company data described in Appendix B. On the surface, there is a good deal of evidence that the Mr. 40 percenters were largely a comprador, intermediary group, which, although it accumulated capital, did not divert any of that capital into productive (noncommercial or consumption) activities. Both Hoogvelt's data and my own interview data suggest that the new joint-venture partners were chosen for their connections, ethnicity, or ability to perform intermediary functions rather than

---

[89] Collins 1977: 129.
[90] "Report of the Industrial Enterprises Panel" 1976: par. 2.27.
[91] Forrest 1982: 337.

their business ability or knowledge about operations. However, even if they had no incentive to involve themselves significantly in operations, they still were in a position to collect dividends. Certainly, those who were lucky enough to purchase the undervalued shares of public companies sold on the stock exchange received a windfall. What they did with this income thus becomes important for an analysis of the potential for accumulation.

The fact that 40 percent of the share capital did not necessarily translate into 40 percent of the profits[92] lends credence to the argument that the new joint-venture partners were not in much of a position to accumulate significant amounts of capital through their participation. However, many received some dividends almost immediately after they acquired the shares, and what they chose to do with this newly found income is most significant. Interviews with indigenous entrepreneurs and joint-venture partners reveal patterns that do not bode well for the formation of a national bourgeoisie engaged in productive activities. Nearly all listed consumption as the first use of the proceeds from joint-venture operations (consumption of imported consumer items, acquisition of a Mercedes, taking a new wife, or throwing a big party). Building a large home in the home village or meeting expenses for extended family members were other common forms of immediate consumption. After consumption, investment in real estate (either land or the acquisition or construction of new buildings) was the most common activity for local capital. Expansion of commercial and service ventures came third, followed by investment in industry. The sectoral data described earlier confirm these general patterns, since the most significant expansion of local capital occurred in commerce and services.

However, before we rule out the possibility of any significant accumulation and productive investment, some countertrends need to be considered. Five years is scarcely enough time to evaluate the consequences of the first decree for the formation of a national bourgeoisie. Although investment in industry ranked fourth among the uses of capital by the Mr. 40 percenters, many were at least contemplating productive investments. As indicated by the sectoral data, indigenous entrepreneurs did expand considerably in the production of furniture and slightly into the areas of food processing,[93] electrical assembly, metals, paint, plastics, printing, and textiles. A few also gained im-

[92] J. Cottrell, "A Legal Approach to Indigenization," *New Nigerian*, 23 March 1973, quoted in Collins 1975: 143.
[93] This was especially pronounced in the North.

portant experience in the management of the large manufacturing ventures found in Schedule II—experience that has long-term consequences that are difficult to gauge over a short time period. Finally, many Schedule I enterprises expanded because they no longer faced competition from foreign capital. Indigenous entrepreneurs like the Ibru Group of companies consolidated their position in certain commercial subsectors (purchasing and taking over a number of Schedule I companies), and subsequently expanded their productive activities in related areas. Their experience was not unique[94] and suggests that local capital was capable of a transformation into productive areas of the Nigerian economy.

For the most part, local capital could be more easily characterized as an intermediary (comprador) bourgeoisie than a productive national one in the period immediately following the first indigenization decree. It was certainly not national in scope or vision, and was primarily concerned with consolidating its position in commerce in the regional economies. Tom Forrest's characterization of the Nigerian bourgeoisie as "weak, small-scale, largely commercial in orientation, fragmented and regional in outlook"[95] is generally accurate for this time period. However, the economy was in constant change, and indigenous entrepreneurs were capable of further transformations. Indigenization accelerated their expansion into a few areas they might otherwise not have entered as early, and in Chapter 6 we will return again to consider the effects of indigenization for the development of a productive national bourgeoisie.

In addition to exacerbating inequality and providing a basis for the creation of an indigenous productive class, the first indigenization decree also facilitated the growth of state expansion in the Nigerian economy. Indigenization was hardly the principal source of this expansion, but it did encourage state involvement in enterprises and sectors it might otherwise have avoided. The decree itself said only that foreign capital had to sell its shares, not that local capital had to buy them. In a number of cases where the enterprises on offer promised low profitability or were otherwise unattractive, they were not picked up by local capital.[96] State or local governments interested in expanding (or at least maintaining) employment were often more than willing to acquire the enterprises, especially if the alternatives

[94] The increase in the share of manufacturing in Chief Christopher Ogunbanjo's investment portfolio indicated by his role in the establishment of the Metalbox–Toyo Glass joint venture is a related example.

[95] Forrest 1982: 324-325.

[96] Arnold 1977: 88.

meant closure of the operations. State governments also purchased shares on the Lagos Stock Exchange, and the largest firm in the country, the United Africa Company, set aside one million shares of its stock for each state government.[97]

For the most part, the first indigenization decree facilitated the expansion of state governments into the economy. The federal government's increasing role in the economy was brought about by its accumulation (and distribution) of oil revenues, and with the reservation of the "commanding heights" of the economy for its productive ventures in petroleum, mining, and manufacturing. In relative terms, state governments in northern Nigeria were more likely to acquire indigenized firms than their counterparts in the rest of the country. Hoogvelt estimates that public financial institutions in Kano State bought 25 percent of the shares on issue and that the Kano State Investment Corporation became the largest single investor in Kano industry.[98] Collins similarly reports that the Benue Plateau State government bought five companies in that state and that both the north-central and northeastern states purchased millions of naira worth of shares, many of them in Lagos-based companies.[99] My own data on cumulative company incorporations indicate that state governments were more active in northern Nigeria than in the rest of the country, especially in the construction industry.

Some of the reasons for state-government acquisitions of shares have already been suggested (the absence of any interested indigenous businessmen; the state's interest in maintaining employment levels). Although for the country as a whole, the Lebanese showed a clear preference for entering into joint ventures with local capital rather than with the state,[100] there are a number of regionally specific reasons why state-government intervention was so common in the North.

First, there was less pressure from indigenous businessmen in the North for indigenization, and state governments were largely concerned with protecting their region's interests and avoiding being left

[97] Collins 1974: 498.
[98] Hoogvelt 1979: 61. This figure includes investment by the Kano State Investment Corporation, as well as by the New Nigerian Development Corporation (NNDC) and Northern Nigerian Investment Ltd. (NNIL).
[99] Collins 1974: 499.
[100] This can be inferred from Hoogvelt's disaggregated data, which reveal that 95 percent of the Lebanese firms entered into joint ventures with no government involvement, while only 54 percent of the British, European, and other non-Lebanese multinationals avoided government participation.

out of the process. This also explains why northern state governments were more active in the acquisition of shares of firms based in Lagos or listed on the Lagos Stock Exchange.

Second, although the shortage of local capital predicted by the multinationals never materialized for the country as a whole, it did in the North. In a number of instances there was insufficient local capital for the acquisition of indigenized firms, and northern state governments were confronted with the prospect of large numbers of enterprises closing down as a result of the process.

Third and finally, there was traditionally a greater role for the state in the economy in northern Nigeria. This stems in part from the larger role of the state in Islamic regions, but more specifically from the fact that the North was unlike the rest of Nigeria in that the highest-quality personnel still advanced through the state sector rather than the private sector. State personnel were accordingly both more interested in control of ventures through indigenization and generally more capable than representatives of local capital. As the least developed region of the country, the North was more likely to continue to use and rely upon the state as a way to mobilize resources for development.

Since indigenization of an economy has essentially a political, rather than an economic, objective, it is hardly surprising that most of the economic consequences of the first decree at the national level are negative, something conservative realists would have expected. There is some evidence that foreign capital shifted some of its operations into areas of the economy where its potential contribution (and comparative advantage over indigenous entrepreneurs) could be greater. Vulgar dependentistas, of course, would dismiss this as less a success than evidence of the multinationals giving up their weakest activities. The increased employment opportunities and experience gained by indigenous managers were also favorable consequences of the decree. For the most part, however, the general economic consequences of the first decree were not beneficial for Nigeria, at least in the short term.

As discussed earlier in this chapter, the salaries, working conditions, and quality of goods and services obtained from indigenized enterprises declined after the decree. As long as indigenous businessmen remained inexperienced, inept, and lacking in technical competence, businesses would remain unprofitable (with possible implications for the growth rate for the country as a whole). But the most obvious short-term negative consequence of the first indigenization decree was its general effect on foreign investment and Nigeria's balance of payments. As the data in Table 3.17 indicate, the decree scared off foreign investors for a short time. There was a marked decline in the inflow of nonoil foreign capital after 1972. (Since it was not affected directly by the first decree, and since oil investments were extremely attractive after OPEC's 1973 price rise, it is not surprising that the decline in new direct foreign investment is restricted to the nonoil sector.) The inflow of foreign capital recovered quite quickly to its previous levels, reaching 149 million naira (or about $238 million) by 1975, largely due to the new attractiveness of the Nigerian market. After the first OPEC price increase, Nigeria was not only a country with a large population, it was a country with a large market (that is, it had a large population, coupled with a great deal of money to spend).

Since most foreign investors had been raising the bulk of their risk capital on local capital markets for some time,[101] indigenization did not mean that the risk capital provided to firms would be shifted to indigenous sources for the first time. Rather, it reinforced the tendency and shifted the burden onto indigenous subscribers. A more direct source of short-term foreign-exchange loss came from the transfer abroad of the payments made by indigenous entrepreneurs for the shares of the enterprises they acquired through the program. In his study of the Nigerian experience with indigenization, Emeka Ezeife

TABLE 3.17
Direct Foreign Investment
Inflows to Nigeria, 1967–75
(in millions of naira)

Year	Nonoil Sector	Oil sector	Total
1967	91.0	N.A.	91.0
1968	142.8	N.A.	142.8
1969	120.0	N.A.	120.0
1970	144.6	N.A.	144.6
1971	148.8	14.0	162.8
1972	132.0	195.8	327.8
1973	128.0	115.5	243.5
1974	95.5	186.2	281.7
1975	149.1	210.5	359.6

SOURCE: Central Bank of Nigeria, *Economic and Financial Review*, various years, and *Annual Report and Statement of Accounts*, various years.

[101] Biersteker 1978: 86.

estimated that the increase in the net factor payments abroad during the 1972–74 period (from around 300 million naira to approximately 600 million naira, or, in current terms, from $456 to $974 million) is "largely explained by the repatriation abroad of the proceeds from those businesses that were disposed of to Nigerians over the period."[102] Finally, foreign-exchange remission from payments for services relative to profits also increased after 1972, probably because of the heightened need of foreign companies to control operations through technology rather than through equity.[103] Some of these tendencies for a short-term foreign-exchange loss from indigenization were offset by the fact that personnel indigenization saved huge sums in foreign exchange (since expatriates both were paid more and were more likely to remit as much of their salaries as possible). On balance, however, the decrease in new inflows of foreign investment and the effects of transfers abroad of payments for shares and technical-service fees had a harmful effect on Nigeria's short-term balance-of-payments position.

To conclude, since most foreign enterprises were capable of maintaining control of crucial aspects of operations at the level of the individual firm and, with the exception of commerce, still maintained a strong position in most sectors of the economy, it appears that the question of control of the economy at the national level has largely been answered. It is clear that the federal government of Nigeria had become explicitly involved for the first time in delineating areas of concentration (and noncompetition) between foreign and local capital, but was it (or Nigerians in general) in any greater control of the economy as a result of the first indigenization decree?

Nigerians were clearly in a stronger position in Schedule I activities, but it would be difficult to contend that these areas were strategically important in terms of control of the economy as a whole.[104] If anything, the state found itself in a position in which it was more difficult to control foreign capital. For after the first decree, the line separating local and foreign capital was increasingly blurred. The joint ventures that were formed involving local and foreign capital might sound indigenous, but they were still predominantly controlled by foreign capital, and they now had a far stronger interest group acting on their behalf. The federal government found itself in a far stronger position in the Nigerian economy when it entered into its own finan-

[102] Ezeife 1981: 176.
[103] Forrest 1982: 328.
[104] Teriba et al. 1977: 111.

cial and productive ventures (many of which were also joint ventures with foreign capital) than it was when it encouraged indigenization. This sounds more like dependent development than the expansion of capitalism or an assertion of host-country bargaining power. However, as we shall see, the first indigenization decree was only the beginning of a very long process. As one of Nigeria's leading indigenous businessmen commented, "It is very difficult to change the color of administration and take control of operations at the same time. You must change the color first."[105] And with the first indigenization decree, that first process was begun.

CONCLUSIONS

In conclusion, what can we say about the consequences of the first indigenization decree for the principal actors identified in Chapter 2? To begin with, many local entrepreneurs were generally satisfied with the outcome. The Lebanese had been forced out of a number of small-scale distributive, service, and manufacturing activities. Some of them left Nigeria, some constructed fronts, and the largest among them diversified into medium- and large-scale manufacturing. Although there was some concern among the indigenous business community that fronting was widespread, those who really wanted effective participation had a great many opportunities in Schedule I enterprises.

Another source of indigenous business satisfaction was the fact that a few well-placed Nigerians (predominantly Lagos-based) obtained access to a share of the proceeds of some of the largest and most profitable multinationals operating in the country. Public company share offerings were available at deflated prices for those with ready access to capital, while the same local entrepreneurs took advantage of their privileged access to either the state or the multinationals to acquire the remainder of the shares of Schedule II enterprises transferred through private placings. Lagos-based entrepreneurs had an advantage because most of the multinationals assigned to Schedule II had their headquarters there.

This meant that there were some important groupings of local capital omitted from the benefits of the first decree. Most northern businessmen were omitted because of their distance from the indigenized enterprises and, as described earlier in this chapter, because such a small number of individuals acquired the shares in that part of the country. The fact that the shares were being made available to north-

---

[105] Interview with prominent indigenous businessman.

ern businessmen just after the drought in 1973 meant that many produce buyers and transporters had relatively little excess capital with
which to purchase firms. Easterners were also largely omitted from
the program because the civil war destroyed many of their potential
acquisitions, they faced massive costs of reconstruction, and, most
important, because they lacked access to the federal government in the
immediate aftermath of the civil war. Even a number of Lagos-based
entrepreneurs missed out, especially when the high concentration of
shareholding and the high degree of oversubscription for public issues are considered.

Thus, after the first decree was promulgated there was some pressure from indigenous businessmen to expand the range of enterprises
assigned to Schedule I (those areas reserved exclusively for Nigerians). There were explicit pressures to include advertising, public relations, real estate, insurance, travel agencies, phonograph production, pharmaceutical distribution, and the purchasing and marketing
of export produce under Schedule I.[106] Local capital also had some
explicit complaints about the exercise. The associations of indigenous
transporters and of clearing and forwarding agents disliked the
amendment to the decree announced in February of 1974 that moved
the haulage of petroleum and most clearing and forwarding activities
from Schedule I to Schedule II.[107] The composition of some of the
state commissions appointed to supervise the administration of the
decree was also criticized by indigenous businessmen outside the inner circles.[108] Finally, the Chamber of Commerce "deplored government participation and competition with indigenous private citizens
in the acquisition of foreign enterprises" and argued that state power
existed for and should be manipulated by enterprising indigenous private businessmen.[109] There was particular concern about the acquisitions by state governments of both supermarkets and municipal bus
services.[110]

Although it was the principal target of the exercise, foreign capital
was not terribly dissatisfied with the consequences of indigenization.
Many of the largest and newest multinationals were not affected at all
by the decree. The Lebanese in commerce and services were the specific target and bore the brunt of the program. Both the Lebanese and

[106] "Report of the Industrial Enterprises Panel" 1976: par. 1.4.

[107] Collins 1974: 505. The state had an interest in maintaining the supply of petroleum in the country, especially after the spot shortages that developed during 1974.

[108] Ibid., p. 506.

[109] "Report of the Industrial Enterprises Panel" 1976: par. 1.4.

[110] Sanwo 1975: 35.

European enterprises affected by the decree complained bitterly about the program throughout its implementation. But since so many were able to obtain exemptions or reclassifications from the NEPB, most had little difficulty complying with the formal requirements of the program. The extensiveness of fronting, nominal transfers of shares, and the other defensive strategies discussed earlier in this chapter meant that most firms had little difficulty retaining effective control of operations.

The biggest complaints about indigenization came from the foreign-owned public companies listed on the Lagos Stock Exchange, especially those caught in the valuation trap. Although they were forced to sell their shares below market levels, the distribution of those shares was very wide, and hence they faced no challenge to their continued managerial control of the enterprises. Profits were still very high, their shares were keenly sought, and since they tended to expand, rather than divide their existing capitalization, most were able to earn as much with 60 percent of the shares as they previously did with 100 percent.[111]

Finally, foreign capital had reason to be satisfied with the assurances it received that no further indigenization would be forthcoming until the end of the Third Plan period (sometime in the early 1980s).[112] More significant, as it turned out, was the protection foreign capital was offered against expropriation as a result of the indigenization program. It would be far easier, and far more popular, for the government to expropriate a wholly-owned foreign subsidiary than an enterprise that had many of its shares in the hands of an influential group of Nigerians.

The state was generally less satisfied with the consequences of the first indigenization decree. To be sure, a number of state officials were quite happy with their access to shares of the most profitable multinationals.[113] The state could also be described as pleased that multinationals had begun to diversify into manufacturing and higher-technology areas of the Nigerian economy as a result of the decree. Indigenization demonstrated clearly that the state had the power to force a one-time sale of equity (even at deflated prices) if it chose. It was much less clear, however, whether it possessed the means to

[111] Interview with prominent indigenous businessman.

[112] Interview with former state official.

[113] Hoogvelt noted that of the top six Alhajis who held 50 percent of the shares of the firms she sampled in Kano, three held important political positions at the time of their selection as joint-venture partners, and the others were relatives of influential politicians (1979: 62).

coerce changes in the effective managerial control of operations, something a faction within the state had wanted the indigenization program to accomplish. The latter objective would prove to be a continuous, and relatively elusive, one.

There were widespread concerns within the state about the extent of fronting, corruption, and inequality associated with the program. The highly skewed distribution of shares to such a small number of well-placed Lagos-based individuals, many of whom were not manufacturers but service-sector professionals (accountants, lawyers, and consultants), was a matter of particular concern in some sectors of the state. There was also great concern within the military and among some civil servants about the regional imbalances associated with the decree, especially the fact that northerners were so left out of the process.

Another source of dissatisfaction within the state stemmed from its inability to use indigenization to further its objective of taking leadership of the "commanding heights" of the economy. Not all segments of the state viewed this as a desirable objective, or agreed on what "commanding heights" meant. The state sector as a whole could be divided into two groups: economic nationalists and limited interventionists. The economic nationalists, represented by a few permanent secretaries, middle level bureaucrats, and a number of individuals in the Central Bank, favored an active role for the state in both production and finance. They would have viewed the state's relative decline in its share and control of enterprises in the manufacturing sector (as indicated by the cumulative incorporation data described earlier) as a defeat. Limited interventionists, represented by most members of the Supreme Military Council, the civilian commissioners in the military government, and several permanent secretaries, would have been satisfied with the growth in joint-venture participation with foreign capital occasioned by the first decree.

By the beginning of 1975, a number of tensions, contradictions, and unresolved controversies had become associated with the first indigenization decree. The inequality occasioned by the program was widely recognized, frequently reported in the press, and had placed General Gowon on the defensive.[114] The magnitude of the inequality had led to new calls for the state to play a more active role in the economy, acquiring the shares itself to avoid their concentration in a few

---

[114] As early as his 1974 annual budget speech, General Gowon felt it necessary to state: "It has never been, and it cannot be, the intention of the Federal Military Government merely to create avenues for a few individuals to grow rich excessively and easily on account of the indigenisation decree" (quoted in Collins 1974: 504).

hands. Controversy over public- versus private-sector leadership of the direction of national development came out in the open again, this time under the guise of complaints from local capital about amendments to the decree, state-government purchases of unbought shares, and the lack of access their business associations had to the state commissions appointed by the NEPB to oversee the indigenization process.[115] These concerns were reflected in statements of dissatisfaction with military rule and growing pressures for some form of redemocratization.

The inability of both northerners and easterners to gain access to the shares being offered provided a regional basis to conflict and tension surrounding the first indigenization decree. Smaller and less well connected local capital in the Lagos area also found itself marginal in the process and joined in calls for redemocratization, complaining of economic mismanagement and excessive patronage under the military.[116]

With the promulgation of the first indigenization decree, a precedent had been set for government intervention in the economy. The decree itself made provision for its extension into other areas of economic activity. As we shall see in the next chapter, it is not until the consequences of the first indigenization decree are fully comprehended (with recognition of the unresolved controversies associated with its implementation), that the sources of the second indigenization decree become fully apparent.

[115] Chief Henry Fajemirokun's warnings about "Fabian socialists' " interpretation of indigenization are germane in this regard. See *Nigerian Business Digest*, November 1973, pp. 7–8, for details.
[116] Collins 1977: 144.

CHAPTER FOUR

The State as Initiator:
The Second Indigenization Decree

NIGERIA'S second indigenization decree grew rather logically out of
the widespread dissatisfaction with the results of the first decree. The
fronting, inequality, and regional imbalances associated with the first
decree were evident to nearly everyone and created an environment in
which new pressures for a revision or extension of the first decree were
inevitable sooner or later. The mere existence of this dissatisfaction
would not have been sufficient to broaden the indigenization program as extensively or as quickly as happened with the promulgation
of the second decree in January of 1977. It took the overthrow of the
Gowon administration in July of 1975 and its replacement by a new
military regime to accomplish this.

The second decree was written with the experience of the first decree firmly in mind. It was a corrective measure, intended to extend
the original program while at the same time improving it and redress-
ing its more obvious defects. As such, it did not stem from the same
sources as the first decree. It was not the product of a compromise reflecting the interests and the collaboration of local capital and the
state. This time the state was the initiator of the program, and the second decree it produced largely reflects its internal controversies and
debates. Local and foreign capital complained, lobbied, and threatened while the second decree was being formulated, but they remained essentially reactive throughout the process.

THE STATE

The coup that brought the government of Murtala Muhammed to
power in July of 1975 ushered in a regime that was far more mobilizational, populist, and relatively insulated from private-sector interests than its predecessor.[1] Like most military regimes, it required

---

[1] Political scientist Richard Joseph has commented that policy measures like indigenization "reflect the degree to which a military-bureaucratic elite during the 1970s was
able to act in an authoritative and often unilateral manner to execute policy and institute reforms." See Joseph 1983: 32.

legitimacy and popular support. This regime, in particular, justified its intervention in the claim that it would rectify the errors of its predecessor.

> The Muhammed regime began with the avowed purpose of improving the tarnished image of the military, eliminating the stigma of corruption with which the society had been tainted during the Gowon regime, and returning the country to a form of civil rule, the pattern of which the people would themselves be free to decide on.[2]

Accordingly, the new regime set up a series of panels to examine the policies and programs of its predecessor. Because the indigenization exercise was so visible and so strongly associated with both corruption and extreme inequality, it was an obvious candidate for government scrutiny—and an obvious source of legitimacy—after the coup.

The new regime was interested in more than just creating legitimacy when it chose to reexamine the indigenization program. There was deep suspicion about the benefits from foreign investment at the very highest levels of the new regime, some of whose members presented arguments closely resembling those of the classic dependency writers reviewed in Chapter 1.[3] Generals Muhammed and Obasanjo in particular were said to be unhappy with the coverage, the implementation, and the distribution of shares following the first decree.[4] In the wake of the continuing boom in international petroleum prices, there was no reason to fear liquidity constraints in the event of a possible extension of the program.

The new military government also received some specific pressure to do something about indigenization. Some pressure came from the press,[5] but the more important pressure came from northern Nigeria. For the reasons discussed in Chapter 3, northerners were dismayed by the extent to which Lagos-based entrepreneurs had been the major beneficiaries of the first decree. Because of their greater access to (and role in) the state, they channeled their requests for further action on indigenization through state mechanisms, specifically through the

---

[2] Dudley 1982: 82.
[3] Interview with prominent former state official.
[4] Ibid.
[5] It is difficult, however, to determine how independent this pressure was, especially when it came from the Lagos-based *Daily Times*, in which the federal government of Nigeria had acquired a majority of the shares by 1975. A good illustration of press calls for a review of the indigenization program can be found in Patrick Sanwo's column "Need to Review Indigenisation," *Daily Times*, 11 October 1975, p. 13.

New Nigeria Development Corporation (NNDC), the holding and investment company for the northern state governments.[6] Although they were not specific in their demands, and although their view was not uniformly held throughout the state sector, they provided a strong constituency for a rectification of the regional imbalances resulting from the first decree.

The state sector was by no means monolithic in its interest (or objectives) in reopening the indigenization program. In addition to the regional divisions just mentioned, there were important ideological and bureaucratic divisions within the Nigerian state when the second decree was composed. The economic nationalists identified in Chapter 3 maintained that further indigenization was justified by the historical development experience of other countries: "It is therefore a natural sequence of events that all nations at various times devise effective strategies to combat and contain the incidence of foreign control."[7] The centrally planned economies provided a model for state leadership of the direction of national development, and economic nationalists maintained that the federal government should have "clearly defined areas of economic endeavor reserved for public ownership only."[8] Many of their specific proposals were summarized in Professor O. Aboyade's closing remarks to a conference on indigenization sponsored by the Nigerian Economic Society in November of 1974. He called for an expansion of Schedule II, an increase in public-sector ownership and control of the economy, the introduction of worker participation in share acquisition, and the raising of the minimum indigenous participation to 75 percent.

Economic nationalists were opposed by limited interventionists within the state. Limited interventionists were largely satisfied with the degree of public sector ownership of productive enterprises and with the progress of indigenization to date. Their view was well represented by Phillip Asiodu's closing remarks to the same session of the Nigerian Economic Society in which he summarized the morning session:

> There was agreement that the present exercise was only the beginning and that sometime in the future, in the light of the fairly successful experience so far, Government should consider what other

[6] Interview with indigenous MNC employee.

[7] Yar'Adua 1976: 10.

[8] Federal Commissioner for Works and Housing Mr. Femi Okunnu, quoted in "Let the State Own a Sector of the Economy—Okunnu," *Daily Times*, 7 September 1973, p. 3.

enterprises should be brought within the scope of the Decree and whether the level of compulsory indigenous ownership should be raised.[9]

Although Asiodu did not remain in the government after the 1975 coup, his views reflected the thinking of large numbers of career civil servants who did remain and who participated in the deliberations about the extension of the first indigenization decree.

As we shall see when we consider some of the specific actions of the state in its review of the first decree, there was also another source of division within the state. Partly generational and partly correlated with the ideological division just discussed, there was also a bureaucratic division between the new appointees of the Muhammed regime and the established civil servants inherited from the Gowon and previous civilian regimes. Members of the new guard invariably proposed the creation of new institutions to implement the policy reforms they proposed (fearing the consequences of their recommendations if implemented by existing ministries), while members of the old guard invariably favored existing channels and mechanisms.

In its pursuit of the second phase of indigenization in Nigeria, the state was relatively insulated from pressures and requests from local and foreign capital, at least in comparison with its military and civilian predecessors. This follows logically from the new regime's effort to distance itself as much as possible from the procedures and activities of the highly penetrated Gowon regime. The Muhammed regime's degree of insulation was manifested most clearly in the way in which it went about extending the decree.

The review panel established to investigate the first indigenization decree was appointed by General Muhammed without any publicity or fanfare on 17 November 1975, approximately two and a half months after he came to power. It was not created in response to any direct form of pressure from outside the government and it operated for nearly a month and a half before being detected by a reporter for the *Financial Times* of London.[10] The so-called Adeosun Commission was chaired by Oluwole Adeosun, who at the time was head of corporate finance at Nigerian Acceptances Limited (a merchant bank associated with Continental Illinois of Chicago). Its members included Alhaji Adebayo Adetunji (president of the Ibadan Chamber of Commerce), Fred Brume (a controller at NBCI), Olisa Chukura, Henry O. Omenai (a former permanent secretary), Alhaji A. M. Sango, and

[9] Asiodu 1974: 53.
[10] Interview with prominent former state official.

Hamza R. Zayyad (managing director of the NNDC). Only one of its members came from the indigenous business community, and a majority had extensive experience in government. Economic nationalists were strongly represented on the commission. Its most influential members favored a larger role for the public sector in production and finance and thought that it was necessary to force foreign companies to conform to and comply with national development objectives.[11] There was also a fair amount of hostility directed toward local capital, much of which was dismissively characterized as "very selfish people."[12]

The commission was appointed as the Industrial Enterprises Panel and given the following mandate. Members were to examine the first indigenization program, considering its implementation (identifying devices employed to circumvent its provisions and suspected cases of fronting) and the basis and spread of ownership resulting from the exercise. They were also asked to make recommendations for amendments to the first decree, including expanding the number of enterprises affected and raising the level of indigenous participation. They were asked to assess the role of key institutions involved in the exercise, namely the Lagos Stock Exchange, the NBCI, the NIDB, and the Expatriate Quota Allocation Board, and to make specific recommendations for the "meaningful and rapid indigenization of Industrial and Commercial enterprises within and outside the scope of the indigenization scheme."[13] Also included in their mandate was to "recommend measures which will ensure that managerial responsibilities are assigned to Nigerian executives."[14] Thus at the outset it was clear that there was high-level government support for the extension of the indigenization program, an extension involving an expansion of the number of industries affected by the program, an increase in the level of indigenous participation, and an increase in the amount of managerial responsibility assumed by Nigerians. The second decree was to go beyond simple ownership of shares and in the direction of effective participation in and increased indigenous control of affected enterprises.

The Adeosun Commission was given ninety days to complete its investigation and began by gathering details from the Nigerian Enter-

[11] Ibid.

[12] Interview with former state official.

[13] This material is taken from the cover letter submitted with the Adeosun Commission's report, "Report of the Industrial Enterprises Panel," to the federal military government in March of 1976.

[14] Ibid.

prises Promotion Board on the levels of compliance with the first decree. The commission also solicited (and/or received) memoranda
from a large number of individuals, associations, organizations, government agencies, and private companies. Indigenous businessmen,
virtually all from the Lagos area, submitted a number of individual
statements. The Lagos Chamber of Commerce and Industry also submitted its views, as did a number of indigenous business interest
groups (e.g. the association of clearing and forwarding agents, char-
tered accountants, the bar association, film industrialists, architects,
and pools stakers). Foreign enterprises and associations made their
depositions, including the large trading companies, banks, accounting firms, and associations like the West Africa Committee, the Bankers' Committee, the Nigerian Employers' Consultative Association,
and the Manufacturers Association of Nigeria. Relevant government
agencies also gave their views and made proposals for reform (among
them, the Capital Issues Commission, the two northern development
corporations, the NNDC and NNIL, the three agencies being inves-
tigated, the NBCI, the NIDB, and the Expatriate Quota Board; the
Central Bank; the NEPB; and the relevant ministries). In all, the
Adeosun Commission received memoranda from fifty-four different
individuals, organizations, and agencies. The majority came from
state agencies and representatives of local capital. The interests of labor were represented by a single statement presented by the Nigerian
Labor Congress.

In addition to considering the documents received from the NEPB
and the memoranda provided by interested parties, the Adeosun
Commission undertook some research of its own into the recent experience of other countries. Several commission members visited the
United Kingdom and the United States gathering information on the
operations of their stock exchanges. Commission members also visited Brazil, Venezuela, India, Japan, and the Philippines in search of
information about the role of their public sectors, their development
banks, and their experiences with indigenization.[15] As will become
clear in the discussion of the commission's recommendations, the
United Kingdom's National Enterprise Board and Brazil's National
Development Bank (BNDE) had the greatest impact on the thinking
of commission members.

The commission was by no means unanimous in its thinking about

[15] Mexico was also to be included in these research visits, but the commission members were unable to obtain entry visas after the coup attempt that resulted in the assassination of General Muhammed in February of 1976.

indigenization and debated many of its recommendations at great length. There was intense debate about the classification of industries into different schedules, probably reflecting the influence of the local and foreign business associations and their numerous memoranda. The recommendation that a second decree be extended to affect the operations of all enterprises operating in Nigeria (i.e. the creation of a third schedule) was also subject to much discussion. At one point a majority of the commission's members favored raising the indigenous equity requirement for Schedule II enterprises from 40 to 51 percent, rather than to 60 percent as the commission eventually recommended. There was also much disagreement about whether the state should push for effective managerial control of operations under the framework of the second decree. Most of these debates mirrored those going on within the state between economic nationalists and limited interventionists, but were generally won at this stage by the nationalists, who predominated on the Adeosun Commission.

The final report of the Adeosun Commission clearly reflected some deep-seated hostility and suspicion toward foreign investors. It characterized multinationals as being controlled overseas and motivated largely by the desire for quick corporate profit which they also quickly transferred abroad.[16] It maintained that only with government intervention could the private sector be expected to perform in ways consistent with state policies. It is for this reason that it called for a large public sector to manage modern productive enterprises.

The report characterized the first indigenization decree with its focus on benefits to local capital as "a major and radical departure both from the intentions of the planners and the explicit approval by government of the basic philosophy of public sector leadership."[17] It expressed doubts and confusion about "the incongruous situation of a people (or rather their government) trying to pursue socialist ends with capitalist instruments,"[18] and after reviewing different models of development concluded that events had vindicated the correctness of the post–civil war model of public-sector leadership of the private sector.[19] According to the commission's report, the failure of the first indigenization decree provided indications of the failure of the attempt to reverse the historical process (of public-sector leadership).[20]

[16] "Report of the Industrial Enterprises Panel" 1976: par. 4.34.
[17] Ibid., par. 1.2. The report cited the Second National Development Plan as an authoritative source for this position.
[18] Ibid., par. 1.3.
[19] Ibid., par. 4.7.
[20] Ibid.

The commission recognized that equality was not an explicit goal or objective of the first indigenization exercise, but questioned whether indigenization need necessarily worsen inequality. As in its sweeping calls for public-sector leadership of the economy, the commission again invoked the Second National Development Plan as an authoritative source. It also expressed concern about the regional concentration (read imbalance) of investment expertise, access to bank facilities, and benefits from the first exercise.

The report broke the most new ground in its calls for effective managerial control of indigenized enterprises, arguing that the government had a duty to ensure that the ownership and management of enterprises whose activities were basic to the control of the economy were placed firmly in Nigerian hands.[21] It urged changes in government policy beyond indigenization that would ensure that "more and more Nigerians get the necessary training and experience to fit them for position[s] on management boards,"[22] the ultimate objective of which was to ensure that more Nigerians were involved in the day-to-day management of enterprises operating in the country.[23]

Thus, when it approached the task of evaluating the first decree and making proposals for a second, the Adeosun Commission did so with the following list of national objectives in mind. First, a dynamic public sector should lead the development of the Nigerian economy, with the participation of the private sector. Second, a rapid pace of development (undefined in the commission report) should be maintained. Third, rapid indigenization of both ownership and control should be encouraged. Fourth, economic self-reliance (to be accomplished by greater reliance on domestic resources) should be promoted. Fifth, the spread of national wealth should be encouraged; sixth, the transfer of technology should be accelerated; and seventh, international levels of production efficiency should be attained.[24] These objectives were legitimized with statements and quotations from General Muhammed's 1975 Independence Day address and an address made by General Obasanjo just a week after the Adeosun Commission was created.

In its assessment of the principal defects of the first indigenization decree, the Adeosun Commission stressed the decree's lack of conformity with national development objectives (especially equality) and emphasized the ease with which its provisions had been overrid-

[21] Ibid., par. 5.42.
[22] Ibid., par. 8.55.
[23] Ibid., par. 8.56.
[24] Ibid., par. 4.9.

den. It criticized the first decree for failing to give the NEPB sufficient powers, for retaining too many loopholes for foreign evasion, and for giving inadequate attention to matching equity participation with management control of indigenized enterprises. The commission also faulted the previous government for its implementation of the program, citing the amendments introduced, the exemptions provided, and the absence of policy coordination with other government agencies.

It was with these concerns in mind that the Adeosun Commission made its specific recommendations for a second indigenization decree. The commission proposed a widening of the program to affect all foreign enterprises operating in Nigeria. This was consistent with the mandate it received from General Muhammed when the commission was appointed, but its specific recommendations went considerably beyond what limited interventionists within the state expected (or thought prudent at the time). A total of twenty-four economic activities were to be added to the revised Schedule I, including all retail and wholesale trade, all shipping, forwarding, and clearing activities, all transportation services, and a number of manufacturing industries (including cosmetics, furniture, printing, and the bottling of soft drinks). Manufacturers' representatives were also added to the areas reserved entirely for 100 percent Nigerian-owned enterprises.

The commission identified twelve industries "which for reasons of public policy should be controlled by Nigerians in equity and management terms."[25] Accordingly, it proposed that the minimum equity held by Nigerians in the revised Schedule II be raised to 60 percent and that key economic activities be added to it (such as banking, insurance, petroleum, mining, plantation agriculture, large-scale construction, and the manufacture of steel, cement, petrochemicals, paper, and fertilizers). All other enterprises not identified in Schedule I or II were to be classified in Schedule III and required to make available for Nigerian subscription a minimum of 49 percent of their equity.

To make the revised indigenization program more egalitarian (or at least more participatory) than under the first decree, the Adeosun Commission recommended that all companies in Schedules II and III be required to offer a minimum of 10 percent of their paid-up share capital to their employees.[26] The commission also stipulated that all

[25] Ibid., par. 1.70.

[26] This proposal to widen the distribution of benefits from indigenization came from the ranks of the commission, not from the Nigerian Labor Congress (the NLC). The NLC was concerned, in fact, that the 10 percent requirement would make it more dif-

Schedule II and III enterprises above a certain size (unspecified in the report) should become public companies, in an obvious attempt to ensure greater participation by the Nigerian public.

The most controversial of the commission's proposals to promote egalitarianism was its recommendation that no single Nigerian citizen could acquire more than 5 percent of the share capital (or 50,000 naira equivalent; not quite $80,000) from any fresh sale of capital made to comply with the revised decree. This was obviously meant to ensure that the same small number of well-placed individuals not reap the disproportionate share of benefits from indigenization a second time around. The only exception the commission recommended was in Schedule I enterprises in which the same individual was both the owner and manager of the venture.

To accomplish this extending and widening of indigenization, the Adeosun Commission recommended that the NEPB be upgraded considerably in its total power, level, staff capabilities, and general responsibilities.[27] It recommended that the NEPB be given sweeping powers of enforcement, including the power to seal up and take over defaulting foreign enterprises. More significantly, however, the commission advised that the NEPB be made an autonomous institution accountable to the Cabinet Office. The members of the commission clearly had some reservations about the degree of support their proposals would obtain from the federal ministries. They also wanted the state committees to report directly to the NEPB secretariat, rather than to the state ministries of industries as they had under the first decree.

The Adeosun Commission had more than just a revised regulatory agency in mind when it made its proposals for institutional change in the NEPB. Its members were influenced by the idea of the United Kingdom's National Enterprise Board and wanted to see the NEPB upgraded to become the government's major holding company and initiator of enterprises.[28] Accordingly, the commission recommended that the public sector control the board, providing sixteen of its twenty-one appointed members. It recommended that four members of the NEPB be appointed from the ranks of local capital and that one member represent the interests of labor.

In their proposals for other institutional changes to support indigenization, the commission members suggested that the NIDB be restructured along the lines of Brazil's National Development Bank. By

---

ficult to create a unified working class in Nigeria (interview with Nigerian labor official).

[27] "Report of the Industrial Enterprises Panel" 1976: pars. 4.26–28.

[28] Ibid., par. 4.40.

doing so, the commission underscored its preference for active public-sector intervention in the economy and leadership in the direction of national development. It also proposed that the Lagos Stock Exchange provide incentives to encourage all Schedule II and III companies to list their stock on public exchanges, regardless of their size.

The commission wanted to have its recommendations acted upon immediately, in order to minimize the effectiveness of the countervailing measures it expected from foreign enterprises. As one of its members suggested, "The multinationals could hold us to ransom. If you gave them six months to a year, they could adjust and render the exercise ineffective."[29] It also wanted its recommendations to be considered as a single, comprehensive package. It feared that its program could be neutralized, if only portions of it were accepted and enacted by the federal military government.

Like the reports of the other review commissions established by the military government at the time, the report of the Adeosun Commission was never published in its entirety.[30] However, it did manage to generate a good deal of discussion and debate within the state in the three months between the time the report was submitted (on 25 March 1976) and the release of the federal military government's views on the commission's recommendations (on 29 June 1976), which were published in the form of a White Paper. The Cabinet Office obtained the comments and reactions of the ministries and the in-house policy research group, the National Policy Development Center. The difference between the government's published views and the original recommendations of the Adeosun Commission tell us a great deal about the nature and the substance of that debate.

Most of the debate was focussed on four issues, three of them substantive and one largely procedural. The substantive issues involved (1) the degree to which egalitarianism should be promoted by the exercise, (2) whether managerial control of indigenized enterprises should be sought, and (3) the nature and meaning of public-sector leadership of the commanding heights of the economy. The procedural issue involved the extent and pace of the revised indigenization program. On each of these issues, limited interventionists within the state took issue with the Adeosun Commission's more stridently economic-nationalist recommendations. As one senior ministry official described the panel, "There was a vengeful spirit . . . there was a desire

---

[29] Interview with prominent former state official.

[30] A considerable number of its specific recommendations were published in *Federal Military Government's Views on the Report of the Industrial Enterprises Panel* 1976, popularly referred to as the White Paper.

to do us one better. It destroyed the careful engineering of the first decree."[31] Another added, "We had to do a lot of rescue work to save the second decree."[32]

The senior military officers in control of the Nigerian government in the middle of 1976 had good reason to want to have indigenization promote, or at least be identified with, greater egalitarianism. It would give them increased legitimacy at a time when they especially needed it (having just survived an unsuccessful coup attempt that had resulted in the assassination of General Muhammed earlier in the year). They were not afraid of alienating the Lagos-based professionals who benefited disproportionately from the first decree,[33] and hence readily accepted the commission's recommendation that a 5 percent (or 50,000 naira) limit be placed on the acquisition of new shares by individuals. They also agreed that an allotment committee should be created to ensure the spread of shares and amended the panel's recommendation that 10 percent of the shares be reserved for employees to read "at least half of which should go to non-managerial staff."[34]

Although they generally supported its egalitarian thrust, the top military officials did not go as far as the Adeosun Commission would have liked in at least one important area. They did not accept the recommendation that the 5 percent equity limitation (and other capital requirements) be made to apply retroactively. Not only would this have generated intense opposition from the indigenous business community, but many of the exemptions and rulings allowed under the first decree had been cleared by (and perhaps even benefited) the Federal Executive Council, some of whose members formed the new military government.

There were much greater conflict and debate within the state over the issue of whether indigenization should be designed to obtain effective managerial control of indigenized enterprises. The Adeosun Commission clearly supported this objective, proposing that there be an explicit link between the level of indigenous equity participation and its representation on the managerial board of the enterprise. The commission had a great deal of support within the state for this posi-

[31] Interview with prominent former state official.

[32] Ibid.

[33] Their attitude is reflected in the way they rejected the recommendation of the inclusion of a Nigerian Association of Chambers of Commerce, Industries, Mines, and Agriculture (NACCIMA) representative on the Lagos Stock Exchange as "superfluous." See *Federal Military Government's Views* 1976: 13 for details.

[34] *Federal Military Government's Views* 1976: 19.

tion, but also encountered stiff opposition from limited interventionists, who argued that "the government should be committed not to interfere on a day-to-day basis" in the management of foreign firms.[35] The latter were worried about a loss of foreign investment and contended that managerial control would ultimately grow from ownership of enterprises.

There was an obvious trade-off between pursuing egalitarianism with the 5 percent limitation on new share acquisition and pursuing local managerial control of indigenized enterprises. Although both remained important in the second decree, the objective of control appears to have lost out in priority to "the goal of creating a more equal distribution of wealth in Nigerian society."[36] The White Paper summarizing the federal military government's views on the Adeosun Commission's recommendations mentioned "its observation in paragraphs 8.51 to 8.58" but failed to identify those paragraphs as containing the strongest case made for the pursuit of managerial control in the entire report.[37] It also concluded that it would be "unrealistic in the present circumstances to require all posts of Chief Executive to be Nigerianized in the suggested time frame."[38] Although temporarily set back, advocates of the pursuit of managerial control remained undeterred within the state and were responsible for the introduction of managerial guidelines by the NEPB in 1980. Hence, the state could be best characterized as having been divided on the issue of control when the second decree was being formulated.

There was also disagreement within the state about the meaning of the phrase "public sector leadership of the economy" and the extent to which indigenization should further the objective. Advocates of state intervention in productive and financial enterprises wanted to see Schedule II expanded and levels of indigenous participation raised to 60 percent. Top military officials accepted this recommendation and also agreed that the state (through the offices of the CIC) should be engaged in the determination of prices for the shares of all enterprises sold to Nigerian citizens and associations.

However, some officials thought that government leadership of the commanding heights of the economy need not necessarily mean government ownership of productive ventures. The official comments published in the White Paper omitted any discussion of the Adeosun

[35] Interview with state bureaucrat.
[36] Ibid.
[37] *Federal Military Government's Views* 1976: 21.
[38] Ibid.

Commission's strong plea for public-sector leadership,[39] and rejected its proposal that 50 percent of the shares of Schedule II enterprises be acquired by the state. It also rejected the suggestion that the NEPB be converted into a national enterprises board autonomous of the ministries and responsible for the creation of new industries after the indigenization process was completed. Rather, the governing military council recommended that the proposal be referred to a committee made up of Cabinet Office and ministry officials to "study the issue . . . and make practical recommendations"[40]—a move certain to kill the proposal.

The rest of the debate was procedural in nature and centered on the issue of the scope and timing of the new decree. The military leaders wanted to retain the appearance of acting decisively in important matters of economic policy and hence moved swiftly to endorse the stern measures proposed for enterprises still in default from the first decree.[41] They also increased the number and range of industries affected by indigenization by a substantial amount, and they held firm against arguments from within the ministries that indigenous shareholding in Schedule II operations be raised only to 51 percent, rather than to 60 percent as recommended by the Adeosun Commission.

The final determination of which industries would be assigned to each of the three schedules generated the greatest amount of procedural controversy, subject as it was to the most lobbying. As shown in Table 4.1, it is clear that the military government was not willing to go as far as the Adeosun Commission did in its recommendations for an extension of the program. For example, it left room for minority foreign participation in large-scale retail activities, in the wholesale distribution of imported goods, in shipping and handling, and in many areas of domestic transportation. It also moved the entire construction industry into Schedule II and textile manufacturing into Schedule III, and exempted the petroleum sector from coverage. (Petroleum was appropriately deemed so central to the economy that it was to be treated by special legislation.)

Some of the other differences between the Adeosun Commission's recommendations and the government's White Paper were less important. The difference between acquiring 49 percent of Schedule III enterprises and 40 percent was insignificant, as was the decision to allow more time for the implementation of the revised decree. The latter had more to do with delays in acting on the report after the con-

---

[39] "Report of the Industrial Enterprises Panel" 1976: 8.48.
[40] *Federal Military Government's Views* 1976: 20.
[41] Ibid., p. 5.

TABLE 4.1
Differences between the Recommendations of the Industrial
Enterprises Panel (The Adeosun Commission) and *The Federal
Military Government's Views on the Report of the Industrial Enterprises
Panel* (The White Paper)

Adeosun Commission report	*White Paper*

To be added to Schedule I

All department stores and supermarkets	Only those under 2m naira turnover (greater than 2m naira added to Schedule II)
Internal air transport	Omitted; added to Schedule II
Printing of books and stationery	Printing and stationery (books added to Schedule II)
All wholesale distribution	Only that of locally produced goods and manufactures (imported goods added to Schedule II)
Shipping and shipping agencies	Omitted
Forwarding and clearing	Omitted
Lighterage	Omitted; added to Schedule II
Brokerage	Omitted
Bottling soft drinks	Omitted; added to Schedule II
Coastal and inland shipping	Omitted; added to Schedule II

To be added to Schedule II

Petroleum	Omitted; covered by other legislation
Large-scale construction	Entire construction industry
Omitted	Textile manufacturing (added to Schedule 3 in final version of decree)
Omitted	Oil milling and crushing
Omitted	Distribution and service of motor vehicles, machinery, equipment, tractors, spare parts

SOURCE: "Report of the Industrial Enterprises Panel" 1976; *Federal Military Government's Views on the Report* 1976.
NOTE: The classifications proposed above were described in the Adeosun report as enterprises that "Should be controlled by Nigerians in equity and management terms." The White paper made only an oblique reference to the Second National Development Plan and the importance of public-sector control.

fusion surrounding the succession of General Muhammed than it did with any attempt to water down the decree.[42]

On balance, although the White Paper reflects a considerable toning down of the thrust of the Adeosun Commission, it was certainly not a total defeat of the economic nationalists. In fact, in many ways those who had been defeated in their attempts to promote public-sec-

[42] Interview with prominent former state official.

tor leadership with the first indigenization decree came back with a vengeance in the second and made considerable inroads in policy. They had a mandate from the military leadership to extend the program, a mandate they used to place limited interventionists and private capital (both local and foreign) on the defensive. The White Paper released by the military government mirrored the ongoing debates within the state about the timing of pursuing managerial control of enterprises and the meaning of public-sector leadership. The agenda calling for egalitarianism, greater control, and state intervention was not at issue for the time being.

The White Paper provided the basis for Nigeria's second indigenization decree, but the process did not end here. The government allowed time for "informed discussion of the various proposals in the White Paper"[43] and encouraged the influential indigenous businessmen's association, the Nigerian Institute of Management, to hold a conference to examine the proposals from their vantage point. We will examine both in detail below when we consider the reactions of local and foreign capital to the proposed revisions.

In summary, then, what were the principal objectives of the state in developing a second indigenization program so quickly after the 1972 Nigerian Enterprises Promotion Decree? First and foremost, it wanted legitimacy. The Adeosun Commission was established to investigate the implementation of the first indigenization decree and assess "the extent to which the aims and objectives of the Federal Military Government in establishing the scheme [have] been achieved."[44] By investigating and correcting the wrongs of its predecessor, the new military regime justified its intervention and its continued existence.

Second, there was genuine concern about the amount of inequality occasioned by the first decree and a desire to do something about it. The extreme concentration of ownership resulting from the first program was "not consistent with the government's national objective of egalitarianism."[45] Furthermore, the exacerbation of regional inequalities produced by the exercise both was personally distressing to the new leadership and posed an important political problem for it.[46]

Third, although there was some disagreement within the state on the pace of this objective, an important and influential faction wanted indigenization to accomplish effective managerial control of affected enterprises. In his 1979/80 budget speech, General Obasanjo asserted that the objective of indigenization was to get Nigerians "to deter-

[43] *West Africa*, no. 1137 (16 August 1976).
[44] *Federal Military Government's Views* 1976: 3.
[45] Chikelu 1976: 24.
[46] Interview with former state official.

mine their own economic future by using equity participation to control board and management decisions."[47] This meant that the state wanted fronting to be eliminated in Schedule I firms, and that it wanted the degree of effective participation at the managerial level in Schedule II firms to reflect the 60 percent share of the equity held by Nigerians.

Fourth, an important segment within the state wanted to assume public-sector leadership of the direction of development, especially in critical sectors of the economy such as finance and the production of basic materials (including petroleum, steel, cement and food products). This is a familiar theme and of course was one of the principal objectives of the state in the first indigenization decree. A few of the authors of the Second National Development Plan still in the civil service continued to hold this position, but the most zealous advocates of extensive state intervention came from the ranks of civil servants and advisors more recently recruited by the new military regime.

Fifth, the state wanted to encourage the creation of new enterprises in general, and more specifically to create opportunities for indigenous businessmen. It wanted to encourage more than just the acquisition of existing foreign-controlled enterprises; it also wanted to create an environment in which local capital could break new ground.

And sixth, the state wanted to be sure to provide a few assurances to foreign capital. There was no intention of expelling foreigners from Nigeria:

> We will continue to need their expertise, we will continue to need their technology and we will in fact also continue to need their investment capital.
>
> What we are trying to do is to establish genuine partnership between those who own the resources and our foreign friends who control the expertise and technology.[48]

As in the past, fair and adequate compensation would be provided to indigenized enterprises.

LOCAL CAPITAL

Most of the Lagos-based beneficiaries of the first indigenization decree were satisfied with the program and were hardly clamoring for its extension in 1975. They did, of course, have a number of complaints

[47] Collins 1981: 122 n. 1.
[48] Ya'Adua 1976: 11.

about the exercise. Many thought they were not adequately consulted by the government, and that the NEPB and its state committees contained too many civil servants.[49] Most thought that indigenization had facilitated an unhealthy expansion of state intervention in the economy. Some were crowded out of financial markets by state governments buying shares,[50] while others complained that enterprises with state participation had competitive advantages such as easier access to expatriate quotas.[51]

However, most of the complaints from local capital concerned the classification of industries into particular schedules under the first decree. Some complained that there were not enough opportunities for local capital in the existing list of Schedule I activities; that the program "created no new opportunities for indigenous entrepreneurs since these areas (Schedule I) had enjoyed intensive Nigerian participation before the Decree's promulgation."[52] There were also complaints about the number of exemptions obtained by foreign capital, especially the largest trading companies and their affiliates.[53] Accordingly, there were specific calls for the moving of a number of activities from Schedule II to Schedule I (including the hauling of petroleum goods by road, advertising and public relations activities, estate agencies, pharmaceutical retailing, clearing and forwarding agencies, and the marketing of export produce). Not all of the proposals for schedule changes recommended moving from Schedule II to Schedule I, however. There were also a few complaints from small businessmen about increases in concentration of ownership that had taken place in their sector after indigenization. They found themselves cut off from their former foreign partners (or suppliers) and not integrated with the supply or marketing system being established in the new highly concentrated Nigerian-controlled sector. Hence, they called for a reclassification in order to maintain their links to their former foreign suppliers and remain in business.[54]

[49] Silva 1976: 37.

[50] Akinkugbe 1974: 41–42.

[51] This was an issue generally discussed in Nigerian Economic Society 1974: 46.

[52] Akinkugbe 1974: 38.

[53] Memorandum from the Pharmaceutical Society of Nigeria, National Secretariat, presented to the chief of staff of the federal military government, 17 December 1976 (unpublished), p. 1. There were also some specific complaints from indigenous distributors about the fact that both Dunlop and Lever Brothers had managed to retain their distributive activities under their Schedule II classification (interview with prominent indigenous businessman).

[54] In its memo to the Adeosun Commission (dated 20 January 1976, p. 2) the Western State Football Pools Stakers Association complained that the increased concentra-

Despite its complaints about the indigenization program, local capital did not provide a mandate for the wholesale extension of the scope, the range, and the objectives of the exercise as envisaged by the Adeosun Commission. As we have already seen, indigenous businessmen did not initiate the proposals for an extension of the first decree. Rather, they were largely reactive, and devoted their attention to toning down the scope and the language of the state-initiated program. They were not prepared for the role being created for them by the state.

The reasons for their reluctance to pursue further indigenization in 1975 stem from the degree of their recent success in breaking down barriers to entry in equity participation with multinationals, the size of their recent dividend benefits, and their success in closing the Lebanese out of certain retail operations. The state of the Nigerian economy in 1975 and early 1976 dulled any enthusiasm indigenous businessmen might have had for an extension of indigenization. The recession stimulated by government import controls made them wary of embarking on new economic ventures,[55] and many local businessmen were still reeling from the effects of the Udoji Commission's public-sector wage recommendations that had made the operations of many of their newly acquired firms so much more costly.[56] The government's restrictions on the size of dividend payments (to 16.5 percent of net income) also made equity participation in joint ventures with foreign capital far less attractive than it had been at the time of the first decree.[57] Finally, a number of indigenous businessmen who relied on foreign enterprises for their supply of goods and services had fears about the consequences of additional indigenization for the performance of those enterprises.[58]

Of course, not all fractions of local capital were equally unenthusiastic about an extension of the indigenization program. For example, those left out of the exercise the first time around had a great deal to gain from and did favor an expansion of the exercise. This included both marginal and small-scale local capital in the Lagos area that had

---

tion of ownership following the first decree forced its members to become fronts for Lebanese businessmen in order to remain in business themselves.

[55] Collins 1983: 422 n. 28.

[56] Beatrice Fisher, "Udoji Awards: What Effects of Indigenisation Policy?" *Daily Times*, 25 March 1975, p. 21.

[57] Interview with prominent indigenous businessman.

[58] This was especially true of local capital in the distributive trade. See Dupe Adeogun, "How to Ensure the Success of Indigenised Enterprises," *Daily Times*, 22 March 1974, p. 7.

been either unable to afford or, more commonly, unable to obtain access to the appropriate vendor of the shares made available to the public following the first decree.[59] These small-scale entrepreneurs were never in the running for the private transfers of shares that took place in 95 percent of the enterprises affected in Schedule II. They were joined by an equally dissatisfied regional fraction of local capital—northern businessmen. They were concerned that Lagos-based entrepreneurs had bought all the shares the first time around, and they wanted a chance to acquire a few for themselves.

A few indigenous businessmen joined senior Nigerian managers employed by multinationals in wanting the program extended to ensure greater Nigerian participation in decisionmaking in Schedule II firms. They were joined by entrepreneurs active in Schedule I who wanted local-content requirements to be incorporated into the scheme.[60] They were few in number, however, and were not particularly important in the lobbying that took place after the government's White Paper was released.

Finally, some pressure for additional personnel indigenization came from the ranks of middle and junior management. The first indigenization decree had raised the expectations of junior staff, many of whom viewed their own promotion within the firm blocked by the presence of an expatriate manager in their division. Thus, the junior staff was often more aggressive in its demands for personnel indigenization than the senior staff members to whom the additional benefits were most likely to accrue.

Despite the existence of some interest in an extension of the indigenization program from the ranks of small-scale businessmen in the Lagos area, northerners left out of the process the first time around, a few local manufacturers interested in local-content requirements, and a number of junior staff members in foreign-controlled firms, these groups did not form an effective alliance or lobby for their position. Local capital was not a driving force behind the second decree, as it had been behind the first. These groups were the principal beneficiaries of the second decree, and they accorded the military government both legitimacy and support for its extension of the program. However, as we shall see, the groups historically most influential in representing local capital were opposed to most of the specific recommendations for an extension of the decree being discussed during 1976.

[59] The heavy oversubscription of all of the public shares made available by Schedule II enterprises after the first decree (discussed in Chapter 3) indicates the potential number of small-scale indigenous businessmen left out the first time around.

[60] Banjo 1976: 35.

By the time the second indigenization decree was being considered, the Lagos Chamber of Commerce and Industry was no longer controlled by expatriate businessmen and had become the principal spokesman for the interests of private capital in general, and local capital in particular. It was among the first of the groups submitting memoranda on indigenization and it provided its views to the government on several occasions during 1976. Its first memo was submitted to the Adeosun Commission on 20 January 1976; its contents indicate the reluctance of local capital to pursue indigenization significantly beyond the levels already reached with the first decree.

It began by characterizing the first decree as "a major landmark," "marked by a commendable sense of realism" whose "execution was no less remarkable."[61] The Chamber expressed its general satisfaction with the first decree and observed that most of the decree's objectives had been achieved. The current government was commended, however, for undertaking a review of the exercise, especially since "a number of problems and shortcomings that tended to inhibit its effectiveness have come to light."[62]

The Chamber stated its appreciation of "the concern of the government that the spread of ownership of the shares of companies being transferred should be as wide as possible,"[63] but it certainly did not suggest that the 5 percent limitation be introduced or that any revisions of the program be made retroactive. Rather, the memorandum suggested (1) that the CIC rules be changed to encourage (not force) more companies to go public, (2) that 10 percent of the shares offered be set aside for a company's employees (level not specified), (3) that the government severely curtail its participation in share acquisition (to enable more Nigerian entrepreneurs a chance to acquire shares), and (4) that insurance laws be amended to allow companies holding pension funds to invest in businesses on the stock exchange.[64]

There was certainly no sweeping call in the Chamber's statement for pursuing managerial control of (or even much greater participation in) foreign enterprises.

> We are firmly of the view that while there is a good case for taking a step forward to increase the proportion of indigenous ownership, it would be imprudent at this juncture to attempt to secure domi-

[61] Lagos Chamber of Commerce and Industry, Memorandum to the Industrial Enterprises Panel, 20 January 1976, p. 1.

[62] Ibid. This was apparently to the surprise of the Chamber.

[63] Ibid., p. 5.

[64] Ibid., pp. 5–6.

nance in one fell swoop. The next few years in the industrial development of Nigeria will probably be most crucial and nothing should be done to prejudice the inflow of foreign technology and to some extent foreign capital which, provided the terms are right, can facilitate the transition to the stage of self-sustained growth.[65]

Local capital for the most part did not view its relationship with foreign capital as antagonistic and was particularly interested in expanding the opportunities for additional joint ventures with multinational corporations in Schedule II activities. Thus, it not only opposed seeking a majority of the equity in Schedule II, it also proposed that the minimum limit on the equity capital required for foreign companies assigned to Schedule II be lowered from 400,000 naira (about $638,000) to 100,000 naira (about $160,000).

There was also little interest on the part of the Chamber in pursuing further personnel indigenization. Rather, its memorandum called for an easing of the restrictions on importing expatriate manpower, especially for sophisticated industrial sectors. Local-content requirements were not mentioned anywhere in its recommendations.

The Chamber's first lobbying attempt ended with its usual complaints about the operations of the CIC (with a special plea to include more representatives of local capital), about the numerous administrative bottlenecks faced by entrepreneurs trying to set up a new firm, and about the insufficiency of capital available to indigenous businessmen. The regional imbalances resulting from the first decree were mentioned only once, in an oblique criticism of the limited geographical coverage of the NBCI.

After the Adeosun Commission report was submitted and the government's White Paper released, local capital complained about its lack of consultation in the process and wanted copies of the commission's full report to be distributed for its input. Rather than make the report or its internal deliberations public, the federal military government asked the Nigerian Institute of Management (NIM) to hold a conference to assess the problems and prospects of indigenization. The institute did so in early September of 1976, just two months after the White Paper was released and four months before the second decree was issued. The timing of the conference was propitious, as was recognized explicitly by its organizers. Michael Omolayole, then chairman of the NIM's council, suggested when he opened the session: "There is the possibility that constructive comments and suggestions which will emanate from the conference can reach the Fed-

65 Ibid., p. 6.

eral Government in good time before a decree is drafted and promulgated."[66] The military had found a way to respond to complaints about its insulation from the private sector in the revision of the indigenization decree, and local capital had found another channel to register its misgivings about the program.

Although the NIM conference included statements by state officials (including Brigadier Shehu Yar'Adua, then chief of staff of the Supreme Military Council, and G.P.O. Chikelu, then permanent secretary in the federal Ministry of Economic Development), most of the presentations were made by indigenous businessmen. Several were made by individuals representing their own Schedule I enterprises, and several were made by indigenous executive directors of multinational companies operating in Nigeria. In the NIM's summary of the conference recommendations (from papers and contributions of participants), the views of both classes of indigenous businessmen were present. For the purposes of the present discussion, the views of indigenous businessmen will be highlighted where possible (i.e. when clearly distinct from those of foreign capital).

The NIM's summary began with a statement supporting indigenization, "a policy which every right-thinking Nigerian should wholeheartedly support."[67] However, it continued, the greatest doubts and fears among the indigenous business community concerned the pace of indigenization, the extent of the program, and the frequency with which decrees were being promulgated. Their greatest source of concern was the impact it would have on foreign capital, specifically the fear that further indigenization would induce a flight of foreign capital from the country and would deprive Nigeria of research facilities and access to technology.

In general, the conference recommendations concluded that the government was pushing too fast with the program. A simple majority of the equity (or 51 percent) of Schedule II firms would be enough to satisfy indigenous businessmen, and jumping from 40 percent to 60 percent in such a short time was considered unnecessary and probably a mistake. Although the conference recommendations supported the idea of having "able and competent" Nigerians participate effectively at both board and management levels, one indigenous conference participant suggested that the NIM had been trying to tell the government to proceed with caution in Nigerianizing all senior posi-

[66] Omolayole 1976: 9.

[67] Nigerian Institute of Management 1976: 13. This is similar to the way the Lagos Chamber of Commerce began its first representation to the federal military government in January of 1976.

tions.[68] The conference also cautioned against sending inconsistent signals to foreign capital and cited changes in indigenous participation in the insurance industry as an example of what not to do.[69]

Indigenous businessmen had specific complaints about the proposed classification of industries into Schedules I, II, and III, and expressed the fear that assigning the biggest trading companies to Schedule I would deprive some small distributors of essential financial resources. A number of small distributors relied on the big trading companies for credit facilities. There were also some doubts expressed about the ability of indigenous businessmen to take over some of the manufacturing industries assigned to Schedule I (especially the manufacture of cosmetics).

Finally, like the Lagos Chamber, the NIM was highly critical of state intervention in the economy and warned of further encroachments from the proposed extension of the decree. The institute complained about its exclusion from the review process, called for a more "balanced" representation on the NEPB (meaning greater representation of local capital), and suggested that both the banking and insurance industries be fully denationalized:

> . . . banks and insurance companies are not only strategic but extremely sensitive institutions and as such care should be taken to ensure that shares in these institutions held at present by the government are transferred to individual Nigerians at the earliest opportunity.[70]

They were particularly concerned that key financial institutions might become politicized after the scheduled return to civilian rule.

A few weeks after the NIM conference, the Lagos Chamber of Commerce submitted its second memorandum to the government on proposals for a revision of the indigenization program. By this time, however, the Chamber had given up on any hopes of limiting the scope of the exercise. It was clear that the government was going ahead with most of the revisions outlined in the White Paper—including extending the program to all enterprises, raising the equity levels, and pursuing managerial control of Schedule I and II firms.

---

[68] Interview with official of the Nigerian Institute of Management.

[69] The state acquired 49 percent of the equity in insurance companies in 1975 and provided its new foreign partners with assurances that there was no plan to increase this percentage of participation "in the foreseeable future." In its White Paper, released the following year, the percentage was increased to 60 percent.

[70] Nigerian Institute of Management 1976: 15.

Thus, the Chamber focussed its attention and energies on minimizing the effectiveness of the new decree.

Some of its specific proposals were simply repetitions of its previous memorandum and echoed the recommendations of the NIM conference. There were again calls for local business representation on the NEPB and stock exchange, warnings about carrying the wider spread of share ownership too far, and complaints about state intervention in the economy. Government participation in the banks again came under fire, as did "government participation in share acquisition in other businesses."[71] Perhaps in response to the Adeosun Commission's argument that its proposals for a widening of the share distribution be made retroactive, the Chamber argued that its proposals for government divestment of shares also be made retroactive. Thus it urged the state banks to "sell the present shares held by the state governments to the public,"[72] a move that would have had a significant impact on the blocks of shares held by the northern state governments. Even if they were not serious about this proposal, it was a clever bargaining maneuver designed to prevent the government from reopening the terms of the first decree.

Most of its specific recommendations, however, concerned the details of the implementation of the revised decree. The Chamber was concerned that the schedules be clearly defined, that the government be flexible in its application of the new classification rules, and that the CIC share-pricing mechanisms be reviewed. It also requested a streamlining of the bureaucratic requirements for the creation of new enterprises, a reform which, as we shall see in Chapter 5, was to have an important impact on the ability of local capital to circumvent the 5 percent or 50,000-naira limitation placed on the acquisition of shares of indigenized enterprises.

Finally, the Chamber introduced a series of demands (some of them quite familiar) for subsidies and government support. It suggested that "[s]ubstantial investment in warehousing, transportation and other facilities will be required if Nigerian distributors are to effectively take over the distribution of locally manufactured goods."[73] It also once again called for financial support, specialist advisory services, and intensified manpower training programs for indigenous businesses.

As we shall see below, many of the Chamber's recommendations

[71] Lagos Chamber of Commerce and Industry, Review of Government White Paper on Industrial Enterprises Panel's Report, 14 September 1976, p. 2.

[72] Ibid., p. 8.

[73] Ibid., p. 1.

were consistent with, similar to, or no different from the comments of multinational corporations on the proposals for a revision of the indigenization program. Foreign capital was equally interested in a clarification of the schedule definition, was opposed to a mandatory rule forcing companies above a certain size to go public, favored an open door on remittance of royalty, patent, and technical fees, and worried about the ability of indigenous businessmen to handle the entire distributive trade. In part, this apparent consonance of interests reflects the continuing influence of foreign businessmen in the Chamber's deliberations. It also reflects the fact that many indigenous businessmen were closely tied to a multinational company's distribution network and worried that rapid indigenization would disrupt their own businesses.

Throughout 1976, local capital was fairly consistent in its position on further indigenization. With the exception of a few individuals, it was certainly not pushing for managerial control of enterprises, but rather stressed the need to be judicious and pursue a gradual approach.[74] A minority of the equity of Schedule II enterprises was still sufficient for most indigenous businessmen. They wanted to maintain access to foreign technology, expatriate expertise, and the distribution networks established by the largest foreign trading houses. Finally, they worried that the state's concern with the distribution of equity would undermine their capacity for capital formation.

What, then, were the principal objectives of the indigenous businessmen confronted by the certainty of a state-led extension of the indigenization program? First, they wanted to contain the most radical economic nationalists within the state and maintain a gradualist approach to indigenization. Having initiated the first decree, local capital wanted to consolidate its position and maintain the principle of state-sponsored support for protection from foreign competition. It was not prepared to move for majority equity or managerial control at this time. There was support for only a gradual increase in personnel indigenization and for an increase in the number of companies listed on the stock exchange.

Second, local capital wanted to ensure that it would continue to be able to retain its access to foreign capital and expertise. It did not favor assurances to foreign investors, clarifications of the proposed revisions, and flexibility in implementation simply because indigenous businessmen were acting as compradors or fronts for foreign interests. There was a considerable interdependence between the two

[74] Ogunbanjo 1982: 13.

groups, and local capital feared that foreign companies might disinvest as a result of the revised decree. It needed continuous access to foreign expertise and to possible joint-venture partners. The continued inflow of foreign capital was viewed not as a threat to local capital, but as a source of reassurance and profitable alliance.

Third, local capital wanted to minimize state intervention and encroachment on sectors it already operated in (or intended to expand into). In many ways, the state was perceived by indigenous businessmen as more of a threat than the continued presence of multinational corporations in most sectors. The revision of the indigenization program was seen as an attempt by the state to move into areas previously occupied by the private sector in general, rather than as an attack on foreign capital in particular. To most indigenous businessmen, the proper role of the state in the economy was to assist the development of local capital, providing subsidies and building infrastructure rather than embarking on productive investments of its own. As one indigenous businessman argued, "State Capitalism as an economic experiment has left a continuous record of failures."[75] In an argument surprisingly close to that of classical Marxists, he continued that Nigerians had "become ensnared in the ideological niceties of our time, under the cloak of that monster—'nationalism.' "[76]

Finally, local capital wanted to keep the demands for greater equity and distribution of the benefits of indigenization from getting out of control. Indigenous businessmen recognized the unpopularity of the first indigenization decree and the need to increase the number of beneficiaries of the second decree (hence their support for additional public listings of companies). However, they also wanted to ensure that the distribution of shares from the first decree would remain unchallenged and that the allocation rules proposed for the second decree not be applied retroactively.

FOREIGN CAPITAL

Most multinational corporate executives were caught off guard by the 1975 coup, the sudden flurry of review panels, and the sweeping proposals for an extension of the indigenization program. They were still implementing and adjusting to the first indigenization decree, and most continued to operate with the assumption (or at least the hope) that the guarantees provided by the Gowon regime about no further

[75] Ibid., p. 26.
[76] Ibid., p. 28.

indigenization until the end of the decade would remain in force. Since the second decree did not come from the initiative of local capital, with which the multinationals had considerable contact in joint ventures and sessions of the Lagos Chamber of Commerce, foreign capital had little advance notice of the proceedings or proposals being considered by the state. Thus, it was largely reactive to proposals and, even more than local capital, remained on the sidelines throughout the process.

In general terms, foreign capital had far less access to the state under the Muhammed–Obasanjo regime than it had had under the Gowon regime. This was in part because the new regime had been in power for less time than its predecessor had when it initiated its indigenization decree. New contacts and new channels of communication had to be established before the multinationals could participate effectively in the proceedings. However, their difficulty in penetrating the state also stemmed from the fact that the new regime based its legitimacy on its reformist, mobilizational character. The widely recognized corruption of the Gowon regime was condemned, and the new regime tried to distance itself from what it perceived as the sources of corruption under its predecessor, both its highly visible ties to established indigenous business and its obvious penetration by foreign capital.

In addition, the new military leadership did not believe that it actually needed to go out of its way to satisfy the concerns of multinational corporations in Nigeria in late 1975 and in 1976.[77] With the oil wealth it accumulated in the wake of the 1973 OPEC embargo, Nigeria had little need for additional capital (even in the unlikely event that multinationals would consider importing capital into Nigeria). Economic nationalism was high on the agenda at the international conferences Nigeria was attending in the mid 1970s, and the country knew its oil wealth and large internal market made it attractive to foreign capital (in part because the multinationals told it so). Therefore, it had no reason to go out of its way to attract new firms to the country or, for that matter, to worry about retaining existing investors.

Finally, because representatives of local capital had gradually taken over more of the offices and programs of the Lagos Chamber of Commerce,[78] foreign capital had fewer channels open to it for lobbying for changes in the revisions proposed for the indigenization program. Some of its views were expressed in Chamber documents, but foreign

[77] Interview with prominent former state official.
[78] Interview with prominent indigenous businessman.

capital did not play the role in the deliberations and official statements of the Chamber in 1976 that it had in the early 1970s.

There were a few channels open to foreign capital to present its case, however. Representations were made to the government by industry associations in which foreign capital predominated and through the auspices of the Manufacturers Association of Nigeria (MAN). Manufacturing was a principally foreign-managed and foreign-controlled activity in Nigeria, and, as a senior representative of the Indigenous Businessmen's Group of the Lagos Chamber of Commerce described it, "The MAN largely represented the expatriate business interests in Nigeria, and they used it as a lobby for their interests."[79] Individual companies, particularly the largest and most influential trading firms, also made their own representations directly to the government.

In its memorandum on the White Paper, the Manufacturers Association warned that many manufacturing companies about to be affected by the revised decree operated in more than one schedule. To dispose of either their Schedule I or Schedule II activities would break up the corporate entity and could have severe repercussions for production levels, productivity, and employment levels, and might lead some firms to cease certain production lines altogether. The document asked the government to be flexible and "give special consideration to industries which would otherwise be completely divided or where production would cease in others to ensure the continued well-being of Nigerian Industry."[80]

The MAN's official comments on the White Paper also expressed concern about the higher rates of taxation the government was considering applying to certain companies to get them to list on the Lagos Stock Exchange. It argued that many companies simply could not satisfy the exchange's requirements and recommended that companies in joint ventures with state entities (particularly parastatals and pension funds) be exempted from such punitive taxation.[81]

What appears to have worried the Manufacturers Association the most, however, were the proposals that the distribution of goods made in Nigeria be turned over to indigenous entrepreneurs. Many manufacturers were themselves engaged in the distribution of their own made-in-Nigeria goods and did not want to lose the business.

[79] Ibid.

[80] Manufacturers Association of Nigeria, confidential memo submitted to the federal military government, entitled "Government White Paper on Enterprises As It Affects the Industrial Sector," 1 November 1976, p. 4.

[81] Ibid., p. 4.

The big trading companies also had a strong interest in maintaining their position in the distribution of all goods, both local and imported. A number of multinationals officially classified as manufacturing firms were essentially nothing more than distribution centers for goods imported from the parent company, and so they too worried about the implications of losing control over the distribution of their ostensibly made-in-Nigeria goods. Hence, the document warned that a disruption of supply and price stability throughout the country could result if the state insisted on its proposal.[82]

The association's rather brief document concluded with an expression of concern about "the speed with which phase two [of indigenization] is following the 1972 Decree,"[83] and warned that this created increased uncertainty about the future of manufacturing investment in Nigeria. After observing that Nigerians were increasingly occupying senior managerial roles in manufacturing, it recommended against pushing for complete personnel indigenization too quickly: "No manufacturer on the other hand likes to see his investment jeopardized by too early a removal of specialist help—capital costs are so high as to make it absolutely necessary to ensure that maximum efficiency is obtained from the investment."[84] The only encouraging sign the Manufacturers' Association saw was the government's proposal to streamline the procedures for the incorporation of new enterprises.

In addition to advancing the MAN memorandum, foreign capital made its views on indigenization known to the government through memos from both the Lagos and London offices of the West Africa Committee, an influential lobbying group representing the interests of British capital.[85] The predominantly foreign-based textile manufacturers in Nigeria also made their views known (although they did not make a formal representation to the Adeosun Commission).[86] Among the individual companies submitting memoranda to the Adeosun panel, banks, accountants, and the large trading houses predominated. The banks argued against state acquisition of a majority of their shares, while the trading houses lobbied most strenuously

[82] Ibid., p. 5.
[83] Ibid., p. 7.
[84] Ibid.
[85] The West Africa Committee denies that it ever made any representations to the Adeosun Commission, but both its Lagos and London offices are listed in the first appendix to "Report of the Industrial Enterprises Panel" as having been among the associations, organizations, and companies that submitted memoranda.
[86] Collins 1983: 416. Collins suggests they were "represented by a well-organized manufacturers association" which might well have made statements to the federal military government after the White Paper was released.

against the proposals that would restrict the distribution of made-in-Nigeria goods to indigenous companies.[87]

In addition to lobbying for changes in the proposals being considered, foreign capital also resorted to explicit warnings and threats of possible disinvestment. The Manufacturers Association expressed its concern about the increased uncertainty for the future, while a number of firms delayed their decisions to invest in Nigeria.[88] Two American companies dramatically announced their intention to withdraw from Nigeria even before the final decree was promulgated. The White Paper made it clear that the revised decree would contain provisions for the acquisition of 60 percent of the shares in many activities, and when the state announced its intention to acquire 60 percent of the banks a few days later, Citibank pulled out of the country.[89] IBM made a similar decision that same year (although it retained close ties with distributors still active in Nigeria). For the most part, explicit threats and disinvestment decisions were the exception, rather than the rule, for foreign capital. Although some delayed new investment decisions, most companies chose to lobby through the limited channels at their disposal and waited to see the final decree before deciding ultimately what to do.

What, then, were the principal objectives of foreign capital with regard to the proposed revisions of the indigenization program? In the first instance, it wanted to block the most radical provisions of the decree, particularly the indigenous acquisition of a majority of the shares in so many sectors of the Nigerian economy. American multinationals in particular were concerned about this aspect of the revision of the first decree. Their European counterparts worried more about the personnel indigenization discussed in the Adeosun Commission report and considered in the White Paper. Many feared that the state was interested in managerial control of enterprises and planned to use the equity requirements and expatriate quotas for this end.[90]

[87] They warned not only about supply and price disruptions, but also identified other problems that might develop. For example, they argued that textile manufacturers relied on the marketing information supplied by the large trading companies to know what designs to produce for the Nigerian market. See Nigerian Institute of Management 1976: 13.

[88] This is especially true of a number of large American firms contemplating their first major investments in Africa outside of South Africa.

[89] This was a decision Citibank came to regret, as evidenced by its unsuccessful attempts to reenter the Nigerian financial market in 1981 and 1982.

[90] This concern was expressed explicitly in interviews conducted with British, German, Dutch, and Israeli multinational executives.

Second, once it became clear that it would be difficult to affect the equity levels, foreign capital wanted clear definitions of the schedules, flexibility in implementation, and allowances for companies operating in more than one schedule. Manufacturers wanted to retain their retail outlets, large trading firms wanted to continue the distribution of locally obtained as well as imported goods, and they both wanted to avoid having all of their activities automatically classified in the lowest-numbered schedule in which they operated.

Third, a number of firms wanted specific exemptions from the provisions of the revised decree. The largest trading companies wanted special treatment, as did companies engaged in joint ventures with state corporations. Fourth and finally, just as it had when the first decree was being written, foreign capital wanted assurances that it would be fully and fairly compensated and that there would be no further extensions of the indigenization program in the foreseeable future.

THE SCOPE OF THE 1977 DECREE

Even though it was initiated by the state, the second decree contained some of the provisions and clarifications sought by local and foreign capital. As in the case of the first decree, policymaking was a political process, a process in which the representations by industry associations and business groups played an important role. In its final form, the second decree closely resembles the first decree in its language, form, and structure. On closer examination, however, there are some very important differences that indicate how much more radical and sweeping a document the second decree really was in its final form.

It began by giving the Nigerian Enterprises Promotion Board (the NEPB) general power "to advance and promote enterprises in which citizens of Nigeria shall participate fully and play a dominant role."[91] This was the same language used in the first decree, but it was stated with more conviction this time around. For in addition to calling for a dominant position of Nigerian entrepreneurs at the enterprise level,

[91] Nigerian Enterprises Promotion Decree 1977 (NEPD 1977), *Supplement to Official Gazette*, no. 2, vol. 64, 13 January 1977, Part A, sect. 1.(2). Until the publication of the second indigenization decree, all of the relevant documents (the Adeosun Commission report, the memoranda submitted to the commission, and the government White Paper) used roman numerals when describing the schedules of the decree. In the published form, arabic numerals were used to denote the three schedules. In the textual references that follow, I will use the notation employed by the published (and unpublished) documents.

the second decree also conferred upon the NEPB powers to advise the Commissioner of Industries "on measures that would assist in ensuring the assumption of the control of the Nigerian economy by Nigerians in the shortest possible time."[92] Thus, among the stated objectives of the second decree was the assumption of indigenous control of enterprises, of sectors, and even of the national economy.

In terms of its general scope, the most significant feature of the second decree was its extension to affect all enterprises operating in Nigeria.[93] Unlike the first decree, which contained no third schedule and had little or no direct effect on most of the largest European and North American multinationals, this time every foreign company would be forced into a joint venture with local capital or the state. Schedule 1, containing areas reserved entirely for Nigerians, was expanded from twenty-two industries in the original version of the first decree to forty in the second. Schedule 2 was similarly expanded (from thirty-three to fifty-seven industries), and the minimum equity to be acquired by Nigerians was raised to 60 percent. A third schedule was also added, which affected all other foreign enterprises and required them to make a minimum of 40 percent of their equity available to local subscribers.

The classification of industries into schedules was nearly identical to the designations published the year before in the government's White Paper. In its final form, Schedule 1 consisted primarily of service-sector, commercial, and small-scale (low-technology) manufacturing establishments. The controversial sector covering distribution of petroleum goods was transferred from Schedule 2 to Schedule 1, as were department stores with an annual turnover of under 2 million naira, estate agencies, poultry farming, and travel agencies. A number of service-sector activities previously unaffected by indigenization were added to the first schedule, including repair shops, a number of distribution and spare-parts agencies, film distribution, office cleaning, and security services. Of greatest significance for foreign companies were the addition of manufacturers' representatives and the wholesale distribution of locally manufactured goods to the list of Schedule 1 firms.

The most significant changes contained in the second decree involved Schedule 2. Not only was it nearly doubled in size (from thirty-three industries to fifty-seven), but the equity levels for com-

[92] Ibid., sect. 1.(2)(b).
[93] The only exception to this was the case of one-time ventures (or single, nonrenewable contracts) with no intention of incorporating in Nigeria, usually involving consultancy arrangements with the federal military government.

pliance were also raised to 60 percent. This was of particular concern for the vast majority of the multinationals that were virtually unaffected by the first decree, many of which now faced the prospect of losing a majority of their equity. In general terms, Schedule 2 contained more complex, higher-technology, and larger-scale firms than Schedule 1. Many intermediate-technology, large-scale manufacturers were assigned to this schedule, as were nearly all financial-service enterprises.

The most significant additions to Schedule 2 were the banking and insurance industries. Both had been exempted from the first decree and now faced the prospect of going into a minority equity position.[94] Also added to the new Schedule 2 were industries designed to give the Nigerian state control of "the commanding heights of the economy." Thus, iron and steel, mining and quarrying, petrochemicals, plastics, rubber, and fertilizer production were added to the list of basic industries that the state had previously reserved for itself (and for a small number of enterprising indigenous businessmen). A large number of food-related industries were added to Schedule 2, as were business services (both areas in which local capital would begin playing an important role). Large department stores and the wholesale distribution of imported goods were also assigned to Schedule 2, a move that essentially maintained the position of the large trading companies in the economy.

Schedule 3 contained the higher-technology manufacturing activities (chemicals, synthetics, pharmaceuticals, machinery, communications equipment, and vehicles), the oil-servicing sector, data processing, and hotels. Textile manufacturing, although usually not identified as high-technology manufacturing, was also assigned to Schedule 3. A total of thirty-eight industries were included in the third schedule, as were "all other enterprises not included in Schedule 1 or 2 not being public sector enterprises."[95]

The only exceptions to the classifications described above were contained in Article 7 of the second decree. Article 7 overrode the classifications of specific industries into Schedules 1 through 3 and ostensibly assigned any enterprise or holding company with an annual

---

[94] Both sectors had previously experienced some indigenization, subject as they were to special sectoral decrees and scrutiny. As already discussed, the state acquired 40 percent of the shares of the three largest commercial banks in 1971. This was the first time, however, that the entire banking sector faced a mandatory sale of the shares. In the case of insurance, the second decree simply reaffirmed the decisions taken in the 1976 insurance decree.

[95] NEPD 1977, sect. 6, p. A-33.

turnover of over 25 million naira and operating in ten or more states in Nigeria to Schedule 2. Thus, the article allowed the largest holding companies in Nigeria, specifically the United Africa Company, to continue their unified corporate activities, including their Schedule 1 activities. Article 7 could not apply to any enterprises not already established in Nigeria by the end of June 1977, and hence it became known as "the UAC article."

In addition to extending indigenization to every foreign enterprise operating in Nigeria, the second decree also set out to correct some of the more obvious defects of the first decree. In particular, it contained provisions that forbade fronting, eliminated private transfers of shares, and forced a more equitable allocation of shares. The first decree had also declared fronting illegal, and the language used in the second was nearly identical. It might have had more force this time, however, coming as it did in the wake of the allegations in the press (and the evidence in the Adeosun Commission's report) of widespread fronting associated with the first decree.

More significant, however, were the provisions in Article 9 that prohibited the sale or transfer of enterprises without the approval of either the NEPB or the Capital Issues Commission, or in some cases both. The NEPB was given the authority to approve "the terms and other conditions of and pertaining to the sale or transfer" of all private companies, while the CIC was principally responsible for the price at which shares could be sold, the timing of the sale, the manner of selection of buyers, and the allotment of shares for public companies.[96] Thus, the NEPB and the CIC were far more involved in share pricing and allocation. Nominal transfers of shares and other informal changes in ownership (e.g., transfers of shares without any payment) were made much more difficult.

More controversial were the provisions designed to ensure a more equitable allocation of shares in both public and private companies. Both the NEPB and the CIC were given the following general guidelines in Article 11 of the second decree: "Ownership of the enterprises affected should be as widespread as the circumstances of each case would justify and deliberate efforts must be made to prevent the concentration of ownership in a few hands."[97] Accordingly, except in the case of owner-managers, no enterprise could be sold to a single individual, and no owner-manager could acquire more than a single enterprise. When allocating shares, the NEPB and CIC were instructed

[96] Ibid., sects. 9.(1) and 9.(2).
[97] Ibid., sect. 11.(1)(a).

by the decree to ensure that no individual acquired more than 5 percent (or 50,000 naira worth, whichever was higher) of the shares offered. The 5 percent was not limited to the acquisition of new shares offered; an individual holding 5 percent of the existing equity would also not be allowed to acquire any additional shares.

To make sure that more Nigerians benefited from indigenization, the decree also stipulated that 10 percent of the total equity shares of any Schedule 2 or 3 enterprise be reserved for the employees of that enterprise. As a populist move designed for the urban working class, at least half of the amount set aside was to be reserved for the non-managerial staff.

To enforce all of these measures, the NEPB was given more authority. It retained the power to call witnesses to hearings, and its inspectors retained the right of access to the premises of affected enterprises, access to their internal accounts, and the right to demand information. Its power to seal up, take over, and distribute the proceeds of defaulting enterprises was reaffirmed in the second decree (though it had more force in the aftermath of the coup, the new military government's decisive anticorruption campaign, and the report of the Adeosun Commission). Its new authority included the power to conduct prosecutions of offenses committed under the decree, as well as its considerably expanded role in the determination of the value of shares sold, their allocation, and the timing of their sale.[98]

CONCLUSIONS

Like the first decree, the second was the outgrowth of a political process. Accordingly, the interests, objectives, and positions of different factions within the state, local capital and foreign capital can all be found in the final text of the decree. This time, however, the state figured much more prominently in the process. The decree it initiated mirrored the debates (and compromises) underway between economic nationalists and limited interventionists within the state far more than it resembled the kind of collaboration between the state and local capital that produced the first decree. Both local and foreign capital had far less access to the state while the decree was being formulated and were forced to compromise, react, and try to contain some of the more radical proposals under consideration by the state.

On the surface, this characterization of the sources of the second decree sounds very much like a liberal-internationalist or structuralist

[98] *Ibid.*, sect. 9.

interpretation, but it is different in at least two important respects. First, the state is disaggregated into ideological factions in this account, rather than considered as a unitary actor. Second, the decree is described as primarily the outgrowth of the struggle between these two conceptual factions (modified by some effective lobbying), rather than the product of some rationally motivated actor trying to maximize its bargaining power or some other developmental objectives. The implications of this conceptualization will be developed further in Chapter 7.

When it comes to evaluating the degree to which the principal actors attained their central objectives, this time the state was relatively successful. First, the review process and resulting decree accorded the new military regime legitimacy. Although there were complaints about the speed with which it produced a revision of the much flawed first decree, the military government acted swiftly by appointing the Adeosun panel only a few months after it came to power, and it did, after all, have to contend with the assassination of its head of state in February of 1976. The White Paper, issued in June of that year, kept the issue on the public agenda. Hence, the state gave the appearance of acting decisively, though not impetuously, on the issue for an extended period of time.

Second, the state managed to ensure that the benefits of the revised decree would be better distributed. The enhanced role for both the NEPB and the CIC effectively eliminated the nominal transfers of shares associated with the first decree and gave the state a direct hand in the regional distribution of shares. Similarly, the allocation guidelines (including the 5 percent rule and the reservation of shares for employees) ensured that the same small number of Lagos-based individuals could not benefit as they had in the past.

The economic nationalists within the state were successful in having the indigenization program extended to apply to all enterprises. The requirement that 60 percent of the shares of Schedule 2 enterprises be obtained by Nigerians also went a long way toward their objective of indigenous managerial control of the vast majority of firms doing business in the country. The second decree did not stipulate the number of Nigerians who had to be in managerial positions on the boards of indigenized firms, but that was only a temporary setback for economic nationalists, since management guidelines were issued by the NEPB in 1980. The biggest loss for economic nationalists was an administrative one. They were unable to have the NEPB separated from the Ministry of Industries and made accountable directly to the Cabinet Office. They had wanted to have the new board upgraded and made responsible for new business development as "the government's major holding company."

Finally, the state wanted to resume its leadership role in the direction of national development, a role first outlined by the authors of the Second National Development Plan and now eagerly adopted by the inheritors of the state apparatus. The assignment of banking and financial activities to Schedule 2, with the accompanying announcement in July of 1976 that the state would acquire the mandated 60 percent of the major banks, was an important step in its drive to assume leadership of the direction of national development. The addition of most basic manufacturing activities to the second schedule also furthered this objective.

Since it was largely removed from the policymaking process, local capital gave its reactions to proposals and compromised where necessary. It certainly did not control the state apparatus when it came to formulating the second decree, and it was unsuccessful in its attempts to contain the economic nationalists within the state. Its proposals for retaining a minority position in Schedule 2 enterprises went unheeded, as did its opposition to the pursuit of managerial control of enterprises in general, and to further personnel indigenization in particular.

Local capital was even more unsuccessful in its attempt to minimize (or reduce) state intervention in the economy. It accurately saw the second decree as a move by the public sector on the private sector, but could do little to prevent the state from acquiring the banks, major manufacturing firms, and mining ventures (in addition to its holdings in the dominant petroleum sector). Flush with its mushrooming revenues from petroleum, the state saw little reason to relinquish its position in (or its growing power over) the economy.

Although they worried that an extension of the indigenization program might scare off future foreign investors, indigenous businessmen did manage to maintain their access to foreign capital. The creation of Schedule 3 forced all multinationals into joint-venture relationships with local capital or the state and cemented the former's growing relationship with foreign firms in many higher-technology areas. Local capital was successful in its bid to increase its representation on the NEPB, the CIC and the state committees, and it also achieved some of the reclassifications it had been seeking (from Schedule 2 to Schedule 1).

Perhaps the biggest accomplishment of local capital was to keep the compliance and allocation rules set down in the second decree from being applied retroactively. In its final form, the second decree stipulated that the NEPB and CIC would be involved in the approval of prices, shares, selection of buyers, and timing of sales only for those sales taking place "as from the commencement of this Decree" (29 June 1976).[99] Despite its displeasure with the regional and national inequalities occasioned by the first decree, the state was not about to risk the disruption to the economy (nor the burden of determining a fair allocation of shares) that would be produced by reopening the certified cases of compliance with the first decree. It was content to be identified with having set things right for the future.

Foreign capital had the least influence on the writing of the second decree and probably lost the most as a result. This time around, the decree was not targeted on the weakest segment of foreign capital (the Lebanese), and most foreign companies found themselves faced with the prospect of having to sell a majority of their equity to Nigerians. There were relatively few wholly owned multinational subsidiaries operating in Nigeria in the mid 1970s (or anywhere else in the world, for that matter), so the idea of joint ventures was not new or entirely abhorrent to most multinationals. What they disliked the most was the prospect of losing control over the selection of joint-venture partners, the timing of the sale of their shares, and the price at which their shares were sold. Foreign companies operating in Schedule 3 faced the same loss of control (and probably short-term revenues), although they did not have to contend with a loss of the majority of their equity.

Another source of dissatisfaction for foreign capital stemmed from its inability to obtain either clear definitions of the activities assigned to different schedules or the NEPB's operating procedures on these matters. This was particularly a problem for the vast majority of multinationals operating in more than one (often all three) of the schedules of the second decree. As we will see in the next chapter, the uncertainty produced by the ambiguities in the decree was more of a problem for them than the terms of the decree itself.

The only tangible accomplishments of foreign capital were obtained by the UAC and a few other trading companies affected by Article 7 of the second decree. They, however, were the exception. From the perspective of most multinational corporations, the only good thing about the second decree was the fact that the state did not act on the recommendation of the Adeosun panel that would have required

[99] NEPD 1977, Decree Number 3, reprinted from *Supplement to Official Gazette*, no. 2, vol. 64, 13 January 1977, Part A, par. 9, p. A-22.

all companies above a certain size to become public companies listed on the stock exchange.

Unlike the first decree, the second decree had clear winners and losers. In many ways, the decree was a move on the part of the public sector on areas occupied by the private sector in the Nigerian economy. As such, the state was the major winner, and foreign capital was the major loser. Local capital compromised where it could to maintain its position, but did not join in the public enthusiasm for the economic nationalism directed against the multinationals. The principal response of both foreign and local capital to the second decree came not in its formulation but in its implementation. As we shall see in Chapter 5, foreign capital teamed up with local capital to defeat the economic-nationalist faction within the state whose views predominated in the writing of the second decree.

CHAPTER FIVE

Maintaining Control:
Multinational Responses to the Second Decree

AT the outset, reactions to the second decree appear to have been very similar to reactions to the first. The measure was once again broadly popular with the Nigerian public and attracted the explicit enmity of the multinational corporations. The multinationals were more numerous and more concerned than they had been after the first decree, since this time every foreign enterprise was forced to sell a major portion (or a majority) of its equity to Nigerian subscribers. Indigenous businessmen made supportive comments about the process, but tended to avoid making specific statements about the revised program. Their reticence in speaking out in favor of the second decree had important implications for its consequences at the level of the individual firm.

Although they were caught off guard by the timing and scope of the second decree, foreign companies wasted little time developing countervailing measures designed to neutralize or minimize its effects. While the newly reformulated NEPB and the rejuvenated CIC were sorting out their jurisdictional differences and devising procedures for the implementation of an unusually vague decree, multinational corporations found ways to create joint ventures with indigenous businessmen which provided the latter with an important source of accumulation, while at the same time having little immediate effect on either control or operations at the enterprise level.

The companies affected by the decree were assigned deadlines for compliance with its provisions, depending on their size and sector of operation. Banks were singled out for special attention two days after the White Paper was released in 1976 and informed that they would have until September of that year to sell 60 percent of their equity to the federal government. The big trading companies affected by Article 7 of the decree (which applied to companies with an annual turnover in excess of 25 million naira [$38.4 million] operating in at least ten states) were given only until the end of June 1977 to comply. The rest of the alien enterprises had until the end of 1978.

Only 14 companies qualified for the Article 7 exemption, and they each offered for sale or subscription 60 percent of their equity by the 30 June deadline.[1] This accounted for the transfer of 79.5 million shares to indigenous subscribers, worth 55.3 million naira (approximately $85 million). An additional 835 companies were valued by the Capital Issues Commission and given until the end of the following year to transfer their 40 or 60 percent to Nigerian subscribers. Thus, by the end of 1978, an additional 443.9 million shares had been traded, valued at 343 million naira (approximately $530 million), bringing the total of shares traded to 523.4 million, worth 398.3 million naira (or just over $615 million) by the initial deadline for compliance.[2]

The implementation of the second decree did not end in 1978. For reasons that will be discussed more fully below, not all of the companies expected to comply with the new decree had managed to meet its provisions by the end of that year. Eighty companies failed to submit applications for compliance on time, and new companies were still being incorporated in the country after 1978. By the end of 1979, the CIC had valued a total of 958 companies worth 477.6 million naira (or $852 million). Two years later, at the end of 1981, the total had reached 1,078 companies, whose shares transferred to Nigerians had been valued at 551.2 million naira (or $865 million). Table 5.1 summarizes the number of companies affected, the total number of shares exchanged, and the value of the shares traded.

The second decree did not affect many more enterprises than the

TABLE 5.1
The Scope of the Second Decree

	Dec. 1978	Dec. 1979	Dec. 1981
No. of enterprises complying	849	958	1,078
No. of shares traded	523.4m	631.6m	787.0m
Value of shares traded (in naira)	398.3m	477.6m	551.2m

SOURCES: *Report of the Securities and Exchange Commission, 1977–1979*, and a paper presented by its acting executive director to the NEPB, 9 August 1982.

[1] They were John Holt (Nig.) Ltd., Leventis Motors Ltd., Leventis Technical Ltd., Leventis Stores Ltd., R. T. Briscoe (Nig.) Ltd., SCOA (Nig.) Ltd., CFAO (Nig.) Ltd., Bewac Ltd., Bata (Nig.) Ltd., K. Chellerams, Bhojsons Ltd., UAC, UTC, and PZ.

[2] *Report of the Securities and Exchange Commission 1977–1979* (Lagos: CBN Press, 1980), p. 10.

first. By the end of 1979, 1,106 companies had been affected by the second decree (958 had received provisional compliance, 80 still had applications pending, and the NEPB had allowed 68 companies to undergo liquidation).[3] The number of enterprises affected by the first decree at a comparable date (mid 1975) was 952. However, since the enterprises affected by the second decree were on average so much larger, and since the ratio of compliance with the second decree was higher (92 percent of the firms affected had complied within a year of the deadline, as opposed to only 78 percent with the first decree), the total value of the shares traded was nearly five times as much (551.2m naira versus 122m).

The overwhelming majority of the enterprises affected by the second decree were located in Schedule 2. According to the NEPB's annual report for 1981, 68.8 percent of the affected alien enterprises were to be found there, while 25.8 percent were in Schedule 3, and only 5.3 percent were in Schedule 1.[4] Thus, although a total of eighteen new industries were added to the first schedule, it is clear they did not contain many enterprises. Most of the 100 percent indigenization had apparently been accomplished under the first decree.

Of the 1,078 enterprises valued by the CIC by the beginning of 1982, 916 were private and 162 were public companies. Although smaller in number, public companies tended to be larger on average and accounted for about two-thirds of the shares offered for sale or subscription.[5] Contrary to early estimates of the relative number of shares offered for sale,[6] out of the 551.2 million naira ($865 million) that had been raised to acquire foreign enterprises by the beginning of 1982, only 138.1 million (or 25 percent) had been applied to offers for sale, while the remainder had been taken up by offers for subscription.[7]

IMPLEMENTING THE SECOND DECREE

As in the case of the first decree, the Nigerian Enterprises Promotion Board was assigned central responsibility for the implementation of the second decree. However, this time the Capital Issues Commission

[3] Ibid.

[4] Nigerian Enterprises Promotion Board, *1981 Annual Report*, Lagos, 1 May 1981, app. VII, p. 85.

[5] Akamiokhor 1982: 7. G. A. Akamiokhor was acting director of the Nigerian Securities and Exchange Commission.

[6] Balabkins 1982: 236–237 estimated that two-thirds of the shares acquired had come from offers for sale.

[7] Akamiokhor 1982: 7.

played a much more prominent role, especially from the perspective of the multinationals. The CIC was responsible for the valuation of all companies affected by the decree, not just those that had chosen (or been forced) to go public, as under the first decree. In addition, a number of ancillary measures, rulings, and procedures of the federal military government had significant implications for the implementation of the second decree.

The Powers, Performance, and Procedures of the NEPB

The language used to describe the powers and responsibilities of the NEPB in the text of the second decree was very nearly identical to that used in the first decree. Both decrees gave the board power to obtain information, inspect enterprises, and to take over, sell, or otherwise dispose of enterprises still operating without transferring the requisite equity to Nigerian subscribers by the assigned compliance date. The major administrative difference in the second decree was the upgrading of the chairmanship of the board from being just another of the many responsibilities of the permanent secretary of the Ministry of Industries to being a full-time executive director appointed from outside the public service. The only substantive increase in the NEPB's power was according it authority to seal up and seize any goods of enterprises in which it detected fronting. (In the first decree, explicit cases of fronting only carried a penalty.)

The principal functions of the NEPB were to assign all alien enterprises to Schedule 1, 2, or 3, decide whether (and when) a private company should go public, monitor the allotment of the shares from private company sales, and inspect companies for compliance. The NEPB was also given (or in some cases assumed) sweeping discretionary power to determine what to do when the 10 percent reserved for employees was not fully subscribed.[8] The CIC, discussed more fully below, was principally responsible for the valuation of the shares of all companies sold to Nigerians, and for the allotment of the shares from the sale or transfer of public companies.

It was widely thought that the NEPB had been upgraded and revitalized for the implementation of the second decree,[9] and it was given both increased staff and funding after 1977. After the decree was promulgated, the NEPB hired an additional 134 employees, 82 of whom were new inspectors of operations.[10] There had been a total of

---

[8] For a good discussion of its discretionary authority, see Ejiofor 1980.
[9] Chikelu 1976: 24.
[10] Balabkins 1982: 208–209.

176 employees when the first decree was being implemented (in the 1973/74 fiscal year), and that number had been increased to 369 in the 1977/78 fiscal year.[11] The total budget for the NEPB increased more than twofold between the 1976/77 and 1977/78 fiscal years, from just 400,590 naira (about $635,000) to 862,040 naira (about $1.3 million).[12] NEPB staff members continued to complain about inadequate staff and financing by the government,[13] but the injections of both after 1977 demonstrated the seriousness with which the government took the implementation of the program.

The appointment of Malam Ali Al-Hakim as the NEPB's first full-time executive director further underscored the government's seriousness about the exercise. Al-Hakim was an economist, formerly associated with Ahmadu Bello University in Zaria, and he pursued the implementation of the second decree vigorously. Al-Hakim had previously led a very thorough investigation of Kano state companies (and the Kano State Investment Corporation [KSIC] in particular) after Gowon was deposed in 1975. Thus, he had first-hand experience both with the consequences of the first decree and with the problems of mismanagement and corruption in state corporations. In his NEPB post he quickly established a reputation for being a "hard bargainer" and someone "difficult to obtain access to."[14] He was described by a friend as very committed to indigenization, and as someone who worked very hard developing guidelines for its implementation.[15] He believed strongly in the 5 percent limitation on individual shareholding, and he saw to it that it was strictly enforced.[16] Al-Hakim oversaw the major part of the implementation of the second decree and stayed with the NEPB as its executive director through March of 1979.

The seriousness of the NEPB was apparent to the multinationals seeking to comply with the provisions of the second decree, and it appeared in stark contrast to the impression of the board developed during the implementation of the first decree. Among the multinationals interviewed in the course of this research (and identified in Appendix A), the overwhelming majority (75 percent of those addressing this issue) described the NEPB as "very serious," "quite effective," "impressive," or "nothing to fool around with." Only those enterprises with very little physical plant in Nigeria (like bankers' representatives,

[11] Ibid., p. 208.
[12] Ibid.
[13] Interview with NEPB official.
[14] Interview with foreign embassy official, 1977.
[15] Interview with prominent state official.
[16] Interview with NEPB official.

Japanese importing firms, and small Italian construction companies) tended to minimize the effectiveness of the implementation. Hoogvelt reports similar findings based on her interviews with industrial companies in Kano, many of whom "felt harassed by the officials and methods of the NEPB."[17]

Despite its seriousness of purpose and the initial impressions it conveyed, the NEPB still confronted significant infrastructural difficulties. It had to get information out to prospective indigenous buyers, process information on nearly a thousand companies immediately affected by indigenization, and continuously monitor compliances throughout the country. One American multinational manager described a product life cycle of Nigerian government regulations which, as we shall see in this chapter, applies well to the implementation of the second decree. "At first everyone talks seriously, they (the regulations) are implemented. Then people wait and see. Follow-up slows, regulations are casually enforced. Eventually they are all but ignored, except when some political opportunity presents itself."[18] Nevertheless, most companies were forced to sell or transfer their shares within two years of the decree's announcement in 1977 and experienced the most serious phase of the regulatory cycle. In the end, there is little question that the NEPB as upgraded for the implementation of the second decree was more capable than its predecessor.

Although many of the NEPB's rulings and procedural decisions had an impact on the implementation of the second decree, four stand out as having been the most significant for an assessment of the decree's consequences. First, it actively tried to get large multinational companies to go public and list their shares on the Nigerian Stock Exchange.[19] By the end of 1979, 112 companies (or roughly 10 percent of the total number affected) had been directed to go public. Of that number, only sixty-four managed to satisfy the stock exchange's standards for qualification and be listed.[20] The decision about who would be told to go public was made largely on the basis of size of

[17] Hoogvelt 1979: 56–68.

[18] Interview with American MNC executive. This kind of thinking about effective enforcement of Nigerian governmental regulations is very similar to that of a senior member of the Adeosun panel when describing the probability that its recommendations would be acted on.

[19] The Nigerian Stock Exchange (NSE) was formed on 2 December 1977 when the Lagos Stock Exchange merged with new branches opened in Kaduna and Port Harcourt.

[20] They included the largest companies in Nigeria operating in all sectors (commerce, manufacturing, construction, services, and primary extraction).

companies involved (i.e. all companies with greater than a million shares being offered for sale or subscription at 50 kobo per share).[21] The NEPB was carrying out the recommendation made originally in the Adeosun report that more companies go public to allow a larger number of Nigerians to participate in the indigenization exercise.

Second, in an attempt to ensure that wider participation be obtained, the board tried to give advance notice of pending sales of shares, recommended that shortened prospectuses be prepared for potential purchasers, and required that application forms be dispersed throughout the country by the state committees before the application dates.[22] The 5 percent limit was strictly enforced, and the NEPB gave preference in its allotment of the shares of privately traded companies to small shareholders applying to buy into companies for the first time. It was also concerned about the regional distribution of shares, kept track of the state of origin of prospective buyers, and refused applications on the basis of state of origin if individuals from that state were already overrepresented. However, the NEPB did not apply the 5 percent limitation and other allocation rules to new foreign enterprises choosing to incorporate in Nigeria after February of 1977. All other aspects of indigenization applied to them (assignment to Schedule 1, 2, or 3 and mandatory sale of their equity to local subscribers), but the board applied the 5 percent limit only to those firms already located in Nigeria at the time of the second decree.

Third, in May of 1980, the NEPB announced that in addition to all of the other documents required for certification of compliance with the second decree (e.g. evidence of the transfer of shares, evidence of payment for the purchase of shares, copies of a company's business permit, expatriate quota, and tax clearance), companies should also submit copies of any approved or proposed management, technical, or consultancy agreement and copies of company articles of association (including amendments made since the promulgation of the second decree).[23] Its requests for this additional information were understandable, given the use of management and technical agreements to maintain expatriate control of affected enterprises after the first decree and given the dramatic increase in applications for foreign exchange clearance for management and technical fees (and increase in the number of firms rewriting their articles of association) after the second decree. However, requesting the information did not mean

---

[21] *Report of the Securities and Exchange Commission, 1977–1979*: 9–10.

[22] Balabkins 1982: 235–236.

[23] NEPB press statement, printed in full in *West Africa*, no. 3,284, 30 June 1980, pp. 1,200–1,201.

that it would be scrutinized very carefully or used to deny compliance of any foreign firm with the decree's provisions. By late in 1982, the NEPB had not refused a certificate of compliance to any foreign enterprise on the basis of its management agreements or changed articles of association.[24] It required copies of the new agreements, but apparently did not use them for anything.

Fourth and finally, in the same announcement in which it requested copies of management agreements and articles of association, the NEPB requested a list of reconstituted boards of directors "to reflect the new alien/indigenous equity participation."[25] More specifically, "For a Schedule 2 (two) enterprise at least two of the Nigerian directors must be executive, while for a Schedule 3 (three) enterprise at least one of the Nigerian directors must be executive."[26] This new requirement came out of a review of the role of expatriates in the economy undertaken by the Ministry of Internal Affairs and was widely viewed as the first explicit measure designed to ensure that Nigerian participation in management was more real than cosmetic.[27] In 1982, the NEPB made a request to the government that there be an amendment to the decree (or some more explicit guidelines articulated) which would follow up on this initiative and ensure that greater Nigerian managerial control of indigenized enterprises be obtained.[28] The board was looking for assurances (or rejuvenated legitimacy) from the civilian government before it proceeded to pursue effective indigenous managerial control of enterprises any further (even though that objective was implied in the definition of its power in the introductory paragraph of the second decree). The Shagari government never acted on the board's request.

The CIC, the Allotment Committee, and the Valuation Controversy Revisited

The Capital Issues Commission was more active with the second decree than it had been with the first. This time, it was responsible for the valuation of all enterprises affected by the program, not just the relatively small number that chose to go public. It was also given the responsibility of allocating the shares of all public companies in the country. Although public companies were relatively few in number, they were on average much larger and had many more shares to allo-

---

[24] Interview with NEPB official.
[25] NEPB press statement, p. 1,201.
[26] Ibid.
[27] Interview with official of an indigenous business association.
[28] Interview with NEPB official.

cate than the private companies handled by the NEPB. Accordingly, the CIC was responsible for the allotment of nearly 78 percent of the total shares offered for sale or subscription by the end of 1979.[29] It was obviously very busy during 1977 and 1978 and grossly understaffed for the valuation of nearly a thousand enterprises and the distribution of nearly 490 million shares.[30]

Throughout the critical implementation period for the second decree (from January 1977 through December 1978), the CIC was not autonomous, but functioned as a department of the Central Bank of Nigeria. It was not separate until the Securities and Exchange Commission Act of 27 September 1979 dissolved the Capital Issues Commission and created the Nigerian Securities and Exchange Commission (NSEC) modelled after the U.S. Securities and Exchange Commission. The fact that it remained under the control of the Central Bank did not inhibit the effectiveness of the CIC in any way, but rather gave it considerable human and financial resources to draw on for its valuation and allotment activities. The Central Bank during this period was generally viewed as "one of the best-run government institutions in Nigeria."[31]

The CIC worked closely with the NEPB in developing implementation procedures, and the two occasionally collaborated in directing companies to go public. The CIC's role would be to threaten a company with a lower valuation (discussed more fully below) if it refused to be listed on the Nigerian Stock Exchange. Like the NEPB, the CIC also favored offers for subscription of new shares, rather than offers for sale of existing shares. If a company had an expansion program underway, had a poor liquidity position, or had historically depended heavily on Nigerian bank facilities for raising capital, the CIC usually directed it to offer shares for subscription.[32] Most companies preferred to sell the requisite portion of their existing equity, but the government was concerned about foreign exchange loss if the offers were unregulated and therefore favored offers for subscription.

Because it was responsible for the allotment of so many shares, the CIC formed an allotment committee made up of its own representatives and representatives of the NEPB, the Nigerian Stock Exchange, and the issuing houses. The need for guidelines on the allotment of shares arose initially during the first phase of implementation, when

[29] *Report of the Securities and Exchange Commission, 1977–1979*, app. vi, p. 25.
[30] Ibid., p. 5.
[31] Interview with MNC banking executive.
[32] *Report of the Securities and Exchange Commission, 1977–1979*, p. 6.

the fourteen large companies affected by Article 7 of the decree were selling their 79 million shares.[33]

Since the allocation of shares was not spelled out specifically in the decree, the Allotment Committee was given considerable discretion in the development of allocation guidelines. It developed procedures that would ensure that shares were widely distributed and began by requiring companies to print at least one prospectus for every hundred shares offered. The committee "adhered strictly to the provisions of the Decree which stipulated 50,000 naira or 5% of the equity of the enterprise, which ever was higher, as the maximum allotment meant for any individual under the Decree."[34] Accordingly, it gave preferential treatment to applications for shares from small investors.[35] Multiple applications were cancelled, and, as one of the committee's members described its proceedings,

> Nearly everyone received some shares, but usually only a percentage of the amount they applied for. If someone applied for 100 shares, he might get 90 percent and receive 90 shares. An applicant for a larger number of shares would get a lower percentage (for example, an applicant for 500 shares might have only 60 percent approved and be limited to 300 shares). This was all done in the name of equitable distribution—the larger the application, the lower the percentage allotted.[36]

The regional distribution of shares by state was an equally—perhaps even more—important criterion for allotment of shares by the committee. State governments were given preferential allotment of shares available according to the following formula. For companies offering 5 million (or more) 50 kobo shares, one and a half percent of the total shares on offer were reserved for each of the nineteen state governments in the country. One percent of the shares was allotted to state governments in cases where fewer than 5 million shares were available.[37]

These guidelines did not operate without some difficulty. Some state governments did not have adequate funds to take up the percentage of shares allocated to them, and hence regional development organizations like the NNDC in the North picked up the unsub-

[33] Ibid., pp. 4, 17.
[34] Ibid., p. 13. However, in exceptional cases institutional applications for shares in excess of the 5 percent limit were approved.
[35] Akamiokhor 1982: 12.
[36] Interview with member of the CIC.
[37] Akamiokhor 1982: 10–11.

scribed shares reserved for northern governments. By some estimates, the NNDC acquired 27 million shares worth about 14 million naira in the process.[38] The extensive role of the NNDC was criticized by other regional development organizations (particularly by O'Dua, the western states' development corporation) that did not have enough money to play a comparable role for their regions. The Allotment Committee did not want to politicize (i.e. regionalize) the issue, and argued instead that since northern individuals and states were underrepresented in the acquisition of shares, the NNDC should be allowed a larger share than other regional development institutions.[39]

Although well intentioned, the Allotment Committee's procedures managed to tie up a considerable amount of indigenous capital while it was making its distributional decisions. Since it required that payment accompany applications for shares and since nearly all of the offers for sale of public companies were again oversubscribed (to be discussed more fully in the next section), the committee had to determine how much of each application to grant and how much money to return. It paid no interest on the amounts of capital tied up in the process (much to the consternation of indigenous businessmen who had borrowed the money from the banks at high interest rates), and it was slow in returning most of the money not used to buy shares.[40]

Despite these and other problems, the Allotment Committee managed to distribute the bulk of the shares of public companies according to its guidelines. In its allocation of the 79 million shares offered by the fourteen large companies affected by Article 7, the committee ensured that 43.6 million shares (or about 54.8 percent of the total) were distributed to individuals acquiring between 100 and 500 shares. Sixteen and a half million shares (or about 20.1 percent) went to state governments and their agencies, while 9.2 percent were set aside for employees of the affected companies. Thus, in the end only about 15.9 percent of the shares went to what could be described as large shareholders.[41]

By far the most controversial aspect of the Capital Issues Commission was its role in the valuation of the assets of companies required to comply with the second decree. Just as they had in the valuation controversy surrounding the first indigenization decree, multinational corporations complained that they were systematically under-

[38] Interview with former executive of the NNDC.

[39] Ibid.

[40] Akamiokhor 1982: 10.

[41] *Report of the Securities and Exchange Commission, 1977–1979*, app. II, p. 18. Large shareholders are defined as those obtaining more than 500 shares each.

TABLE 5.2

Spread of Allotment of Shares for Fourteen Companies
Affected by Article 7 of the Second Decree

	No. of shares acquired	%
Small shareholders (100 to 500 shares)	43,588,955	54.8
State governments	16,494,039	20.1
Large shareholders (over 500 shares)	12,153,342	15.3
Staff	7,298,124	9.2
Total	79,534,460	100.0

SOURCE: Computed from *Nigerian Securities and Exchange Commission Report, 1977–1979*, app. II, p. 18.

valued,[42] while the CIC maintained it was being scrupulously fair.[43] However, this time the reasons for the dispute were different.

Before it determined the value of a company's shares, the CIC asked each firm to supply it with documents, including audited annual accounts for the five years preceding the application for valuation, detailed profit and loss accounts for the same period, a brief history of the enterprise, a full description of the nature of its business and operations, a statement about its staff and management, information on any pending litigation, and a copy of its articles of association.[44] The commission examined the five-year record of accounts and earnings and accepted only audited accounts. Full disclosure was very important to the CIC, especially since it undertook no physical inspections of affected companies.[45] Companies were asked to attend valuation hearings with representatives of their issuing houses, but their

[42] Only 20 percent of the multinational firms I interviewed on this question (described in Appendix A) characterized their treatment at the hands of the CIC as fair (e.g. "We got what we asked for"). Some complained that they had received as little as one-fifth of what they had expected. Hoogvelt's respondents in Kano generally believed that the CIC undervalued shares by an average of 30 percent. For details, see Hoogvelt 1979: 58.

[43] The acting executive director of the Nigerian Securities and Exchange Commission, G. A. Akamiokhor, wrote in 1982: "In spite of complaints by both vendors of shares and market intermediaries that the Commission does under-value shares of companies, I am of the strong view that the Commission is the only disinterested party whose decision is bound to be more objective" (1982: 7).

[44] Capital Issues Commission 1977: 1.

[45] Akamiokhor 1982: 5.

presence did not always help their case. As one CIC staff member complained:

> Many conventional methods couldn't be used. Records were inconsistent or nonexistent. There were some companies with 400 to 500 percent dividends. Therefore, we couldn't use their records. . . . If management had been more forthcoming in presentations, upward valuation in their assets would have taken place.[46]

Again, however, there was more involved in the CIC valuation procedures than displeasure with foreign companies' lack of candor.

The CIC considered both the net asset value of companies and estimates of their maintainable annual profit when making its valuations. For the most part, however, it relied more heavily on maintainable annual profit than on net assets. It did so primarily because most of the companies affected by the second decree were located in Schedule 2 or 3 and therefore would have the bulk of their shares widely distributed among the Nigerian subscribers rather than concentrated in the hands of a single owner-manager (as in the case of many Schedule 1 enterprises). Thus,

> Although the net asset valuation is computed, the Commission, especially in case of public companies, operates on the principle that the value of a business as a going concern does not depend on the assets it owns but on how efficiently the assets are being utilised as measured by profits records.[47]

The commission favored the maintainable-annual-profit method of valuation because it assumed that the value of any assets to an individual investor in a minority position in the firm would be the earning capacity of the assets, rather than the assets themselves.[48]

Multinationals complained that by favoring the maintainable-annual-profit method, the CIC systematically underestimated the true value of the shares being transferred to indigenous owners. Companies reinvesting recent profits were penalized, as were companies reluctant to declare large profits in recent years because of restrictions on repatriation. Profits for a number of companies had also been understated in the mid 1970s, as other means of transferring capital out of the country (including licensing fees, overinvoicing, and tradi-

[46] Interview with former CIC staff member.
[47] CIC 1977: 4.
[48] Akamiokhor 1982: 6.

tional forms of transfer pricing) were developed and perfected.[49] (This, of course, was not an argument the multinationals were about to make on the record.)

The CIC relied more heavily on the net asset value method of valuation for some enterprises. It did so in the case of most banks, whose assets are principally cash, and in the case of many Schedule 1 private companies, "where 100% or the controlling interest is to be sold to an owner-manager or a handful of investors who from the point of sale would have full control over the assets of the company."[50] These cases were the exception, however, and represented only a small number of the total enterprises affected by the second decree.

Even when net assets were taken into consideration by the CIC, multinationals complained of a treatment that systematically underestimated their true value. Because so many companies had undertaken upward revaluations in their equity either at the time of the first indigenization decree or after they first became aware of the appointment of the Industrial Enterprises Panel in early 1976, the CIC assumed they had done so in anticipation of indigenization and in the hope that they might attract higher prices when their shares were sold.[51] "The Commission has been very sceptical of revaluations, as such revaluations neither enhance the value of the asset to the business nor in any way improve its profitability by the mere fact that the book value has been raised."[52] Hence, the CIC did not want to reward revaluations and discounted, on a graduated basis, the amount of surplus from revaluation it allowed in computing a firm's net assets.[53] This procedure further irritated multinational firms, which maintained that their revaluations had been overdue and that the CIC's discounting was both too rigid and at too high a rate.

In the end, like the first valuation controversy, the second resulted from incommensurable differences in the financial interests of those

---

[49] The CIC apparently uncovered numerous cases of overinvoicing and excessive buying commissions when it began to review the audited accounts of affected companies. The commission maintained that in many cases these practices had led to an overstatement of the cost of doing business and an understatement of profits, and hence further justified its decision to rely most heavily on the maintainable-annual-profits method of valuation (Balabkins 1982: 226).

[50] CIC 1977: 4.

[51] Akamiokhor 1982: 5.

[52] CIC 1977: 1.

[53] Ibid., p. 2. The percentage of a revaluation allowed by the CIC in the computation of a firm's net asset position was: for revaluations made in 1971, 80 percent allowed in computation of net assets; in 1972, 60 percent allowed; in 1973, 40 percent allowed; in 1974, 20 percent allowed; in 1975, 15 percent allowed; in 1976, 5 percent allowed.

selling the shares and those buying them. Multinational corporations wanted to receive as high a price as possible for the shares of companies they had built up and were now forced to sell, and they bristled at the other "political" pressures placed on them to go public or to comply with the decrees on a hurried schedule. In terms of current market value alone, many shares were undervalued and yielded windfall gains for their Nigerian purchasers. However, neither the indigenous businessmen, who wanted the shares priced as cheap as possible, nor the bureaucrats, who wanted to ensure that the Nigerian public would not be taken advantage of in the pricing of shares, had much sympathy for the multinationals. From their perspective, the valuation controversy was just a part of a bargaining process in a nonmarket situation. Their conception of a fair price has to be considered in broader historical terms. The CIC in particular was interested in remedying past wrongs (such as transfer prices) and hence its conception of a fair valuation had to go beyond narrow market terms.

Ancillary Measures and the Financing of Indigenization

No public policy exists in a vacuum, and indigenization was no exception. Its implementation and the responses of multinational corporations to the program were both affected by other policies and decrees of the Nigerian government. In part because of the history of huge dividends declared after the first decree (and in part because of foreign-exchange needs and a desire to control inflation), the federal government restricted dividend payments to 30 percent of gross earnings in 1976. The ceiling on dividend payments was gradually increased to 40 percent in 1977 and to 50 percent in 1979.[54] However, one immediate effect of these measures was to reduce the incentives for banks to provide loans for the acquisition of shares (loans which had been extremely secure for them in 1973–74, largely because of the average size of the dividends declared).[55] Another immediate consequence was that the dividend restrictions made indigenous businessmen less interested in acquiring the shares of foreign companies (given the large returns from other activities).[56]

Faced with the possibility of a potential shortage of capital and a serious undersubscription of shares on offer, the federal military government moved simultaneously on two fronts. First, it used the Central Bank's credit guidelines to direct bank loans to indigenous busi-

---

[54] In 1977 the government excluded all bonus issues made after 30 September 1976 from the payment of dividends (Odife 1977: 29).

[55] Nwankwo 1977: 527.

[56] Interview with prominent indigenous businessman.

nessmen. The credit guidelines were first introduced in 1971 and were designed to influence patterns of lending in the country. Each year the Central Bank set lending targets by sector of the economy for each class of major bank (commercial, merchant, and development) and penalized individual banks unable to meet those targets.[57] By adding certain classes of businessmen to the guidelines (i.e. mandating that a certain percentage of banks' loans go to indigenous businessmen or to businesses with an indigenous participation of a set amount), the Central Bank ensured that a shortage of bank capital would not inhibit the indigenization program. The other thing the federal government did to keep the banks active in the program was to buy out the foreign holdings of development banks like the NIDB,[58] broaden the scope of their portfolios,[59] and provide financial assistance to underwrite the shares of viable companies offered for sale to the general public.[60]

At the outset, it appeared that there would be a problem of undersubscription of shares, despite the Central Bank's credit guidelines and the other measures taken by the federal government. The sheer volume of the shares on offer was so great that there were no lines of eager buyers struggling to get their hands on a copy of a company's prospectus, as there had been at the time of the first decree.[61] Concerned that it might be left with large numbers of unsubscribed shares, the federal military government established a consortium of underwriters led by the NBCI to purchase and warehouse unbought shares for future resale to individual subscribers.

Toward the end of 1978 it appeared that the market was, indeed, becoming saturated and that the consortium would be needed. Individual members of the consortium, like the NNDC, had been acquiring shares for some time, but in the rush to complete compliance with the second decree, "the capital market in Nigeria was almost stretched to [the] breaking point."[62] In the end, however, the consortium was never activated. The allotment of undersubscribed shares was spread

[57] If an individual bank failed to meet these targets (i.e. if it were unable to direct x percent of the value of its loans to manufacturing establishments), it would be penalized and have its unexpended funds for that sector taken out and deposited with the Central Bank of Nigeria without interest (interview with MNC banking executive).

[58] The shares of the World Bank's IFC and the big three commercial banks (Standard, Barclays, and Société Générale) in the NIDB were bought out by the federal military government after the second decree (Asabia 1982: 12).

[59] Ibid., p. 13. The NIDB lowered the capital requirements for individual loans to 10,000 naira and granted 80 percent of its loans to Nigerian-managed enterprises.

[60] Ibid., p. 14.

[61] Ejiofor 1980: 38.

[62] Ibid., p. 36.

over 1979, and by the end of that year only a little over 8 million shares (or about 1.7 percent of the total public shares offered) were still unsubscribed.[63]

Because of the CIC's detailed involvement in the valuation process, the nominal transfers that accounted for most of the shares acquired during the first decree were impossible the second time. Most of the capital raised by indigenous businessmen for the acquisition of shares came from the banking system, but even the Central Bank is not sure how much was borrowed and how much was taken from savings.[64] There appear to have been no regional differences in this pattern, and many indigenous businessmen used property they had acquired after the first decree as collateral when borrowing from the banks.[65] In a few cases, loans were guaranteed by the multinational joint-venture partner, but most firms stayed away from this practice, since there were enough indigenous businessmen around to contribute capital and guaranteeing loans came precariously close to the type of fronting that was explicitly prohibited by the second decree.[66]

In addition to raising money from the banks, indigenous business-men had access to other sources of finance. Some plowed back earnings from enterprises acquired during the first decree, though usually not until after going on a major consumption binge.[67] Small businessmen interested in acquiring the assets of Schedule 1 firms occasionally raised money from village associations:

> One person collects money from many people in his local district, say 50 naira from each of 25 people, and that one invests it. It's a form of forced savings, especially for small business development. This was common, especially in the East; very, very common.[68]

Finally, some indigenous businessmen went to the vibrant informal financial sector in Lagos and other parts of the country to raise funds for the acquisition of shares. They were forced to pay interest rates well above the maximum allowed by the Central Bank in the heavily regulated formal banking sector, but these undocumented sources of

[63] Computed from apps. v and vi of *Report of the Securities and Exchange Commission, 1977–1979*: 24, 25. As will be discussed in more detail in Chapter 6, most of the shares warehoused by the NNDC were never redistributed to the Nigerian public.

[64] Most of the thirty-five financial analysts interviewed in the course of this research estimated that overdrafts from commercial banks accounted for most of the bank borrowing, and that the banks provided somewhere between 75 and 85 percent of the total capital involved in the financing of the second decree.

[65] Interview with branch manager of MNC bank.

[66] Interview with American MNC manager.

[67] Interview with MNC bank manager.

[68] Interview with prominent indigenous businessman.

finance did offer an additional source of funds. (The effective interest rates were probably lower than they initially appeared, since the moneylenders were recipients of a great many curses and often died a violent death.)[69]

Indigenous businessmen were, of course, not the only recipients of the shares on offer from the multinationals. The state sector (in particular the state governments) was also very active and was ultimately responsible for a considerable amount of the capital provided for the purchase of shares. In addition to state governments, regional development institutions were also very active in acquiring shares. "The NNDC went into portfolio investment in a big way after the second decree."[70] In many cases, the 5 percent of the shares set aside for nonmanagerial employees were placed as a donation in employee trust funds and never fully paid for, accounting for a further percentage of the shares transferred.

In the end, no one, including senior officials in the Central Bank and the NSEC, knows precisely what percentage of the financing of the second decree came from the banks, from savings, from the informal financial sector, or from the state. As will be discussed further in Chapter 6, a considerable amount of the money involved was contributed directly by the state via purchases by state governments, development institutions, and development banks or by the warehousing of shares. It is unlikely, however, that the state was responsible for most of the financing. In May of 1982, the shareholding structure of all the companies quoted on the Nigerian Stock Exchange was 42 percent expatriate, 35 percent individual Nigerian investors, 15 percent government, and 8 percent institutional investors.[71] Although it had increased its involvement in the national economy after indigenization, the state still only accounted for a little over a quarter of the total indigenous participation in the companies listed on the stock exchange.[72]

CONSEQUENCES FOR THE INDIVIDUAL FIRM

Since the second decree created three schedules (and therefore three different kinds of joint ventures), it is necessary to examine its conse-

[69] Interview with board member of the Central Bank of Nigeria.

[70] Interview with NNDC official.

[71] These figures were recorded in a council memo of the Nigerian Stock Exchange, dated 25 May 1982 (interview with government official).

[72] Recall that 78 percent of the value of all companies affected by the second decree was quoted on the stock exchange.

quences separately for each schedule. The countervailing measures taken by firms, and the consequences for their operations, obviously differ according to whether they were required to sell a minority, a majority, or all of their equity to local subscribers.

Schedule 1

Although eighteen new economic subsectors were added to Schedule 1, most of them were already fully indigenized before the decree was published. Only 57 enterprises (or 5.3 percent of the 1,078 companies affected by the decree by the end of 1981) were assigned to the first schedule and forced to sell their remaining equity to Nigerians. Their strategic responses were similar to those employed during the first decree: They tried to get reclassified, took out Nigerian citizenship, and attempted fronting. However, this time it was more difficult to get reclassified, and fronting for foreigners was nearly impossible. Taking out Nigerian citizenship for a family member was still allowed and became a modal response for Lebanese family firms assigned to Schedule 1 in the North.[73] Multinational companies straddling Schedules 1 and 2 merged their existing operations under a single heading and applied for a Schedule 2 classification.

The only new countervailing measure designed to neutralize a portion of the second decree was developed by indigenous businessmen interested in acquiring Schedule 1 enterprises, not by the foreign owners of those companies. A new form of fronting was introduced by businessmen trying to get around the 5 percent limitation on the number of shares an individual could acquire. It became routine for local businessmen, many of whom had gained their wealth during the first decree, to provide temporary loans or gifts to their drivers or housekeepers to acquire shares on their behalf.[74] In many ways, they mimicked the foreign businessmen who had originally developed these techniques to maintain their control over Schedule 1 operations during the first decree. This is a good illustration of the kind of learning going on as a result of indigenization.

Since the countervailing measures at their disposal were more limited this time, foreign businessmen operating in Schedule 1 spent more of their energies obtaining the best possible price for the transfer of equity than they did trying to retain control. As a result of their low valuation (and faced with the prospect of losing all of their eq-

[73] Hoogvelt 1979: 61. This point was also made in an interview with a university lecturer.
[74] Hoogvelt 1979: 58.

uity), some Schedule 1 companies attempted asset stripping (that is, selling off assets piecemeal to realize the best possible price for the enterprise as a whole). Thus, Nigerians acquiring the ownership of the enterprise might inherit an empty shell. Although the practice of asset stripping was specifically outlawed by the government, the NEPB did allow a few companies to liquidate in this manner.[75]

The operational changes in fully indigenized Schedule 1 firms were not significantly different from those observed after the first decree. In addition to the companies' experiencing discontinuities in management, short-term productivity declines, and difficult access to both finance and suppliers, labor again suffered disproportionately from its new employers. Because of their interest in building up capital (some for the very first time), indigenous businessmen tended to increase their rate of accumulation after they acquired Schedule 1 enterprises by paying lower salaries, offering fewer benefits, and postponing improvements in working conditions.[76] They also went to great lengths to block unionization: "[M]any Nigerian employers are prepared to spend more money fighting against a union in their company than it would cost them in additional benefits and pay."[77]

Schedule 2

Of much greater interest, and of much greater significance for the Nigerian economy, were the strategic responses and changes in operations of Schedule 2 enterprises. The second schedule of the second decree affected 742 companies, or nearly 70 percent of the total. Many of these were large multinational companies, headquartered in Europe or North America, and a significant number of them were confronted with the prospect of entering into a minority position in a joint venture for the first time. Thus, their strategic responses, and the changes that took place in their operations as a result of indigenization, are of considerable interest.

Many of the commercial and manufacturing multinational firms locating in Nigeria during the 1970s (and many of those already doing business there) were primarily motivated by a desire to increase their market share in a potentially large market. They were attracted by Nigeria's considerable oil revenues and its potentially large domestic market. There was little else of intrinsic value about investing in Nigeria, given its poor infrastructure, poorly trained and expensive labor, and its innumerable bureaucratic requirements for doing busi-

---

[75] *Report of the Securities and Exchange Commission, 1977–1979*: 9.

[76] Interviews (this point was made independently by two labor consultants).

[77] Interview with journalist specializing in labor.

ness. Many of the companies locating (or located) in Nigeria were interested primarily in "export pull-through" (i.e., exporting from their parent company and its affiliates) rather than producing exclusively for the Nigerian market. The fact that it was easier to export to Nigeria after establishing a manufacturing or assembly operation in the country explains why so many firms were able to remain in Nigeria even though their local ventures were operating at a loss.

For this reason, it was extremely important for multinational firms to maintain control over their Schedule 2 operations after indigenization. If they did not, it would be difficult to guarantee that already unprofitable operations might not become even more so. Control of finance was crucial, since it enabled the multinationals to fend off demands from their new indigenous partners for high dividend declarations at a time when restrictions on capital repatriation were severe. It also facilitated transfer pricing, if necessary. Ultimately, unless the multinationals kept control of finance and essential aspects of operations, the costs of maintaining a physical presence in Nigeria might begin to exceed the benefits from export pull-through. Foreign and local capital shared an interest in maintaining an efficient operation in Nigeria, but the multinationals had an added interest in export pull-through and market share in a populous and (thanks to OPEC) relatively wealthy country. Thus, multinational enterprises assigned to Schedule 2 devised a broad array of countervailing measures designed to ensure they maintained effective control over operations with a minority of the equity.

In order to document the range and effectiveness of countervailing measures employed by multinational firms, I conducted interviews with senior managers in fifty-eight companies operating in Nigeria between 1979 and 1982. The firms were selected to ensure a representative sample of companies investing in Nigeria during this period by sector (commerce, manufacturing, construction, services, and primary) and by nationality. Details of the selection procedure and identity of the firms interviewed can be found in Appendix A. Of relevance for the current discussion, however, is the fact that in most cases at least one senior expatriate and one senior Nigerian manager (or in some cases, indigenous partners) were interviewed about the status of effective control, the nature of the countervailing measures employed, and changes in operations that could be attributed to indigenization.

When the expatriate managers were asked whether they were slowly losing control over their Nigerian operations,[78] in thirty-five of the

---

[78] Control was defined for them as it was in Chapter 3, in terms of managerial responsibility for financial, technical and commercial aspects of operations.

forty-four enterprises assigned to Schedule 2 (or nearly 80 percent of the total in this sample) they answered with an emphatic "No!" Of the remaining firms, five said they might possibly be losing control, while only four answered clearly in the affirmative. Of the nine who thought they might have lost (or might be in the process of losing) control, six were in the service sector, and all of those were in banking. The consequences of indigenization, controlling for sector and nationality of the companies involved, will be examined more fully below. For the time being, however, let us examine the countervailing measures employed by the successful Schedule 2 enterprises, that is, those that had not lost effective control of their operations after selling 60 percent of their equity to Nigerian subscribers.[79]

The first thing many multinationals did in response to indigenization was reorganize their Nigerian operations. For companies doing business in activities assigned to both the first and second schedules of the decree, a regrouping and merging of operations took place, and the Schedule 1 activities were brought under the umbrella of the Schedule 2 enterprise. For companies straddling Schedules 2 and 3, the company reorganization involved a division, rather than a merging, of their operations. By pursuing what I have described elsewhere as a "two-company strategy,"[80] multinationals incorporated two companies in Nigeria, one located in Schedule 2, and one in Schedule 3. Since they could retain 60 percent of the equity in the Schedule 3 operation, they were able to retain uninhibited (or majority equity) control over as many product lines they could assign to their Schedule 3 entities.

TABLE 5.3
Responses to the Question "Are You Slowly Losing Control over Your Nigerian Operations?"

	Yes	Possibly	No	Total
Commerce	1 (7%)	0	12 (93%)	13
Manufacturing	1 (7%)	0	12 (93%)	13
Construction	0	1 (20%)	4 (80%)	5
Services	2 (15%)	4 (31%)	7 (54%)	13

SOURCE: Interview material described in Appendix A.

[79] It should be noted that this typology of countervailing measures does not define mutually exclusive strategies. Most firms employ a combination of several of these measures to retain effective control over operations.

[80] Biersteker 1980: 216.

Meanwhile, control could be exercised over the Schedule 2 company in a number of ways. The two subsidiaries were usually established with identical organizational structures, often with overlapping memberships on their boards of directors, and in most instances with the same indigenous partners holding the equity in each of the subsidiary companies. It was not unusual for the Schedule 2 enterprise to negotiate a technical- or managerial-services agreement with its Schedule 3 counterpart, and often the two companies existed solely on paper. Only one plant would be constructed, with a single administration building housing both companies. Having the Schedule 2 company located physically across the hall from its Schedule 3 affiliate made it easier to control.

Two-company arrangements offered other benefits to the multinationals. The Schedule 2 firm could manage the distribution and servicing of products for both companies, and having two companies in the country allowed multinationals to divide their government contracts in ways that minimized their tax liability in Nigeria.[81] In the end, nine of the thirty-five Schedule 2 companies that retained control (or a little more than 25 percent of the sample) employed some kind of company reorganization in response to the second decree. However, no company's response was restricted to a single measure. Most employed a combination of this and some other countervailing measures.

By far the most common way to retain control over ventures in which companies were reduced to a minority equity position was to take great care in the selection of joint-venture partners. In twenty-nine of the thirty-five companies surveyed (or nearly 83 percent), expatriate managers stressed the importance of "choosing the right local partners," "making the right selection," and the need for "sensible directors." It made good business sense for multinationals to search for local partners who agreed with their business objectives and could conform to their standard operating procedures. The selection of such a partner was likely to minimize conflicts on the board and create the kind of "affinity" observed by Hoogvelt in her interviews with manufacturing multinationals in Kano.[82] However, most expatriate multinational managers were interested in more than just minimizing local conflicts—they were deliberately looking for individuals with little or no interest in management.

When asked specifically what evaluation criteria they used in the se-

[81] Interview with American MNC executive.
[82] Hoogvelt 1980: 260.

lection of local partners, expatriate managers emphasized their search for people with "no political drive," with "little experience in the production of the firm," or with "no interest in management."[83] In short, "[T]hey were chosen to be quiet."[84] Some were deliberately chosen because they had money. This was a prudent criterion for multinational managers because local partners with their own source of income would tend to be less interested in overnight wealth from the firm, in addition to being more capable of raising capital on local money markets.

Even more important than financial resources, however, were the political clout and connections of potential joint-venture partners. Local partners could play an important role in obtaining contracts, helping the subsidiary out with government restrictions, and lobbying on behalf of the industry in which the firm operated. As one executive described the situation, "Make investments with the most powerful people, not so that they control operations, so that they can provide access. It's important to spread your risk. This [Nigeria] is the most corrupt country in the world. Therefore, it's necessary to buy protection."[85] Although this might have been an effective strategy during the late 1970s when the second decree was being implemented, it created a few more problems than it solved for some companies during the Second Republic. In several cases, the people chosen for their political clout under the military eventually became clearly identified with particular political parties. This was fine if you were an NPN company (i.e. identified with the ruling party), but a distinct liability if you were identified as an NPP or UPN company (identified with one of the opposition parties).

In the end, most companies employed a combination of these factors in choosing joint-venture partners. One internal company memorandum of a manufacturing multinational assigned specific weights to the contributions it expected from its local partners. The financial resources and political clout or connections of the local partners were valued most highly and each was assigned a weight of 40 percent. Within the remaining 20 percent, management ability and knowledge of manufacturing were valued least and assigned a value of only 2 percent. As an expatriate with another firm summed up his company's strategy, "We chose our partners for their political ability, their business connections, and on the basis of merit—in that order."[86]

---

[83] Interviews with American and German MNC executives.
[84] Interview with German MNC executive.
[85] Interview with multinational oil company executive.
[86] Interview with British MNC manufacturer.

Not all the multinationals affected by the second decree had this much latitude in selection of joint-venture partners. The banks, the insurance companies, and some of the manufacturing firms in the North had their directors chosen for them by the government. In a few cases where a single individual had acquired the bulk of the shares after the first decree, that individual played an important role in the selection of the additional partners required to comply with the second decree. However, they tended to be as interested in silent partners as the multinational managers. As one expatriate manager described the attitude of his principal local partner, "He wanted shareholders who wouldn't make any trouble for *him*."[87]

After selecting local partners (or having them selected for you), the next task facing the multinational manager was to keep them happy. Some expatriates described the regular contact they had with their board members, socializing with them and visiting with them in their homes. Others stressed that a continual flow of dividends was usually enough to keep them satisfied and uninterested in the management of the firm. If that didn't work, many Nigerian partners were satisfied with other perks, such as a car and driver, housing, a night watchman, and occasional trips to board meetings in Europe or North America.

As long as they were kept happy, local partners could occasionally be called upon for political contacts, connections, or to handle liaison with Nigerian government agencies. They could be particularly helpful in obtaining additional expatriate quotas (discussed more fully below) or with other "business-practice problems" such as the paying of bribes for procuring large contracts.[88] Thus there was a genuine division of labor between the expatriate and local directors, a comparative advantage both recognized and utilized by the expatriate managers.

Finally, if a company had chosen the wrong (i.e. meddlesome) local partners during the first decree when it gave up 40 percent of its equity—and some clearly did—it could use the allocation of an additional 20 percent of its equity from the second decree to dilute their influence. At least four companies among the thirty-five Schedule 2 firms who contended they still maintained control used the second decree to tighten their control in this manner. In several other cases, firms selected additional partners from different parts of the country

[87] Interview with Dutch MNC executive.

[88] None of the expatriate managers I interviewed admitted to paying any bribes in Nigeria, but several described the process whereby their partners "assisted" in procuring large contracts. One manager was also able to quote the going rates for individual permanent secretaries and ministers.

to try to play them against one another. They did so in the name of "federal character" (that is, ensuring that all major ethnic groups in Nigeria were represented on the board). Their intention was somewhat less benign, however. They did so in the hope that disputes between board members from different regions would distract them from trying to manage the company.

There were many variations in this general strategy. Small one-man family operations in Nigeria tended to rely on friends and old networks in their search for local partners, while companies operating in northern Nigeria tended to opt for their former distributors or a small group of "big Alhajis."[89] The bottom line was the same, however, irrespective of company size, sector, nationality, or location. They all wanted to keep their Nigerian partners out of day-to-day management. As one expatriate manager put it, "We never want to hear from them."[90]

After reorganizing the company and taking great care in the selection of local partners, a third countervailing measure pursued by many companies was to spread their shares as widely as possible. Thirteen companies (or 37 percent of the sample) fractionalized their share distribution to ensure that no single indigenous subscriber would hold a block of shares anywhere near the 40 percent the multinationals were allowed to retain. The most obvious way of doing this was to go public. Government pressure to go public was greater during the second decree, the costs of doing so were less, and the potential benefits for a foreign firm allowed to retain only 40 percent of its equity were obvious. As one expatriate executive advised, "Once you've made the decision to go public, spread your shares as widely as possible."[91] Another added, "The broader the distribution, the easier it is to control the operation."[92] A number of Nigerian officials have pointed to the impressive growth of the number of companies listed on the Nigerian Stock Exchange as an illustration of the success of the second decree (which brought an additional seventy-eight companies onto the exchange).[93] However, in addition to responding to overt government pressure, one of the main reasons so many companies were willing to sell publicly after the second decree was that this time they were required to relinquish a clear majority of their equity. They

---

[89] Hoogvelt 1979: 62. The term "big Alhajis" is Hoogvelt's and refers to the wealthiest businessmen in the Kano area (all of whom had been to Mecca).

[90] Interview with American MNC executive.

[91] Interview with British MNC manufacturing executive.

[92] Interview with American MNC executive.

[93] Alile 1982: 8.

had a greater need for direct control and a greater incentive for fractionalizing their share distribution by going public.

Another way multinationals fractionalized their indigenous equity was to allocate shares sold privately among a large number of shareholders. This was encouraged by the distributional reforms written into the second decree, and companies were generally not sympathetic to the new form of fronting begun by wealthy indigenous businessmen trying to get around the 5 percent limitation. They were equally willing to allocate 10 percent of their stock to their Nigerian employees, in part because it served to atomize the indigenous equity even further.

A fourth countervailing measure employed by at least eight companies (or nearly a quarter of the sample) was to rewrite their company articles of association, make contractual agreements with their Nigerian partners, or change key voting rules or other operational procedures to ensure that the foreign partner either (1) retained effective managerial control or (2) maintained an effective veto over essential decisions. Some firms rewrote their articles to ensure that the foreign partner would be responsible for commercial, financial and technical management of the enterprise, that the managing director would be appointed by the foreign partner, that the use of the company's trademark could be discontinued at the foreign partner's request, and even that the company could be liquidated if the foreign partner lost effective managerial control.

Other firms changed their voting rules on key decisions to prevent important policy changes from being made without their consent. The typical formula would be to raise the number of votes required for passage of major motions from a simple majority to two-thirds or three-fourths. As one expatriate executive manager described his company's policy, "We don't want to give the control of the company to Nigeria at the present time. The company can write voting rules any way it wants."[94] An internal memorandum from another company to its parent office was equally explicit. It identified a number of measures to ensure that it would retain "a suitable measure of control over its investment," including proposals to amend its articles "so that no decision can be taken without [our] consent, i.e. 2/3 or 3/4 majority required" in the annual general meeting. Another amendment ensured that in meetings of the board of directors "all decisions require the affirmative vote of at least one of the non-resident Directors, i.e.

[94] Interview with American MNC executive.

affirmative vote of 6 Directors."[95] Not every company had to rely on making changes in existing articles, agreements, or decision rules, however. As one manager described his company's position, "The accounting procedures we use within [the company] worldwide maintain our control over the financial decisions of the firm."[96]

More than half of the Schedule 2 companies surveyed (eighteen of thirty-five) had technical- or managerial-services agreements between their Nigerian subsidiaries and their home offices, many of which were negotiated (or renegotiated) after indigenization. Technical agreements tended to give the multinationals responsibility for technology choice, maintenance, and innovation. As Hoogvelt points out from her survey of manufacturers in Kano, many companies used the additional capital obtained from the sale of shares to increase the technical specificity of their operations,[97] something that enabled them both to import machinery from the parent company (often at inflated prices) and to increase the reliance of the firm on expatriate technicians and technical advice.

Management-service agreements tended to serve the same function as changes in articles of association. As one expatriate manager put it, "We have a management agreement which effectively gives the [foreign] shareholder the authority to run the company: appoint a general manager and the top three positions in the company."[98] An expatriate banker commented,

> Our management-services agreement allows [us] to run the bank as we see fit. There is no interference, political or otherwise, from board members in management decisions. Our management-services agreement is a lengthy document negotiated with the Central Bank and the Ministry of Finance. It governs expatriates, guarantees control for [us], and ensures that credit judgement is in [our] hands.[99]

Other firms used management agreements to routinize seeking advice from the parent company, to appoint an expatriate managing director, or to ensure that all of the important decisions would be made by the foreign partners. One multinational manager characterized his

[95] Internal company memorandum supplied by an American MNC executive during an interview.
[96] Interview with Swiss MNC executive.
[97] Hoogvelt 1980: 263.
[98] Interview with Dutch MNC executive.
[99] Interview with American banking executive.

company's management agreement as "another way to tie things up."[100]

A less legalistic way of accomplishing some of the same objectives as rewriting articles or negotiating a technical or management agreement was to rely on training programs to socialize indigenous senior managers to "think like us." Sending Nigerian managers for training in Europe or North America could assure an expatriate management that its structure and standard operating procedures would remain unchanged even after complete personnel indigenization. One manufacturing multinational executive maintained that "Nigerian managers of fifteen to twenty-five years are part of us."[101] Another suggested that by bringing up Nigerian management through the ranks and by providing training programs abroad his firm had been able to create local managers who were so thoroughly socialized they only thought in terms of the company. If a company could get local people to carry out policy from the home office, it could run the operation with a minority of the equity and save a lot of money on personnel.

Most companies were not yet willing to run the risk of thoroughly indigenizing their personnel in Nigeria, however. Only three companies (or under 9 percent of the sample) relied on management loyalty of their indigenous employees to maintain control for the head office after indigenization. A much more common response was to increase the number of expatriates working for the indigenized firm. Thirteen of the companies in the sample (or more than 37 percent) increased their expatriates after the second decree. The Expatriate Quota Allocation Board monitors and regulates the employment of expatriates through the issue of work permits, but there are both legal and not so legal ways of adding extra expatriates to a firm.

It was not at all unusual for a company to apply for additional expatriates to install and service capital goods imported to Nigeria after the second decree. This was a perfectly legitimate thing for companies to do, given the number of firms that used capital raised from indigenization to increase plant capacity. However, many brought in additional expatriates deliberately to tighten their control over operations as they passed from a majority equity to a minority equity position. Some firms relabelled positions to sound technical, some lied, and nearly all bargained with the Expatriate Quota Allocation Board for additional expatriates. A number of firms relied on their local partners to obtain an increased quota, or "hired the right lawyer"

---

[100] Interview with American MNC executive.
[101] Interview with Canadian MNC manufacturing executive.

to handle the bribes for the board. Some companies blatantly brought in additional expatriates on tourist visas, while others came up with an ingenious system for shifting employees around from one subsidiary to another in a procedure analogous to transfer pricing. For example, one company obtained permits for what it claimed were necessary but were in fact redundant employees for its subsidiary assigned to Schedule 3. Once they were in the country, these expatriates were reassigned (transferred) to one of its subsidiaries assigned to Schedule 2.

If a company had difficulty importing additional expatriates, it gave existing employees additional responsibilities. Many of the foreign executives interviewed complained about their increased work load after indigenization. Deputy general managers served in effect as general managers, while managing directors often assumed the responsibility of technical directors. Some firms systematized more of their operations to maintain control, while others responded by importing a different type of expatriate manager to Nigeria, a manager capable of dealing flexibly and creatively with difficult business conditions. Well-seasoned managers with a "frontier mentality" became the norm in American companies, many of whose expatriates had previously managed operations in Teheran or Saigon.

As a last resort, a small number of companies chose to invoke their embassies for support against indigenization. One Japanese firm used its embassy to negotiate its way into Schedule 2, while one American firm threatened to invoke the Hickenlooper Amendment after it received its share valuation from the Capital Issues Commission. However, these were the exceptions rather than the rule.

When all else failed, a few companies chose to ignore the decree altogether. One trading-company representative that should have been assigned to Schedule 1 labelled its sales activity "technical" and obtained expatriate permits for salesmen. A construction firm that should have sold 60 percent of its equity sold only 40 percent and in 1982 was still waiting for the NEPB to catch up with it. A number of service-company representatives maintained legitimately that, since they had no equity in the country, the second decree should not apply to their operations. Nevertheless, even after being informed that they were in violation of the decree, they failed to file papers with the NEPB. As one executive confidently stated:

We have never properly registered with the NEPB, never produced a balance sheet for them. If they pursue it, we'll pay the penalties for not filing. Or we could type up the documents later, say the NEPB lost the copy we sent them, and produce an "original."[102]

This says as much about the enforcement capacity of the Nigerian government, however, as it does about the efficacy of the countervailing measures employed by multinational companies.

Figure 5.1 summarizes the strategic responses of multinational companies assigned to Schedule 2 of the second decree. It should be recalled that these are the responses of the successful firms, that is, those that were able to maintain effective control over their operations with 40 percent of the equity. These countervailing measures are not mutually exclusive. In fact, most firms employed at least two, and some as many as six, in their attempts to maintain effective control over operations. Their combination of strategies depended on their sector, their nationality, and their internal corporate structure. It is possible, however, to provide summary characterizations of strategic responses by sector and by nationality.

Commercial-sector companies relied most heavily on carefully selecting joint-venture partners to maintain control of operations. They tended to combine this with company reorganizations (usually mergers or regroupings of their Schedule 1 and 2 activities), spreading shares widely through private distribution, bringing in extra expatriates, and negotiating management-service contracts. Only the big trading companies were prominent enough to go public, and because commercial ventures have relatively few technical advantages to offer, they have relied more on management than on technical-service agreements to maintain control.

Manufacturing firms, by contrast, have relied most heavily on a careful selection of joint-venture partners in conjunction with going public and negotiating a technical-services agreement. Many of the largest manufacturers have a recognizable product and have had no difficulty finding purchasers for their publicly offered shares. They also have technological advantages that enable them to negotiate technical service agreements in addition to management ones.

These findings are similar to the results of Hoogvelt's survey of manufacturing firms in Kano. She found that sixteen of her twenty-four firms relied on a careful selection of partners (what she termed "fronting") and/or a wide dispersal of shares (or what she called "fragmentation").[103] Management contracts were the principal corporate

---

[102] Interview with American banking executive.

[103] These figures are based on a disaggregation of the data used by Hoogvelt in her two papers cited previously.

FIGURE 5.1
Strategic Responses of Schedule 2 Enterprises
(Percentages indicate % of companies in sample employing this countervailing measure)

Step One   Reorganize the company (26%)
                  If straddling Schedules 1 and 2, regroup activities
                  If straddling Schedules 2 and 3, divide activities

Step Two   Choose the "right" joint-venture partners (83%)
                  Select partners with no interest in management
                  Socialize with them and keep them happy with dividends
                  Dilute the share of "problem" partners
                  Divide and rule

Step Three   Spread shares widely (37%)
                  Go public
                  Disperse private shares

Step Four   Rewrite articles of association (23%)
                  Revise partnership agreements
                  Change voting rules

Step Five   Negotiate a technical-services agreement (51%)
                  Stipulate roles of local and foreign partners
                  Negotiate management agreement

Step Six   Rely on management loyalty (9%)
                  Provide training programs
                  Bring up managers through the ranks

Step Seven   Increase the number of expatriates (37%)
                  Lie, bargain, or bribe for additional expatriates
                  Increase workload and responsibilities of existing expatriates
                  Bring in seasoned expatriates

Step Eight   Invoke the embassy (6%)
                  To assist with regrouping or rescheduling
                  To assist with obtaining a fair valuation

Step Nine   Ignore the second decree (9%)
                  Sell less than 60%
                  Refuse to file with the NEPB

strategy in four of the companies in her sample, while seeking naturalization was an equally viable approach, at least for Lebanese family firms.

Service-sector companies have relied equally on importing additional expatriates, negotiating managerial service agreements, and carefully selecting partners. Since so many of the service-sector companies were not able to select their own joint-venture partners, they were more prone to bring in extra expatriates, increase the workload on those expatriates already working in Nigeria, negotiate managerial service agreements, and rewrite their articles (for bankers, their loancommittee rules). Construction firms relied almost exclusively on choosing the right partners, at least in part because of the importance of well-connected local partners in securing big contracts in Nigeria.

Most of the countervailing measures described in Figure 5.1 were employed by multinational companies, irrespective of national origin. However, a few significant differences can be seen when comparing the strategies of American firms and European firms, or when differentiating multinational companies from Lebanese family firms.

American firms were more likely to concentrate on legalistic countervailing measures (like rewriting the articles of association or negotiating precise management-service agreements) than their European counterparts. This stems in part from the fact that the U.S. multinationals operating in Nigeria tend to assign relatively young managers to head their Nigerian operations and because their international corporate structure tends to allow these managers relatively little discretionary authority to make decisions. In contrast, British multinationals distinguished themselves by placing senior managers in the country (some of whom had been in Nigeria since colonial days) and giving them broad discretionary authority. The British firms are the only companies that relied on "informal understandings" between expatriate and indigenous managers, and they were also the only companies that seriously counted on training and management loyalty for continued home office control.

Another distinctive characteristic of American firms was their tendency to employ as many as five or six different countervailing measures at a time in what appeared to be a desperate search for something that would work to maintain their control of operations in Nigeria. This stemmed in part from the fact that American firms tended to be larger on average than their European counterparts and to have less experience both with minority participation in joint ventures and with government participation. Americans distinguished themselves by being the most visibly reluctant to sell a majority of their equity to indigenous subscribers, they complained the most publicly, and they provided the most celebrated cases of resistance to indigenization (thanks to Citibank and American International Insurance). Several American firms described their Nigerian affiliates as a test case for the home office, because they were the first of their subsidiaries in the world to be forced into a minority equity position.[104]

Lebanese firms employed most of the same countervailing measures as European and North American multinationals, with one exception. They were virtually the only Schedule 2 companies that responded to the second decree by taking out Nigerian citizenship.[105] This was a strategy ordinarily utilized only for Schedule 1 ventures, but was surprisingly common among Lebanese Schedule 2 manufacturers in the Kano area.[106] Among Schedule 2 manufacturing firms in Kano, the Lebanese were more likely to go into a joint venture with only one or two prominent local individuals, while the European and North American multinationals were more likely to spread their shares among many smaller holders.[107]

Although there were some sectoral and national differences in the types of countervailing measures employed, the final consequences were the same. The overwhelming majority of Schedule 2 enterprises had little difficulty retaining effective managerial control of enterprises in which they were reduced to a 40 percent minority share of the equity. The only exceptions to this were to be found in an occasional commercial or manufacturing company and, more significantly, in several of the banks. Six of the nine Schedule 2 companies in my sample that suggested that they either had lost or might possibly be losing control over their Nigerian operations as a result of indigenization were banks. (This accounts for two-thirds of the total of nine banks included in the sample.)

These companies had employed many of the countervailing measures described above. Nearly all had negotiated management services agreements and most had tried to bring in additional expatriates. However, banking can be distinguished from most subsectors after the second decree on several counts. First, the federal government acquired the mandatory 60 percent, and it appointed the indigenous directors. Second, the form of the state's participation in banking could

---

[104] Interviews with American manufacturing MNC executives.

[105] One Italian company did so as well.

[106] Hoogvelt 1979: 61. From a disaggregation of her Schedule 2 manufacturing companies, it appears that 27.3 percent of the Lebanese companies obtained Nigerian citizenship, while only 7.7 percent of the European multinationals did.

[107] Ibid., p. 63.

be distinguished from the form of its participation in other sectors of the economy. It placed several representatives from the Central Bank of Nigeria in the senior management of each indigenized company, where they operated as executive directors. And third, the entire sector was strictly regulated by the Banking Decree with its mandatory credit guidelines (which effectively structured the outcome, if not the particularities, of what would normally be decisions made exclusively by the senior management of a firm).

The affected banks tried to maintain their position by expanding training programs in their home countries, by creating credit committees which effectively give them vetos on key loan decisions, and, more significant, by trying at all costs to avoid potentially divisive votes in those same committees. However, although it may be limited to one subsector of the economy, the second decree has had (or is having) an impact on the effective control of a majority of the banks in Nigeria. As the Nigerian managing director and chief executive of Nigeria's largest commercial bank wrote in 1981:

> The Federal Government now owns substantial part of the equity of all the major banks and total Nigerian equity holding in all of the commercial banks put Nigerian's participation in the majority. The revolution in equity structure and loans policy has also been carried into management; thus executive management of practically all of the banks is now firmly in the hands of Nigerians.[108]

Although changes in effective managerial control have been restricted to a relatively small number of Schedule 2 companies, they are located in a strategic sector of the economy, something that has a significance we will examine more thoroughly when we consider the sectoral and national consequences of the second decree.

What do these conclusions about control of Schedule 2 enterprises mean for changes, if any, in their operations? Among the banks, personnel indigenization has been speeded up to the point where nearly all of the senior management positions are now occupied by Nigerians. In 1975, the three largest commercial banks in the country employed a total of 153 expatriates, or a little more than 9 percent of their total number of bank officers. By March of 1982, after a period of significant growth in deposits, loans, assets, and number of branches, the three largest commercial banks employed only 41 expatriates (or just a little over one percent of the officers).[109] Most ex-

---

[108] Asabia 1981: 5.
[109] Computed from Table 4 of Asabia 1982. Data are available only for December of

patriate bankers accordingly complained about a loss of efficiency in operations as a result.

There is also a clear sense that more decisions are now being made in Nigeria. Several expatriate bankers observed that because they had less influence or because they had been overruled on several occasions, different decisions were now being made in the banks. More small loans were being made to indigenous borrowers, more loans were going to rural areas, and longer-term lending was on the increase. These findings are corroborated by other observers of Nigeria's banking sector. As Asabia has written,

> Lending practices and techniques of credit evaluation of banks in the country have changed substantially since the early seventies following purposeful intervention by the Central Bank and the changes which have taken place in the pattern of asset ownership in commerce and industry in the country.[110]

There was evidence that the Central Bank's credit guidelines were more rigorously enforced (e.g. there was less deliberate falsification of records) after indigenization, since many banks began to exceed the Central Bank's assigned minimum percentages.[111] Finally, it appeared that political considerations had become more important in credit decisions, at least during the Second Republic.

Companies in other sectors that thought they might have lost (or were in the process of losing) control described similar kinds of changes in operations. Most complained about declines in the efficiency of their management and service, while one observed that it was now more difficult to cut back on employee benefits. Fights between indigenous and expatriate shareholders (usually over the size of dividends) were more common, and pressure to indigenize senior management increased from within the firms. At the same time, labor relations in general improved, it was easier to obtain local financing, and, because of its increased knowledge about and willingness to use local materials, one firm reported increasing its local content after indigenization.

Because more than 80 percent of the Schedule 2 companies I interviewed maintained they were not in the process of losing control over

---

1980 for one of the three banks (Union Bank); the number of expatriates remaining in 1982 was assumed unchanged for that bank. Given previous trends, however, this probably overestimates slightly the number of expatriates remaining in managerial positions in Nigerian banking.

[110] Asabia 1981: 10.

[111] See Table 7 in Asabia 1982.

operations, it is not surprising that over a quarter of them indicated that nothing had changed in their operations as a result of indigenization. However, many reported cosmetic changes in operations due to the sale of a majority of their equity to indigenous subscribers. More board meetings were held after indigenization, and preparation for the annual general meetings of public companies occupied more of the time of senior management. For the most part, however, increases in Nigerian participation amounted to little more than allowing Nigerians to countersign checks or giving them copies of internal company reports. Several firms reported increasing the benefits paid to their Nigerian directors (consistent with the strategy of keeping them happy). Pressure for increasing local content was acknowledged by several expatriate managers, but because of the scarcity of locally available raw materials (or their substantial cost) there was little more than talk about it.

There were several more substantive changes in operations following indigenization, even among those firms confident that they had retained effective managerial control of operations. Among the most common was an increase in personnel indigenization at the senior management level. More than 17 percent of the successful Schedule 2 companies indicated that the pace of personnel indigenization had increased, often from internal pressure from the junior and middle managerial ranks within the company.[112] Indigenization raised the expectations of middle and junior managers for promotions, and they became the most effective advocates for continuing personnel indigenization.

A second change in operations during the period was that nearly all companies increased employee benefits, increases that might have served to placate employees dissatisfied with the absence of changes in other aspects of the operation (like personnel indigenization). From a survey of microeconomic data gathered on the operations of sixteen Schedule 2 firms before and after the second decree (see Appendix C for details), in all but one instance individual enterprises increased their employee benefits. In 1974, the average value of annual per employee benefits was 77 naira ($125). In 1980, this same figure was 616 naira ($1,130). This increase took place during a period in which wages also increased considerably. Inflation accounted for some of

[112] Interviews with American manufacturer and executives of American and Swiss service-sector companies. Similar pressures from within the ranks were reported in the Nigerian press. See *Nigerian Observer*, 25 August 1976: "No Indigenisation in Jebba Paper Mill," p. 5, and *Nigerian Herald*, 17 February 1977: "Is This Slavery?" p. 2, for illustrations.

the increase, as did collective bargaining after the new unitary labor organization (the Nigerian Labor Congress) was set up in 1978. Nevertheless, indigenization probably had some effect on the bargaining power and confidence of employees.

A third change in operations was the outgrowth of indigenization and the restrictive foreign-exchange regulations in effect during the late 1970s. Since so many Schedule 2 firms increased their share capital to comply with the decree, they had an excess of liquidity after receiving 60 percent of the value of their shares from their indigenous partners. When this excess liquidity was combined with strict limitations on the size of dividends that could be declared and lengthy delays in Central Bank approval for the remittance of foreign exchange, companies generally responded in one of two ways. They either used the excess liquidity to expand the size of their plant in Nigeria, or they developed elaborate transfer pricing mechanisms to get their money out of the country. Sometimes the two solutions could be neatly combined when a company expanded its plant with overpriced imported capital goods.

There is plenty of evidence for the first response, and even some for the second. Seven companies in the sample of thirty-five I interviewed suggested that they had expanded the size of their operations after indigenization (though three said they had no plans to expand, had postponed plans to expand, or were divesting certain operations). The microeconomic data from the sixteen Schedule 2 firms described above also suggest that a great many companies expanded their operations. When the labor/output ratios of the sixteen firms in 1974 are compared with those in 1980, twelve of the sixteen companies show increases, ten of which are substantial (i.e. greater than by a factor of two). This implies that more than just increases in labor productivity were recorded for ten of the sixteen firms. Hoogvelt's survey of Kano manufacturing firms yielded a similar conclusion. Two-thirds of the companies she examined that had been established before the second decree modernized and expanded their operations (and were running under capacity) when she interviewed them.[113]

The consequences of expanding plant capacity were many. The importation of capital goods required for expansion provided a ready channel for transfer pricing. The capital intensity of production increased, and the employment effects might have been negative (depending on the counterfactual assumptions one makes about alterna-

[113] Hoogvelt 1980: 264–265.

tives to multinational investment in Nigeria).[114] Other consequences of increasing the capital intensity of production were to give the foreign partner more latitude in negotiating a technical-services agreement, create expanded markets for exports from the parent company (i.e. enhance export pull-through), and make it more difficult to utilize Nigerian raw materials in production (i.e. reduce the possibility of increasing local content).[115]

The only other changes in operations were specific to particular industries. Insurance companies indicated that they had to be more careful to comply with government legislation after a majority of their shares were acquired by state governments in Nigeria. The 1976 Insurance Decree was analogous to the Banking Decree in that it stipulated the minimum percentages of insurance premiums that were to be held in Nigerian investments and affected other aspects of operations.[116] The major reason the operations of the insurance companies were not as significantly affected as the banks was that their senior management was not installed by the Central Bank. Another industry-specific change in operations occurred in the publishing industry, where forms of pidgin English were printed for the first time by the indigenized publishing houses.

Some of the changes in the operations of Schedule 2 enterprises, such as the increase in personnel indigenization or increases in the capital intensity of production, would eventually have more significance (and will be considered again in Chapter 6). However, none of the changes in the operations of the vast majority of Schedule 2 enterprises was of any immediate significance.

Schedule 3

It was far easier to maintain control of Schedule 3 enterprises than of Schedule 2 ones. Since they only had to sell 40 percent of their equity to local subscribers, several multinational managers indicated that indigenization was "of no concern at all."[117] However, two of the ten Schedule 3 companies interviewed indicated that Nigerians con-

---

[114] See Biersteker 1978: 54–58 and 122–129 for a discussion of the employment effects of the introduction of capital-intensive means of production. It may be difficult to sustain the argument that unemployment had been exacerbated, given the sectors in which many operated and the considerable growth of employment that accompanied these expansions in production.

[115] Hoogvelt 1980: 265 provides some examples of this from a blanket and a match factory.

[116] Asabia 1982: 17–18.

[117] Interview with Indian manufacturing executive.

trolled the operations. Significantly, in both of these cases the firms had been initiated by the Nigerian joint-venture partners after the promulgation of the second decree (and were hence not restricted to the 5 percent limitation).

Among the vast majority of firms in which control had not been affected, countervailing measures similar to those employed by Schedule 2 companies were employed. Although 50 percent of the companies relied principally on their dominant equity position for control, few were sufficiently confident to rely on a majority of the equity alone. After all, indigenization might be extended again, or they might find themselves reclassified under the existing decree as Schedule 2 enterprises. When the second decree was being implemented in the late 1970s, many firms were also worried about the uncertainties that might develop after the return to civilian rule.

Accordingly, like their Schedule 2 counterparts, more than half of the Schedule 3 firms interviewed engaged in a careful selection of joint-venture partners. They too were looking for "low-profile people," people too busy to interfere with management, or as one manager put it, "We're looking for noncontroversial people with money."[118] Nearly half of the firms rewrote their articles of association and a similar number regrouped and employed a two-company strategy. Approximately a quarter of the firms negotiated technical-services agreements and spread their shares widely.[119]

In the two Schedule 3 enterprises in which Nigerians appeared to have effective managerial control, that control was not lost by the multinationals, but was negotiated at start-up. Both were companies in which a single Nigerian entrepreneur had 40 percent of the equity and both were initiated by the Nigerian partner.[120] The Nigerian partners were previously the principal distributors for the goods produced by these enterprises; hence these are examples of the movement

[118] Interviews with American manufacturing executives.

[119] The sample of ten is too small to say very much about sectoral or national variations in the countervailing measures employed. There was very little sectoral variation in any event, since virtually all of the Schedule 3 enterprises were engaged in some form of manufacturing. With regard to national differences, some of the same patterns described for Schedule 2 firms emerge. From an analysis of the disaggregated data from Hoogvelt's survey in Kano, Lebanese firms were unique in the taking of Nigerian citizenship, and they again had a preference for joint ventures with a few "big Alhajis" (as opposed to spreading their shares as widely as possible, which multinationals tended to prefer).

[120] A single Nigerian could own more than 5 percent of any company incorporated after 1979, since the 5 percent limitation applied only to the indigenization of companies already incorporated in Nigeria (interview with NSEC official).

FIGURE 5.2
Strategic Responses of Schedule 3 Enterprises
(Percentages indicate the % of firms employing this
countervailing measure)

Step One   Rely on majority equity position (50%)

Step Two   Select joint-venture partners carefully (50%)

Step Three   Rewrite articles of association (38%)

Step Four   Regroup and employ a two-company strategy (38%)

Step Five   Negotiate a technical-services agreement (25%)

Step Six   Spread shares widely (25%)

of Nigerian entrepreneurs from commerce into manufacturing
(something that will be examined in greater detail in Chapter 6). The
terms of the joint-venture agreement for one of the firms defined a
clear division of labor, since it restricted the expatriate personnel to
technical aspects of production and required that the directors of the
firm representing the foreign partner be Nigerian citizens and be approved by a unanimous vote of the board.

Since three of the Schedule 3 firms in the sample started up production only after 1979, there have been no changes in their operations
attributable to indigenization. However, none of the seven other
companies affected by the decree reported any significant changes in
operations either. There was some evidence of an increase in personnel indigenization, accompanied by an increase in employee benefits.
For a small sample of Schedule 3 enterprises, the average annual per
employee benefits increased from 29 naira ($47) before indigeniza-
tion to 175 naira ($320) after the decree.[121] In both cases, these fig-
ures are less than the comparable averages for Schedule 2 firms in the
same years.

When the labor/output ratios of Schedule 3 firms are examined to
see whether they expanded their operations after indigenization (a result of their excess liquidity), they again appear to have responded

[121] Appendix C contains details about the source of this data. There were only six
Schedule 3 firms on which both 1974 and 1980 data were available at Nigeria's Federal
Office of Statistics.

somewhat differently from their counterparts in Schedule 2. Although a majority of the companies in the sample did display increases in their labor/output ratios, only a third of them were substantial increases (which would have implied expansion rather than simple productivity gains). This evidence is corroborated by the interview data which suggested that Schedule 3 companies were more inclined to postpone, rather than accelerate, their expansion. These differences, though slight, do suggest that the greater amount of equity acquired by Nigerians in Schedule 2 did indeed have an effect on operations, even though the multinationals retained effective control of the vast majority of enterprises in both schedules.

Companies Exempt from the Second Decree

Because of the efforts of the Adeosun panel to reduce the number of allowable exemptions from indigenization, only a small number of companies were not affected by the second decree. Companies doing one-time contract work for government ministries were exempt from the decree as long as they limited their work to a single contract. The number of companies applying for and receiving this kind of exemption increased substantially under the civilian regime, in part because of the continuing construction of the Federal Capital Territory in Abuja (and in part because the civilian government had not sponsored the second decree and was in the process of relaxing some of its provisions).

The other major area of the economy exempt from the second decree was the vital petroleum sector. The petroleum industry was governed by other decrees, which effectively mandated the government's share of production and, in some cases, equity investment. It is difficult to generalize about the indigenization of the petroleum sector, since the pattern and terms of joint-venture arrangements in this sector have varied over time, vary according to production levels attained, and have been subject to renegotiation whenever the oil market softens (as it did especially after 1982). In some multinational oil companies the Nigerian National Petroleum Company is a portfolio investor holding only a percentage of stock and is not engaged at all in management. In others, a new entity has been created and the percentage share of the NNPC holding varies (as does its degree of effective participation) from 60 percent to 80 percent.[122] In still others,

---

[122] The figure of 80 percent is derived from the Shell/NNPC joint venture (formerly the Shell-BP/NNPC joint venture). Before BP's share was taken by the federal government of Nigeria in 1979, Shell-BP/NNPC was a typical 40%/60% joint venture. For a

the foreign companies retain 100 percent of the stock and have a pro-
duction-sharing agreement with the NNPC.

Of relevance for the present discussion is the fact that by the end of
1982 all of the multinational oil companies in Nigeria (whether engaged in exploration, refining, or marketing) operated in a minority
position. That is, even though a few retained 100 percent of their equity, they operated with a participating-interest agreement (splitting
costs and profits and, in some cases, production), with a production-
sharing contract (dividing output), or with a service contract (where
the multinational pays for initial expenditures and the arrangement is
renegotiated once oil is found).[123]

Despite the fact that they operate in a minority position in an industry that provides 90 percent of Nigeria's foreign exchange earnings, two out of three of the multinational oil companies interviewed
maintain that they have retained effective control over their operations. One expatriate manager who thought his company might be
losing control indicated that his company was only occasionally overruled by the NNPC, usually in matters involving the allocation of
contracts and construction bids.[124]

One reason why multinational oil companies are able to retain effective control over some of the operations in an industry as vital as
petroleum is that they still have significant comparative advantages in
the exploration process. A second reason stems from the fact that the
extreme drop in the real price of petroleum after 1982 enabled the oil
multinationals to renegotiate the terms of their agreements in countries like Nigeria so dependent on oil revenues for foreign exchange.
A third reason stems from the nature of the Nigerian government's
participation in the oil industry.

In contrast with banking, where the Central Bank places its people
inside each corporate entity, the NNPC only holds a share of the equity, receives a share of the profits, or receives a share of the production from the multinational oil companies. The NNPC looks after the
entire industry, attends meetings with individual companies, and
monitors their operations from its headquarters. It does not, however, have enough senior (and competent) personnel to assign to each
company, as the Central Bank does in the banking sector. As one expatriate manager described the nature of Nigerian participation:

---

partial taxonomy of forms of state participation in the petroleum sector as of 1977, see
Adeniji 1977.

[123] Interview with multinational oil company executive.

[124] Ibid.

[We] look after six blocks [of offshore exploration]. NNPC looks after all blocks in the country. Therefore, it has a management problem. NNPC scarcely has 20 percent of the personnel in the oil industry, although it has 60 percent participation in operations. We have fifty people. NNPC probably has two on [us]. We may have ten engineers. They may commit one. Therefore, in negotiations the multinational oil companies can predominate. All they [the NNPC] can do is work on general matters.[125]

Thus, it appears that the form of government participation makes a difference for control of the enterprise. The Nigerian government participates to the same degree (60 percent) in both banking and petroleum, but not in the same manner.

CONCLUSIONS

In the final analysis, no real change took place in the effective control of the vast majority of enterprises affected by the second indigenization decree. Undoubtedly a few changes took place in Schedule 1, there were some significant changes in the banks and an occasional Schedule 2 enterprise, and even a few Schedule 3 firms reported changes in control. Only 5.3 percent of the companies affected by the second decree were located in the first schedule, and it would probably be an overestimate to suggest that control was affected in as many as 20 percent of the Schedule 2 and 3 enterprises.

Why was the second decree so ineffective in creating significant change at the enterprise level? First, it is clear that the range of strategies and countervailing measures available to multinational corporations was considerable. Whether they involved company reorganization, personnel changes, legal adjustments, or not-so-legal arrangements, multinational firms had a broad array of means at their disposal to neutralize some of the state's objectives. The evidence from Nigeria's indigenization experience diverges considerably from the general expectation of liberal-internationalist writers that multinationals are losing control over operations. However, more than just the cleverness of the multinational managers was required to maintain their control over operations. They also required the assistance of their Nigerian joint-venture partners.

As we saw in Chapter 4, much of the indigenous business community was opposed to extending the indigenization program as quickly or as far as the second decree went. Yet it was precisely those same in-

125 Ibid.

dividuals who would have to be relied upon to assume managerial control of enterprises if that objective of the second decree were to be accomplished. Although they were not in a position to influence significantly the formulation of the policy, they certainly were in a position to affect its implementation.

Hence, indigenous businessmen had few qualms about being silent partners and staying out of management. They were more than willing to help their joint-venture partners obtain additional expatriates, to negotiate away their managerial responsibilities in technical-service agreements, to accept the rewritten articles of association, and to ignore some of the unilateral violations of the decree committed by their foreign partners. It was not that local businessmen were venal, ignorant, or unpatriotic. It is just that they had an acute sense of how to maximize their own interests and did not share all the objectives of the state technocrats who constructed the second decree. It is ironic that although state officials knew they were opposed by the indigenous business community on the issue of control, they ultimately had to rely on them to accomplish that objective.

The combination of the countervailing measures employed by the multinationals and the opposition of indigenous businessmen made it extremely difficult to affect the control of operations, even when a majority of the equity was acquired by Nigerians. However, the fact that the state itself was divided on the issue effectively eliminated the possibility that significant changes in control could take place at the enterprise level. The 5 percent limitation was not consistent with the objective of control, and the state never established the mechanisms required to implement a real change in control in a large number of companies.[126] Making political appointments to the boards of indigenized companies also did little to advance the cause of securing control. Given the strategies of the multinationals, the opposition of the indigenous businessmen, and the divisions within the state, it is surprising that any changes in effective control took place.

Those changes that did occur tended to stem from one of the following situations. First, if Nigerians acquired 100 percent of the equity with their own capital, they were likely to assume control over operations. This condition applies only to a small percentage of the Schedule 1 enterprises affected by the second decree, however. A second way to accomplish a change in effective control was for the state

[126] Recall that the CIC did not assume that control was a central objective of the program in either its valuation or its allocation procedures, and even the NEPB was less vigilant on the issue of control after Al-Hakim's tenure.

to assume the majority of the equity. Under those conditions, the state did not have to rely on others (especially on reluctant local businessmen) to accomplish some of its objectives (like managerial control). As we saw in the case of the petroleum sector, however, this is not a sufficient condition for obtaining effective control. The form of the state's participation is important, as is accompanying legislation like the Banking Decree with its credit guidelines. This implies that the insurance industry and possibly petroleum might be the most likely candidates for changes in effective control in the future. The third condition under which a change in effective control is likely is when the joint venture is initiated by indigenous businessmen, rather than by the multinational corporation. A change in control is more likely if the local businessmen put up their own capital and if they have some experience with the production or distribution of the product involved. These types of enterprises are still few in number, but they do exist—even in Schedule 3.

Aside from a few cases of changes in effective control, there were very few operational changes of any immediate significance at the enterprise level. Board meetings became more frequent and annual general meetings became more lively, but these were largely cosmetic changes. The picture is not quite as grim (or static) as many dependency writers would maintain, however. A few changes in operations that do not appear significant at present may have important long-term implications.

The increased pace of personnel indigenization at the senior levels has simultaneously increased learning about operations and created a vocal constituency for further personnel indigenization from the ranks of middle managers. The increases in wages and employee benefits have had an important effect on urban wages in general and on the growing disparity between urban and rural income in the country. The capital-intensive expansion of industry has potentially significant implications for Nigeria's foreign-exchange position and provided one of the constraints in its 1986 financial crisis. Finally, the shift of some indigenous businessmen from managing their own commercial ventures to initiating productive joint ventures with foreign capital is of considerable importance for the development of a domestic bourgeoisie, something we will consider more fully in the next chapter.

CHAPTER SIX

The Control of Finance and the Development of Capitalism in Nigeria

ALTHOUGH no real change took place in the effective control (and operations) of the vast majority of the enterprises affected by the second indigenization decree, the program was not entirely without effect at the enterprise level. Some changes did take place in each of the schedules, and especially in a number of the banks. When we begin to evaluate the consequences of the program at higher levels of aggregation (i.e. at the sectoral and national levels), a somewhat different pattern emerges. Some significant changes have taken place at both levels.

To an extent far greater than before 1975, Nigerians now effectively control their domestic financial system. Like other large debtor countries, they are still severely constrained by their international financial obligations. However, the state has a greater capability (and responsibility) for domestic finance than it had prior to the indigenization program, something that has significance for the direction of national development. In addition, there has been a significant movement of indigenous businessmen into productive economic activities, at least up through 1982. An accumulating indigenous bourgeoisie engaged in productive economic activities is not exactly thriving in Nigeria, but something of a more than ephemeral nature was underway before the oil glut and Nigeria's economic downturn of the middle 1980s began.

The indigenization program was by itself not entirely responsible for these changes, but in combination with other foreign and domestic economic policies (such as the banking decree, import controls, and the austerity measures) it has had a significance that transcends the immediate objectives of any of the central actors considered in Chapter 4. These changes would not have taken place to the degree they have, or as quickly as they have, had the second indigenization decree never been enacted.

CONSEQUENCES AT THE SECTORAL LEVEL

To assess the sectoral consequences of the second decree, we must again turn to the company data set described in Appendix B. By examining the patterns of investment for the 1,230 firms for which complete data on the year of incorporation, principal economic activity, and ownership can be obtained, we can at least begin to evaluate the sectoral consequences of the decree. These data are only indicators or approximations of underlying trends and must be interpreted with caution. Given the paucity of reliable statistical data on the Nigerian economy, however, I can think of no more reliable nonanecdotal source of information on these issues. As was the case in Chapter 3, the data will be supplemented (and in this case updated) with information from the interviews described in Appendix A.

The first striking feature from this sample of companies is the fact that fewer companies were incorporated between 1976 and 1980 than in the preceding five-year period.[1] A total of 340 firms were incorporated around the time of the first decree (between 1971 and 1975), while only 139 new companies came on stream during a comparable period around the second decree (between 1976 and 1980).[2] Half of the new incorporations were foreign companies, while 44 percent were indigenous firms. Only 4 percent were state firms.

The absolute number of indigenous businesses incorporated declined from 170 in the first period (1971–75) to 64 during the second (1976–80), and their relative share declined from 50 percent to 46 percent. This pattern is not surprising, given the amount of indigenous capital employed to purchase the shares of existing foreign ventures. One of the short-term opportunity costs of indigenization was the disincentive it provided for the establishment of new indigenous companies. At the same time, the second decree appears to have made foreign companies hesitant about making new investments in Nigeria. The absolute number of new foreign companies locating in Nigeria fell from 151 in the first period to 69 in the second.[3] New state

---

[1] The period 1976–80 was chosen because it is of comparable length and coincides with a period comparable to that used to evaluate the first decree in Chapter 3. Recall that a year before the promulgation of the first decree, most members of the indigenous and expatriate business communities were aware of the impending 1972 decree and were given until 1974 to comply. The White Paper for the second decree was released in 1976, the decree in 1977, and the implementation period extended until 1979. Both of the periods under review (1971–75 and 1976–80) include an additional year to allow for consolidation of the trends initiated during the implementation process.

[2] A total of 261 companies were incorporated between 1965 and 1970.

[3] Their relative share increased slightly, however, from 44 percent to 50 percent.

companies accounted for only 4 percent of the sample in the 1976–80 period; however, the measure of new incorporations does not adequately capture the significance of the growth of state intervention through portfolio investments. It also does not consider the size and significance of the state's investments, something that will be considered in more detail below.

Most of the indigenous companies incorporated after 1975 were engaged in commerce, suggesting that the second decree had little immediate effect on the sectoral proclivities of local capital. In fact, new commercial ventures accounted for 53 percent of their new incorporations in both the 1971–75 and 1976–80 periods. Their spread among three other sectors was again divided roughly equally. Approximately 17 percent established service-sector firms, 16 percent went into construction, and 13 percent created manufacturing companies. Under 2 percent of the new incorporations were in the primary sector, consistent with the decline of agriculture and the reservation of the petroleum sector for the state. The manufacturing sector showed the greatest growth, but it was of only 2 percent and was built on a very small base.

During the 1976–80 period, foreign capital showed an increased tendency to go into construction ventures. Construction accounted for 34 percent of the new foreign companies established between 1971 and 1975, and it grew to 39 percent at the time of the second decree. There was a slight decline in new manufacturing firms (from 18 percent to 17 percent) during the same period, while service-sector activities experienced a similar decline (from 21 percent to 20 percent). The biggest decline in new incorporations occurred in the primary sector. Foreign incorporations in commerce were virtually unchanged.

These data on new incorporations give us a general sense of the direction of both local and foreign capital immediately after the second decree was issued, but they do not tell us anything about the cumulative impacts of these sectoral shifts, or, more important, whether indigenous or foreign capital was concentrated in any particular industries. To answer these questions, we again have both to examine cumulative incorporation data and include information from the research interviews described in Appendix A.

The Service Sector

Although the cumulative data do not indicate it, the most important sectoral consequences of the second decree are to be found in the service sector. Cumulatively, in the service sector as a whole there was

TABLE 6.1
Distribution of Newly Incorporated Firms
during the Implementation of the
Second Indigenization Decree, 1976–80

	Local capital		Foreign capital	
	No.	%	No.	%
Commerce	34	53	14	20
Manufacturing	8	13	12	17
Construction	10	16	27	39
Services	11	17	14	20
Primary	1	2	2	3

SOURCE: Company data set described in Appendix B.

TABLE 6.2
Cumulative Incorporation of Service-Sector Firms in Nigeria,
1970–80

Year	Local	Foreign	State	Total
1970	49 (33%)	77 (51%)	24 (16%)	150
1975	84 (38%)	109 (49%)	29 (13%)	222
1980	95 (38%)	123 (50%)	30 (12%)	248

SOURCE: Data described in Appendix B.

a very slight, statistically insignificant, increase in the relative share of
foreign capital after the second decree. By 1980, foreign companies
accounted for 50 percent of the incorporated companies in the service
sector, up less than one percent from 1975. Most of this was accounted for by several new foreign-managed hotels, growth in the
number of foreign business-consulting firms, and the introduction of
agricultural irrigation services. Foreign capital lost ground in the
banking, insurance, shipping, and transportation subsectors.

The single most important change in the service sector cannot be
captured by looking only at cumulative incorporation data, however.
One has to look inside the enterprises to assess the operational significance of changes in control. As discussed in Chapter 5, the greatest
change in control and operations took place in the banks. Given the
identity of the banks affected, the number involved, the nature of Nigerian state participation, and the combined effects of indigenization
and the Central Bank's annual guidelines, it is fair to say that the sec-

ond decree enabled the Nigerian state to assume control over its domestic financial system.

This is no mean accomplishment. Banking is a sector of strategic economic importance, and, as indicated earlier, "prior to 1972, the major banks had operated practically as if they were external to the Nigerian financial system."[4] It was not until after the second decree, when the state appointed the managing directors of the major commercial and merchant banks, that it could be described as being able to control the banking system as a whole. Before the appointment of indigenous managing directors, the banks were able to find ways to falsify their allocation records to comply with the Central Bank's credit guidelines.[5] This has become more difficult since the appointment of Nigerians to senior managerial positions, and the banks have become more diligent about carrying out the Central Bank's policy and guidelines. This suggests that the Banking Decree by itself was not sufficient for attaining indigenous control of the sector and that the second decree played a central role in the "radical changes" through which the banking industry has gone in structure and attitude in recent years.[6]

In addition to the dramatic changes in banking, the insurance industry has witnessed significant change. State governments acquired a majority of the shares of the largest companies, while insurance brokerage has become an important area of growth for indigenous businessmen (thanks in part to its relatively small capital requirements).[7] Indigenous stock-brokerage firms also experienced a boom after the second decree, since they managed the sale of shares of the many large foreign companies forced by the CIC (and later the NSEC) to offer public subscriptions. Thus, the growth and control of enterprises were not restricted to banking, but were experienced throughout the financial sector.

The second decree not only produced state control of the Nigerian financial system, but also spurred the institutional development of that system. The Capital Issues Commission that had been created at the time of the first decree was transformed into the Nigerian Securities and Exchange Commission (NSEC).[8] It was responsible not only for valuing every firm affected by the second decree, but also proved largely responsible for the substantial growth of the number of com-

[4] Asabia 1981: 28.
[5] Interview with multinational bank manager.
[6] Asabia 1981: 5.
[7] Asabia 1982-17.
[8] Akamiokhor 1982: 8.

panies listed on the Nigerian Stock Exchange. As many as fifty-three new companies were added to the exchange at the time of the second decree. Thus, the NSEC contributed to a further institutional development—the development of the Nigerian Stock Exchange (NSE), formerly the Lagos Stock Exchange. The exchange grew from having only seventeen firms listed in 1971 to ninety-six by the end of 1981,[9] and it opened branches throughout the country by 1980. This in turn stimulated the growth of indigenous stock-brokerage firms and made it easier for small businesses to raise capital.[10]

In the rest of the service sector, there was relatively little change after the second decree. Local capital continued to dominate areas associated with commerce (freight forwarding and customs services), and it maintained control over advertising, domestic transportation, and real estate. By the early 1980s, real estate and property development were widely regarded as among the best investments for local capital in Nigeria.[11] They offered the highest rates of return, especially in the Lagos and Kano metropolitan areas, and even some of the largest trading families started to pursue property investments when the advance deposits on imports being levied by the Central Bank became too costly (they reached levels of 200 percent).[12] Indigenous entrepreneurs also managed to maintain a competitive position with foreign capital in some of the newer, most rapidly growing, areas of the service sector such as architecture, accounting, planning, business consulting, and legal services.

Foreign capital dominated the oil services sector, foreign shipping, and telecommunications. It also pioneered new technical-service activities in irrigation, engineering, and agricultural equipment. As described above, the state dominated only in banking, though it also played an important role in the insurance and hotel industries. For the most part, aside from the significant developments in banking and finance, the service sector experienced relatively little change immediately after the second decree.

Manufacturing Sector

After services, the most significant developments took place in the manufacturing sector. Again, these developments do not show up very clearly in the cumulative incorporation data, although the slight trends that do emerge at the sectoral level are at least in the right di-

---

[9] Asabia 1982:Table 9.
[10] Interview with indigenous senior manager with a MNC.
[11] Interviews with several indigenous businessmen and multinational bankers.
[12] Interview with indigenous businessman.

rection. Foreign companies continued to dominate the manufacturing sector as a whole, but they yielded a little ground to indigenous business. The 1970–80 period shows a consistent, though very gradual, decline in the relative share of foreign enterprises. As was the case for the service sector as a whole, most of the ground gained by indigenous enterprises took place between 1971 and 1975, probably because so much local capital was tied up in the acquisition of existing companies at the time of the second decree.

Unlike the first indigenization decree, the second affected the manufacturing sector very directly. Most of the lower- and intermediate-technology manufacturing activities were assigned to Schedule 2, so it is important to investigate whether local or state capital gained a foothold in any specific manufacturing industries after 1976. The 337 manufacturing enterprises in the sample were distributed in forty-three different activities (e.g. textiles, food processing, automobile assembly), nineteen of which were large enough to have at least five incorporated firms. Of those nineteen activities, foreign capital continued to dominate all but two of them. However, the data suggest a trend toward an increased concentration of local capital in a number of low-technology manufacturing activities. Although their number may not show up as significant in the aggregate data for the manufacturing sector, local businessmen may have created a niche for themselves in a number of areas.

By 1980, indigenous businessmen had increased their position in the furniture and electronics-assembly industries to a point where they dominated those activities. They were at parity with foreign capital in the printing, publishing, and rubber-processing industries and they were strongly competitive with multinationals in the production of household goods and appliances, textiles, packaging materials, paints, plastics, and shoes. State productive enterprises dominated in none of the nineteen industries examined, although several strategic

TABLE 6.3
Cumulative Incorporation of Manufacturing Firms in Nigeria, 1970–80

Year	Local	Foreign	State	Total
1970	59 (23%)	181 (70%)	19 (7%)	259
1975	78 (25%)	208 (66%)	27 (9%)	313
1980	86 (26%)	220 (65%)	31 (9%)	337

SOURCE: Data described in Appendix B.

industries like oil refining, petrochemicals, and iron and steel were either reserved for future state development or had only a few incorporated companies on stream by 1980. State enterprises were competitive with foreign ones in brewing and soft-drink bottling, cement, and food processing. Figure 6.1 summarizes some of the subsectoral shifts within the manufacturing sector since indigenization. A ten-year period is appropriate for this purpose, because of the longer gestation of manufacturing investments relative to other activities and the extended period required for returns in manufacturing.

The story does not end here, however. When multinational managers in all sectors were asked where local capital was strongest in the early 1980s (and where local firms were competitive with them), some of the trends outlined above become even more apparent. In the twenty-four interviews in which a multinational manager or banker responded to a question about where indigenous business was most competitive, the strengths of indigenous business in manufacturing were ranked as follows. Nearly half mentioned food processing, furniture, beer brewing, and soft drinks. Eight respondents listed textiles, while one-fourth listed electrical assembly, metal fabrication, and printing. Other areas of clear growth or prominence of indigenous business were plastics and building materials. Only three respondents suggested that indigenous firms were "not strong in manufacturing whatsoever."[13]

The results for the same question asked of fourteen indigenous businessmen were similar, at least at the top of the scale.[14] Thus there is a growing amount of evidence both from the company data set and from the research interviews that by the early 1980s indigenous businessmen had carved for themselves a niche in the production of a number of low-technology consumer goods (like foods and beverages, textiles, furniture, and electronics) and low-technology processing industries (like metal fabrication, plastics, building materials, and chemicals). Indigenization was not entirely responsible for this development. Many of these subsectors were identified as areas of indige-

[13] Interview with MNC executive. The responses of twenty-four multinational managers interviewed (see Appendix A) were as follows: thirteen, food processing; eleven, furniture; ten, beer brewing and soft drinks; eight, textiles; six, metal fabrication, electrical assembly, and printing; five, plastics and building materials. (The frequencies do not add to twenty-four, since most respondents listed more than one industry, and few rank-ordered them.)

[14] The detailed rankings were as follows: ten, food proceesing; nine, beer brewing and soft drinks; four, textiles and chemicals; three, furniture; two, building materials, shoes, metal fabrication, and plastics. (The frequencies do not add to fourteen, since most respondents listed more than one industry, and few rank-ordered them.)

nous business strength in the extensive literature on Nigerian entrepreneurs generated in the 1960s.[15] It would probably be more accurate to suggest that indigenization reinforced and accelerated a process already underway.

There is a good deal of evidence that manufacturing was increasingly perceived as offering the best opportunities for indigenous business, a marked change from the 1960s and 1970s. When indigenous businessmen were asked in mid 1982 what they thought were the best investments for local firms, a clear majority ranked manufacturing first. Thirteen out of the twenty-four respondents answering this open-ended question described manufacturing as the fastest-growing investment area for local capital. Six individuals ranked property investments first, while five maintained that commerce still offered the best returns. But several of those listing commerce first declared they intended to use commercial ventures to accumulate capital before investing it in manufacturing activities.[16] Indigenization was credited by many with having created investment opportunities for indigenous businessmen in manufacturing, though it was not the sole source of this development. The federal military government's import controls were also cited by several as having convinced "those who build up capital through importation . . . to go into manufacturing."[17] The Shagari government's austerity program had very much the same effect in the early 1980s. In addition, the Central Bank's credit guidelines were modified to stimulate indigenous investment in manufacturing.[18] The combined effect of indigenization plus import controls, the austerity measures, and the easing of credit made manufacturing investments far more attractive to indigenous entrepreneurs.

Most of the new investment that did take place was in the low-technology consumer-goods and processing industries described above. The investment tended to be small or medium scale in size,[19] low value added, and heavily reliant on imported raw materials.[20] By some estimates, up to 75 percent of the raw materials employed in production in these industries was imported,[21] contributing substantially to

[15] The contributions of Peter Kilby (1969), John R. Harris (1967), Sayre P. Schatz (1977), and E. Wayne Nafziger (1977) come especially to mind.

[16] Interview with indigenous senior manager with MNC bank.

[17] Ibid.

[18] Asabia 1981: 14.

[19] Ogunbanjo 1982: 14.

[20] Forrest 1982: 333.

[21] Interview with indigenous senior manager with MNC bank.

FIGURE 6.1
Shifts in the Pattern of New Incorporations in the Manufacturing Sector after the Indigenization Decrees

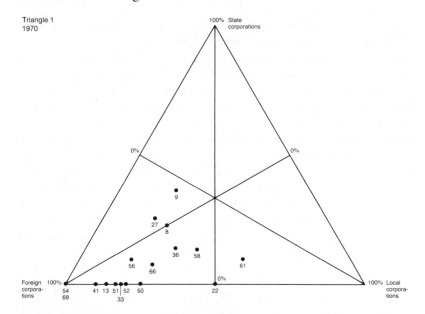

Key to business activities
8 Brewing and soft drinks
9 Building materials and cement (including block molders)
13 Chemicals (batteries, industrial gases, adhesives)
22 Electrical and electronic equipment
25 Food and food processing (includes bakeries/confectioneries)
27 Furniture (including interior decorating)

33 Household goods and appliances
36 Leather and shoes
41 Metals, metal processing and fabrication
44 Motor vehicles and components
50 Packaging
51 Paint
52 Paper and paper products
54 Pharmaceuticals and medical supplies and services

56 Plastics and plastic products
58 Printing and publishing (books and newspapers)
61 Rubber and rubber goods
66 Textiles and clothing and textile equipment
67 Timber industries, sawmills
69 Toiletries and cosmetics

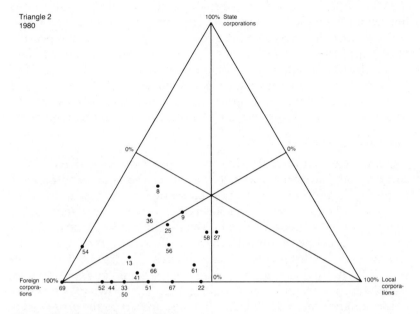

Triangle 2
1980

100% State corporations

0%

0%

8

36

9

25

58 27

54

56

13

66

61

41

Foreign 100%
corpora-
tions

69

52 44 33
50

51

67

22

0%

100% Local
corpora-
tions

NOTE: See note to Fig. 3.3, p. 137.
SOURCE: Company data set described in Appendix B.

Nigeria's huge recurring import bill. The only exception to this appears to be in the furniture industry, where local materials are more readily employed.

Many of the new enterprises initiated and controlled by indigenous businessmen employ expatriate technicians on contract. Most also seek and are able to receive tariff protection. (This has been especially important for the expansion of beer brewing and furniture production.) Thus, although there is mounting evidence that local capital began carving out a niche in some manufacturing areas after the second decree, this development is not without some evident costs (due to import intensity and the amount of protection apparently required).

Commercial Sector

Commerce continued to attract the majority of new indigenous incorporations, at least up to 1980. Most of the new manufacturers identified in the previous section continued to keep a foothold in commerce. At the sectoral level, local capital consolidated its position slightly at the expense of foreign capital. The state's participation in the sector remained minimal. The rate of expansion of indigenous commercial establishments, which was fairly constant between 1960 and 1975 (more than doubling every five years), slowed considerably after 1975. This is due largely to the general slowdown in new incorporations after the second decree, but also in part to the growing attractiveness of manufacturing and property investments.

By 1980, foreign capital still dominated large-scale commerce (department stores) and the sale of technical goods (such as oil equipment, telecommunications, and chemicals), but local capital was at parity with it or dominated all other areas of commerce by that time. Indigenous businessmen were starting to go into wholesale trade, to import their own goods directly, and to expand supermarket chains (like Domino, Ilupeju, and Globe Fish).

TABLE 6.4
Cumulative Incorporation of Commercial Firms in Nigeria, 1970–80

Year	Local	Foreign	State	Total
1970	89 (45%)	103 (52%)	5 (3%)	197
1975	179 (56%)	133 (41%)	10 (3%)	322
1980	213 (57%)	147 (40%)	11 (3%)	371

SOURCE: Data described in Appendix B.

The general consolidation of the position of local capital in commerce was not restricted to any particular activities, but was spread throughout the sector. The largest gains of indigenous business growth after the second decree were found in companies specializing in the sale of agricultural equipment, food, hardware, timber, office equipment, and computers. Slight gains in the relative position of local capital were recorded in building materials, cement, pharmaceuticals, and general trading companies. The largest loss of relative position was only of a magnitude of 5 percent (in the sale of electronic goods) and was caused by the establishment of a state government company, not the expansion of foreign capital.

Thus, the second decree further consolidated the position of local capital in commerce, and by 1980 no new foreign companies were being incorporated in that sector. Figure 6.2 summarizes the shifts in the patterns of new incorporations for some selected activities in the commercial sector between 1971 and 1980.

Other Sectors

The relative share of local capital, foreign capital, and the state remained virtually unchanged in the construction industry in the years immediately following the second decree. There was a very slight gain of local capital in the industry, largely at the expense of the state. As in the other sectors we have examined, however, there are some subsectoral concentrations of local businessmen which suggest that they are establishing a position in the construction sector as well.

For example, although local capital accounted for only about one-fourth of the total construction companies incorporated in the country in 1980, the companies specialized in small-scale projects that the larger foreign companies tend to pass up.[22] They are likely to be found in the construction of buildings, access roads, and nontechnical projects. Local engineering firms are also increasingly competitive with foreign ones and have reached parity with them (at least in the number of incorporated companies) in both electrical and mechanical engineering.

The construction industry boomed as long as the oil money was flowing, since it received so much public spending. Local firms benefited considerably from the federal government's practice of giving preference to construction bids from foreign companies working in association with indigenous companies. However, in the majority of these cases the local firm contributed more in the way of a name and

[22] Interview with indigenous manager with MNC.

FIGURE 6.2
Shifts in the Pattern of New Incorporations in the Commercial
Sector after the Second Indigenization Decree

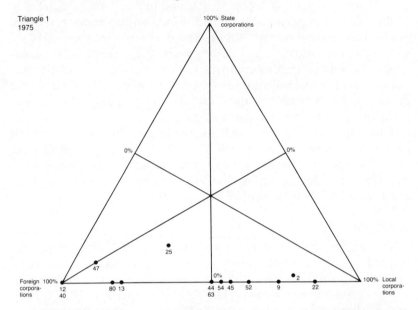

Key to business activities
2 Agents and general
   trading companies
3 Agricultural equipment
   and services
9 Building materials and
   cement (including
   block molders)
12 Chain stores
13 Chemicals (batteries,
   industrial gases,
   adhesives)
22 Electrical and
   electronic equipment

25 Food and food
   processing (includes
   bakeries/
   confectioneries)
27 Furniture (including
   interior decorating)
31 Hardware
40 Mechanical
   engineering plant
44 Motor vehicles and
   components
45 Office equipment and
   supplies

47 Oil and gas services
   and equipment and
   pipeline contractors
   (supplying them or
   distributing their
   products)
52 Paper and paper
   products
54 Pharmaceuticals and
   medical supplies and
   services
63 Scientific instruments
65 Telecommunications
80 Diversified

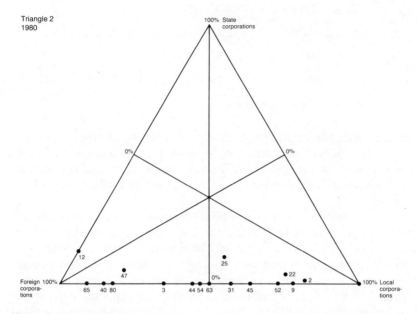

Triangle 2
1980

100% State corporations

0%   0%

12

25

47   22

0%   2

Foreign 100%
corpora-
tions

65   40 80   3   44 54 63   31   45   52 9

100% Local
corpora-
tions

NOTE: See note to Fig. 3.3, p. 137.
SOURCE: Company data set described in Appendix B.

TABLE 6.5

Cumulative Incorporation of Construction Firms in Nigeria, 1970–80

Year	Local	Foreign	State	Total
1970	16 (16%)	82 (83%)	1 (1%)	99
1975	41 (23%)	134 (76%)	1 (1%)	176
1980	51 (24%)	161 (76%)	1 (0%)	213

SOURCE: Data described in Appendix B.

useful political contacts than it did in technical expertise.[23] There is not yet much evidence to suggest that indigenous construction firms have used their position in small-scale construction (and the benefits of association with foreign firms) to expand into other areas of the sector.

Primary production has experienced the least change of any sector from the perspective of local capital. The purchase of agricultural produce continues to be a monopoly of the state, there has been little growth in the position of local mining firms, and the most important subsector, petroleum, is entirely run by foreign companies and the state. The data on the number of incorporated companies in the sector as a whole do not really tell us very much about the important role of the state in the largest industry in the sector, the petroleum industry, since foreign capital continues to control essential aspects of production (based on the interviews discussed in Chapter 5). The state's role is also concentrated in a single company, the NNPC, which makes the cumulative number of incorporations a particularly poor indicator of involvement of the major actors for this particular sector. Nevertheless, as shown in Table 6.6, the data do indicate the extent to which (with a few notable exceptions) local capital has divorced itself from large-scale corporate investment in agriculture and raw-materials development, especially in the years since the indigenization process was begun.

CONSEQUENCES AT THE NATIONAL LEVEL

Among the national-level consequences of the second decree, the economic and financial effects of the program have generated the most debate and controversy within Nigeria. By the early 1980s the lines of

[23] Interview with official of a foreign embassy.

TABLE 6.6
Cumulative Incorporation of Primary-Sector Firms in Nigeria,
1955–80

Year	Local	Foreign	State	Total
1955	6 (32%)	13 (68%)	0 (0%)	19
1960	7 (30%)	16 (70%)	0 (0%)	23
1965	13 (39%)	20 (61%)	0 (0%)	33
1970	15 (33%)	31 (67%)	0 (0%)	46
1975	16 (28%)	41 (71%)	1 (2%)	58
1980	17 (28%)	43 (70%)	1 (2%)	61

SOURCE: Data described in Appendix B.

this debate were fairly clearly drawn. On one side were critics of the program from the indigenous business community who argued that the second decree had reduced the inflow of new foreign capital from direct investment, had retarded the growth of new investment in both Schedules 1 and 2, and had only provided a stimulus to greater state involvement in the economy. There was general support for this position at the highest levels of the Shagari administration.

The strongest disagreement with this assessment of the second decree came from retired officials of the Muhammed–Obasanjo military government, a number of high-level civil servants, and several senior indigenous managers working for European and North American multinationals. They generally agreed that foreign investment was down, but disagreed strongly that total investment in the economy had declined, and contended that state intervention performed a critical function by mediating among potentially disruptive ethnic economic interests and keeping any single group from dominating the economy. The latter argument was particularly prevalent among northern Nigerians.

In the immediate aftermath of the second decree there is some evidence that multinationals "shied away from new investments," as charged by some critics of indigenization.[24] As mentioned in Chapter 5, a number of firms delayed decisions to invest or expand their operations in Nigeria. However, the aggregate data on foreign investment inflows into Nigeria suggest that this was a temporary phenomenon. The data displayed in Table 6.7 and Figure 6.3 indicate that sharp declines in inflows of foreign capital took place in the years immediately following the promulgation of each decree (declining in

[24] Ogunbanjo 1982: 14.

1973 and 1978). However, in both cases, within one or two years after the decree was announced, inflows of foreign investment exceeded levels attained prior to the decree.[25]

In the years immediately following the first indigenization decree, most of the inflow of foreign capital was accounted for by the oil sector, a sector that was not affected by the program and that operated according to its own dynamic. Oil investment accounted for between 47.4 percent and 66.1 percent of the total foreign investment inflows for each year between 1972 and 1975; thus critics of the program are on stronger ground when they criticize the first decree for dampening the interest of foreign capital. With regard to the second decree, the same argument cannot be made. The increase that took place in investment inflows after 1978 cannot be accounted for by an expansion of oil-sector investment. In fact, new investment in oil as a percentage of total direct investment dropped consistently between 1975 and 1979 before levelling off at around 25 percent of annual foreign in-

TABLE 6.7
Inflow of Direct Foreign Investment into Nigeria, 1967–81 (millions of naira)

Year	Nonoil sector	Oil sector		Total
1967	91.0	N.A.		91.0
1968	142.8	N.A.		142.8
1969	120.0	N.A.		120.0
1970	144.6	N.A.		144.6
1971	148.8	14.0	(8.6%)	162.8
1972	132.0	195.8	(59.7%)	327.8
1973	128.0	115.5	(47.4%)	243.5
1974	95.5	186.2	(66.1%)	281.7
1975	149.1	210.5	(58.5%)	359.6
1976	197.9	157.8	(44.4%)	355.7
1977	245.0	147.5	(37.6%)	392.5
1978	231.8	92.1	(28.4%)	323.9
1979	322.0	100.3	(23.8%)	422.3
1980	325.0	109.2	(25.1%)	434.2
1981	375.6	117.2	(23.8%)	492.8

SOURCE: Central Bank of Nigeria, *Economic and Financial Review*, various years, and *Annual Report and Statement of Accounts*, various years.

[25] In fact, there may have been some learning going on for the multinationals, since the rate at which inflows picked up was much higher after the second decree than it had been after the first. Even though the second decree was far more extensive, many multinational managers had seen this kind of program (and responded to it) in Nigeria before.

FIGURE 6.3
Inflow of Direct Foreign Investment into Nigeria, 1967–81

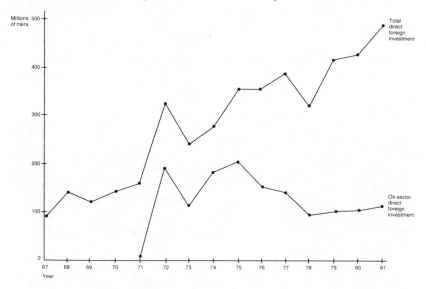

SOURCE: Central Bank of Nigeria, *Economic and Financial Review*, various years, and *Annual Report and Statement of Account*, various years.

vestment inflow. Thus there is not a great deal of empirical evidence to support the contention that foreign investment inflows diminished considerably after the second decree. Critics of the program need to justify their counterfactual assumption that direct foreign investment has decreased from levels it would have reached in the absence of indigenization.[26]

Data from interviews with multinational managers also challenge the argument that foreign investment declined because of indigenization. The argument might be sustained after the first decree, but not after the second. In research interviews conducted with multinational managers in 1981, only a few years after the promulgation of the second decree, it was apparent that few, if any, were concerned about indigenization. In answer to an open-ended question about which Nigerian government regulations affected their operations the most, it was rare to hear anything about the program. For the reasons that were identified in Chapter 5, most were satisfied that they retained

[26] Interview with former government official. This counterfactual assumption was apparently widespread within the Shagari administration.

control over operations, and hence were more likely to respond to the question by complaining about foreign exchange restrictions, import restrictions, expatriate-quota regulations, Form M, or the myriad of governmental decrees affecting specific industries (the Banking Decree, the Insurance Decree, etc.). In the end, it is the sum total of these bureaucratic regulations plus infrastructural difficulties (like obtaining a consistent supply of electricity, clean water, or accessible roads) that provide the greatest disincentive to foreign investment in Nigeria.

With regard to the total amount of new investment in Schedule 1 and 2 activities, critics of indigenization are on stronger ground. It is clear that there were at least short-term, and possibly long-term, opportunity costs incurred by the indigenous acquisition of existing companies. The level of incorporations of new firms between 1976 and 1980, discussed above, was clearly below that obtained in the two previous five-year periods. It is unfortunate that data are not available after 1980 to determine whether this was a temporary or lasting phenomenon.

Aggregate investment figures, however, do not indicate a sharp decline in total investment over the period in question. Using commercial bank loans and advances as a rough proxy for investment, between 1968 and 1979 total investment grew nineteenfold in current naira. These Central Bank data do not distinguish between investment as an acquisition of existing enterprises (brought on by indigenization) and investment as the creation of new establishments, and they do not take account of funds generated internally and reinvested by firms. They also fail to distinguish between public- and private-sector investment. Thus, although they indicate the total amount of investment in the Nigerian economy, these data cannot be used to address the central questions about the program posed by its critics (i.e. its contribution to the establishment of new enterprises and the growth of the state's intervention in the economy). From the interview data described in Appendix A, observers of the Nigerian economy are divided along the lines defined earlier.

One thing on which most agree, however, is that more capital has been retained in the country in recent years. As in the case of some of the other sectoral and national consequences of the program, indigenization is not solely responsible for this development. The repatriation restrictions in place at the time of the implementation of the second decree played a primary role, and the establishment of the National Reinsurance Corporation also contributed by requiring that certain classifications (or percentages) of insurance premiums be held in Nigerian investments.[27] Both indigenous business critics of the program and multinational bankers agree that more money now stays in the economy for reinvestment as a result of the second decree and these associated measures.[28]

The concern about the foreign exchange implications of the second decree observed immediately after the initial valuations by the CIC now seems unwarranted.[29] The concern was usually expressed in terms of the percentage of shares offered for sale rather than for subscription, but by the end of 1981 the NSEC reported that nearly 75 percent of the naira value of the shares had been offers for subscription rather than offers for sale which could eventually be repatriated.[30] If one compares the value of paid-up capital of all the firms affected by the second decree prior to the valuation undertaken by the CIC with the value of the same firms after the valuation process in 1979 (subtracting the total value offered for sale on the assumption that it could be remitted, and adding the total value offered for subscription), the net gain in potential foreign-exchange savings is more than 50 million naira.[31] The final calculations of the foreign-exchange implications of indigenization are far more complex, and would have to take into account counterfactual alternative uses of capital (i.e. alternatives to buying shares in existing companies) as well as the intangible effects of transfer pricing, something which was bound to, and in fact did increase under the conditions prevailing in Nigeria (that is, the forced sale of assets at below market prices, combined with severe repatriation restrictions).

One final national-level economic consequence of the second decree that might well have important political implications in the long run was the stimulus it gave to middle- and upper-level management training. In addition to promoting a number of Nigerians to senior management positions, most companies embarked on extensive training programs. They either sent employees through their own programs, often at the parent headquarters, or they participated in the programs offered by the Center for Management Development and

[27] Asabia 1982: 17–18.

[28] Interviews with one MNC bank manager and three indigenous businessmen.

[29] See Balabkins 1982: 230–231 for an example of this concern, and the low estimate of only 40 percent of share transactions being offers for subscription reported in Forrest 1982: 337.

[30] Akamiokhor 1982: 7.

[31] This assumes that money raised by offers for subscription might otherwise have left the country, a not unreasonable assumption given the past performance of Nigerian entrepreneurs.

the Industrial Training Fund, the two training institutions created after the first decree. The costs of maintaining expatriates in Nigeria undoubtedly played a major role in the thinking of many of these companies, but indigenization served to reinforce the tendency.

Many of the multinational firms described in Appendix A embarked on new training programs after the second decree, a trend particularly prevalent among West European firms.[32] Similarly, all of Hoogvelt's Kano respondents (most of whom were Lebanese or West European), provided "some sort of 'on the job' training of technicians and junior managerial staff."[33] Although it was not formally incorporated into the second decree, an expansion of training for Nigerian managers was recommended by the Adeosun Commission. Several commission members were strongly influenced by their information-gathering trip to Brazil and contend that their recommendations contributed to the Obasanjo government's crash program of sending 117,000 Nigerians abroad for technical training in the late 1970s.[34]

The major national-level political consequence of the indigenization program (which alarms its critics and is applauded by its supporters) is the contribution it has made to the growth of state involvement in the economy. Indigenization is certainly not the principal source of the growth of state intervention, something which has deep historical sources that were exacerbated by the explosion of the international oil market and the importance of petroleum for Nigeria after the early 1970s. However, the program was seized upon by advocates of greater state involvement in the late 1960s, and it has clearly facilitated the growth of the state portfolio investments since that time.

Indigenization has facilitated the growth of state intervention in the economy in two ways. First, because of the widespread concern about the regional imbalances associated with the first decree, the second decree established mechanisms (like the 5 percent limitation and the CIC's allocation guidelines) that ensured a wide, and generally representative, geographical spread of shares. The resulting purchasing and warehousing of shares by state governments and state development corporations contributed significantly to state-government participation in the economy. Second, the reservation of certain of the leading sectors of the national economy for the federal government (e.g. the banks, large-scale manufacturing in high-growth areas like

[32] European firms accounted for more than three-fourths of the examples of expanded training programs I was told about in my interviewing, a disproportionate number in terms of their percentage of the total sample (42 percent of the total sample).

[33] Hoogvelt 1980: 271.

[34] Interview with member of the Industrial Enterprises Panel.

petroleum, petrochemicals, refining, iron and steel, and vehicle assembly) led to an expansion of its role that far exceeded its previous levels of involvement in utilities and the occasional acquisition of failing companies.

It is difficult to assess how extensive this expansion of state intervention has been. According to one observer of the national economy, "There is certainly greater government involvement after the second decree, but it's almost impossible to know the details."[35] State governments are notoriously bad at keeping accurate records of their activities, but even the federal government had not compiled a list of its portfolio investments as many as six years after the decree.[36] According to one observer, the federal government is the leading shareholder, followed by the regional development corporations (NNDC for the North and O'Dua for the West), and state governments in Bendel, Ogun, Lagos, Oyo, Kano, and Kaduna states.[37] Total government shareholding (both state and federal) on the Nigerian Stock Exchange accounted for only 15 percent of the shares in 1982.[38] Government shareholding in public companies was distributed fairly widely, and when all state agencies are combined, they hold more than 20 percent of the shares in only thirteen of the fifty largest companies listed on the exchange. However, one indicator of the significance of the growth of state intervention throughout the economy was that following indigenization the NIDB had to alter its policy of not investing in government controlled projects.[39]

State governments and their development corporations accounted for 20.1 percent of the shares of the fourteen large trading companies listed on the exchange, while the NNDC alone acquired a total of 27 million shares, more than 3 percent of the total shares transferred during the process.[40] There is little expectation that any of these state-owned shares will ever be sold, since to sell "would create too much intense interest [in the public-private distributional issues] again."[41] It might also raise regional distribution questions. Even after the second decree, it appears that eastern state governments in Nigeria were

[35] Interview with spokesman for indigenous business group.
[36] Interview with senior state official.
[37] Interview with spokesman for indigenous business group.
[38] Nigerian Securities and Exchange Commission, internal memorandum from a meeting held on 25 May 1982, obtained from interview with government official. Individual investors accounted for 35 percent, while foreign investors held 42 percent of the total.
[39] Asabia 1982: 13.
[40] Interview with former state official.
[41] Ibid.

still largely left out of the process. None of them ranked alongside those in the West or North when it came to acquiring shares, and their equivalent of the NNDC (the Central Investment Company) was reportedly "not very active" at the time the shares were allocated.[42]

The federal government tends to specialize in acquiring shares in large-scale, high-growth enterprises in the strategic sectors of the national economy identified above. Most of their investments involve capital commitments beyond the capabilities of indigenous businessmen or state governments. State governments, on the other hand, specialize in smaller-scale manufacturing enterprises like breweries and textiles or service-sector activities like transportation. They are also more likely to end up with ownership of nonperforming enterprises that no one in the indigenous business community will buy. This is one of the reasons why state intervention resulting from indigenization has been so inefficient in Nigeria.[43] It is not that state management is necessarily less efficient, but that the state intervenes for noneconomic reasons (e.g. to maintain production or employment levels) and is therefore more likely to end up acquiring unprofitable enterprises.

One of the most interesting, and potentially most important, consequences of the entire indigenization program was its contribution to the growth of an accumulating bourgeoisie in the country. There is little point in searching for a unified national bourgeoisie in Nigeria, since if any aggregations of accumulating entrepreneurs exist, they are still likely to be divided along regional or ethnic lines. However, the continued salience of regional distinctions should not rule out the question of an accumulating bourgeoisie (or bourgeoisies) altogether, and the answers to some of the most interesting and important questions about the direction of Nigerian development are contingent upon its existence or nonexistence.

Inequality is a necessary condition for accumulation in contemporary capitalist political economies, and there is little question that the first indigenization decree contributed to inequality in Nigeria. The second decree, however, contained the 5 percent limitation and was implemented by the CIC's Allotment Committee with careful attention to the regional and national distribution of shares. It also affected both public and private companies. Thus, the distribution of shares

---

[42] Interview with spokesman for indigenous business group.

[43] Hoogvelt 1979: 62 reports that the Kano State Investment Corporation showed zero or negative returns between 1972 and 1978, "when everybody else, profiting from the Nigerian boom, has been able to make a 20% return on capital at the least."

from the second decree was certainly more egalitarian than from the first.

However, procedural fairness of the kind associated with the implementation of the second decree can be misleading. Those in power at the time realized the political importance of creating "the impression that a fair distribution has taken place."[44] They also realized that even with the 5 percent limitation, indigenization is not a program of national egalitarianism or redistribution of wealth. The ownership of shares is still highly concentrated, and there is a general consensus that those in business first, especially those around at the time of the first decree, benefited the most from the second.[45]

There are three major reasons for this. First, only a small percentage of the Nigerian population had either the savings or access to capital through the banking system to purchase shares. Some of the issuing houses required that shares be purchased with checks drawn on Nigerian banks, a procedure that effectively eliminated 90 percent of the Nigerian population. Second, a new form of fronting was developed at the time of the second decree. As described in Chapter 5, the practice of wealthy Nigerians' having relatives and trusted employees purchase shares on their behalf had "become an established routine."[46] Third, despite the fact that more companies were affected and more capital involved, for many Schedule 2 enterprises the 5 percent limitation and other distributional safeguards applied only to the 20 percent of additional shares transferred at the time of the second decree. The bulk of the shares involved (40 percent) had been traded when the 5 percent limitation was not in effect.[47]

Without doubt, more people acquired shares at the time of the second decree than at the time of the first. Small shareholders holding between 100 and 500 shares acquired 54.8 percent of the fourteen large public enterprises sold in phase one of the implementation. The reservation of 10 percent of the shares for employees, the 5 percent limitation, and the Allotment Committee saw to it that the program was less inegalitarian. However, it was only a matter of degree. The cumulative effect of the first and second decrees provided at least a theoretical basis for indigenous capital accumulation in the country.

While it provides a theoretical basis for accumulation, inequality

[44] Interview with former state official.

[45] Interviews. The point was made in at least eight interviews with members of the indigenous business community.

[46] Hoogvelt 1979: 58.

[47] Recall also that the measures were not applied retroactively. See also Hoogvelt 1979: 63 on this point.

does not ensure that accumulation or investment in productive enterprises actually takes place. As we saw in Chapter 3, immediately after the first indigenization decree most of the dividends received went into consumption or real estate rather than into productive accumulation. The same general trends could again be observed after the second decree, but some of the indigenous joint-venture partners began accumulating and going into productive ventures of their own.

The smallest shareholders tended to spend the bulk of their dividend earnings on personal or extended family consumption. As a general rule, larger shareholders spread their risk and invest their dividends in property development, other securities, and small-scale manufacturing. When multinational managers of the sixty companies described in Appendix A were asked what their joint-venture partners did with their dividends, only thirteen were confident enough to be able to say. Of that number, six listed investment in other securities first, five listed property, and only two mentioned consumption. This suggests a change from the patterns observed after the first decree, when consumption was much more evident.

When indigenous joint partners were asked what they personally did with their share earnings, the few that answered were divided equally between property and investment in other securities. Several of those investing in other securities described their movement into investments in manufacturing.[48] One of the reasons investments in property continued to attract so much local capital is best expressed in one of the interviews, worth quoting at length:

> Everyone has the feeling that the maximum returns come from investments in buildings, property and land. People build houses [even with a loan] and when they finish, they can receive rent for five years in advance. Thus, they can pay off the loan immediately and increase their assets at the same time. One acquaintance built six shops [7' by 13'] for which he received 7,000 naira per year for each shop, five years in advance! That's 7,000 × 5 years = 35,000 × 6 shops = 210,000 naira for 546 square feet![49]

The rates of return for investments in manufacturing were not as high, but real-estate investments were limited, the market was difficult to break into, and real estate did not carry the kind of prestige associated with manufacturing. Most of the indigenous businessmen using their dividends to go into manufacturing expected to recover

---

[48] Interviews with several indigenous businessmen.
[49] Interview with Indian multinational manager.

their entire investment in two to three years, and by the end of 1982 there was growing evidence that investments in manufacturing were receiving a growing amount of dividend income.

This is consistent with the sectoral trends in manufacturing described earlier in this chapter. There is a great deal of circumstantial evidence to suggest that a significant number of Nigerians were moving into productive activities by the early 1980s. Not only were indigenous businessmen concentrating in a number of low-technology, small- and medium-sized consumer-goods and processing industries, but many of them also appear to have made that move after participating in joint ventures with multinationals as a result of indigenization.[50] According to one observer, "Most of the young [in their thirties and forties] businessmen are thinking of going into manufacturing. Indigenization has given people experience with all areas of the economy."[51] Thus, although there is evidence that this transition was only beginning in 1982, one senior Nigerian banker working for a multinational merchant bank described how widespread the tendencies were:

> On a recent visit to my home in [———] I was approached by three alhajis saying they realize that manufacturing is in the future. They sought my advice on where to invest in the sector. These tendencies are very widespread.[52]

There are a number of cases of indigenous businessmen going into their own manufacturing after an earlier association with foreign capital. One multinational manager complained about the loss of several local managers who were trained by his home office in Europe and upon their return to Nigeria went off and set up their own competing concerns, one in the production of toothpaste, another in the production of paints.[53] Another foreign manager complained about a similar incident in which one of his former employees established a food-processing company that copied the packaging and labelling of one of his firm's most successful consumer products.[54] None of these foreign managers described these new companies as posing a serious threat to their market position in Nigeria, but these local firms are still in the

[50] Interview with senior indigenous bank manager employed by large multinational commercial bank.

[51] Interview with senior official of NSE.

[52] Interview with senior indigenous bank manager employed by multinational merchant bank.

[53] Interview with European multinational manufacturer.

[54] Interview with European multinational manager.

early stages of production and have already proven sufficiently competitive for expatriate managers to take notice.

Another route taken by local capital has been to begin in commerce, usually with the monopoly distribution of a particular product, and then to initiate production of that same item in Nigeria. To be sure, the import controls and austerity measures have contributed the most to this development. However, indigenization can be credited with having reserved certain industries for majority-owned indigenous businesses. The items are usually produced under license, with an expatriate technical assistant. However, control of finance is distinctly Nigerian, something that distinguishes these firms from their indigenized counterparts which operated in the same sectors prior to the second decree.

Another form of indigenous manufacturing activity similar to the type just described is for local businessmen to initiate a project, raise the capital, select the technology, and search abroad for an expatriate technician willing to work under contract for the new firm for a specified period. These are genuinely indigenous ventures, in which local capital controls the enterprise and makes the major decisions about both technology and finance. They are likely to be found in medium-scale, intermediate-technology areas, though there is at least one in a relatively high-technology activity.[55] In a few cases, these new ventures were initiated by individuals sent abroad for technical training during the 1970s. There is no way to know how widespread this phenomenon is, although one multinational bank manager suggested in 1982 that "this type of 100 percent Nigerian firm accounts for 10 percent of [our] loan applications."[56]

The largest indigenous firms—the family holding companies like Ibru, Dantata, Rabiu, Fanz, Ashamu, Stephens, Mandilas,[57] and Ugochukwu—are variously rated by multinational managers and local capital, but they are generally regarded as "quite strong" or "increasingly important" in the country.[58] They are strong enough to be characterized as "strong competitors" to multinational firms in some ac-

---

[55] Interview with Nigerian-initiated firm in high-technology sector.

[56] Interview with multinational bank manager.

[57] Non-Nigerians who have taken up Nigerian citizenship (like Mandilas and G. Cappa) and whose principal basis of accumulation is in Nigeria are classified as local capital for the purposes of this discussion. Their firms are not affiliates of companies based outside of Nigeria, and they are not strongly linked to trading partners located in a single foreign country (like most of the Lebanese firms). They act, therefore, according to the same logic as local capital.

[58] Interviews with multinational manager and official at a foreign embassy.

tivities (e.g. construction, food processing, furniture, and soft drinks), and to have "great potential."[59]

All began primarily in commercial activities, and have only a small percentage of their business in manufacturing. However, most are expanding in that area. In general, these firms are described as one-man operations, with little delegation of authority, highly diversified, and difficult to do business with. They are generally recognized, however, as having better contacts with the state and being better able to obtain lucrative contracts than their multinational counterparts. Although there are significant variations in their manufacturing activities, there is a fair amount of market segmentation in Nigeria, and these companies tend to produce for the lower end of the consumer market (that is, lower-quality products, with less sophisticated packaging, for a less well-to-do consumer). This is a market with great potential, given Nigeria's population of nearly 100 million, and the fact that several of these companies have expressed an interest in manufacturing at intermediate levels prompted one multinational manager to suggest that they "may provide a future base for industrialization."[60] Some of these firms say they have plans to look outside Nigeria for additional markets, but thus far there has been more talk than anything of substance to those plans.

In addition to a growing interest in manufacturing and both case-study and aggregate evidence of a diversification of local capital from commerce and services into production, there is macroeconomic evidence that finance for this transition has been available from the Nigerian banking system. The Central Bank's credit guidelines have allocated an increasing amount of finance to productive activities in manufacturing and agriculture, and they appear to have had significant effect, especially since the state assumed control over domestic finance.

Using commercial banks' loans and investments as an approximate measure for Nigerian investment, total investment grew nineteen-fold in current terms between 1968 and 1979, while investment in manufacturing grew thirty-two-fold (from 460 to 14,725 million naira) during the same period. In 1968, about 30 percent of all Nigerian investment went into the "production" sector (including manufacturing, agriculture, fishing, forestry, mining and quarrying, construction, and real estate). That percentage increased constantly to about 38 percent in 1973, but grew substantially after that, reaching

[59] Interview with British multinational manager.
[60] Ibid.

nearly 60 percent by 1979 (nearly half of which was accounted for by manufacturing alone).[61] During the same period, investment in general commerce declined from over 50 percent to under 20 percent.

In its more recent annual reports, the Central Bank has complained about the extent to which its credit guidelines in agriculture and manufacturing have not been attained.[62] However, given the limited number of credit-worthy proposals being received by the banks in

TABLE 6.8
Analysis of Commercial Bank Loans and Advances by Sector, 1968–79 (in millions of naira)

Year	Production	Commerce	Services	Other	Total
1968	783.5	1,338.2	134.6	386.2	2,642.5
	(29.6%)	(50.6%)	(5.1%)	(14.6%)	
1969	780.6	1,123.5	129.6	408.7	2,442.4
	(32.0%)	(46.0%)	(5.3%)	(16.7%)	
1970	1,039.1	1,437.4	187.0	513.9	3,177.4
	(32.7%)	(45.2%)	(5.9%)	(16.2%)	
1971	1,961.1	2,152.1	335.2	792.0	5,240.4
	(37.4%)	(41.1%)	(6.4%)	(15.1%)	
1972	2,467.6	2,391.9	494.9	1,148.0	6,502.4
	(37.9%)	(36.7%)	(7.6%)	(17.6%)	
1973	2,974.2	2,633.7	668.2	1,494.1	7,770.2
	(38.3%)	(33.8%)	(8.6%)	(19.2%)	
1974	4,157.0	3,018.9	727.8	1,866.7	9,770.4
	(42.5%)	(30.9%)	(7.4%)	(19.1%)	
1975	6,279.2	4,240.7	1,097.2	2,613.2	14,230.3
	(44.1%)	(29.8%)	(7.7%)	(18.4%)	
1976	10,772.6	5,649.1	1,874.6	2,993.5	21,289.8
	(50.6%)	(26.5%)	(8.8%)	(14.1%)	
1977	16,498.9	7,293.4	2,854.2	4,230.6	30,877.1
	(53.4%)	(23.6%)	(9.2%)	(13.7%)	
1978	24,134.8	9,448.8	3,658.0	6,305.5	43,547.1
	(55.4%)	(21.7%)	(8.4%)	(14.5%)	
1979	30,129.7	9,925.2	4,262.1	7,019.0	51,336.0
	(58.7%)	(19.3%)	(8.3%)	(13.7%)	

SOURCE: Central Bank of Nigeria, *Economic and Financial Review*, various years.

[61] Central Bank of Nigeria, *Economic and Financial Review*, various years. These data include loans and advances to all borrowers, not just local capital, and they include nonproductive activities like real estate. Nevertheless, they do illustrate a general shift in priority and an allocation of capital away from commerce in the direction of manufacturing. As such, they are consistent with the general point that finance has been available from the Nigerian banking system for this transition.

[62] Central Bank of Nigeria. *Annual Report and Statement of Accounts for the Year Ended 31st December 1981* (Lagos: Central Bank of Nigeria, 1983), p. 53.

these sectors, and given the difficulty the banks now have in falsifying allocation records, the growth of credit to manufacturing alone is astonishing. The sector now receives more investment capital than any other in the economy, reaching 30.9 percent in 1981, slightly under the prescribed target of 36 percent for that year.

There is a wealth of evidence to suggest that local capital is in the process of diversifying from nonproductive to productive activities in Nigeria. There is a concentration of local capital in certain manufacturing activities, manufacturing is generally recognized as an increasingly prestigious and attractive area for investment, the case studies demonstrate the movements of indigenous companies into productive activities following indigenization, and the amount of finance available for such purposes is considerable. However, this does not add up to a thriving, dynamic, productive, and accumulating domestic bourgeoisie in Nigeria. The development is only in its infancy, but the extent and duration of the movement are such that it is of a more than ephemeral nature. Something is going on, and those who have correctly described Nigerian local capital in the past as weak, fragmented, and largely commercial in nature need to take account of (or address) the phenomenon.[63]

There are plenty of incentives against local capital making this transition; thus it faces an uncertain future at best. Manufacturing investments in Nigeria involve more capital, require more expertise, entail higher risk, and provide slower returns than investments in other sectors. Like foreign capital, indigenous businessmen need to be self-sufficient in infrastructure, have to contend with inconsistent government policy,[64] and have had to compete with smuggled imports.

[63] Paul Collins has come to a similar conclusion (although based on a different kind of evidence) in his most recent published analysis of indigenization: "Doubts about their origins, existence or credentials notwithstanding, the 1970s in West Africa have seen the emergence of a significant class of indigenous industrialists, particularly in Nigeria. This class, despite some overlaps, is distinct from the now famed 'comprador' class of distributors who are seen to have locked themselves into their foreign suppliers' capital structure, as well as distinct from the more 'passive' shareholders-Directors drawn from the ruling group and allied classes. Investments on the part of this group are often of at least N 1 million and well into double figures in some cases, usually but not always following government policies in terms of product" (1983: 421).
The analysis is, I think, correct. But the evidential thread on which it rests is slim. Further, the cause of the change, allegedly "the more decisive and meaningful state indicative planning that has emerged of late" (p. 424), is curious and unsubstantiated. Planning and the poor coordination of government policy have more often interfered with the transition.

[64] The most vexing of these inconsistencies stems from the struggle between the tariff-minded Ministry of Industries and the free-trade-oriented Ministry of Commerce.

These inherent difficulties were compounded by the severity of the recession in Nigeria following the drop in oil prices after 1982. Thus, any prognosis of the health of the emerging bourgeoisie must be guarded, at best. The seeds are there, however, and that may ultimately be the most significant contribution of the indigenization program.

The extent to which indigenous businessmen are accumulating capital and making a transition from the sphere of circulation to the sphere of production suggests that indigenization has contributed to the development of capitalism in Nigeria (as defined by classical Marxists). As in the case of the other sectoral and national consequences of the program, however, indigenization is certainly not solely responsible for this development. The opportunity costs of the exercise also need to be considered, even if in the abstract, before its contribution to the development of capitalism can be fully appreciated.

For the most part, indigenization has shifted the financial burden of existing enterprises onto Nigerian investors without any appreciable increase in their control over the operations of those firms. The capital that was used to purchase shares of existing companies could have been used for many other things; hence the opportunity costs of the program could theoretically be quite high. But would the capital have been used more productively in the absence of indigenization? Without an elaborate program of incentives to induce local capital into productive areas of the economy along with an effective enforcement mechanism from the state, there is little evidence that such a development would have taken place. An effective state enforcement mechanism for programs deemed essential to national development has evaded most Nigerian governments since independence, and there is not much evidence that local capital would have gone into manufacturing without the protection of the state. Neither the research interviews with indigenous businessmen nor the earlier survey work conducted by Akeredolu-Ale in the early 1970s provide much of a basis for optimism on the latter point.[65]

In the final analysis, what have the first and second decrees taken together meant for control of the national economy? First, the Nigerian state now has greater control of finance than it did before the pro-

---

To the disappointment of most manufacturers, the latter is politically stronger (interview with prominent indigenous businessman). This fact undoubtedly contributes to the import intensity of manufacturing in Nigeria, discussed in more detail in the conclusion of this chapter.

[65] Akeredolu-Ale 1975: 62–96 (chap. 4).

gram. Second, more companies have been forced to go public, making it easier for the state to monitor their activities (they must file additional information with an unusually effective state agency, the NSEC). Third, indigenous businessmen have consolidated their position in commerce and found niches in construction, services, and manufacturing. At the same time, the state has reserved for itself an important position in the vital petroleum and high-growth manufacturing sectors. Taken together, these trends suggest that the Nigerian state has greater control of the national economy than it did before the indigenization program was begun, but it is important to keep this change in perspective before endorsing the views of liberal-internationalist writers. The change is, at best, a slight one, since it is probably more difficult for the state to regulate joint ventures of local and foreign capital than it was for it to regulate them separately. Indigenous businessmen can form a very effective lobby against the designs of the state, and in combination with foreign capital can effectively neutralize state policy (as they demonstrated so well with the implementation of the second decree).

As I cautioned in Chapter 3, the first indigenization decree was only the beginning of a very long process. Most of the research on which the argument of the succeeding chapters is based was conducted within five years of the promulgation of the second decree. Thus, the tendencies identified may in the end prove to be more important than any definitive conclusions that can be made about the general ineffectiveness of the program. As one of the architects of the second decree commented, "We achieved as much as we could under the circumstances."[66] This is not exactly a ringing endorsement of the effectiveness of the program, but although it did not change very much at the enterprise level, some of the changes initiated at the sectoral and national levels suggest that indigenization has had an effect that will be observed over a longer period.

CONCLUSIONS

The economic nationalists within the state who pushed so hard for the expansion of the indigenization program were more successful in the formulation of policy than in its implementation. Their principal objective of assuming effective managerial control of individual enterprises was not obtained. With the exception of the banks, they were foiled by the resistance of foreign capital and the lack of interest ex-

---

[66] Interview with member of the Industrial Enterprises Panel.

pressed in the issue by local capital. Hence, "the economic fortune of this nation is still not being determined by Nigerians as envisaged by the architects of the indigenisation scheme."[67] The program had a certain political utility, since it created the impression that Nigerians were "increasingly the managers of the economy,"[68] but in the final analysis all the economic nationalists could claim was that a start had been made in securing their principal objective.

They did somewhat better in having the state assume the leadership of the national economy. They secured control of domestic finance, through a combination of the Central Bank's credit guidelines and having the state acquire a majority of the equity of the banks. Indigenization reserved the principal high-growth areas of the economy for state firms (even though most would be in joint ventures with foreign capital), and the 1979 constitutional provisions ratified the reservation of the "commanding heights of the economy" for the state, identifying many of the same sectors originally described in the Second Plan.[69]

In general, the state accomplished its objective of making the program slightly less unfair. The second decree ensured that many more people participated in the exercise, even if they were still only a tiny percentage of the Nigerian population. The most glaring regional imbalances resulting from the first decree were addressed in the second by having state-government portfolio investment increase substantially. Finally, new opportunities were created for local capital. Most of them were not realized in the short term, since so much local capital initially went into the acquisition of existing companies. After the second decree, however, indigenous businessmen began to find safe places for themselves in sectors other than commerce.

Local capital found itself in a stronger position in its relationship with foreign capital following the two indigenization programs. At the time the second decree was being formulated, indigenous businessmen were concerned that foreign capital might flee the country, undermining their own position, since local and foreign capital were so heavily interdependent. Because foreign capital was only momentarily frightened by the second decree, the program not only retained the access of local capital to foreign capital, but also strengthened it in ways the indigenous businessmen did not envisage at the time.

The biggest defeat for local capital has come from the expansion of

[67] Akamiokhor 1982: 14.
[68] Interview with senior official of the Shagari administration.
[69] Ogunbanjo 1982: 14–16.

the state. Indigenization further legitimized the reservation of certain classes of economic activity in the Nigerian economy for different actors, and occasioned a significant growth of state-government portfolio investment. The oil economy is the principal source of the growth of state intervention in Nigeria, but indigenization has reinforced it.

As we saw in Chapter 5, foreign capital succeeded in blunting attempts to have Nigerians assume managerial control of individual enterprises, and was also successful in its effort to obtain particular exemptions and some flexibility in the implementation of the program over time. Foreign companies eventually managed to obtain permission for Schedule 2 holding companies in which the foreign partner held only 40 percent of the equity to take a majority share of new companies established after the second decree.[70] This allowed them to avoid diluting their equity excessively and was something which had been of major concern among companies unable to remit their earnings or proceeds from the sale of shares following the second decree.[71]

However, foreign companies were generally dissatisfied with the compensation they received from the sale of their shares, and have had their sphere of capital accumulation restricted by the indigenization program.[72] They have been effectively moved out of most areas of commerce and face increased competition from local capital in other sectors of the economy. These developments have not affected the capacity of multinational firms to accumulate capital in Nigeria, but only forced them to concentrate in certain areas. Foreign capital has not voted with its feet, as indicated by the nonoil inflows of foreign investment over time.

Although each of the principals (multinationals, local capital, and the state) has accomplished some of its objectives, on the central issue of control of indigenized enterprises, local and foreign capital have prevailed. The available evidence suggests they will continue to do so for the foreseeable future. The economic nationalists within the state have had to satisfy themselves with the fact that they have made a start, a beginning in their objective of securing greater Nigerian control at the sectoral and national levels of the economy.

By the early 1980s, significant, though not always readily apparent, changes had been set in motion as a result of the indigenization program. The two decrees were by themselves not entirely responsible for

[70] Collins 1983: 413.

[71] Interview with large multinational holding company.

[72] On this point I take issue with an otherwise excellent assessment of Nigerian industrialization written by Tom Forrest (1982: 341).

these changes, but they contributed to them in a significant way. The state was in a position where it could increasingly control the direction of finance in the country. Its control of the banks produced changes in their operations which have in turn contributed to a second important development: the easing of financial constraints on the movement of local capital into productive areas of the economy.

Indigenization has also contributed directly to that process. By reserving certain areas of the economy for local capital, it has had an important psychological effect. It has opened people's eyes to business opportunities and increased their self-confidence about the capability of Nigerians to manage firms.[73] There is a general sense that the economy has opened up a little for indigenous business in the decade following the first decree.[74]

Third, a considerable amount of managerial training was stimulated by the second decree. The significant increase in the amount of in-house training, combined with the number of Nigerian students receiving technical training abroad, will have long-term implications for the development of the country. The architects of the second decree were aware of this possibility and point to the fact that in Brazil, one of the countries which provided the Adeosun Commission with a model for state-led development, there had been a major commitment to extensive managerial and technical training in the late 1940s and early 1950s.

> They sent their first batch of petrochemical engineers abroad after their first refinery was established in 1948. By the late fifties, they had returned and designed subsequent refineries which are fully Brazilian-run. We are just now beginning to reap the benefits of this program. By 1990, we'll have a new generation of technicians.[75]

In the end, conclusions about a dynamic process like indigenization can never be definitive. They can only stop at a certain point and identify what has changed and the extent to which it has changed. These conclusions are based on an analysis of the changes observable in the mid 1980s. The second decree, like the first (and like any government policy), has sown contradictions that have laid the basis for subsequent government action in this area.

The inequality associated with the first decree is less apparent, but

[73] Several indigenous businessmen described how the decrees had "opened their eyes" to new investment opportunities, and one also mentioned the increase in self-confidence the program has created.

[74] Interview with indigenous employee of multinational merchant bank.

[75] Interview with member of the Industrial Enterprises Panel.

it is still there. A very small percentage of the population continues to control most of the wealth in the country. The regional distribution issue has abated somewhat, although the eastern states are still largely omitted from the process.

The conflict over public- versus private-sector leadership of the national economy continues, despite the apparent success of the state in reserving the most productive areas of the economy for itself. Much of the controversy is fought out not on the grounds of policy formulation, but in the areas of policy implementation. The public–private-sector debate was prominent in the retrospective on indigenization underway in 1982, and it was reflected in the middle of the decade in positions on devaluation and negotiations with the IMF.

The combined effects of token personnel indigenization at the very top of indigenized firms and the anticipated return of large numbers of trained and highly qualified Nigerian managers will provide pressure for further personnel indigenization. There has already been a great deal of pressure within companies to speed up the process, especially from the junior ranks dissatisfied with the pace of promotion. This kind of tension will intensify unless relieved by other policies or programs.

Finally, the state incentives designed to induce local capital to move into productive areas have not been coordinated with policies in other areas, producing anomalous forms of indigenous enterprise. Many of the Nigerian manufacturing ventures created thus far are so import-intensive that they only serve to exacerbate already unacceptably large foreign-exchange losses.

These contradictions contain the seeds of the long-term consequences of indigenization, and they serve to identify the parameters of future policy in this area. For the foreseeable future, the program is likely to be relaxed. Like so many other developing countries affected by the recession in the world economy in the 1980s, Nigeria is extremely short of foreign exchange, its trade has slowed considerably, and its nonoil exports have nearly disappeared. The world oil glut and Nigeria's continued dependence on the export of petroleum for 90 percent of the state's revenue have compounded the effects of the world recession in its case. Hence, some sectors of the economy are being quietly moved from Schedule 2 to 3, while, for the short term at least, it has been easier to obtain expatriate permits.

The contradictions identified above will have their greatest impact in the longer term. The inequality inevitably associated with a program of this kind could be used to mobilize a constituency in favor of a third decree, but because of a retrenchment of foreign capital internationally, it will probably be some time before such a program gains widespread favor within the state. Even the state's most ardent supporters of the second decree are more concerned with consolidating the program (and defending their role in its creation) than they are in extending it. The fact that easterners continue to be largely left out of the process will not provide much impetus for an expansion of the program, at least until they obtain political influence commensurate with their numbers in the country. Most easterners prefer the opportunities available to them through open competition to the elaborate system of quotas that was developed to allocate shares with indigenization. Hence, they are not interested in making an argument for indigenization based on regional deprivation.

The extent to which the state acquired portfolio investments after the second decree has sensitized local capital to the dangers of producing another decree. Local capital may not be in a position to influence the formulation of future policy directly, but it certainly will make its case against further expansion of the state in the national economy. For the time being, at least, it is joined in its efforts by the international financial community (both the transnational banks and the IMF), something that is likely to strengthen its position in the argument.

Given the widespread, and growing, realization that equity participation does not readily translate into control of enterprises, future programs in this area are not likely to stress equity participation. Increasing indigenous Schedule 2 equity participation from 60 percent to 80 percent is not likely to yield any tangible benefits, and would cost a great deal in terms of indigenous opportunity costs and lost foreign capital. Thus, any future programs in this area are likely to emphasize effective personnel indigenization and local content. Nigeria's economic crisis dampened temporarily the enthusiasm of middle-level managers for rapid promotions, but the pressure for upward mobility from within the indigenized enterprises will return, especially after large numbers of Nigerian students begin to return home from their studies abroad.

The calls for increased local content emanating periodically from both military and civilian governments since the mid-1970s are likely to gain more force in the future for two reasons. First, the anomalous, highly import-intensive forms of indigenous manufacturing enterprise stimulated by indigenization are going to create persistent and increasingly large demands for foreign exchange. They are joined in this need for foreign exchange by most of the large multinational manufacturers, many of which are equally import-intensive and have been so for many of the same reasons. Second, because this persistent need for imports is accompanied by an increased foreign-exchange scarcity brought on by the slackening world demand for petroleum, the state will have a strong incentive to impose effective local-content requirements. To some extent, the 1980s recession has already imposed these requirements on the Nigerian economy. If the recession succeeds in forcing backward linkages without bankrupting most manufacturing activities, the state is likely to promote local content as a central part of any future programs in this area.

CHAPTER SEVEN

The Dialectics of Indigenization: Stagnation and Transformation at Alternative Levels of Analysis

ON the basis of the arguments and analyses of Nigerian indigenization presented in Chapters 2 through 6, it is possible to construct a general model of the process. Like any public policy (in any country), the program is not entirely rational or consistent. It is part of a political process, the outgrowth of recurring combinations and recombinations of prominent political-economic actors in the country operating to maximize their conceptions of group, national, and occasionally international welfare. Thus, the successive indigenization decrees were essentially compromises, and each contained contradictions which planted the seeds of future policy initiatives.

Throughout the process, each of the three generic types of political-economic actors (local capital, foreign capital, and the state) mounted a counteroffensive or defensive strategy every time it deemed its central objectives threatened in some way. This idea has important implications for conceptions of state power, the sources of state power, and assessments of the bargaining capacity of multinational corporations. Thus, after the state was defeated in obtaining some of its objectives toward the end of the first decree, it managed to come back with a vengeance with the creation of a second decree. When local capital was defeated in the formulation of the second decree, it responded at the implementation stage, ensuring that the control objectives of the economic nationalists within the state would not be attained. And every time their effective control of enterprises was potentially threatened, multinationals responded with an impressive array of countervailing measures designed to ensure they maintained effective control over operations.

This observation is not meant to imply that although change appears to take place, nothing really changes. From Nigeria's experience with indigenization it is clear that some significant changes have taken place in control of the economy, even if they are not immediately evident at all levels of analysis. Although each significant actor has an impressive supply of defensive or countervailing measures, they are not equally or consistently effective. The more difficult problem is how to develop criteria to assess the direction of what change is taking place at different levels.

Nigeria's first indigenization decree came out of a temporary alliance of local capital and elements within the state. The two groups were themselves divided and did not agree on all aspects of the program; however, there was sufficient agreement to allow them to move together against foreign capital operating in the country at the time. Because the program came from an alliance of these two groups at a time when the state was relatively penetrated (and because it did not stem from a populist alliance of economic nationalists and labor), it was not very radical. Only the weakest elements of foreign capital were affected, and most multinationals were able to continue operating in the country with virtually no change. The first decree was developed with relatively little influence from (or knowledge of) the experience of other developing countries, and it probably would have been enacted earlier had the Nigerian civil war not intervened.

The first decree set in motion a number of changes which at first appeared insignificant, but would subsequently prove to have greater force. It was also replete with contradictions and distortions which laid the basis for the second decree. Since the second decree stemmed principally from an unpenetrated state sector both interested in and informed about the experience of other developing countries during the economically nationalist 1970s, it was both more consistent and more radical than the first decree. It was also explicit in its intention to right the wrongs of the first program. Hence it stressed a broader distribution of shares, more effective indigenous participation, and a greater role for the state in the economy.

The second decree was not without its own contradictions (especially between policy formulation and policy implementation) and hence set the stage for the relaxation of the program and some of the other recent policy manifestations. However, since it affected so many of the largest multinationals operating in Nigeria, it elicited more imaginative countervailing measures from foreign capital than did the first decree. Most proved to be effective, with the important exception of finance, where the state intervened in a distinctive and particularly effective way. In the final analysis, the most significant changes that did occur were not equally apparent at all levels of analysis, suggesting the importance of employing multiple levels of analysis in the study of international political economy.

It would be possible to develop a more detailed model of the sources and consequences of Nigerian indigenization, deriving hy-

FIGURE 7.1

A Schematic Summary of the Sources and Consequences of Nigeria's Indigenization Decrees

	1972	1977	1982
Sources of Indigenization	Alliance of local capital and the state (military gov't)	Principally a state-led initiative (military gov't)	Relaxation of the program (civilian gov't)
Consequences at the level of the firm	Fronting (most MNCs not affected) Relatively few changes in operations	Effective counter-vailing measures developed by most MNCs Few changes in operations	
Consequences at the sectoral and national levels	Consolidation of local capital in commerce Inequality	State control of finance Evidence of local capital movement into productive areas	

potheses to link sources to consequences as identified in Figure 7.1, or summarizing over time the principal combinations of actors and the conditions under which their alliances and recombinations are likely to take place (and to what effect). This, however, would not do justice to the detail presented in Chapters 2 through 6; besides, the Nigerian experience with indigenization is not necessarily generalizable to other policies or countries. Not every country has had two indigenization decrees, and there is no reason why Nigeria's experience should be generalizable in such a manner.

Nigeria has had a distinct history, is composed of distinctive ethnic, economic and political actors, and has a particular mode and degree of integration with the world economy. There is little point in fabricating an abstract model of Third World economic nationalism out of Nigeria's indigenization experience and trying to force it on every other country and potentially relevant policy area. Too many of the theorists and authors of empirical studies identified in Chapter 1 do this, routinely dismissing the contributions of all other schools because the specifics of their arguments do not apply to *their* case. This kind of argument is not a basis for cumulation of knowledge, hence I propose a somewhat more abstract form of generalization.

Even if Nigeria's indigenization experience is not readily generalizable, I think the method used to evaluate it in this book is. As I mentioned in Chapter 1, I have tried to construct a partial synthesis of noncontradictory aspects of six theoretical approaches into an explanation of the sources and consequences of a prominent aspect of developing country foreign economic policy: indigenization. In general terms, I have employed a quasi-dialectical, historical analysis of a concrete situation, obviously borrowing heavily from the method of the three radical approaches (especially of sophisticated dependency writers).[1] For the identification of principal actors, I began with (and modified) the principal categories employed by sophisticated dependency writers. I looked to neoclassical conservatives for an initial identification of the principal countervailing measures employed by multinationals. For my concern with the changing MNC–host country bargaining relationship and my general analysis of the determination of policy (what one commentator has described as "radical pluralism"),[2] I owe a debt to liberal-internationalist writers. The emphasis on policy implementation came from a careful reading of contemporary structuralists, while concern about accumulation and the development of capitalism was derived from a reading of classical Marxists.

An attempt to synthesize aspects of these different approaches is necessary for a full comprehension of contemporary change in North–South relations in general and of Third World economic nationalism in particular. The preceding analysis would have been too narrowly restricted without consideration of their various analytical distinctions, different definitions of problems, alternative emphases, and diverse insights. Too much contemporary academic work is littered with narrow considerations of issues and sham put-downs of alternative theoretical perspectives. The recent spate of attacks on dependency approaches is one of the latest manifestations of this tendency.[3] Dependency approaches are certainly not flawless, needed

[1] By "dialectical" I mean a holistic approach that assumes constant change, the existence of contradictions and significant oppositions that drive that change, and the primacy of qualitative change or transformation over quantitative and incremental change, and that leads to the discovery of the revealed or hidden essences underlying social phenomena. For an elaboration of the meaning of dialectics, see Biersteker 1986.

[2] The term is that of Irving Leonard Markovitz, introduced in a very informative commentary on Chapter 2 of this manuscript at the Annual Meeting of the American Political Science Association in Chicago, September 1983.

[3] See, for example, Becker 1983 or Smith 1978. There have also been a number of recent Ph.D. dissertations in political science devoted to identifying the logical, histor-

some careful scrutiny, and were themselves polemical in their treatment of modernization theorists a decade and a half ago. There is, however, little point in reversing the polemic and dismissing the entire approach out of hand, however fashionable it might be at present. This is not a way toward the cumulation of knowledge. It would be far more constructive to integrate some of their insights into contemporary analysis, rather than scoring cheap victories, reverting to the past, or rediscovering the wheel (a point dependency writers themselves should have considered in the past). As a start, let me suggest a few modest guidelines for a synthesis, identifying more explicitly (though rather undialectically) some of the components of the method employed in this book.

First, the foreign economic policies of states create contradictions that set the parameters for future policy initiatives. Nigeria's first indigenization decree did not emerge in a vacuum or out of imitation of programs found in other Third World countries. It was the culmination of years of frustration experienced by indigenous businessmen, combined with the nationalist and developmentalist aspirations of the political leadership. The principal components of the first decree were outlined in documents written prior to independence, and the basis of the initial program can be found there and in the tensions, frustrations, and contradictions in Nigeria's development experience of the 1960s.

Similarly, the second decree grew rather logically out of the first. It was designed to rectify the imbalances brought on by the contradictions of the first decree. Since inequality, fronting, and regional imbalances were the legacy of the first decree, the second was designed to correct them (hence the emphasis on the Allotment Committee, the 5 percent limitation, and explicit warnings about fronting). As identified at the end of Chapter 6, the parameters of future policy initiative in indigenization can be found in the contradictions visible in the aftermath of the second decree.

As a method of analysis, a dialectical and historical approach cannot predict the future. It can, however, give a good indication of the parameters of future developments, as well as a good basis for compre-

---

ical, and/or empirical deficiencies of dependency "theory." Not every theoretical subfield in international political economy is equally dismissive of alternative perspectives. For example, contemporary regime theorists in the United States have for the most part avoided a polemical dismissal of their principal rival by attempting to subsume most of the "realist" approach in their analyses. They have not avoided the narrowness characteristic of much of the literature, however, since they have ignored most of the neo-Marxist literature on contemporary capitalist crises.

hending these developments. It also has great utility for evaluating other issues in international political economy. It manages change especially well (since it assumes it is constant), thus making it appropriate for the mercurial subject of political economy. It also lends itself especially well to organic, holistic conceptions of problems in international political economy, where a systems level of analysis is often especially useful. Topics such as the likely course of the international debt crisis, the sources of opposition to (and consequences of) stabilization programs, and the future role of multinational enterprises in the world economy can best be understood by paying careful attention to the identification of key actors, their objectives, their actions, and the contradictions they engender. The same could be said for the important subject of the breakdown and transformation of international regimes.

A second methodological generalization suggested by the analysis of Nigerian indigenization is that it is often necessary to differentiate among different levels of analysis when making an assessment of the consequences of a policy, program, or phenomenon. If Nigerian indigenization had been evaluated solely at the level of the enterprise, with sectoral and national consequences assessed only by way of projection from trends observed at the enterprise level, a very different conclusion about the program would have been reached in Chapter 6. Since the vast majority of enterprises were not significantly affected by the two decrees, the significance of state control of finance and the movement of indigenous businessmen into productive areas of the economy might have been lost.

This methodological point is not likely to be disputed by any of the six approaches outlined in Chapter 1. However, it would not have been brought home with the same force if any one of them had been used to guide the analysis at the outset. Different approaches emphasize different levels of analysis when they characterize the consequences of indigenization. Most neoclassical writers tend to emphasize changes at the level of the firm, while radical writers concentrate on consequences at the national level. Only the liberal internationalists have much to say about sectoral-level consequences. Each school tends to concentrate on those levels relevant to its theoretical assumptions (and supportive of the central thrust of its argument). By contrasting the diverse assessments of indigenization in Chapter 1, the need to separate levels of analysis for analytical purposes became strikingly apparent.

A third methodological point suggested by the analysis of Nigerian indigenization is that foreign economic policymaking (and most probably policymaking in general) is a political process, not the out-growth of rational actors attempting to maximize national interests. Again, this is not a novel point, but it is striking to note the frequency with which detailed bureaucratic analysis of the sort common to stud-ies of the United States and other advanced industrial economies is not attempted in the case of developing countries. Developing coun-tries are certainly not any less complex, although they are significantly more difficult to gain detailed access to.

The sources of Nigeria's two indigenization decrees, and the proc-ess through which compromises were struck (and ignored) under-score the importance of viewing policymaking as political and not rational. In both cases, the final versions of the decrees were inconsis-tent, vague, and contradictory in places. This was not due to the in-competence of the civil servants or military decisionmakers in Ni-geria, as is commonly believed by most expatriate observers. Drafts of each decree were circulated for comment and each was reviewed by a number of key actors in the public and private sectors (including the multinationals). In the end, each of the decrees reflected some of the positions and arguments of all the protagonists involved in the program.

Thus, it is striking to note the degree to which most structuralists, liberal internationalists, and neoclassical realists assume these policies are the outgrowth of rational governments acting to maximize na-tional economic and political objectives, be they regime survival, for-eign-exchange retention, or vague development objectives. There is no reason to expect that policymaking in Nigeria is any more rational and consistent than policymaking on the budget or tax reform in the United States.

It is equally striking to note the extent to which most dependency and classical Marxist writers are trapped by their theoretical con-structs into denying the possibility of state-initiated programs. As the analysis of the sources of Nigeria's two very different indigenization decrees indicates, there is no single theoretical explanation for the sources of programs of this sort (e.g. capital does not always capture the state and the state does not always have the capacity for au-tonomy). Things are more complex than most of our theoretical constructs.

In general, scholars of international political economy would do well to begin by identifying the actors with effective channels of influ-ence in each issue area, and then attempt to determine their principal objectives, concerns, and disputes. Once these objectives are better understood, it will be easier to comprehend the statements, actions, and policies that ultimately ensue.

It is equally important to be aware of significant differences within key actors, especially within the state. Functional distinctions within the state are usually identified (e.g. between central bankers and the established ministries), but occasionally other distinctions are offered, such as those between politicos and technicos, or between reds and experts in socialist regimes. It might be profitable to go beyond these binary distinctions and suggest divisions along the broader lines of developmental ideology. In the Nigerian context it is clear that there have been genuine disagreements about the proper role for the state in development, divisions that go beyond the distinctions between politicians and technocrats in the civil service. In the end, a number of normative questions about what makes the good society are involved in the disputes. It would be instructive to try to identify these conceptions and analyze policy initiatives as the outgrowth of political struggles among competing sets of ideas—in this case, different conceptions of development.

The suggestion that policymaking or the actions of states are inevitably the outgrowth of a political process has relevance for a number of other topics of concern in international political economy. World Bank and IMF economists would do well to ponder the point before they castigate recalcitrant Third World regimes for resisting their good advice on matters of devaluation, food subsidies, or demand management. Training more technocrats or sending another team of persuasive experts will not convince states to accept market discipline voluntarily. There is more involved in their resistance than lack of will—it is the constraint of politics.

A fourth and final methodological point suggested by the analysis of Nigerian indigenization is that the formulation and the implementation of policy are two very distinct things. Again, this is not a particularly original observation, except that it has been overlooked in too many analyses of state power in the liberal tradition and in too many analyses of state autonomy in the radical literature.

The discussion of Nigeria's second indigenization decree in Chapters 4 and 5 demonstrates that the power of an actor like local capital is not confined to one part of the policy process. Although much of their advice was ignored while the second decree was being formulated, indigenous businessmen found a decisive way to affect the program at the implementation stage. Because the state tacitly relied on them to implement a portion of the decree they strongly opposed (the managerial-control provisions), they ultimately had far more power to affect outcomes than might have been expected had one focussed exclusively on their role in policy formation.

As we shall see in greater detail below, this point has important implications for discussions of state power and sovereignty. For while individual states are legally sovereign in that they can do almost anything to actors like multinational corporations operating within their borders (i.e. can formulate policies about anything), very few have a comparable capacity to implement such programs effectively. To focus on only one part of the policy process, either formulation or implementation, is to miss an important part of the whole. This is yet another reason for pursuing the kind of detailed, holistic, and dialectical analysis of issues in the international political economy of North–South relations proposed at the beginning of this section.

OTHER LESSONS

Nigeria's experience with indigenization also suggests some substantive generalizations of interest to students of international political economy. Despite the evidence available from resource-extractive industries in the 1970s, it is now apparent that the "inexorable" shift in the balance of bargaining power from multinationals to host countries may have been reversed. To be fair, sophisticated liberal internationalists like Bergsten, Horst, and Moran never claimed that the growing competition among multinationals of different nationalities and the movement of developing countries up the learning curve would have equally decisive effects in all countries. They did imply, however, that an important shift was at least underway.

The countervailing measures employed by multinationals in response to Nigeria's indigenization program in the 1970s and early 1980s suggest that the shift set in motion in the 1970s could be reversed, or at least slowed considerably. Further, it is apparent not only that multinationals have responsive capacities that have been widely underestimated in much of the literature, but also that they too are capable of moving up a learning curve. Some of the strategies invoked in response to the second decree were based on lessons learned from the first decree (such as spreading additional equity sold to dilute the influence of problem partners, developing new regrouping strategies like the two-company formula, or simply ignoring aspects of the program in the hope that the product life cycle of Nigerian policymaking would run its normal course).

By emphasizing the significance of multinationals' countervailing measures, I do not mean to imply that there is no change taking place in the bargaining relationship between host countries and multinationals, but only that the balance of bargaining power has not shifted either as far or as quickly as most liberal internationalists maintain. There is indeed host-country learning going on, but that learning is accompanied by learning going on within the multinationals as well. A few of the corporate strategies identified in Chapters 3 and 5 are specific to the Nigerian case, but many are also evident in other Third World countries.[4]

As soon as the state does x, to counter the n^1 strategy of the multinationals, the multinationals respond with n^2. In Nigeria, Lebanese firms and a few multinationals developed fronting as a means of neutralizing the first indigenization decree. The second decree specifically forbade fronting and developed enforcement mechanisms to deal with it. Hence, the multinationals responded with regroupings, the two-company formula, and the careful selection of joint-venture partners. I have little doubt that a third decree, or the issuance of more explicit industrial policy guidelines, could address these countervailing measures. But I am equally convinced of the capacity of most firms to develop yet another response.

Figure 7.2 represents graphically the dynamics of this process. Control of multinational enterprises is not beyond the reach of some repressive states in the contemporary world economy, but it is beyond those with a political-economic composition comparable to Nigeria's. In the much longer run, a combination of extensive technical and managerial training plus a political coalition interested in controlling multinationals could make a difference in the balance of bargaining power. However, that shift is still a long way off for most developing countries.

The dynamics of the bargaining relationship between states and multinationals summarized in Figure 7.2 need to be placed in a broader historical context. For while the multinationals may have been able to retain effective control over their operations in most countries, over the longer term it may not make that much difference. Direct foreign investment was a phenomenon of the 1960s, just as economic nationalism, efforts to control multinationals, and mandatory joint ventures were phenomena of the 1970s. As we have seen, multinationals were able to develop a complex variety of countervailing measures in response to these measures, but they have also simul-

[4] See esp. Lall and Bibile 1977; Weinstein 1976; Gereffi 1983; and Bennett and Sharpe 1985.

FIGURE 7.2
Dynamics of the Changing Bargaining Position of Host States and Multinationals

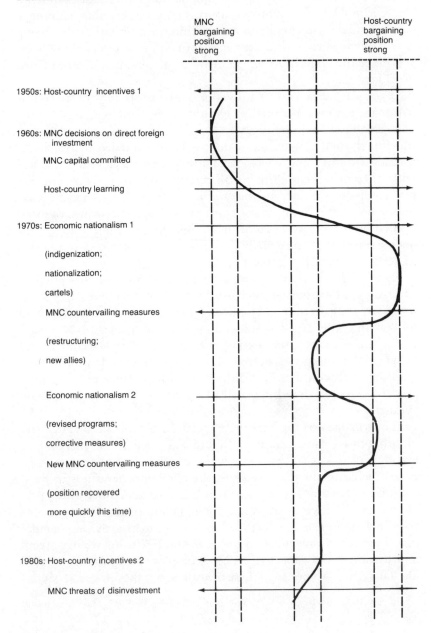

taneously reduced the flow of their investments to the developing world.

The 1980s have witnessed a return to the rhetoric of the 1950s and 1960s (at least in the United States) with regard to the benefits of foreign investment, the costs of state intervention and economic nationalism, and the need to provide an environment conducive to private-sector development. However, the context of these prescriptions and the situation of developing countries are very different today. Developing countries may be frustrated with the failures of state-led development, but they have not forgotten the failed promises of the liberal economic regime of the 1950s and 1960s. At the same time, transnational corporations are not eager to jump back into direct foreign investments in the Third World, and some are even contemplating disinvestment from the developing countries at the present time.

While multinational corporations will continue to play an important role in the world economy in general and in the developing countries in particular, our analyses of direct foreign investment and economic nationalism will have to be revised to take account of phenomena like disinvestment, multinational alliances, worldwide sourcing, nonequity arrangements, technology licensing, countertrading, barter agreements, and the proliferation of special economic zones. A qualitative change in the relationship between multinationals and developing countries is underway, again underscoring the need for dialectical, historical analyses of phenomena in international political economy.

A second substantive generalization suggested by the Nigerian experience with indigenization is that foreign economic policy is not always directed primarily or exclusively against an external entity like the multinational corporation. To be sure, indigenization has a direct effect on multinationals, and its study clearly belongs in the subfield of international political economy. However, in assessing the sources of the program, it was necessary to examine domestic politics in great detail, something (usually restricted to the domain of comparative politics) that yielded some occasionally surprising results.

Although the theoretical approaches identified in Chapter 1 consider indigenization policies either the rational outgrowth of states maximizing national objectives or the outgrowth of pressure from a local bourgeoisie dissatisfied with its position in the domestic economy, the Nigerian example suggests that neither may be entirely the case. Nigeria's indigenization program was not exclusively designed to assert the national will against the interests of foreign enterprises. Economic nationalism was used in part as a disguise for a redistributional struggle underway within the country. The state technocrats interested in the first decree were not only responding to indigenous business pressure, but they were also building up the leadership role in the national economy they had designated for the public sector in the Second National Development Plan. The opposition of local capital to the second decree described in Chapter 4 was couched primarily in terms of its concern about the growth of the public sector. Even in the retrospective debate on indigenization underway in 1982, most of the discussion dwelt on the proper role of the public and private sectors in the national economy. Indigenization enabled public-sector officials to increase their role in the economy without subtracting directly from the role of the existing indigenous private sector. Since the proceeds of the program were theoretically open to both parties and hence offered opportunities to each of them, it was relatively easy to produce a consensus about the first decree. Once indigenous businessmen saw what the economic nationalists within the state had in mind, a comparable consensus about the second decree never materialized.

The fact that economic nationalism can be used in part as a disguise for a redistributional struggle within the country is not restricted to Nigeria. Canada's National Energy Program required multinational energy companies to sell a major share of their equity to Canadian subscribers, but it essentially served to transfer power and revenues from the western provincial governments to Ottawa.[5] Similarly, Malaysia's New Economic Program, which also required foreign companies to sell their equity during the 1970s, was also intended to redistribute wealth and economic opportunity from the nonindigenous Chinese and Indian communities to the indigenous Malay community (the Bumiputras).[6] Hence, the equity of multinational corporations acquired through mandatory joint-venture programs is often used to accomplish other redistributive goals within the indigenizing country.

Finally, Nigeria's experience with indigenization suggests that a state's capacity to implement policy is at least as important as (and possibly more important than) its capacity to formulate policy. As we saw in Chapters 4 and 5, whereas the Nigerian state proved fully capable of designing a much improved and more far-reaching second decree, it lacked the capability to implement the program as its origi-

[5] Jenkins 1986.

[6] Mansor Othman, "The Politics of Indigenization: The Making and Implications of Indigenous Capitalism in a Multi-Racial State," draft Ph.D. dissertation, Department of Political Science, Yale University.

nators intended. With the exception of the banks (where it took great pains to appoint the right managers to senior positions), the state ultimately relied on local capital to accomplish its objective of greater indigenous control of enterprises. Since the vast majority of indigenous businessmen did not share its interests or objectives, it was impossible for the state to implement the program effectively. In the final analysis, the capacity of the state to monitor, to regulate, and to implement is far more important than its legal basis to act in a sovereign manner.

This point has important implications for conceptions of state power, and it also has relevance for other areas of controversy in international political economy. In many ways, the failures of stabilization programs and IMF standby agreements are not really very different from the failures of states to effect changes in control of enterprises with indigenization. Just as any sovereign state can formulate an indigenization program, any state can agree to a stabilization program or standby agreement. The real test of state power comes when it attempts to implement a program. Even authoritarian regimes in Latin America have found themselves unable to meet many of the terms they have agreed to in negotiations with the IMF and the World Bank.[7] While these failures could be attributed to a lack of will on the part of the state leadership, or to the possibility that they have been negotiating in bad faith, their inability to meet the terms of agreements may stem more from their general lack of capability to implement programs. Even though the state is more widely involved in the economy, it is not necessarily more effective. States often appear to be endowed with more power than they actually possess.

All of this implies that if a state's capacity to implement a program like indigenization is not present, it might be better off without the program. By developing a program it cannot implement, all it does is create channels for corruption, consume valuable resources that could be put to better use, and create unrealistic expectations about its capacity. A good case can be made for programs like indigenization. The social and economic costs of multinational corporations can be significant, as can the potential benefits of effective indigenous participation. In addition, the state does learn and increases its capabilities over time. But with ineffective programs, the state loses at least four times over. It does not receive an appreciable increase in its control of

[7] Konrad Stenzel, "The Politics of Debt and the Dependent State: The Cases of Chile and the Dominican Republic," draft Ph.D. dissertation, Department of Political Science, Yale University.

enterprises or economy, it can discourage future investment (which offers some clear benefits as well), it creates channels for corruption, and it undermines its own credibility.

This is not meant to suggest that all indigenization programs are a mistake. After all, Nigeria's indigenization exercise has yielded some tangible benefits. However, if the state cannot enforce or implement its programs, it should probably consider the costs before enacting them. It might be better for it to target strategic sectors, concentrate its resources and efforts, and effectively implement its program in those areas. In a sense, Nigeria did this with the banking industry after the second decree, but it could probably have taken control of its financial sector and created incentives to push local capital into productive activities without promulgating the two sweeping indigenization decrees. While some important changes either took place or were set in motion, they were not accomplished very efficiently.

THE ISSUE OF CONTROL

In the final analysis, what can we say about the issue of control? Are Nigerians in greater control of enterprises, sectors of their economy, or their national economy as a whole because of the indigenization program? In short, the answer is yes, but not much. While the program has yielded all sorts of unintended, and a number of undesirable, consequences, Nigerians are now obtaining important experience at the top levels of management and are participating effectively in important decisions in a few firms. While they may effectively control no more than a small percentage of them, their influence and role have increased and they are at least now in a better position to control them than they were before the exercise began.

For better or for worse, the state has assumed managerial control of most of the domestic financial sector, especially the banks. This is probably the most significant consequence of the entire program. Finance is a strategic sector, and the indigenization program has given the state an opportunity to increase, however slightly, its control over the national economy by directing financial resources to certain sectors. This fact, combined with local capital's accumulation from indigenization and some external factors like import controls, has stimulated indigenous business interest in more productive activities. Although not yet fully realized, this has significant implications for the development of capitalism, and the long-term direction and ultimately the control of the national economy by Nigerians.

Although important, these changes are not substantial, especially given the amount of time committed, the financial resources expended, and the attention accorded the indigenization program over the last decade. While it has had some effect, indigenization has certainly not contributed significantly to Nigerians' control of their economy. The state and a few indigenous businessmen have been the principal beneficiaries of the program. A small percentage of the country's formal sector labor force received the benefits of shares reserved for company employees, and, despite complaints, foreign capital will discover in the long run that it has found a graceful way to exit from its major equity investments in Nigeria. However, the vast majority of the country's population has been excluded entirely from the process, from start to finish.

Controlling multinationals has proven to be almost as elusive as other Third World efforts to control resources, markets, enterprises, or organizations that affect a country's material well-being. Few countries have been able to emulate the export-led strategy of the newly industrializing countries, the New International Economic Order negotiations are a relic of the past, nationalization has provided only temporary (and reversible) gains, and a record number of countries have found themselves subject to the dictates of the International Monetary Fund and its market discipline. Even OPEC, previously the most successful example of Third World efforts to acquire control over international markets, has fallen into disarray. In theory, it should have been easier for states to control subsidiaries of foreign companies operating in their sovereign territory than to attempt to control something as elusive as an international market. Even these efforts have had at best only modest success.

These developments are not uniformly undesirable for the majority of developing countries or their populations. Most suffered either directly or indirectly from OPEC's success. A majority could probably benefit from a moderate increase in the kind of market discipline required by the IMF. And the direct benefits of indigenization programs were not widely realized in any country. The issue of control, however, is separate from these welfare concerns, and the evidence to date does not suggest that developing countries are in much greater control of resources, markets, enterprises, or organizations than they were before any of these efforts were begun. It is ironic that the dependency perspective has become so widely assailed precisely at a time when the experience that originally gave it meaning has gained so much force in the lives of most of the world's population.

APPENDIX A
Research Methods and Sampling of Companies of
Individuals Interviewed

IN THE course of the research for this book, interviews were conducted with multinational managers, their local joint-venture partners and employees, Nigerian state officials, indigenous businessmen, representatives of labor groups, officials of foreign embassies, and academics. A few people fit into more than one of these categories, but in the final analysis a total of 157 individuals were formally interviewed. Most of the interviews were conducted during research visits to Nigeria in 1979, 1981, and 1982, although several were also conducted in the United States and the United Kingdom. None of the interviews were tape-recorded, and all of the subjects were assured of the confidentiality of their remarks. It is for this reason that I have developed functional descriptions (e.g. "British multinational manager" or "prominent state official") as the source of each of the interviews cited in the text.

Of the 157 individuals interviewed, 96 were expatriate or indigenous employees of multinational corporations, 18 were state officials, 18 were indigenous businessmen or representatives of indigenous business associations, 12 were academics or journalists, 10 were officials of foreign embassies, 2 were labor representatives, and 1 was an official of a political party. Table A.1 summarizes the distribution in more detailed categories.

Interviews with multinational managers were begun in 1979, while I was working as a consultant for the General Electric Company, then contemplating an investment in Nigeria. It was that experience that originally gave birth to the project, since I was asking other companies how they had been affected by or had dealt with indigenization. The bulk of the interviews with multinational managers were conducted on a return visit to Nigeria in 1981, though a few were also conducted in 1982. The sample of companies selected for interviews was drawn up in 1981 after the company data set described in Appendix B was completed. Since that data set contains nearly the entire population of large incorporated companies in Nigeria, I was able to ensure that the companies interviewed were broadly representative of the total population of foreign investors, at least in terms of sector of operation and nationality. Several firms were also selected because of

TABLE A.1
Individuals Interviewed in the
Course of Research

Multinational managers (expatriate and indigenous)		96
(Commerce	19)	
(Manufacturing	22)	
(Construction	8)	
(Services	43)	
(Primary	4)	
State officials (classified by government with which they were primarily associated)		18
(Gowon	3)	
(Muhammed–Obasanjo	8)	
(Shagari	7)	
Indigenous businessmen		18
(Officials of associations	5)	
(Individuals	13)	
Academics and journalists		12
Foreign embassy officials		10
Labor representatives		2
Politicians		1
Total		157

the importance and visibility of their experience with indigenization and/or because of the articulateness of their senior managers.

A total of fifty-eight companies were interviewed. In most of them, more than one individual was interviewed and in several there were follow-up interviews. The sample of companies by principal sector of operation is quite representative of the total population. Nineteen service-sector companies were interviewed, seventeen manufacturers, fourteen commercial enterprises, five construction firms, and three primary producers. Table A.2 summarizes the distribution and compares it with the population of incorporated companies described in Appendix B.

Although construction firms were underrepresented and service-sector companies overrepresented, the sample of interviews is generally representative of the total population. The overrepresentation of service-sector enterprises stems from the number of interviews conducted within the banks, for reasons that are clear from Chapter 6.

The sample of companies interviewed is also broadly representative of companies in Nigeria classified according to nationality. American

TABLE A.2
Sample of Companies Interviewed,
by Sector

Sector	No.	%	% from Appendix B
Commerce	14	24	23
Manufacturing	17	29	28
Construction	5	9	24
Services	19	33	19
Primary	3	5	6
Total	58	100	100

TABLE A.3
Sample of Companies Interviewed
by Nationality

Nationality	No.	%	% from Appendix B
American	27	46	25
British	12	21	38
European	14	24	23
Other	5	9	14
Total	58	100	100

firms are clearly overrepresented, while British firms are underrepresented (owing to the nature of networks, my own nationality, and the sheer number of British enterprises in the country). The number of European and other companies included in the sample is more representative of the total population. Table A.3 summarizes these distributions.

For the majority of companies interviewed, the following interview schedule was employed. In most cases, not all of the questions were asked, though all were asked at some point in the research. Since the questions were open-ended, respondents were allowed to expand on certain points, especially when their experience was particularly germane to an issue. Bankers and petroleum-sector executives were given supplementary questions appropriate to their activities, which have been appended to the general interview schedule for multinational managers listed below.

1981 INTERVIEW SCHEDULE FOR FOREIGN CAPITAL

A. *Basic Information*
1. Interviewee
2. Company name
3. Principal function:

1	2	3	4	5	6
commerce	manuf	const	service	primary	conglom

4. Principal activity (1–80, using coding scheme described in Appendix B)
5. Other activities
6. Schedule of indigenization decree: 1   2   3
7. Ownership structure (percentage of which is:
Foreign capital   Local capital   State   Other)
8. State of principal operation in Nigeria (1–19, using coding scheme described in Appendix B)
9. Other affiliates in Nigeria? Yes   No   Names:
10. Amount of paid-up capital:
11. Sales turnover:
12. Employees
a. Total number:
b. Number of expatriates:
c. In what positions?

B. *History of Operations in Nigeria*
1. Date of 1st contact with Nigerian market
2. Nature of 1st contact (trade, contracts)
3. Date of start-up/major involvement/establishment of operations
4. Why invest/locate in Nigeria?
5. What determined location within Nigeria?
6. What were the principal sources of capital? (% imported /% raised locally) (identity of foreign company)

C. *Local Partners*
1. Who are your local partners? (get as much information as possible—what other ventures do they have?)
2. How were local partners chosen? (criteria employed)
3. What do they do for the firm? (former distributors?)
4. What are they most effective at?
5. What do you think are their motives for entering a joint venture with your firm?

6. How are they compensated? (what do they get out of it?)
7. What do they do with their earnings?
8. Can you refer us to them?

D. *Government Regulations*
1. Which Nigerian governmental regulations most affect your operations? (indigenization, repatriation, import restrictions)
2. How seriously are they taken by the Nigerians? (for popular consumption or genuine economic nationalism? try to get differentiation by regulation type)
2a. Public/Private-sector splits?
3. How effective is enforcement? (how competent are Nigerians in enforcement? do they follow through?)

E. *Indigenization* (defined most broadly to include indigenization of share capital [equity] and personnel)
1. Which of the following has had the greatest impact on your operations?
   a. Indigenization decrees (1972 and 1977)
   b. Expatriate quotas
   c. Other
2. What was your firm's experience with indigenization? (tailor to fit context: number of years in Nigeria, type of firm, etc.)
3. How did you respond to/manage/cope with indigenization? (how to maintain efficient operation with fewer expatriates)
   Negotiate?
   Two-company formula?
   Technical consulting arrangements?
   Voting rule changes in articles of association?
   Other?
4. In what areas of your Nigerian operation have things changed the most since indigenization?
   a. Personnel quality
   b. Efficiency (production/output)
   c. Increased local content
   d. Employee benefits
   e. Labor relations
   f. Marketing
   g. Financing
   h. Technology (acquisition/use)
   i. Greater reliance on managerial/technical consultants
   j. Expansion
5. In what areas of your operation do Nigerians have the most responsibility? (what do Nigerian managers do?)

Labor relations?
Marketing?
Advertising?
Production?
Finance?

6. Are you slowly losing control over your Nigerian operations? (control is defined as managerial responsibility for financial, technical, and commercial aspects of operations)

7. What are the principal sources and objectives of indigenization? (who is behind it? bureaucrats, military, business?) What do they want?

8. What do you think are the effects of indigenization in Nigeria?
   a. Has indigenization reduced challenges from local firms in your industry?
   b. Is it providing an important training base for indigenous managers? (significant for long-term development?)

9. What are the future trends in indigenization? More stringent? (local-content requirements?) Relaxation?

10. How will you react?

F. *Sectoral Questions*

   1. Who are your major competitors?
      a. Identify
      b. Mostly local capital? Foreign capital? State capital?

   2. How do you differ from your competitors?

   3. Which MNCs are best at doing business in Nigeria? Why? (Lebanese? Indians?)

   4. How would you assess the role of public corporations in the economy? How important are state–foreign capital joint ventures in the economy?

   5. How common are joint ventures among MNCs, local firms, and the Nigerian government? (triple alliances—is this a trend?)

   6. How significant/important are the large Nigerian groups of companies (Fanz, Ibru, Ugochukwu, Dantata, Odua)?

   6a. Do they provide a foundation for future industry?

   7. In which areas of the economy are local Nigerian firms strongest? (ask specifically about manufacturing)

   7a. How is your firm compensated? (what do you get out of the investment?)

   7b. How important are Nigerian-initiated/managed firms with expert technical partners?

   8. What is your firm's future strategy? (expand/cut back) Why?

G. *Conclusion*
    1. Whom else would you recommend I talk to?

Supplement I—Questions for Bankers
    1. Where is big money for investment coming from? (the state, foreign capital, local capital)
    2. Where is local capital for indigenous enterprises coming from?
    3. Does oil money trickle down to local private sector? How?
    4. Where are local firms investing their earnings from joint ventures? (post-indigenization)
        a. Land?
        b. Imports?
        c. Other firms? What types?
        d. Switzerland?

Supplement II—More Questions for Bankers
    S1. What percentage of your current loan applications come from Nigerian-initiated, Nigerian-run firms in commerce; in manufacturing; in construction; in services; in primary activities?
    S2. What percentage of your recent loans approved for Nigerian-initiated, Nigerian-run (genuinely indigenous) firms are in commerce; in manufacturing; in construction; in services; in primary activities?
    S3. Do the lists of indigenous manufacturers, indigenous insurance companies, indigenous banks, finance and investment companies compiled in the data set described in Appendix B have any important omissions?
    S4. Has there been a significant growth of any small industries not included in the major directories of companies? In which areas?
    S5. What percentage of new indigenous manufacturing firms are joint ventures with foreign companies? What percentage are Nigerian-initiated and -managed, with foreign technical consultants only?

Supplement III—Questions for Multinational Oil Companies
    G1. Do you think it would make much difference if you had private Nigerians as joint-venture partners rather than the government?
    G2. Are the Nigerians serious about controlling the oil companies? What aspects?
    G3. Are they capable of doing so?
    G4. What is the area of greatest controversy between (company name) and your Nigerian joint-venture partners?

Below is an alphabetical listing of companies interviewed between 1979 and 1982. Nearly all of these firms have complied fully with the provisions of the 1972 and 1977 decrees. The countervailing measures described in Chapters 3 and 5 were employed by some of them, but not by all. Often in the course of an interview the managers or owners described the countervailing measures employed by other companies in addition to their own responses to the measures.

Abbott Laboratories
Alpha Management
American International
    Insurance Group
Arthur Anderson
Ashland Oil
BASF
Bankers Trust
Bank of America (Savannah
    Bank)
Barclays Bank (Union Bank)
Bata Shoes
Blackwood-Hodge
Bofam
Brown Bovari
Cadbury
Chase Manhattan Bank (Chase
    Merchant Bank)
Continental Illinois (Nigerian
    Acceptances Limited)
Dizengoff
Elf Petroleum
Ferguson Associates
First Boston (Nigerian–
    American Merchant Bank)
First Chicago (International
    Merchant Bank)
Fougerolle Construction
GEC
General Electric
Guinness
ICI
ITT
Johnson & Johnson

Johnson Products
Lever Brothers
Leyland
Life Flour Mills
Merle International
Morgan Guaranty (ICON)
NAAFCO Scientific
Nestlé
New Products and Processes
Nichimen
PRC Associates
Pfizer
Philip Morris
Phillips Petroleum
Raychem Labs
SCOA
Sadelmi Construction
Shawmont
Sisselman
Société Générale (United Bank
    for Africa)
Taylor Woodrow
T-Comm
Tower Aluminium
UAC
Union Carbide
Utilgas
Van Leer Containers
Volkswagen
Wallace, McHarg, Roberts &
    Todd
Westinghouse

The following interview schedule was used for the majority of the interviews conducted with indigenous businessmen or representatives of indigenous business associations. A slightly adjusted form of the schedule (concentrating on selected questions in sections C and D) was used for interviews with Nigerian state officials, academics, labor representatives, and politicians.

As in the case of the interviews with multinationals, not all of the questions were asked in every interview. And occasionally, when the personal experience of the respondent was especially germane to a particular topic (such as the response of an indigenous business group to a draft of a decree or the role of a prominent state official in the formulation of policy), special questions were drawn up. Since to reveal those questions would also reveal the identity of the individuals quoted in the text, I have chosen not to list every question asked. The interview schedule captures the central issues addressed in all interviews, even those in which special questions were drawn up.

1982 INTERVIEW SCHEDULE

A. *Background Information*
　　1. Interviewee
　　2. Address
　　3. Date
　　4. Biographical sketch
　　　　a. How did you get started in business?
　　　　b. Father's occupation?
　　　　c. Education?
　　5. Principal business activities today (PRINFCN) (1–6, using coding scheme from Appendix B)
　　6. Principal activities (1–80, using coding scheme from Appendix B)
　　7. State of principal operation in Nigeria (1–19, using coding scheme from Appendix B)

B. *General Economic Survey*
　　1. Where are Nigerian businesses strongest (most important) today? (Nigerian business = Nigerian-initiated and -run . . . without foreign subsidiary link)
　　　　PRINFCN 1　2　3　4　5　6
　　　　PRINACT (using coding scheme from Appendix B)

2. What are the fastest-growing sectors/areas for Nigerian business?
   PRINFCN 1   2   3   4   5   6
   PRINACT (using coding scheme from Appendix B)
3. What do *you* think are the best investments for Nigerian businesses today?
   PRINFCN 1   2   3   4   5   6   7   8   9
                                         land   abroad   other
   PRINACT (using coding scheme from Appendix B) Why?
4. (If relevant) What prevents Nigerian businessmen from going into manufacturing?
5. Where does local capital for Nigerian business come from?
   State banks? Other sources? Federal banks (NIDB, NBCI)? Accumulated earnings? Commercial banks (merchant banks)? Savings?
6. Would you rather invest on your own or create a joint venture with a foreign company? Why?
7. What type of foreign management/expertise do you want in a joint venture?
8. Does the oil money filter down to Nigerian businessmen? How?
   Licenses/contracts?
   Construction contracts?
   Exclusive supply contracts?
   Service contracts?
9. Are state governments important intermediaries (between the federal government and yourself) in the distribution of the oil wealth?
10. What areas of national economic policy create the most controversy in Nigeria?
    Tariffs? Licenses? Revenue allocation? Industrial location?

C. *Indigenization*
   1. Who were the strongest backers/supporters of indigenization in 1972? Which groups? Which individuals?
      Who pushed for its extension in 1977? Which groups? Which individuals?
      Why?
   2. Did everyone in the local Nigerian business community support it? Manufacturers (Manufacturers Association of Ni-

geria) as well as importers and distributors? (Chamber of Commerce)

Did anyone in the business community oppose it? Who? Why?

3. Which ministries, agencies, or government officials backed the exercise most enthusiastically?

4. What were (are) the principal objectives of the indigenization exercise?

 Control? Share of profits? Training? Others?

5. Were there any differences between Nigerian government officials and the Nigerian business community on these objectives?

6. What has changed the most (in general) as a result of indigenization?

7. What has changed the most in *your* operations (or operations with which you are most familiar) since indigenization?

 a. Personnel
 b. Efficiency
 c. Local content
 d. Employee benefits
 e. Labor relations
 f. Marketing
 g. Financing
 h. Technology (acquisition/use)
 i. Greater reliance on consulting (managerial/technical)

8. In what areas of the operation do Nigerian managers have the most responsibility?

 a. Labor relations
 b. Marketing
 c. Advertising
 d. Production
 e. Finance
 f. Others (connections, contracts, land)

9. Are you slowly gaining control over operations that were formerly foreign-run? (control is defined as managerial responsibility for financial, technical, and commercial aspects of production)

10. What is the role of the Nigerian directors of indigenized companies? (how active in management? in investment decisions? profit determination?)

11. How did you get involved with the foreign firms with which

you are associated? (did you initiate? did foreign company?
did banks?)
12. Who benefited the most from indigenization? Which groups?
(old trading families? politicians? civil servants? military?)
In which regions?
Which individuals? (only rarely ask this)
13. What have they done with their share earnings?
Reinvest in other foreign companies? Buy land? Consume?
Establish new enterprises? in commerce? in manufacturing?
14. What have *you* done with *your* share earnings? (use same categories as in 13)
15. What do you think are the long-term effects of indigenization
in Nigeria? Training? Learning? Base for business development? Other?

D. *State Capital*
1. Where are Nigerian government enterprises most heavily
concentrated? (in what activities?)
PRINFCN 1   2   3   4   5   6
PRINACT (using coding scheme from Appendix B)
2. Do state governments and the federal government invest in
different activities? (where are they concentrated?)
3. What is the proper role of government involvement in the
economy?
4. Which ministries, agencies (or individuals) are most wary of
foreign investment? (i.e. want greater controls, monitoring)

E. *Contacts*
1. Whom else would you recommend I talk to?
2. May I use your name?

Below is an alphabetical listing of the former state officials, indigenous businessmen, representatives of indigenous business groups, academics, labor representatives, and representatives of political parties
inteviewed in Nigeria or the United Kingdom between 1979 and
1983. None of them is entirely responsible for the interpretations I
have presented in this book, and most would disagree with portions
of my argument. Reconstructing the political economy of Nigerian
indigenization has been at times as much of an artistic as a scientific
venture. Each of them is again thanked for his or her time and many
insights.

Alhaji Abubakar Abdulkadir
Professor Ladipo Adamolekun
Justice S. D. Adebiyi
Professor Haroun Adamu
Professor Tunde Adenirin
Chief O. A. Adeosun
O. J. Adewumi
G. A. Akamiokhor
Olu Akinfosile
S. 'Sola Akingbohungbe
Chief J. Akin-George
Professor A. A. Akinsanya
H. I. Alile
Professor Mai Aliyu Muhammed
Professor Nur Alkali
Professor Olajide Aluko
S. O. Asabia
P. C. Asiodu
A. A. Ayida
Chief M. Balogun
M. F. Bello
Hammond Bello Mohammed
Chief Kola Daisi
Professor E. C. Edozien
Professor Fred Ekeh
Uma O. Eleazu

M. O. Funmilayo
M. W. Gadzama
Alhaji Aminu Gidado
W. O. Goodluck
General Yakubu Gowon
Professor Ankie Hoogvelt
I. O. Ihejirika
T. O. Ilugbuhi
M. O. Kayode
Chief A. O. Lawson
Arthur C. I. Mbanefo
General Olusegun Obasanjo
Cornel C. Obi
Chief C. O. Ogunbanjo
Professor Ayo Ogunsheye
M. A. Oke
Chief Oladotun O. Okubanjo
Dr. M. O. Omolayole
Gamaliel O. Onosode
Gregory I. O. Osude
Malomo Owonuwa
B. Richard Ranshaw (financial controller for Alhaji Aminu Dantatta)
Akintola Williams
Hamza R. Zayyad

In addition to the interviews cited above, a few interviews were also conducted with officials of foreign embassies, usually commercial or economic officers. The questions asked tended to be among the most general items listed on the two interview schedules (for 1981 and 1982) described above. American, British, Canadian, French, and German officials were interviewed.

Finally, in addition to the 157 interviews conducted by me and/or one of my research assistants, several other scholars also generously gave me access to their raw data, interview materials, or research notes. I am especially grateful to Joseph LaPalombara of Yale University for giving me access to transcripts of interviews from his Conference Board project on elite perceptions of multinationals. Ankie Hoogvelt of Sheffield University also gave me a chance to examine her research interviews and notes from her work in Kano.

APPENDIX B
Methodology and Codebook for Data Set Assembled on
Incorporated Enterprises in Nigeria

BECAUSE reliable statistical data are so hard to come by in Nigeria, I assembled basic data on 2,328 companies incorporated in Nigeria at the end of 1980. The data were compiled from twelve different business directories and were used intensively for the sectoral analysis of the consequences of the two indigenization decrees. Each company was assigned an identification number and classified according to its principal sector, principal economic activity, ownership and origin, and joint-venture type. Basic economic data on paid-up capital, sales turnover, and number of employees were also gathered. The year of the company's incorporation in Nigeria was obtained from the 1980/ 81 edition of the Registrar of Companies' *Directory of Incorporated (Registered) Companies in Nigeria.*

Every datum was carefully cross-checked by a research assistant who looked for differences recorded in different directories. The list of discrepancies was then discussed with me by a research assistant who had accompanied me on several research trips to Nigeria, and we decided together what the appropriate classification should be (or whether an item should be recorded as indeterminate, not available, or missing). We also made all of the decisions about the principal sector in which each company operated (labelled "principal function") and the principal economic activity of each firm.

The following business directories were examined in the course of assembling the company data set:

1. *Accounting and Banking Firms* (Lagos: United States Embassy, 1981).

2. *American Firms, Subsidiaries, and Affiliates in Nigeria* (Lagos: United States Embassy, October 1979).

3. *Canadian Firms Operating in Nigeria* (Lagos: Canadian High Commission, May 1980).

4. *Companies in the Oil and Gas Industry in Nigeria* (Lagos: United States Embassy, January 1980).

5. *Directory of American Firms Operating in Foreign Countries* (New York: Simon and Schuster, 1979).

6. *Directory of Incorporated (Registered) Companies in Nigeria* (Lagos: ICIC [Directory Publishers] Ltd., 1981).

7. *Principal International Businesses, 1982* (New York: Dun and Bradstreet International, 1982).

8. *Lagos Chamber of Commerce and Industry List of Members of the Indigenous Businessmen's Group* (Lagos: Lagos Chamber of Commerce, 1981).

9. *Major Companies of Nigeria* (London: Graham and Trotman Ltd., 1979).

10. *Nigeria Company Handbook, 1980* (Ikeja, Lagos State: Jikonzult Management Services Ltd., 1980).

11. *Some British Connected Firms in Nigeria* (Lagos: British High Commission, 1980).

12. *Top Twenty British Associated Companies in Nigeria* (Lagos: British High Commission, 1980).

What follows is an item-by-item description of each of the variables for which data were obtained, including the full classification scheme and general decision rules used.

1. *Principal Function*

Each company was assigned to a single sector of the economy in which it principally operates, identified as 1–6 below. This classification was most difficult in cases where the company straddled sectors (as many do) and where the principal sector was not immediately apparent.

0 No information
1 Commerce (suppliers, importers, exporters, distributors, wholesalers, retailer agents, dealers, merchants)
2 Manufacturing (manufacturers, producers, assemblers, processors, fabricators, smelters, refiners)
3 Construction and engineering (contractors, engineers)
4 Services (bankers, insurance, financiers, investors, consultants, accountants, lawyers, architects, planners, repairs, hotels, caterers, broadcasters, telecommunications, tourism, transport, travel, shipping, oil services, company representatives, plant hire)
5 Primary production (agricultural production, fishing, mining, quarrying, exploration, extraction)
6 Conglomerate (holding company for eight or more companies operating in more than three different activities, 1–5 above)

Decision rules:
(1) Directory 4 supersedes all other directories for petroleum sector only.

2. *Principal Activity*

Each company was also assigned a principal area of economic activity, identified as 1–80 below. When combined with the variable for principal function, this classification enables us to differentiate a textile retailer (coded 1–66) from a textile manufacturer (coded 2–66). Again, this classification proved difficult, since so many firms operate with several product lines. Hence, a principal activity was chosen for each.

  0 No information
  1 Accountants and lawyers
  2 Agents and general trading companies
  3 Agricultural equipment and services
  4 Agricultural produce (most under 25)
  5 Air conditioning, heating, and refrigeration
  6 Architecture and town planning
  7 Banks, finance, and investment companies
  8 Brewing, soft drinks, and wine
  9 Building materials and cement (including block molders)
10 Carpets
11 Ceramics and sanitary fittings (usually under 9)
12 Chain stores
13 Chemicals (batteries, industrial gases, adhesives)
14 Civil engineering and construction
15 Commercial and industrial institutes and associations
16 Computers
17 Construction plant (often under 14; refers to construction machinery)
18 Consultants (business) (services include advertising, PR)
19 Consultants (engineering) (construction under 14)
20 Defense and armaments
21 Educational equipment and training services (includes books)
22 Electrical and electronic equipment (includes assembly)
23 Electrical engineering
24 Fishing and fish processing
25 Food and food processing (includes bakeries, confectioneries)
26 Freight forwarding and customs agents (see shipping, unless customs agent only)
27 Furniture (includes interior design, decorating)
28 Glass
29 Government bodies
30 Handicrafts, pottery, and jewelry
31 Hardware (sometimes with metals)
32 Hotels and catering

33 Household goods and appliances (detergents and soaps, matches, candles, watches)
34 Insurance and reinsurance
35 Irrigation services and equipment
36 Leather and shoes
37 Leisure goods (includes records, musical instruments)
38 Livestock and animal feeds
39 Mechanical engineering (see also construction plant, where plant-machinery)
40 Mechanical engineering plant (see also construction plant)
41 Metals, metal processing and fabrication (including windows/doors/sidings, galvanized metal sheets)
42 Mining, mineral processing, and quarrying
43 Motorcycles and bicycles
44 Motor vehicles and components (includes 43)
45 Office equipment and supplies (includes adhesives, cleaning services)
46 Oil and gas exploration and production
47 Oil and gas services and equipment and pipeline contractors (supplying them or distributing their products)
48 Oil refining
49 Optical and photographic equipment
50 Packaging
51 Paint
52 Paper and paper products
53 Petrochemicals
54 Pharmaceuticals and medical supplies and services
55 Plant hire
56 Plastics and plastic products
57 Power equipment (construction—power generation)
58 Printing and publishing (books and newspapers)
59 Property or real estate, surveyors
60 Publishing, broadcasting, films, and advertising
61 Rubber and rubber goods (includes tire retreading)
62 Safety and security equipment (includes nightwatchman services)
63 Scientific instruments
64 Shipping, shipbuilding, and shipping services (see also 26)
65 Telecommunications
66 Textiles and clothing and textile equipment (including the manufacture of piece goods)
67 Timber industries, sawmills
68 Tobacco

69 Toiletries and cosmetics (often with pharmaceuticals; may be slight bias towards pharmaceuticals owing to alphabetical location)
70 Transport (some shipping firms)
71 Travel and tourism
72 Utilities and public services
73 Fertilizers
74 Advertising
75 Technical equipment (general)
80 Diversified (principal function known; three or more possible activities)

Decision rules:

(1) Whenever there was a choice, we picked the more general listing.

3. *Ownership and Origin*

Each company was also classified according to its ownership and origin, according to the following scheme. Like the principal-function and principal-activity variables described above, this is a two-part classification. The ownership is the most general category, primarily differentiating foreign, local, and state capital. The origin component identifies the national identity of the foreign firm or whether the government involvement is state or federal. That is, any enterprise with a 200-level coding is predominantly foreign-controlled, but an American firm (210) can be differentiated from a British one (230).

Ownership	*Origin*
0	00 Undetermined
1 *Local*	00 Undetermined
2 Predominantly *Foreign* (20% and more)	00 Undetermined
	10 American MNC
	11 Canadian
	20 Comecon
	30 British
	40 Undetermined European
	41 German
	42 Swiss
	43 French
	44 Dutch
	45 Italian

Ownership	*Origin*
	46 Belgian
	47 Scandinavian
	48 Israeli
	50 Undetermined Asian
	51 Japanese
	52 Korean, Taiwanese
	60 Indian, Pakistani, Malaysian
	70 Lebanese, Syrian, Sudanese, and other Arab MNCs
	80 Other (Greek, Brazilian, etc.)
	90 British–American
3 *Government*	00 Undetermined (assumed if no other indication)
	10 State government(s)
	20 Federal government
	30 Combination federal, state (and/ or local) governments
4	00 International organization
5	00 Foreign government (aid, not including foreign state corporations such as AGIP or British Leyland)

4. *Combination Type*

Each enterprise was also classified according to its type of joint-venture combination, according to the coding scheme identified below. Again, to have meaning, this coding scheme is a multivariate one, with the first digit identifying the dominant ownership of the firm and the second specifying its combination type. That is, enterprises identified as 21 or 31 are both joint ventures between multinationals and state corporations or agencies, but a firm classified as 21 is likely to be predominantly foreign-controlled, while a firm classified 31 is most likely to be state-controlled.

00	No information
1 *Local*	0 Local 100% (identity clearly indicated, all major shareholders are local)
	1 Local–Foreign (includes 100% local with foreign manager or technical partner)

    2 Local–Government
       (in most cases, we do not have sufficient infor-
       mation to determine whether government or
       local involvement is more important; hence we
       assume that in most government-local combi-
       nations government exercises control—then it
       falls under 32 below)
    3 Local–Foreign–Government
    4 Undetermined

2 *Foreign*   0 Foreign 100%
    1 Foreign–Government
    2 Foreign–Local
       (mostly assumed when no evident government
       involvement)
    3 Foreign–Local–Government
    4 Undetermined

3 *Government*   0 Government 100%
       (assumed when there was no explicit mention
       of foreign or local involvement)
    1 Government–Foreign
       (includes 100% government with foreign man-
       ager or technical partner)
    2 Government–Local
    3 Government–Foreign–Local
    4 Undetermined

Decision rules:

(1) Government institutions are classified according to the follow-
ing general guidelines. State government corporations include the
New Nigeria Development Company Ltd., Northern Nigeria Invest-
ment Ltd., Odu'a Investment Co. Ltd., Kano State Investment Co.
Ltd., Great Nigeria Insurance Co. Ltd., etc. Federal corporations in-
clude the Nigerian Industrial Development Bank, Nigeria National
Petroleum Corporation (NNPC), National Insurance Corporation of
Nigeria, Central Bank of Nigeria, Nigerian National Shipping Line
Ltd., etc.

(2) Undetermined foreign capital (200) has combination type 24,
if the partners are not known.

(3) If there is not any exact information about the shareholders (but
it is certain that they are foreign), code it as 22. No foreign firm has
100% ownership anymore.

(4) Any 000 has 00 as combination type.

(5) If two government institutions own a company, select the most important in equity terms.

(6) Unless otherwise indicated in a combination of foreign and local capital, the foreign shareholder is assumed to be the most important one.

(7) If two MNCs own a Nigerian company, take the most important. Most of the time, the company listed first is more important in cases where exact figures are not given.

(8) If a company is associated with or is a division of UAC, John Holt, or one of the other large holding companies, code as 23.

(9) If an MNC and government corporation own a company, code as Foreign capital (FC) as long as it is clear that FC owns more than 20%. Code as government if the logic of the organization is national.

5. *State of Operation*

To assess the location of enterprises, each firm was also assigned to its state of principal operation, according to the coding scheme described below. Care was taken to ensure that the actual site of production was coded in cases of manufacturers and primary producers; however, there is a tendency to overrepresent Lagos State, since so many companies have their headquarters there.

1. Anambra	11. Kwara
2. Bauchi	12. Lagos
3. Bendel	13. Niger
4. Benue	14. Ogun
5. Borno	15. Ondo
6. Cross River	16. Oyo
7. Gongola	17. Plateau
8. Imo	18. Rivers
9. Kaduna	19. Sokoto
10. Kano	

6. *Paid-up Capital*

Total amount of paid-up capital as of 1977. All figures are recorded in thousands of naira.

Decision rules:

(1) "Sales turnover" is read as "turnover" for insurance companies.

(2) The dates of financial figures vary. Most are from 1976 and 1977, but often no date is given.

(3) If a directory lists the amount as "over x," x is taken as the figure (only one firm with this feature).

(4) If paid-up capital is "to be increased to x," the x figure recorded is recorded (only two or three firms with this feature).

(5) If a range is given, the average of the two figures is computed and recorded.

(6) If the original data are in $'s, convert to naira at the rate of 1 naira = $1.60.

7. *Sales Turnover*

Total amount of sales turnover as of 1977. All figures are recorded in thousands of naira.

Decision rules:

See notes on financial data classifications for paid-up capital above.

8. *Number of Employees*

Total employees (at all levels of the operation) as of 1977.

Decision rules:

(1) If data for number of employees are different, take those of the most recent directory.

9. *Date of Incorporation*

Year of incorporation of each company as recorded in the *Directory of Incorporated (Registered) Companies in Nigeria*, 1980/81 edition.

Decision rules:

(1) In some cases, the entry of a firm in the *Directory* is different from our previous information. This is usually because many firms list start-up rather than incorporation date as more significant from their standpoint. Since the *Directory* contains a larger and more consistent sample, the incorporation date is chosen for all cases.

(2) If there is more than one entry in the *Directory*, record the initial listing (e.g. First Bank of Nigeria was incorporated in 1912 as company no. 1, in 1950 as company no. 789, and in 1969 as company no. 6290).

APPENDIX C
Microeconomic Data Gathered about the Operations
of Manufacturing Firms

To MAKE an assessment of the operational significance of changes in
ownership of Schedule 2 and 3 enterprises after the second decree,
microeconomic data were gathered on twenty-two companies (sixteen in Schedule 2 and six in Schedule 3) for 1974 and 1980. Data
were obtained from the Industrial Surveys Division of the Federal Office of Statistics in Lagos. Data were gathered on each firm's paid-up
capital, number of employees, wages, benefits, total sales, investment
in new machinery, and profitability. The years 1974 and 1980 were
chosen for comparison because they allow an examination of company operations both before and after the second decree.

The number of companies is so small not because of time limitations, but because these twenty-two firms are the entire population of
Schedule 2 and 3 enterprises on which the Federal Office of Statistics
has data for both years. (This is a sad comment on the quality of statistical data available to the Nigerian government and should serve to
warn scholars against relying too heavily on published national statistics. It should also now be apparent why I went to the trouble of assembling my own data set on incorporated companies in the country.
While the Federal Office of Statistics has returns from less than a
hundred manufacturing enterprises for 1980 [and bases its calculations of industrial output on these completed surveys], I have a list of
610 manufacturing enterprises for the same year in the data set described in Appendix B.)

For each enterprise for each year, data were gathered to produce the
following variables:
1. Paid-up capital
2. Total number of employees
3. Total wages and salaries
4. Contribution to the National Provident Fund
5. Other benefits paid
6. Total sales
   a. In monetary figures
   b. In unit figures

7. Value of end-of-year stock
8. Cost of raw materials, fuel, and other expenses
9. Additions to assets
10. Receipts from the sales of assets

From these variables, the following ratios and additional variables were calculated:

11. Ratio of employees/sales (monetary figures)
    Variable $11 = 2/6a$
12. Ratio of employees/sales (unit figures)
    Variable $12 = 2/6b$
13. Total benefits
    Variable $13 = 4 + 5$
14. Net profit/loss for the year
    Variable $14 = (6a + 10) - (3 + 7 + 8 + 9 + 13)$.

From a comparison of these computed ratios for 1974 and 1980, it was possible to make some of the inferences about the operational effects of indigenization discussed in Chapter 5.

APPENDIX D
Chronology of Economic Nationalism in Nigeria

1946 Nigerian Local Development Boards set up
1948 Lagos Chamber of Commerce modifies charter to admit Africans
1951 Aid to Pioneer Industry Ordinance (provides incentives for foreign companies employing Nigerians)
1952 Statement of immigration policy (to increase indigenous participation in distributive trade)
1956 Industrial estates established
     Reiteration of 1952 immigration policy
1958 Mbadiwe sets up commission to examine problems of indigenous businessmen
     Tax Relief Act (requires limited Nigerianization of personnel and management in foreign firms seeking favorable tax treatment)
1959 Report of Advisory Commission on Aids to African Businessmen submitted to federal government
1961 Waziri Ibrahim's statement in parliament calling for the distributive trade and road transport to be reserved for Nigerians
1962 Nationalization debate in parliament
1963 Immigration Act (stipulates that no alien can practice a profession without Ministry of Internal Affairs approval and establishes a quota system for expatriate employees of newly established MNCs)
1964 Government statement on industrial policy (announces preferences to firms with 10% indigenous participation and 45% local content)
     NIDB established
1965 National Commission on the Nigerianization of Business Enterprises set up (August)
1966 Expatriate Quota Allocation Board created
1968 Companies Decree
1969 Banking legislation introduced (banks are required to incorporate in Nigeria and publish audited statements of account)

Petroleum Decree (requires oil companies to Nigerianize not fewer than 60% of jobs at all levels and not fewer than 75% of management positions within ten years of receiving a lease; applies to new concessions only)

National Insurance Company of Nigeria (NICON) established

1970 Second National Development Plan (provides guidelines for training and personnel indigenization and introduces a rationale for equity indigenization

Central Bank of Nigeria introduces credit guidelines

1971 Government acquires 40% of three largest commercial banks (April)

Nigeria joins OPEC (July)

Nigerian National Oil Company (NNOC) established and government acquires majority (and some minority) participation in petroleum companies

Industrial Training Fund Decree (no. 47) announced

1972 Nigerian Council for Management Education and Training reconstituted to coordinate future programs (January)

NIGERIAN ENTERPRISES PROMOTION DECREE (1972) promulgated (23 February)

Plans for NBCI announced (April)

1973 Center for Management Development established (January)

Capital Issues Commission founded (March)

National Bank for Commerce and Industry (NBCI) established (May)

NEPD Amendment (1973) (23 June)

Nigerian Agricultural Development Bank (NADB) created

1974 NEPD Amendment (no. 2) announced (February)

Government acquires 55% of petroleum industry

Government acquires 40% of NICON (National Insurance Company of Nigeria)

Nigerian Economic Society symposium on indigenization (9 November)

1975 Government acquires 49% of insurance companies

Third National Development Plan (declares that government will introduce measures to ensure that indigenous equity holding is reflected in the control of the businesses concerned)

Adeosun panel is convened (17 November)

1976 Adeosun Commission report is submitted (25 March)

Government White Paper commenting on Adeosun report is released (29 June)

Government announces intention to acquire 60% of the banks (1 July)

Nigerian Institute of Management conference on indigenization is held (September)

Dividend payments are restricted to 30% of gross earnings

Capital Issues Commission (CIC) is transformed into the Nigerian Securities and Exchange Commission (NSEC)

1977 NIGERIAN ENTERPRISES PROMOTION DECREE (1977) promulgated (12 January)

Dividend payments are restricted to 40%

Nigerian National Petroleum Corporation (NNPC) established (1 April)

1978 Nigerian Reinsurance Company established

Lending operations of insurance companies brought under Central Bank control

1979 Nigeria hires General Superintendence Company of Switzerland (SGS) to monitor transfer pricing of multinational corporations (February)

Dividend payments restricted to 50% of after-tax profits

Securities and Exchange Commission Decree formally establishes NSEC (27 September)

1980 Fourth National Development Plan

Management guidelines issued by the NEPB as a condition for issue of certificates of compliance (May)

Nigerian industrial policy guidelines announced

1981 Some relaxation of NEPD2 begun, as several industries are reclassified from Schedule 2 to Schedule 3

NNPC reorganized and decentralized into nine subsidiaries

1982 NEPB requests amendment to NEPD2 to clarify guidelines regarding management control

BIBLIOGRAPHY

Nongovernmental Material

Aboyade, O. 1974. "Closing Remarks." In Nigerian Economic Society 1974, pp. 77–78.
———. 1977. "Indigenizing Foreign Enterprises: Some Lessons from the Nigerian Enterprises Promotion Decree." In Teriba and Kayede (eds.) *Industrial Development in Nigeria: Patterns, Problems and Prospects*, pp. 379–388. Ibadan: Ibadan University Press.
Adedeji, Adebayo (ed.). 1981. *Indigenization of African Economies*. London: Hutchinson University Library for Africa.
Adeniji, Kola. 1977. "State Participation in the Nigerian Petroleum Industry." *Journal of World Trade Law* 11, no. 2 (March–April): 156–179.
Akamiokhor, G. A. 1982. Untitled paper presented to a meeting of the chairman of the NEPB and the chairmen and secretaries of the State Enterprises Promotion Committees, Sokoto, 9 August.
Akeredolu-Ale, E. O. 1972. "Environmental, Organizational and Group Factors in the Evolution of Private Indigenous Entrepreneurship in Nigeria." *Nigerian Journal of Economic and Social Studies* 14, no. 2 (July): 247–256.
———. 1974. "Some Thoughts on the Indigenization Process and the Quality of Nigerian Capitalism." In Nigerian Economic Society 1974, pp. 68–72.
———. 1975. *The Underdevelopment of Indigenous Entrepreneurship in Nigeria*. Ibadan: Ibadan University Press.
Akingbohungbe, S. S. 1980. "The Nigerian Securities and Exchange Commission: Its Activities." Paper presented at 3rd Annual Branch Controllers' Conference of the Central Bank of Nigeria, 23 September.
Akinkugbe, Olu. 1974. "Nigerian Enterprises Promotion Degree and Its Implementation." In Nigerian Economic Society 1974, pp. 38–43.
Akinyemi, Chief O.I.A. 1976. "Towards Making Dwellers of Rural Areas Company Shareholders." *Management in Nigeria*, September: 16–17.
Alavi, Hamza, 1975. "India and the Colonial Mode of Production." In Ralph Miliband and John Saville (eds.), *The Socialist Register* 1975, pp. 160–197. London: Merlin Press.
Alile, H. I. 1982. "Efforts at Achieving Spread of Shareholding in Enterprises through the Stock Exchange." Unpublished paper delivered by director general of Nigerian Stock Exchange at meeting of the chairman of the NEPB and the chairmen and secretaries of the State Enterprises Promotion Committees, Sokoto, 9 August.

Amin, Samir. 1976. *Unequal Development: An Essay on the Social Formations of Peripheral Capitalism*. New York and London: Monthly Review Press.

——. 1980. "The Class Structure of the Contemporary Imperialist System." *Monthly Review* 31, no. 6 (January): 9–26.

Arnold, Guy. 1977. *Modern Nigeria*. London: Longman.

Asabia, S. O. 1974. "Share Valuation: The Nigerian Experience." In Nigerian Economic Society 1974, pp. 19–31.

——. 1981. "Development of Commercial Banking in Nigeria." Paper presented to *Daily Times* Banking Seminar, July.

——. 1982. "Impact of the Nigerian Enterprises Promotion Decrees on the Banks and Other Financial Markets." Unpublished paper.

Asiodu, P. C. 1974. "Closing Remarks." In Nigerian Economic Society 1974, pp. 49–56.

——. 1979. "Nigeria and the Oil Question." Address delivered at Annual Conference of the Nigerian Economic Society symposium, Lagos, February.

Ayida, A. A. 1973. *The Nigerian Revolution, 1966–1976*. Presidential address delivered at 13th Annual Conference of the Nigerian Economic Society. Ibadan: Ibadan University Press.

Balabkins, Nicholas. 1982. *Indigenization and Economic Development: The Nigerian Experience*. Greenwich, Conn.: JAI Press.

Banjo, Ademola. 1976. "The Principal Problems of Indigenisation." *Management in Nigeria*, September: 29–35.

Bauer, P. T. 1954. *West African Trade: A Study of Competition, Oligopoly and Monopoly in a Changing Economy*. Cambridge: Cambridge University Press.

Becker, David. 1983. *The New Bourgeoisie and the Limits of Dependence*. Princeton: Princeton University Press.

Beckman, Bjorn. 1982. "Whose State? State and Capitalist Development in Nigeria." *Review of African Political Economy* no. 23: 37–51.

Bello, V. I. 1974. "The Intentions, Implementation Processes and Problems of the Nigerian Enterprises Promotion Decree (No. 4) 1972." In Nigerian Economic Society 1974, pp. 7–18.

Bennett, Douglas and Kenneth Sharpe. 1977. "Controlling the Multinationals: The Ill Logic of Mexicanization." Unpublished paper. February.

——. 1985. *Transnational Corporations versus the State: The Political Economy of the Mexican Auto Industry*. Princeton: Princeton University Press.

Bergsten, C. Fred, Thomas Horst, and Theodore H. Moran. 1978. *American Multinationals and American Interests*. Washington, D.C.: Brookings Institution.

Biersteker, Thomas J. 1978. *Distortion or Development? Contending Perspectives on the Multinational Corporation*. Cambridge: MIT Press.

——. 1980. "The Illusion of State Power: Transnational Corporations and the Neutralization of Host-Country Legislation." *Journal of Peace Research* 17, no. 3: 207–221.

——. 1986. "Dialectical Thinking about World Order: Sixteen Theses on Dialectics." Paper presented at the Annual Meeting of the International Studies Association, Anaheim, Calif., March.

———. Forthcoming. "Indigenization and the Nigerian Bourgeoisie: Dependent Development in an African Context." In Paul Lubeck (ed.), *The African Bourgeoisie: Capitalist Development in Nigeria, Kenya and Ivory Coast*. Boulder: Lynne Rienner Publishers.

Bissell, Richard E., 1978. "Political Origins of the NIEO." In W. Scott Thompson (ed.), *The Third World: Premises of U.S. Policy*, pp. 227–240. San Francisco: Institute for Contemporary Studies.

Brenner, Robert. 1977. "Origins of Capitalist Development: A Critique of Neo-Smithian Marxism." *New Left Review* no. 104 (July): 25–92.

Brewer, Anthony. 1980. *Marxist Theories of Imperialism: A Critical Survey*. London: Routledge and Kegan Paul.

Cardoso, Fernando Henrique. 1973. "Imperialism and Dependency in Latin America." In Frank Bonilla and Robert Girling (eds.), *Structures of Dependency*, pp. 7–16. Stanford: Stanford University, Institute of Political Studies.

———. 1977. "The Consumption of Dependency Theory in the United States." *Latin American Research Review* 12, no. 3: 7–24.

Cardoso, Fernando Henrique and Enzo Faletto. 1978. *Dependency and Development in Latin America*. Berkeley and Los Angeles: University of California Press.

Cassani, K. 1979. "Indigenization in Nigeria: Letter." *Fortune* 100, no. 4 (27 August): 128.

Chattopadhyay, Paresh. 1972. "On the Question of the Mode of Production in Indian Agriculture." *Economic and Political Weekly* (Bombay) 7, no. 13 (25 March): 39–46.

Chikelu, G.P.O. 1976. "Aims and Objectives of the Indigenisation Scheme." *Management in Nigeria*, September: 21–25.

Cockcroft, James D., André Gunder Frank, and Dale L. Johnson (eds.). 1972. *Dependence and Underdevelopment: Latin America's Political Economy*. Garden City, N.Y.: Anchor Books.

Collins, Paul D. 1974. "The Political Economy of Indigenization: The Case of the Nigerian Enterprises Promotion Decree." *African Review* 4, no. 4: 491–508.

———. 1975. "The Policy of Indigenization: An Overall View." *Quarterly Journal of Administration* (University of Ife) 9, no. 2 (January): 135–147.

———. 1977. "Public Policy and the Development of Indigenous Capitalism: The Nigerian Experience." *Journal of Commonwealth and Comparative Politics* 15, no. 2 (July): 125–150.

———. "The Management and Administration of Parastatal Organizations for the Promotion of Indigenous Enterprise: A West African Experience." *Public Administration and Development* 1: 121–132.

———. 1983. "The State and Industrial Capitalism in West Africa." *Development and Change* 14: 403–429.

Donovan, J. F. 1974. "Nigeria after Indigenization: Is There Any Room for the American Businessman?" *International Lawyer* 8, no. 3: 600–605.

Dos Santos, Theotonio. 1970. "The Structure of Dependence." *American Economic Review* 60, no. 2 (May): 231–236.

———. 1971. "Structure of Dependence." In K. T. Fann and Donald C. Hodges (eds.), *Readings in U.S. Imperialism*, pp. 225–236. Boston: Porter Sargent.

———. 1976. "The Crisis of Contemporary Capitalism." *Latin American Perspectives* 3, no. 2 (Spring): 84–99.

Dudley, Billy. 1982. *An Introduction to Nigerian Government and Politics.* Bloomington: Indiana University Press.

Ebong, I. J. 1972. "The Policy of Indigenisation and Its Implications for National Growth." *Management in Nigeria* 7 (March–April).

Eiteman, David K. and Arthur I. Stonehill. 1973. *Multinational Business Finance.* Reading, Mass.: Addison-Wesley.

Ejiofor, Pita N. O. 1980. "The Limitations of Indigenization Decree." *Management in Nigera*, July: 35–41.

Ekundare, R. O. 1973. *An Economic History of Nigeria.* London: Methuen.

Engberg, Holder L. 1975. "Indigenisation of the Business Sector through the Organized Capital Market: The Lagos Stock Exchange." *Journal of Management Studies* 7, no. 4 (October): 3–17.

Evans, Peter. 1979. *Dependent Development: The Alliance of Multinational, State, and Local Capital in Brazil.* Princeton: Princeton University Press.

Ezeife, Emeka. 1981. "Nigeria." In Adedeji (ed.) 1981, pp. 164–186.

Forrest, Thomas. 1982. "Recent Developments in Nigerian Industrialization." In Martin Fransman (ed.), *Industry and Accumulation in Africa*, pp. 324–344. London: Heineman Educational.

———. Forthcoming. "State Capital in Nigeria." In Paul Lubeck (ed.), *The African Bourgeoisie: Capitalist Development in Nigeria, Kenya and Ivory Coast.* Boulder: Lynne Rienner Publishers.

Foster-Carter, Aiden. 1978. "Modes of Production Controversy." *New Left Review* no. 107 (January): 47–77.

Frank, André Gunder. 1969. *Latin America: Underdevelopment or Revolution— Essays on the Development of Underdevelopment and the Immediate Enemy.* New York and London: Monthly Review Press.

———. 1972a. *Lumpenbourgeoisie: Lumpendevelopment.* New York and London: Monthly Review Press.

———. 1972b. "Economic Dependence. Class Structure, and Underdevelopment Policy." In James D. Cockcroft, André Gunder Frank, and Dale L. Johnson (eds.), *Dependence and Underdevelopment: Latin America's Political Economy*, pp. 19–46. Garden City, N.Y.: Anchor Books.

Geddes, Barbara. N.d. "Economic Development as a Collective Action Problem: Individual Interests and Innovation in Brazil." Draft Ph.D. dissertation, Department of Political Science, University of California at Berkeley.

Gereffi, Gary. 1983. *The Pharmaceutical Industry and Dependency in the Third World*. Princeton: Princeton University Press.

Gereffi, Gary and Peter Evans. 1981. "Transnational Corporations, Dependent Development, and State Policy in the Semiperiphery: A Comparison of Brazil and Mexico." *Latin American Research Review* 16, no. 3: 31–64.

Harris, John R. 1967. "Industrial Entrepreneurship in Nigeria." Unpublished doctoral dissertation. Northwestern University.

Helleiner, Gerald (ed.). 1976. *A World Divided: The Less Developed Countries in the International Economy*. Cambridge: Cambridge University Press.

Hirschman, Albert O. 1971. "How to Divest in Latin America, and Why." *A Bias for Hope: Essays on Development and Latin America*, pp. 225–252. New Haven: Yale University Press.

Hoogvelt, Ankie. 1979. "Indigenisation and Foreign Capital: Industrialization in Nigeria." *Review of African Political Economy* no. 14 (January–April): 56–68.

———. 1980. "Indigenization and Technological Dependency." *Development and Change* 11, no. 2: 257–272.

Hutchison, Alan. 1974. "Last Minute Rush to Nigerianise." *African Development* 8, no. 3 (March): 41–45.

Inanga, Eno L. 1975. "Dividend Policy in an Era of Indigenization: Comment." *Nigerian Journal of Economic and Social Studies* 17, no. 2: 133–147.

Jenkins, Barbara. 1986. "Re-Examining the 'Obsolescing Bargain': A Study of Canada's National Energy Program." *International Organization* 40, no. 1: 139–165.

Joseph, A. Richard. 1983. "Class, State, and Prebendal Politics in Nigeria." *Journal of Commonwealth and Comparative Politics* 21, no. 3 (November): 21–38.

Keohane, Robert. 1985. *After Hegemony*. Princeton: Princeton University Press.

Kilby, Peter. 1969. *Industrialization in an Open Economy: Nigeria, 1945–1966*. Cambridge: Cambridge University Press.

Krasner, Stephen. 1985. *Structural Conflict*. Berkeley and Los Angeles: University of California Press.

Laclau, Ernesto. 1971. "Feudalism and Capitalism in Latin America." *New Left Review* no. 67 (May–June): 19–38.

Lall, Sanjaya and Senaka Bibile. 1977. "The Political Economy of Controlling Transnationals: The Pharmaceutical Industry in Sri Lanka (1972–1976)." *World Development* 5, no. 8: 677–698.

LaPalombara, Joseph and Stephen Blank. 1976. *Multinational Corporations and National Elites: A Study in Tensions*. New York: The Conference Board.

———. 1979. *Multinational Corporations and Developing Countries: A Research Report for the Conference Board*. New York: The Conference Board.

Leys, Colin. 1978. "Capital Accumulation, Class Formation and Dependency— The Significance of the Kenyan Case." In Ralph Miliband and John Saville (eds.), *The Socialist Register 1978*, pp. 241–266. London: Merlin Press.

332   Bibliography

Lubeck, Paul. 1977. "Nigeria: A Political Economy." *Africa Today* 24 (October): 5–10.

McMillan, Claude, Jr. and Richard F. Gonzales with Leo G. Erickson. 1964. *International Enterprise in a Developing Economy: A Study of U.S. Business in Brazil*. East Lansing, Mich.: Bureau of Business and Economic Research, MSU Business Studies. Summarized in John Fayerweather (ed.), *International Business Policy and Administration*. Hastings-on-Hudson, N.Y.: The International Executive, 1976.

Nafziger, E. Wayne. 1977. *African Capitalism*. Stanford: Hoover Institution Press.

Nigerian Economic Society. 1974. *Nigeria's Indigenisation Policy*. Proceedings of the November 1974 symposium organized by the Nigerian Economic Society, "Indigenisation: What Have We Achieved?" Ibadan: Department of Economics, University of Ibadan.

Nigerian Institute of Management. 1976. *Problems and Prospects of Indigenisation*. Special issue of *Management in Nigeria*, September.

Nwankwo, G. O. 1977. "Indigenisation or the Debunking of the Economy?" *New African* 11, no. 6 (June): 525–527.

Nylander, Arthur. 1976. "Ownership, Management and Control of Enterprises." *Management in Nigeria*, September: 42–45.

Odife, D. O. 1977. "Dividend Policy in an Era of Indigenization: A Comment." *Nigerian Journal of Economic and Social Studies* 19, no. 2: 25–30.

Odufalu, J. O. 1971. "Indigenous Enterprise in Nigerian Manufacturing." *Journal of Modern African Studies* 9, no. 4: 593–607.

Offiong, Daniel A. 1980. *Imperialism and Dependency*. Enugu: Fourth Dimension Publishing Co.

Ogbuagu, Chibuzo Samson Agomo. 1981. "The Politics of Import Substitution and the Industrialization Process: The Nigerian Experience." Unpublished Ph.D. dissertation, Yale University.

Ogunbanjo, C. O. 1969. "Problems of Ownership and Local Participation in Capital Formation." Paper presented at the 7th National Management Conference of the Nigerian Institute of Management, Lagos, 20 March.

———. 1982. "The Dilemma of Nigeria's Mixed Economy: The Indigenous Entrepreneur's View-Point." Unpublished paper presented at the National Institute for Policy and Strategic Studies, Lagos.

Ogunsheye, Ayo. 1972. "Experience and Problems of Indigenous Enterprises." *Management in Nigeria* 7 (March–April).

Okediji, F. O. 1975. "Indigenization Decree and Income Distribution: The Social Implications." *Quarterly Journal of Administration* (University of Ife) 9, no. 2 (January): 149–157.

Okigbo, P.N.C. 1981. *Nigeria's Financial System: Structure and Growth*. London: Longman.

Olakanpo, O. 1963. "Distributive Trade: A Critique of Government Policies." *Nigerian Journal of Economic and Social Studies* 2 (July): 237–246.

Omolayole, Michael. 1976. "It Is a Timely Conference." *Management in Nigeria*, September: 9.

Onoge, Omafume F. 1974. "Indigenisation Decree and Economic Independence: Another Case of Bourgeois Utopianism." In Nigerian Economic Society 1974, pp. 57–67.

Onosode, G. O. 1974. "Indigenisation Decree and Its Implementation—Patterns of Shares-Acquisition." In Nigerian Economic Society 1974, pp. 32–37.

Osagie, Eghosa. 1975. "The Nigerian Enterprises Promotion Decree: A Philosophical Approach." Unpublished paper presented at the Christian Council of Nigeria symposium on the indigenization decree, 1–3 April.

Othman, Mansor. "The Politics of Indigenization: The Making and Implications of Indigenous Capitalism in a Multi-Racial State." Draft Ph.D. dissertation, Department of Political Science, Yale University.

Owonuwa, Malomo. 1975. "Manpower Implications of Nigerian Enterprises Promotion Decree 1972." Unpublished M.P.A. dissertation, University of Ife.

Palma, Gabriel. 1978. "Dependency: A Formal Theory of Underdevelopment or a Methodology for the Analysis of Concrete Situations of Underdevelopment?" *World Development* 6: 881–924.

Patnaik, Utsa. 1972. "On the Mode of Production in Indian Agriculture." *Economic and Political Weekly* (Bombay) 7, no. 40 (30 September): 145–151.

Penrose, Edith. 1976. " 'Ownership and Control': Multinational Firms in Less Developed Countries." In Helleiner (ed.) 1976, pp. 147–174.

Prebisch, Raul. 1959. "Commercial Policy in the Underdeveloped Countries." *American Economic Review (Papers and Proceedings)*, 49, no. 2 (May): 251–273.

Pribor, Jeffrey. 1979. "Indigenization and the Growth of the African Capitalist Class: Nigeria and Kenya." Unpublished Economics and Political Science senior essay, Yale University.

Rake, Alan. 1975. "Debating the Future of the Stock Market." *African Development*, March: 57–61.

Rapoport, Carla. 1979. "Why Spending Stopped in Nigeria." *Fortune* 100, no. 1 (16 July): 147–154.

Rimlinger, G. V. 1973. "The Indigenisation of Industry." *Quarterly Journal of Administration* (University of Ife) 7, no. 2 (January): 205–215.

Rimlinger, G. V. and C. Stremlau. 1973. *Indigenisation and Management Development in Nigeria*. Lagos: Nigerian Institute of Management.

Robock, Stefan H., Kenneth Simmonds, and Jack Zwick. 1977. *International Business and Multinational Enterprises*. Homewood, Ill.: Richard D. Irwin.

Rodney, Walter. 1974. *How Europe Underdeveloped Africa*. Washington, D.C.: Howard University Press.

Ruggie, John. 1983. *Antinomies of Interdependence*. New York: Columbia University Press.

Sanwo, Patrick. 1975. "Indigenisation: How Has It Worked?" *African Development*, March: 33–36.

Schatz, Sayre. 1977. *Nigerian Capitalism*. Berkeley and Los Angeles: University of California Press.

Schmidt, Wilson E. 1978. "The Role of Private Capital in Developing the Third World." In W. Scott Thompson (ed.), *The Third World*, pp. 269–286. San Francisco: Institute for Contemporary Studies.

Seers, Dudley. 1972. "The Meaning of Development." In Norman T. Uphoff and Warren F. Ilchman (eds.), *The Political Economy of Development: Theoretical and Empirical Contributions*, pp. 123–129. Berkeley and Los Angeles: University of California Press.

———. 1980. "North–South: Muddling Morality and Mutuality." *Third World Quarterly* 2, no. 4 (October): 681–693.

Silva, E. A. 1976. "Advantages and Disadvantages of Indigenisation." *Management in Nigeria*, September: 37–40.

Singer, Hans W. 1950. "The Distribution of Gains between Investing and Borrowing Countries." *American Economic Review (Papers and Proceedings)* 40, no. 2 (May): 473–485.

Smith, Anthony. 1978. "The Case of Dependency Theory." In W. Scott Thompson (ed.), *The Third World*, pp. 207–226. San Francisco: Institute for Contemporary Studies.

Soyode, Afolabi. 1975. "Dividend Policy in an Era of Indigenisation: A Comment." *Nigerian Journal of Economic and Social Studies* 17, no. 2: 149–154.

Stenzel, Konrad. "The Politics of Debt and the Dependent State: The Cases of Chile and the Dominican Republic." Draft Ph.D. dissertation, Department of Political Science, Yale University.

Swansbrough, Robert H. 1972. "The American Investor's View of Latin American Economic Nationalism." *Inter-American Economic Affairs* 26, no. 3 (Winter): 61–82.

Teriba, O. 1975. "Financing Indigenisation." *Quarterly Journal of Administration* (University of Ife) 9, no. 2 (January): 159–176.

Teriba, O., E. C. Edozien, and M. O. Kayode. 1977. "Some Aspects of Ownership and Control Structure of Business Enterprise in a Developing Economy: The Nigerian Case." In O. Teriba and M. O. Kayode (eds.), *Industrial Development in Nigeria: Patterns, Problems and Prospects*, pp. 89–112. Ibadan: Ibadan University Press.

Uzoaga, W. O. 1975. "Dividend Policy in an Era of Indigenisation: A Rejoinder." *Nigerian Journal of Economic and Social Studies* 17, no. 2: 155–161.

Uzoaga, W. O. and J. U. Alozienwa. 1974. "Dividend Policy in an Era of Indigenization." *Nigerian Journal of Economic and Social Studies* 16, no. 3: 461–478.

Vernon, Raymond, 1971. *Sovereignty at Bay: The Multinational Spread of U.S. Enterprises*. New York: Basic Books.

Warren, Bill. 1973. "Imperialism and Capitalist Industrialization." *New Left Review* no. 81 (September–October): 3–44.

————. 1980. *Imperialism: Pioneer of Capitalism*. London: Verso NLB.

Watts, Michael. 1983. *Silent Violence: Food, Famine and Peasantry in Northern Nigeria*. Berkeley and Los Angeles: University of California Press.

Weinstein, Franklin B. 1976. "Multinational Corporations and the Third World: The Case of Japan and Southeast Asia." *International Organization* 30, no. 3: 373–405.

Williams, Gavin. 1976. *Nigerian Economy and Society*. London: Rex Collings.

————. 1980. *State and Society in Nigeria*. Idanre, Ondo State: Afrografika.

Wilson, Ernest J., III. 1981. "Nigeria." In Ken Stunkel (ed.), *National Energy Profiles*, pp. 315–358. New York: Praeger.

————. 1982. "Contested Terrain: A Comparative and Theoretical Re-Assessment of State Owned Enterprise in Africa." Paper presented at African Studies Association conference, Washington, D.C., November.

————. N.d. "Public Corporation Expansion in Nigeria: The Interplay of Political Interests, State Structure and State Policy." Unpublished manuscript.

Yar' Adua, Shehu. 1976. "The Government Is Not Embarking on Creeping Nationalization." *Management in Nigeria*, September: 10–11.

GOVERNMENT DOCUMENTS AND REPORTS

Capital Issues Commission. 1977. *Guidelines for Valuation of Shares of Companies to Be Sold under the Nigerian Enterprises Promotion Decree 1977*. Lagos. March.

Central Bank of Nigeria. *Annual Report and Statement of Accounts* (various years). Lagos: Central Bank of Nigeria.

————. *Economic and Financial Review* (various years). Lagos: Central Bank of Nigeria.

Federal Military Government's Views on the Report of the Industrial Enterprises Panel. 1976. Lagos: Federal Ministry of Information Printing Division.

Federal Office of Statistics. *Industrial Survey of Nigeria* (various years). Lagos: Federal Office of Statistics, Industrial Surveys Division.

International Monetary Fund. *International Financial Statistics* (various years). Washington, D.C.

Nigerian Securities and Exchange Commission. *Reports and Accounts* (various years). Lagos: NSEC.

Report of the Advisory Committee on Aids to African Businessmen. 1959. Federation of Nigeria. Lagos: Federal Government Printer.

"Report of the Industrial Enterprises Panel" (The Adeosun Commission Report). 1976. Federal Republic of Nigeria. Unpublished. March.

Second National Development Plan, 1970–74: Programme of Post-War Reconstruction and Development. 1970. Lagos: Federal Government Printer.

INDEX

Aboyade, O., 146, 161
Adeosun, Chief O. A., 162
Adeosun Commission, 104, 115, 144,
147, 162, 165, 170, 177, 179, 183,
188, 195, 240, 266, 280; appointment
of, 162–163; conception of development, 165–166; debate on, 169–173,
197; evaluation of first decree, 164,
166–167, 193; recommendations (for
second decree), 167–168, 171, 172,
189; report of (issued in 1976),
79n86, 98n7, 103, 107, 113, 116,
125, 128, 146, 180, 194, 205; role of,
163, 174
Adetunji, Alhaji A., 162
Advisory Commission on Aids to Afri-
can Businessmen (1959), 60; report
of, 54, 57, 64
Ahmadu Bello University, 203
Aid to Pioneer Industry Ordinance
(1951), 53
Akeredolu-Ale, E. O., 59, 60, 276
Al-Hakim, Malam A., 203
American International Insurance Com-
pany, 232
Amin, Samir, 28, 29, 44
Andean Common Market, 20
Aramco, 8
Asabia, S. O., 234
Ashamu Group of Companies, 272
Asiodu, Phillip C., 64, 161, 162
Atta, Abdul, 78
Ayida, Alison A., 97

Balance of payments, effects of indigeni-
zation on, 151–153
Bankers' Committee, 164
Banking Decree, 233, 237, 244, 249,
264
Banking sector, 141, 144, 248–249
Baran, Paul, 39
Bargaining power: balance of, 282–295;
of host country, 19, 21–23, 26, 31,

37, 48, 154; of MNCs, and liberal-in-
ternationalist school, 138, 292–293;
of state, 96. *See also* Control
Bata Shoes, 101, 119
Beckman, Bjorn, 44
Bello, V. I., 106
Bendel State, 267
Benin, 114
Benue Plateau State, 150
Bergsten, C. Fred, 44
Biafra, 72
Bight of Bonny, 72
Boots, 101
Brandt Commission, 23, 25
Brazil, 34, 36, 50, 164, 266, 280; Na-
tional Development Bank of (BNDE),
164, 168
Brenner, Robert, 39
Brewer, Anthony, 39, 42
Brume, Fred, 162
Bumiputras, 296

Cabinet Office (Federal Government of
Nigeria), 168, 169, 172, 195
Canada: joint-venture programs in, 8;
National Energy Program, 296
Capitalism, development of, 268–276
Capital Issues Commission (CIC), 88,
90, 95, 101, 105, 108, 120, 129, 164,
179, 180, 183, 196, 199, 200, 202,
207–213, 228, 236, 237, 265, 266
Allotment Committee of, 109, 208–
209, 268–269, 288
allotment of shares by, 207
role of in NEPD 1, 90, 207; valuation of shares, 109–112, 116, 171
role of in NEPD 2, 193, 195, 197;
valuation of enterprises, 209–213,
215
Cardoso, Fernando, 33
Center for Management Development
(CMD), 91, 92, 96, 265
Central Bank of Nigeria, 70, 77, 80, 90,

Library of Congress Cataloging-in-Publication Data

Biersteker, Thomas J.
  Multinationals, the state, and control of the
Nigerian economy.
  Bibliography: p.
  Includes index.
  1. Investments, Foreign—Nigeria. 2. International
business enterprises—Nigeria. 3. Nigeria—Economic
policy. 4. Nigeria—Economic policy—1970–
I. Title.
HG5881.A3B54   1987   338.8′88669   86–25214
ISBN 0–691–07728–2 (alk. paper)
ISBN 0–691–02261–5 (pbk.)